His Truth Endureth

LIFTING THE CURTAINS OF TIME

The spade of the archæologist has pushed our knowledge of early civilizations forward thousands of years into an unknown past of which historians had little more than dreamed.

By permission of The Museum of the University of Pennsylvania

His Truth Endureth

A Survey of the Beginnings
and of
Old Testament History in the Light of
Archæological Discoveries

BY

JAMES C. MUIR

NATIONAL PUBLISHING COMPANY

PHILADELPHIA

To the constantly cheerful Companion
of the author's wanderings,
HAZEL GIBSON MUIR
this book is lovingly dedicated.

CONTENTS

3755*

viii   CONTENTS

His Truth Endureth

INTRODUCTION

*The Lord is good; his mercy is everlasting; and his truth endureth
to all generations.*—Psalm 100:5.

THE Old Testament is a compilation of very ancient books. The
writers of these books were men from greatly varying walks of life.
Priests and prophets, kings and commoners, shepherds and scribes
—men who spent their lives in semi-nomadic wanderings, as well as men
who dwelt in urban communities—contributed to this majestic masterpiece
of literature. These writers also varied greatly in educational attainment,
and in mental and spiritual capacity. Coming from different lands, mingling
with different peoples, their writings reflect, somewhat, their varying environments and life experiences.

In point of time, some of these writers lived centuries apart. A time
distance of hundreds of years lends variety to their combined work. Some
of these writers have been immortalized by their contributions to the
Great Book. Others remain obscure or unknown, even their names having
vanished in the mists of time. Some of the writers, whose work appears
in the Old Testament as we know it today, without doubt had access to,
and used, documents of a wide variety in character in writing their
respective books,—ancient triumphal songs of Israel, ancient histories,
genealogies, time-treasured epics and essays of great religious leaders
whose lives were contemporary with recorded events, records of rulers
and books of kings. The writers frequently refer to literary works now
unknown, such as "the book of the wars of the Lord" (*Numbers* 21:14)
and "the book of Jasher" (*Joshua* 10:13; 2 *Samuel* 1:18). That they
may have used these documents does not detract from the book's historical
value, nor deny the inspiration of the particular writer, but these ancient
documents represent, on their part, the work of unknown and unsung
authors who are not even a "name" to us of today.

The writers of the Old Testament, in telling the story of a spiritually-
minded people's search for the One True God, have written a spiritual
guide for all mankind. Deftly they have woven into their narratives
strands of poetry, philosophy, prophecy, and the distilled wisdom acquired
through thousands of years of everyday life.

2

Aside from its unparalleled position as the spiritual guide of the adherents of two great living religions that worship only one God; aside from its awe-inspiring beauty as a work of literature, the Old Testament is well worth our study as a work of history.

The Old Testament tells the story of a race which lived, and fought, and suffered through the most pregnant centuries of our civilization. This race witnessed the rise and fall of great empires that we of today know only through the pages of history and the monumental ruins of their ancient cities. This race knew the Chaldea in which what we call "our Western Civilization" had its first feeble beginnings. It saw Egypt in its ancient glory. It witnessed the rise and fall of the Assyrian Empire. It knew, only too well, "Babylon, the glory of kingdoms." It watched the Medes and Persians sweep over the Near-East, only to be swept back by the world-conquering march of the Greeks under Alexander the Great. Under the iron heel of the Caesars it knew the midnight gloom before the great dawning, when a star hung over a manger in Bethlehem to herald the coming of Jesus of Nazareth. The writers of the Old Testament had marvelous backgrounds into which they could frame their narratives.

The annalists and recorders of the Old Testament did not lack for characters for their stories. They had their own great galaxy of national heroes: Abraham, the "Father of the Faithful," and his patriarchal descendants; Joseph, prime minister of Egypt; Moses, emancipator and law-giver; Joshua, conqueror of Canaan; saintly Samuel, the king-maker; David, who welded a tribal people into national unity; Solomon, whose glory dazzled the ancient East; Hezekiah, the builder; Nehemiah, the business executive, who raised Jerusalem from ruins; and the great succession of sublime prophets who were the outstanding product of the Old Testament age. Beside this procession of heroic Hebrews marched the great ones of the earth: the mighty Pharaohs of Egypt; the warlike monarchs of Assyria from Tiglathpileser to Ashurbanipal; the great Babylonian family that flamed into prominence with Nabopolasser and Nebuchadnezzar, only to sink to oblivion with the decadent Belshazzar; Cyrus and Darius, Alexander and Antiochus Epiphanes; Pompey and a succession of Caesars; all these, and countless others of the mighty of their day, marched across the horizons of Hebrew history. The writers of the Old Testament needed no fictitious heroes for their narratives. They needed not to resort to tales originating around Oriental campfires for material to decorate their priceless contribution to the historical literature of the world.

The Old Testament was not written as a history. It was written for a more noble purpose. Its purpose was to spread a gospel that would bring about the spiritual regeneration of mankind. Nevertheless, the Old Testament is replete with narratives of historical episodes. These episodes are minor movements in the single major historical movement which forms the background against which the historical narratives are projected. This great movement did not end with the writing of the last chapter of the Old Testament. It did not end with the coming of Jesus of Nazareth. With His coming it broke from the traditional barriers which had circumscribed it for centuries, and took on new life, new trends and forms, and is still going on. Its influence is paramount in the Jewish world. It flows in mighty stream throughout all Christendom. The little that is good in the religion of the Moslems was borrowed from the ideals that motivated the Israel movement. No movement in history has been more vital, more potent, or more important, in shaping the channels along which the human race has moved to its present measure of civilization. Since its inception the great movement has profoundly affected the life, the culture, the material welfare, and the faith of a constantly increasing proportion of mankind.

Many of the earlier Biblical narratives, as we read them today, were written long after the occurrence of the events they purpose to portray. This circumstance has led many commentators on the Scriptures to assume that the subject matter of the narratives was handed down for centuries in the form of tradition, exquisitely beautiful, but completely unhistorical. Other commentators, while admitting that the narratives have a strong background of history, and that the writers probably had earlier documents to which they could refer, have pointed out many seeming anachronisms in the circumstantial details with which the writers have surrounded their narratives. Modern Biblical scholars, through exhaustive research of the component documents, have determined the approximate dates at which the various books were written, and many important facts as to the circumstances under which they were written. Purely linguistic criticism, however, seems nebulous and unsatisfactory to the average Bible reader. He longs for some material evidence which will dispel the mists of unreality with which time has enshrouded many of the Old Testament narratives. Archæology, that branch of science which studies the art, customs, and culture of ancient peoples through the investigation of the material evidence they have left behind them, comes to the aid of the Bible reader who wishes to acquire a broader and more complete knowledge of the historical, geographical, and cultural backgrounds of the Old Testament.

Archæology, which during the past century has thrown so much light upon hitherto obscure or unknown periods in the history of almost every land, has been particularly illuminating regarding the countries which form the geographical backgrounds of the Old Testament narratives. Since most of these regions, particularly Palestine and Babylonia, passed into the control of Great Britain after the close of the World War, increased opportunity has been afforded for the scientific investigation of the ruins of many ancient cities that are mentioned in the Old Testament.

The rediscovery and excavation of many long-lost Biblical cities have revealed abundant material evidence supplementing and expanding previous knowledge, and providing tangible contemporary illustration for many Old Testament narratives and historical records.

Archæological science is today unlocking for us many doors that have been sealed for centuries by the deep dust of battle and decay. Across these thresholds we may mentally enter the temples, the palaces, and the homes of ancient peoples, and read in material evidence fascinating details of the civilization, education, and culture of the people who once thronged these now ruined rooms. Here we may read the multitudinous details of the urban, the rural, the commercial, and the private life of many peoples who influenced the mind and thought, and helped to shape the political fortunes of the Children of Israel.

The Biblical cities varied in importance in accordance with their locations. In agricultural districts the location was frequently determined by the accessibility to caravan trails and roads. Other cities grew to importance because their strategic locations enabled them to dominate the junctions of important trails and highways, and thus establish military and commercial control over a district. The principal controlling factor, however, in the matter of location was convenient water supplies. Cities had to be so located that in times of siege the inhabitants could have access to potable water within the city walls. This was particularly true in Palestine, where water has always been an extremely limited and valuable commodity.

Unlike our modern cities, most of the Biblical cities grew upward as well as outward. Great quantities of food supplies had to be stored within the city limits to prevent starvation in the all too frequent sieges. There was no sanitation in the modern sense of the word. The city wastes were dumped at any convenient place within the city walls, thus starting the upward growth. When a wave of invasion swept over the city walls, the city might be destroyed in part or completely, so the invaders levelled off the site and built anew. Each succeeding wave of invasion left behind it material evidence of the invaders' stay at the site. Sometimes this evidence is marvelously complete. An instance of this is seen at Beth-shan, where the Palestinian Expedition of The University Museum of Philadelphia is now working. Here twenty-one superimposed city levels tell the history of Palestine from the days of the "pit dwellers" to the time of the Crusaders. Cities grew upward at the rate of about five feet a century. Parts of Jerusalem today are eighty feet higher than they were when Our Saviour trod that city's streets!

The scientific investigation of many Biblical cities, particularly those of Assyria and Babylonia, has antiquated many standard histories dealing with those regions. Many scholarly works of Biblical criticism have also been rendered obsolete by the material evidence recovered at the point of the spade of the scientific investigator. The opening chapters of many excellent works dealing with non-Biblical subjects must undergo revision in the light of this new evidence. The early history of accounting, of architecture, and of transportation will have to be revised, but it is worthy of note, not "one jot or one tittle" of the Bible will have to be revised!

The historical movement of the Hebrews, into which two thousand years of Old Testament history are framed, had its inception in a comparatively inconspicuous incident—the migration of a family from Ur of the Chaldees. A concise statement in *Genesis* 11 tells us that "they went forth with them from Ur of the Chaldees, to go into the land of Canaan." From this simple beginning, just as a great river may be traced to its source at a tiny spring, may be traced a great historical movement that has maintained its momentum for four thousand years.

At a time of unsettlement and unrest, when men were ever on the move, this family probably differed little from countless other migrating clan-families; yet from this family emerged the mighty character whose stature has shadowed the centuries—Abraham, the "Father of the Faithful," and "the Friend of God."

Naturally, we think of Abraham as a Hebrew. We think of him as an Old Testament character of outstanding religious and moral excellence. He is the great central figure of the book of *Genesis*. His influence flows through the entire Old Testament. Psalmists sang of him—and prophets invoked his name. Abraham, however, must be counted among the great citizens of the world. Beyond the widest reaches of race and religion; beyond all national or geographical boundaries; beyond the realms of any earthly empire, flows unfettered the influence of the great soul to whom was vouchsafed Divine injunction and mandate, and to whom, in reward for keeping the sacred covenants, was given the promise eternal—"In thy seed shall all the nations of the earth be blessed."

Because Abraham was, in his latter life, a rich flockmaster and herdsman, many of us have assumed that in his early life he was a skin-clad tent-dweller, a wandering nomad, or a member of some semi-nomadic colony which had temporarily settled on the banks of the Euphrates. When, with the uncovering of Ur of the Chaldees, it was discovered that Abraham spent his boyhood and young manhood, the formative years of mind and character, in the midst of a great center of culture and education, in a city whose inhabitants had already evolved that complex mode of life that is called "civilization," all our ideas as to Abraham's early life had to be considerably modified.

When the Joint Expedition of the Museum of the University of Pennsylvania and the British Museum, through thirteen years of scientific exploration, raised the curtains of Time from Ur of the Chaldees, there was revealed a civilization of which science had never even dreamed, and the eyes of the historian were enabled to penetrate centuries hitherto obscure or unknown.

We now know that long before Abraham's day the inhabitants of Ur had invented a method of writing, and evolved a system of mathematics based on the number six, just as our decimal system is based on the number ten. They formulated and codified a system of civil and criminal law, and provided for the administration of municipal and national government. The architects of Ur made use of the arch and dome in building construction, and worked out all the basic architectural forms in use today. Not only did the mechanics of Ur produce the first four-wheeled vehicles, but they made use of the wheel fifteen hundred years before it was imported into Egypt. The jewelers of Ur had discovered the art of polishing, boring, and artistically mounting gems. Expert craftsmen were producing, in gold and silver, in copper and bronze, beautiful objects of art and utility worthy of the craftsmen of any age. The scholars of Ur were already writing and collecting in libraries epics and legends from which the Greeks were to borrow extensively centuries later.

As a boy, Abraham may, or may not, have attended the famous "boys' school" at Ur; but we do know that schoolboys of that time could add and subtract, multiply and divide numbers, could extract square roots by arithmetic; had lessons in grammar, and could draw maps of their city. When we picture the city where the boy was raised, the culture he knew, and the educational advantages that were open to him there, it is no longer possible to picture Abraham as a crude, unlettered, product of some tented tribe of nomads. Projected against such a background as was Abraham's early environment, it is difficult to visualize a man of the mental and spiritual stature of Abraham as being other than an educated, able, broad-minded, sophisticated citizen of the world when he went forth "from Ur of the Chaldees, to go into the land of Canaan."

Although outwardly the migration of the family of which Abraham was a member had a common aspect, inwardly its significance was unparalleled. Here began an historical movement that has influenced the currents of history for four thousand years. Motivated by a Divinely sanctioned mandate to give to the world an inspired conception of the One True God and man's spiritual fellowship with his Creator, the movement survived centuries of semi-slavery in Egypt. Its ideals were framed into the fundamental laws of Israel by Moses in the wilderness, and enshrined in the Ark of the Covenant, the visible symbol of Jehovah's protecting presence with His Chosen People. When the great movement penetrated the Promised Land, and Israel achieved nationhood under David, the religious ideals of Israel became the basis of the national government of the newly-created kingdom. In a material sense, the great movement reached its greatest earthly glory under Solomon, in "the Golden Age of Israel." In the religious sense, and as a civilizing and cultural force, its greatest days were still in the far distant future.

After the death of Solomon the Golden Age of Israel came to an end. The kingdom was divided. The great Hebrew Empire, reaching from the Red Sea to the Euphrates, that David and Solomon had erected on the ruins of Canaanite civilizations, began to disintegrate. Torn by civil strife; bruised by the heel of the conqueror; reduced to vassalage by Assyria; enslaved by Babylon; overrun by Greece; persecuted by Rome, the great movement lost its political power, but never its sacred purpose. Finally the east brightened with a new dawn. The coming of Jesus of Nazareth altered all the currents of history. The movement had reached one of its goals, but not its destination.

Such an historical movement must needs leave material evidence behind it. The wide geographical distribution of this material, and the multifarious nature and great volume of the evidence itself, calls for a wide range of study. We should know something of the geography of the Bible lands, and of the political and economic conditions of these lands during the Old Testament period. We should also know something of the customs and character of the various peoples with whom Israel came into contact while they were weaving the history which forms the framework of the priceless book they have given us.

Material evidence comes under many classifications. There are the ruins of cities with their fortifications, temples and palaces, as well as the homes of the inhabitants. There are monuments and funerary structures with their frescoes and bas-reliefs. There are clay cylinders and tablets and other inscriptioned objects. There are the weapons, the tools, and the household utensils of many peoples, including the common pottery. Pottery, being a product of the earth itself, while easily broken, if buried in the earth is almost everlasting. Of all the remains of handicrafts that the ancients have left behind them, pottery tells most completely the story of man's past.

This book is not written for archæologists. It is not written for theologians. Its purpose is to enable the reader to assimilate more readily the historical, geographical, and cultural backgrounds of the Old Testament narratives, and thus make the reading of the Bible more meaningful. The writer aims to achieve this purpose through a simple, nontechnical presentation of the material evidence that supplements the Old Testament narratives. Naturally, since the Bible and the material evidence throw mutual light on each other, there are many Scriptural references, but the reader will look in vain for any interpretation of the Scriptures or doctrinal matter of any sort.

I

IN THE BEGINNING

In the beginning God created the heaven and the earth.—Genesis 1:1

AS the name implies, *Genesis* is the Book of Beginnings. Since its opening chapters present a picture of the dawn of creation and a survey of the earliest eras of mankind on earth, its name is well chosen. *Genesis* is a book of many beginnings. It records the beginnings of the rise of the descendants of Abraham to world leadership in religious thought, it begins the great, reliable, Religious History of the World, and last, but not least, it forms a fitting introduction to the New Testament and the History of Christianity.

The religious genius who framed the opening chapters of *Genesis* had some wonderful narratives to relate. Although he was a literary pioneer in his divinely appointed field, some of his narratives, in the broader sense, were not altogether new. Long before the earliest of the great prophetic writers of Israel set down the first of his literary gems, earlier scholars had inscribed on clay tablets the story of the creation, of the fall of man, and of a great deluge that wiped out rising civilizations.

The story of the creation seems to have been one of infinite appeal to all early peoples. Ancient peoples, whose history is known only through the material evidence they left behind them in the ruins of their cities, wrote many crude versions of the story of the creation which scholars may read today. When the rising of civilizations made necessary the invention of systems of writing—the placing of connected thought in permanent form—the story of the creation was one of the earliest placed on record. Barbaric and semi-barbaric peoples, whose geographical locations or inferior economic resources denied them until comparatively recent times a knowledge of the art of writing, have handed down the story in the form of oral tradition. It remained, however, for a spiritually minded Hebrew to write a reverent epic of the handiwork of God, and of His overruling relationship with His world and the creatures He had created.

The literary artist who shaped the *Genesis* Epic of Creation lived in a country close to the cradle of mankind. Outside of his own race, all the peoples he knew were pagan. These peoples had gods, many gods. Probably one of primitive man's earliest conceptions was that he possessed a soul, a spirit quite independent of his body. If he possessed a soul with strange unearthly powers, why should not everything he saw about him, the trees, the rocks, the mountains, the storms, the stars, the sun, the moon, have strange powers? Perhaps, he reasoned, in some mysterious manner these outside powers helped or hindered him. When plentiful winter rains brought a favorable summer season his flocks and herds prospered, the gods were kind. When rainfall was scanty, and the white hot winds from the desert dried up the waterholes and scorched the grazing grounds bringing the ever-dreaded famine, the gods must be angry. Some gods were always kind. The miracle of Spring impressed him. Then the earth renewed itself, and his flocks and herds yielded their increase. Surely there must be some especial powers put forth for his benefit at this lovely season. This miraculous seasonal change was to him a purely feminine phenomenon, therefore it must be controlled by a female, a goddess.

The Spring passed but it came again. This was a goddess in whom one could place dependence. This goddess of fertility was seasonal, but her bounty affected his fortunes throughout the year. Here was one worthy of especial worship. Even while she was gone, he must court her favor. He must make some visible symbol of her. Out of clay he made little figurines, with the feminine features greatly exaggerated, and enshrined them as his principal household deity. From such simple beginnings grew the most widespread of all pagan cult worships. With the passing of centuries the goddess of love and fertility grew in stature and took on many strange attributes. Her lineal descendants, in one form or another, as Ishtar, Ashtoreth, Astarte, Antit, and even Venus, were worshipped by many peoples for thousands of years.

As people after people, from the Euphrates to the Tiber, adopted the goddess of love and fertility and claimed her for their own, the fancied powers of the great goddess immeasurably increased. She grew in popular esteem until she was revered as "the Queen of Heaven," against whom generations of Hebrew prophets were to hurl their dire warnings (See *Jeremiah* 7:18; 44:17, 25). Later, the great goddess mothered the "religions of the shadows" of ancient Greece and Rome, which endured until well into the Christian Era. Only the rise of Christianity banished to oblivion the baleful influence of the greatest of pagan deities.

The early gods of the ancients were at first merely personal and household gods. As clan-family merged with clan-family to form tribes, the greatest of the household gods became tribal gods. In regions where the rich soils of the river valleys produced such wealth that trading became necessary, and trading centers grew into cities, the most powerful and popular god became the god of the city. When cities grew to such importance that they controlled a surrounding territory with its lesser towns and villages, thus forming a city-kingdom, the principal god became the ruler, administering through the king.

Far back in the dawning days of civilization, successive waves of nomadic peoples poured over the rim of Arabia and began to spread over the world. These are called Semitic peoples because of their descent from Shem, who was one of the sons of Noah. One of these desert-bred races "journeyed east" and "found a plain in the land of Shinar; and they dwelt there" (See *Genesis* 11:2). These newcomers found themselves in a smiling land. They were in the land which in *Genesis* 24:10 is referred to as Mesopotamia. Mesopotamia means "between the rivers." In this case the rivers were the "twin rivers," the Tigris and the Euphrates, which find their source in the mountains of Armenia and roughly parallel each other as they find their way to their common outlet in the Persian Gulf. The country they had invaded is today officially known as Irak, although it is most commonly referred to as Babylonia.

Much of Irak is desert today, a featureless expanse of drab clay and drifting sand. In places the flat surface of the land around the lower reaches of the "twin rivers" is broken by irregular heaps, or "Tells," which mark the sites of ancient cities. Some of these cities were flourishing when the forerunners of the Hebrews first found their way into the country. No desert country could support such cities. When the Semitic tribes first entered the land it was a rich agricultural country. Its enterprising inhabitants, the Sumerians, had excellent hydraulic engineers who designed and constructed great irrigation systems to bring water from the twin rivers to the fertile alluvial soil. Plentiful water, long days of hot sunshine, and rich soil produced two plentiful grain crops per year. Farms, vineyards, and date orchards lined the canals and the roadways leading to the great walled cities.

These Sumerian cities were doubly products of the soil. The fruits of the soil furnished the wealth with which to build them, and the soil itself furnished the materials of which they were built. The country has no stone, and it never had timber. Clay and bitumen were the only native building materials. Roofing timber had to be imported. From native clay the Sumerians made excellent bricks and splendid pottery.

Clay was an important factor in the economic life of the country. In a land that was without native metals and had no wood, and where water and food had to be conveyed and stored in small lots, the inhabitants were forced to make extensive use of pottery. As a matter of fact, all ancient peoples made extensive use of pottery. There is an interesting tradition in regard to the first making of pottery. It relates that some prehistoric basket maker, having plastered a basket with clay to make it a better container, carelessly left the basket too near the fire which warmed his little hut and, later, was amazed to note the effects of fire on clay.

Sumerian pottery was entirely handmade. The use of the potter's wheel came later. This pottery was sometimes ornamented by combing with a wooden comb, the teeth making lines of varying depths on the surface. Sometimes it was embellished with paint before firing. It is quite possible that the first artists used clay as their working medium. Long before the forerunners of the Hebrews entered the country the Sumerian had learned to reproduce faithfully the outlines of human, animal, and vegetable forms; and it is but natural that he should preserve on his household utensils his early conceptions of art and color and beauty. A joint expedition of the University Museum of the University of Pennsylvania and the American School of Oriental Research at Bagdad, under the direction of Dr. E. A. Speiser, recently recovered at Tepe Gawra, in Northern Irak, an earthenware pot decorated by what is believed to be the world's earliest attempt at landscape painting. This pot was in use many hundreds of years before the time of Abraham.

Evidently the Semitic newcomers liked this rich land. They spread all over it. Some of them worked their way northward along the rivers into the higher lands of Assyria. Here, also, they found cities—Nineveh, the site of which is now marked by the great mound of Kouyunjik, just across the Tigris from the modern city of Mosul; Calah, now marked by the mound of Nimroud; Asshur, which is traditionally associated with one of the sons of Shem. These cities were very ancient (See *Genesis* 10).

Some of these Semites moved south. Of these a portion settled in Ur of Chaldees. From one of the early Semitic families which settled in Ur sprang Terah, whose place in history was established when he became the father of Abram (later known as Abraham) who became the father of Israel.

It was a fortunate circumstance for young Abram that he was raised in Ur of the Chaldees. The scientific exploration of the ruins of that early city reveals that Abram grew up in a great center of culture and education.* Long before his day the art of writing was known and extensively practiced by the scribes and scholars of Ur. When we know that there was at least one excellent elementary school in Ur in Abram's day, and that he probably played on the streets with boys who could read and write, had lessons in grammar, and were so far advanced in mathematics that they could extract square roots of numbers by arithmetic, it is difficult to imagine that the young lad failed to absorb some of the culture of Ur. The boy who later became "the Father of the Faithful" and the "Friend of God" was a product of Ur of the Chaldees.

---

*See Chapter II, page 29.

The Old Testament tells us nothing of Abram's life in "the land of his nativity." Outside of Talmudic tradition, nothing is known of his boyhood. It seems fitting, however, that Abram should have spent his boyhood and young manhood, the formative years of his character, in the greatest center of culture and education of his day. Abram's blood was Semitic, but his culture was Sumerian, or Chaldean. Abram was prepared for his great lifework at Ur of the Chaldees. Here was laid the foundation which enabled him to profit by the great spiritual experiences of his later life. Israel was not fathered by a skin-clad nomad.

Abram's earliest religious instruction was probably purely pagan. The polytheistic religion of Ur was not without ideals of moral living and some crude conceptions of man's spiritual relationships with his many gods. When did Abram first begin to doubt and question the powers of the pagan gods? Probably during his adolescence at Ur. Although the full revelation of man's spiritual relationship with the Unseen did not come to him until he was a mature man living in Haran, it is probable that his mind and soul were being prepared for the divine message that was to come to him later on. Oriental poetry of Mohammedan and Jewish origin makes much of this thought. Although it is mere tradition, an interesting legend comes from Talmudic sources. It relates that Abram, gazing on the glory of the heavens, asked himself, "Who is the maker of all that?" The sun arose, and Abram fell down and worshipped. Evening came, the sun fell, and Abram cried, "This cannot be the Creator, for this is subject to extinction." The moon arose, the stars beaconed the skies, and Abram exclaimed, "Surely the moon is mistress of the universe, and the stars the mighty throng of her attendants." The moon set, dawn dimmed the stars, and Abram was left without his god. Then he arose and cried, "These are but creatures. They move in obedience to some mightier power. Some hand unseen is ordering their course, and His ordering moves them as His messengers." Imaginative poetry, of course, but not without interest. Perhaps the forming mind of Abram was being prepared for the great religious idealism that made him the father of Israel.

Ur of the Chaldees was a city-kingdom.* All the city-kingdoms had their own peculiar gods, who governed through the king. In Abram's home town the ruling gods were the Moon-god, Nannar, and his consort, Ningal. In other cities, the inhabitants had their own selected gods, the ruling god and many lesser gods. The center of state and municipal administration was in the temple of the ruling god. Here was the national treasury, where all taxes and tithes were paid. Since the temple area was also the center of educational activities, there was usually a temple library.

*See Chapter II, page 24.

Several of these temple libraries have been recovered by archæological expeditions. In them many histories, epic poems, mathematical, astronomical, and grammatical texts have been unearthed. These documents now number into the tens of thousands. The first "all American" archæological expedition into the Near-East, that of the University of Pennsylvania Museum, Philadelphia, under the direction of Dr. J. P. Peters, recovered the temple library at Nippur, consisting of upwards of fifty thousand documents inscribed on clay tablets, in cuneiform characters. Here were found business documents of every kind and description. Here were the lessons of schoolboys who lived four thousand years ago. There were also many hymns and prayers to various Babylonian deities, many of them in style and language closely resembling the Psalms. Tablets bearing the story of the creation were found as well as other tablets giving an ancient Sumerian version of the story of the flood. Another notable find was that of Ernest De Sarzec, who, in 1877, uncovered a remarkable library at Telloh, the site of Lagash. Many other expeditions, English, French, German, and last, but not least, American, have contributed their share. Among the many epics have been found versions of the Story of the Creation, Paradise and the Fall of Man, as well as ancient versions of the Story of the Flood.

Several systems of writing were invented by inhabitants of early centers of rising civilizations. The subsequent development of these early systems of writing was governed somewhat by the materials available for the making of records. So far as is now known, the Sumerians were the first to practice the art of writing. They had no pens, no ink, no paper. With sharpened bone or pointed reed they made crude inscriptions on tablets of clay. Their earliest written work was purely pictographic, an attempt at the realistic rendering of the appearance of actual objects. Later their picture symbols became so conventionalized that the original forms were lost. Their writing never reached the alphabetical stage. Among the many epics they passed on to posterity appear several versions of the Story of the Creation.

The Sumerians deserve distinctive mention in history for many remarkable achievements. With only clay as a building material they built great cities. In building these cities they worked out all the basic architectural forms in use today. They may, or may not, have been the earliest people to make use of the wheel, but they certainly invented the first four-wheel vehicles. They, however, deserve no especial credit for their early conceptions of the working out of the great drama of creation. In every land, in every clime, regardless of whether or not they could read and write, early thinkers were striving to solve the riddle of the universe. Some favored few could set down their conclusions, others could only pass them on by word of mouth to their children.

It is but natural that men who had already begun to note and record the movements of the heavenly bodies, who were marking down on clay tablets the regular appearance of certain planets as morning and evening stars, and noting with awe and wonder the majesty of the solar and lunar eclipse, should ponder deeply on the nature of, and reason for, these sublime phenomena. They could see these wonders but could not understand them. Surely these things were the work of great gods. What gods? The greatest gods that Oriental writers knew were the gods of their own city-kingdoms, *ergo,* their own god must have set the universe in motion. Thus, to many gods, in many lands, went credit for the creation.

Among the most interesting of early Oriental epics is the Epic of Gilgamesh. Gilgamesh was a semi-divine being. His body was formed of "the flesh of the gods"—two-thirds god and one-third man. He was the shepherd king of Erech, a city mentioned in *Genesis* 10. He had great knowledge and wisdom. He knew the history of everything that happened before the deluge. This epic is a story of a quest to discover the meaning of life and death. From this story the Greeks borrowed the idea for the stories of Hercules.

According to the Epic of Gilgamesh mankind was created by the goddess Aruru. The epic contains the lines:

The goddess Aruru, when she heard this,
A man like Anu she formed in her heart.
Aruru washed her hands;
Clay she pinched off and spat upon it;
*Eabani, a hero she created.**

The epic most frequently compared with the early chapters of *Genesis* is the Babylonian Epic of Creation. This is a long poem founded on earlier mythical stories. The epic originally contained over one thousand lines, but a few of the lines are so broken as to be illegible. The story is told on seven tablets which are frequently referred to as the "Seven Tablets of Creation." Some people profess to see some relationship between the seven cantos of the epic and the seven days of the *Genesis* account of the creation. Since the longest and best known version of the epic was written in Babylon, Marduk, the great god of Babylon, is given a leading role in the work of creation. It tells the story of the primeval water-dragons emerging from chaos:

When on high the heavens were not named,
And beneath a home bore no name,
And Apsu primeval, their engenderer,

*For complete translations of the Epic of Gilgamesh see *Archæology and the Bible,* by G. A. Barton, American Sunday School Union. See also *The Babylonian Story of the Deluge and the Epic of Gilgamesh,* British Museum.

And the form Tiamat, the bearer of them all,
There mingled their waters together;
Dark chambers were not constructed, and marsh lands were not seen;
When none of the gods had been brought into being,
And they were not named, and fates were not fixed,
*Then were created the gods in the midst thereof.**

The water-gods, Apsu and Tiamat, are overthrown by Ea and Marduk.
Marduk then proceeds to create the heavens and the earth and finally
creates man, by whom he is adored:

What in his heart he had conceived he offered as a plan:
"Blood will I bind, bone will I fashion,
I will produce a man; 'man' is his name;
I will create man 'man';
Verily by the service of the gods he shall give them rest;
Verily I will alter the ways of the gods."

A Babylonian tablet now in the British Museum credits Marduk with
assisting Aruru in the creation. It reads, in part:

Marduk bound a structure of reeds upon the face of the waters,
He formed dust, he poured it out beside the reed-structure,
To cause the gods to dwell in the habitation of their hearts' desire,
He formed mankind.
The goddess Aruru with him created mankind.

Early thinkers and scholars among all the peoples of the earth attempted
to perpetuate their own conceptions of the great drama of the creation.
Peoples parted so far by geographical space that they could have had no
possible means of communication produced versions of the great story
which bear some resemblance to one another. The strange gods of the
South Pacific Islanders are credited with creative powers which the American Indian attributed to the Great Manitou. Many men have created
many gods, and in turn credited these gods with the creation. These
stories of the creation are a part of the literary inheritance of mankind.

Despite the wide divergence of points of origin, all pagan conceptions
of the creation and the appearance of mankind on earth have some points
in common. This could not well be otherwise. The powers of human
expression are limited. Thinking along similar lines, different authors
used expressions of similar meanings. Modern scholars, in translating
these legends into our modern languages, used our nearest lingual equiv-
alents. Resemblances were accentuated in translation. Many words, many

---

*Many translations of the Babylonian Epic of Creation have been made. It may
be found in full in L. W. King's *Seven Tablets of Creation;* Rogers' *Cuneiform
Parallels to the Old Testament;* G. A. Barton's *Archæology and the Bible,* and in
many other works.

FLOOD TABLET FROM NIPPUR

This tablet contains one of the earliest versions of the Story of the Flood and the Fall of
Man so far discovered. The language is Sumerian.

REVERSE OF FLOOD TABLET

By permission of The Museum of the University of Pennsylvania

expressions of thought, are common not only to the pagan legends but also to the great *Genesis* narrative of the Creation.

The early pagan legends of the creation are of great educational value. From them we can learn of the lines along which the ancients thought, and trace the growth of the languages in which they clothed their thoughts. Modern scholars naturally compare the pagan legends with the *Genesis* narratives. It is fitting and proper that they should. St. Paul advises: "Prove all things, hold fast to that which is good" (*1 Thessalonians* 5:21). However, when one attempts to compare the rather ridiculous pagan epics with the sublime opening chapters of *Genesis* the work is somewhat like comparing the feeble flicker of a tallow taper to the glorious light of the sun. The pagans picture a world created by quarreling, jealous gods: *Genesis* reveals a universe coming into being at the simply spoken command of Almighty God.

> *And the Lord God planted a garden eastward in Eden; and there he put the man whom he had formed.*—Genesis 2:8

The story of Paradise is another of the universal stories. In one form or another it is found in the legends and folklore of all ancient peoples. Some of these ancient legends place Paradise and the Fall of Man after the flood. In some Sumerian versions of the story Uta-Napishtam survives the flood and becomes a gardener. Nintud, the earth goddess, advises him as to which fruits he may safely eat. He is forbidden to eat the fruit of the cassia tree. He eats it. For this he is afflicted with bodily weakness and loses the longevity of the prediluvian age.[*]

In the Sumerian Epic of Paradise, now in the University Museum, Philadelphia, a god and a goddess are represented as ruling over paradise:[†]

> *Enki, the water god, and his consort Ninela or Damkina, ruled over mankind and paradise. In that land there was no infirmity, no sin, and man grew not old.*

In ancient Sumerian and Babylonian documents the stories of the Creation, the Fall of Man, and the Flood usually appear together. In a crude, but extremely interesting manner, the writers present a survey of their pagan beliefs regarding the early eras of mankind on earth.

> *And it came to pass after seven days, that the waters of the flood were upon the earth.*—Genesis 7:10

The story of the Flood is still another of the universal stories. If possible, it is even more widespread than the story of the Creation. Between

---

[*]See *Sumerian Epic of Paradise, the Flood and the Fall of Man*, by Stephen Langdon, Philadelphia, 1915, page 6ff.

[†]*Ibid.*

3

the stories of the Creation and the stories of the Flood there is, however, one distinctive difference. The pagan stories of the Creation are pure invention, the blind gropings of heathen minds looking for light on an apparently unsolvable problem. On the other hand, the stories of the Flood had firm foundation in fact. Only a few centuries before the time of some of the Sumerian writers, the rising civilization their forefathers had known was wiped out by an overwhelming deluge of water and its remains buried deep under a blanket of water-borne clay.*

These early stories of the Flood had many points in common, many interesting parallels. Unlike the great mystery of Creation, the Flood was something the pagan writers could more or less understand. They knew of its effects, but understood nothing of its causes. To their minds the Deluge was the work of gods, their gods, who thus vented their wrath on unsatisfactory creatures whom they had created. The writers interpreted the event in terms of their beliefs in their own heathen gods.

Sumerian tablets record that for some reason Enki, god of wisdom, became dissatisfied with man and decided to overwhelm him with his waters. This plan he revealed to Nintud, the earth goddess, who with Enlil, the earth god, had created man. For nine months the flood endured and man dissolved in the waters like tallow or fat. Nintud (or Ninharsag) planned to save the king and certain pious ones. In the epic the story is related to Gilgamesh:†

> I will reveal to thee, O Gilgamesh, the secret story,
> And the decision of the gods will I relate.
> Shurippak, a city which thou knowest,
> Is situated on the banks of the Euphrates.
> That city was old and the gods in it—
> Their hearts prompted them to make a deluge.
> Their father Anu,
> Their councillor, the warrior Enlil,
> Their herald, Enmastu,
> Their hero, Enugi,
> The lord of wisdom, Enki, counselled with them;
> Their words he repeated unto the reed-hut:
> "O reed-hut, reed-hut, O wall, wall,
> O reed-hut hearken; O wall, give heed!
> O man of Shurippak, son of Ubaratutu,
> Pull down thy house, build a ship,
> Leave thy possessions,
> Take thought for thy life,

---

*See Chapter II, page 24.

†See British Museum Booklet, *The Babylonian Story of the Deluge and the Epic of Gilgamesh*, page 31ff. See also *Archæology and the Bible*, by G. A. Barton, Part II, Chapter VI.

Leave thy gods, thy life save!
Embark seed of all kinds on a ship!
The ship which thou shalt build,
Measure well its dimensions,
Make it correspond its breadth and length;
Upon the ocean thou shalt launch it.

A tablet from Nippur, now in the Imperial Museum in Constantinople, contains a vivid description of the deluge which reads:

Once on a time the spirit, the wrathful Word,
The Deluge gathered all.
The raging storm uttered its roar with terror.
The devastating spirit with its seven winds caused the heavens
*   to moan.*
The violent storm caused the earth to quake.
The storm-god in the vast heavens shrieked.
And there were little hail-stones and great hail-stones.

What are probably the earliest known versions of the flood story are found on tablets from Nippur now in the University Museum, Philadelphia. These date from about 2200 B. C.* According to Langdon's translation a part of the lines read:

Her herald the divine anointed ones called.
The sons of men who were pious she was not wroth against.

.   .   .   .

My king who was filled with fear,
His foot alone upon the boat set.
Two humbles as watchmen he placed on guard.
Doubly he caulked the ship, torches he lighted.
Enki devastated the fields.
The fields received the waters of Enki.

Naturally, there is wide latitude in the opinions of modern scholars in regard to the flood. The discoveries of Wooley at Ur of the Chaldees and of Mackay and Langdon at Kish would seem to render untenable the position of those who simply dismiss the matter as mythical legend and say, "There was no flood." The story certainly has historical foundation. While it is no longer possible to doubt the reality of the Flood, scholars will continue to debate as to its extent and duration. Men naturally read the story in the light of varying predilections in religious opinion.

Those who accept the *Genesis* narrative as written stand in good company. The enlightened Isaiah, greatest of all writers, declares: "For this is as the waters of Noah for as I have sworn that the waters of Noah

*See *Museum Journal,* published by University Museum, Philadelphia, Vol. IV, No. 2.

should no more go over the earth" (*Isaiah* 54:9). St. Paul added his testimony: "By faith Noah, being warned of God of things not seen as yet, moved with fear, prepared an ark to the saving of his house" (*Hebrews* 11:7). Peter, in his *First Epistle* (See 1 *Peter* 3:20), speaks of Noah and the ark, while in his *Second Epistle* he writes of a universal flood: "Whereby the world that then was, being overflowed, perished" (2 *Peter* 3:6). Jesus of Nazareth, in His great lessons on faith, speaks of Noah as a personality (See *Matthew* 24:37), and uses the Flood as an illustration (See *Luke* 17:27).

One of the purposes of *Genesis* was to visualize the emergence of Israel out of a dark background of pagandom. Abraham, the father of Israel, had been reared in an idolatrous city. When he left Ur of the Chaldees he had broken with idolatry. He had found the faith of the people among whom he was raised unsatisfactory. Later, as he communed with his God in the quietude of the hills of Haran, he had been given an inspired conception of man's spiritual relationship with his Creator. Here the mighty intellect of Abraham became conscious of the all-pervading Presence of the One True God. God found Abraham; Abraham found God. This God whom Abraham had come to know could not be defined or described by any term within the mental range of mankind, yet, since He was the God of mankind, He must be given a name that could be understood by men. The name given was *Yahweh*, or Jehovah, which means, "he was, he is, and he will be." From Jehovah came the call to Abraham: "Get thee out of thy country, and from thy kindred, and from thy father's house, unto a land that I will shew thee" (*Genesis* 12:1), "and he went out, not knowing whither he went" (*Hebrews* 11:8), into the land we today call Palestine.

Abraham is the central figure in most of the great picture-narratives of *Genesis*. Through Abraham the writer introduces the Hebrews as a people into written history. The writer, however, contemplated a concise, but comprehensive survey of pre-Abrahamic history as an introduction to his narratives of how the Chosen People came to know and recognize the sovereignty of Jehovah.

The great wonder-drama of the Creation, which had puzzled the philosophers of the ages, was divinely revealed to the illumined mind of the great Hebrew writer as a sublime synthesis of the supreme Intelligence and Authority whom the Hebrews knew as Jehovah. The writer knew that he was but the instrument of revelation, his mind but the means of conveying to mankind the working out of God's eternal laws. To him was given the undying distinction of presenting to a waiting world the true picture of the universe in the beginning, and of man as a creature fresh from the hand of his Creator.

II

IN ANCIENT CHALDEA

And they went forth with them from Ur of the Chaldees.—Genesis
11:31

THE epiclike style used by the writer of *Genesis* called for little
in the way of dates or exact geographical delimitation. The writer
was interested in portraying the human dimensions of the found-
ers of a great religious movement, and visualizing by picture narratives
the backgrounds in which the recorded events took place. In introducing
the Hebrews as a people into written history, he chose as his working
medium a series of sermonettes in biography. With loving art he presents faithful portraits of the early religious leaders of his race. In un-
surpassable word-pictures he depicts the parts they played in the great
human drama that gave to the world a new conception of man's relationship with God and a new pattern for righteous living.

Fortunately, he did not choose the uncompromising methods of the
Occidental historian. Such methods would have been utterly alien to him.
He was essentially an Oriental, and chose, naturally, the Oriental style of
writing.

His fascinating, human interest stories illuminate the beginnings of a
great religious movement. In these stories he has given us the ground-
work on which, through the later Biblical narratives and external and
contemporary supplementing evidence, the historian and the archæologist
are enabled to weave into a continuous pattern the glorious history of
the Chosen People.

The portraits of the patriarchs presented in *Genesis* are by no means
the earliest biographical sketches in existence. Archæological and linguistic research has revealed many interesting documents of a biographical
nature that long antedate the *Genesis* narratives of Abraham and his
descendants. Compared with the crude efforts of contemporary biograph-
ers, however, the immortal stories told in *Genesis* shine like beacon lights
of literature. No writer, in any age, has ever equalled the genius displayed in *Genesis* for portraying the greatness of individuals without
neglecting their human frailties. As character studies, the *Genesis* narratives of the patriarchs stand alone in literature.

Of Abraham's boyhood the Bible tells us nothing. Talmudic and
Mohammedan traditions picture him as having been the son of an idol

maker of Ur of the Chaldees; but on Abraham's life before he left Ur the Old Testament is silent. In *Genesis* 11, however, it is made clear that Abraham spent his boyhood and young manhood at Ur of the Chaldees. Abraham was a son of Ur, a child of Chaldea.

Sometime about B. C. 2000, Terah, the father of Abraham, decided to migrate to Haran, far to the north on the left bank of the Euphrates. Terah was the head of the clan-family at this time. Abraham's adventures in Canaan did not begin until long later, "when he was called to go out into a place which he should after receive for an inheritance" (*Hebrews* 11:8). The latter day Hebrews always thought of Chaldea as being the home of their ancestors. Joshua, addressing the assembly at Shechem, pointed out: "Your fathers dwelt on the other side of the Flood" (the Euphrates) "in old time, even Terah, the father of Abraham . . . and they served other gods" (*Joshua* 24:2). It is to this crossing of the Euphrates by Abraham and his followers that the word "Hebrew" owes its origin. They were the first *'ebirim,* "crossers over," "Hebrews."

If "the child is father to the man," and if a man is in part the product of his early environment, the Bible reader should be interested in the city where Abraham spent his boyhood, his impressionable years. If you will glance at a map you will see that Chaldea stretches northward from the head of the Persian Gulf. It is a great alluvial plain through which flow the "twin rivers," the Tigris and the Euphrates. You will find that Ur is located about ten miles west of the present course of the Euphrates and almost midway between Bagdad and the Gulf. The scene about Ur is one of desolation and decay. Drab clay and yellow sand shroud the ruins of a realm that has dried to desert.

Undisturbed for centuries there stood out in this desert waste a low mound called "Tell al Muqayyar," which means in Arabic, "the Mound of Pitch." In 1854 this mound was investigated by J. F. Taylor, then the British Consul at Bazra. Taylor merely scratched the surface in his operations, but he took from the mound a number of clay tablets and cylinders, and other inscriptioned articles. These he shipped to the British Museum, and when the authorities there had deciphered the inscriptions on the tablets and cylinders it became known that the Mound of Pitch undoubtedly covered a portion of the site of the long-lost City of Abraham, Ur of the Chaldees.

Two or three attempts were made to carry the work of excavation further, but, owing to unsettled political conditions and the hostility of the natives, work had to be abandoned until after the close of the World War, when all of Babylonia passed into the control of Great Britain under a mandate. In 1921 a joint expedition was fitted out by the University Museum of Philadelphia and the British Museum to explore thoroughly the ruins of the city from which Abraham went forth "to go into the land of Canaan." To the years of labor expended by this expedition we owe practically all our knowledge of Ur, the boyhood home of Abraham.

The excavation of Ur of the Chaldees opened up one of the most fascinating chapters in the history of archæology. Not only did it bring to light interesting information as to the civilization, education, and culture of the people, thus enabling us to form a clear conception of the daily life of Abraham's neighbors; it also enabled us to read in material evidence the story of Ur from long before Abraham's day down to the time of the Persian invasion, when the ill-fated Belshazzar met his death at the hands of the Medes and Persians.

The country about Ur was not always the scene of such desolation as exists there today. What are now ruins in a parched plain, Abraham saw as a great city in the midst of one of the richest agricultural districts the world has ever known. In order to form a clear conception of the home city of Abraham it is necessary to let the mind travel back beyond the first dim dawnings of human history in the great river valley back to a time when the plain between the twin rivers was merely a great tidewater marsh. Each year the rivers brought down vast quantities of silt from the hill country to the north, and deposited it over the marshes. Gradually the rivers took more definite courses, and dry land appeared in the form of low banks and hummocks. Into this low country came a semi-barbaric people who subsisted largely by hunting and fishing. For shelter they built little wattle huts, that is, huts made of branches plastered with Mesopotamian clay. They were a skin-clad people, although toward the end of their day they had some slight knowledge of the use of the loom for weaving.

After a time a more advanced people entered the country, and proceeded to crowd the original settlers from the choicer portions of the land between the rivers. This early start toward civilization was interrupted by a great disaster which destroyed the inhabitants of the country and all their works. This calamity was in the form of a deluge that buried the entire district under a blanket of water-borne clay eight feet thick, and left the country depopulated. "The windows of heaven" had opened to spread a shroud of clay over a rising civilization and leave it sepulchred in timeless silence to await the day when, in 1928, the spade of the scientific investigator would penetrate its resting place to reveal to the world a hitherto unknown people, and prove that the story of Noah and his adventures had a sound basis in fact.

During the season of 1928-1929, the excavators at Ur, while sinking a test pit, came upon this bed of clay, and thought at first they had reached an ancient bed of the river.* Subsequently, on digging through this bed of alluvial deposit, they came upon the remains of this early start toward civilization, showing burnt bricks of a size and shape previously unknown. Although the investigation of the material evidence left behind by this early people, who were destroyed by the great inundation, is largely a problem for the future, this find at Ur and other more recent finds at other sites indicate a flood of great extent and considerable duration. This was no mere river flood. This great disaster brought all life and all movement toward civilization to a sudden stop, and left that region depopulated for a long period. The story of a deluge, as found in *Genesis* and on Sumerian tablets, is not pure legend as many have supposed, but has a strong basis in actual history. The most drastic critic must admit that the story of Noah now takes on a new aspect.

Long after the Flood a new people came into the country between the twin rivers. This people is commonly called "the Sumerians." They were probably attracted by the rich agricultural possibilities of the district. They turned the country into a "farmers' paradise" by cultivating intensively the rich alluvial soil, which they irrigated with great systems of canals and lateral ditches. This great agricultural wealth naturally brought about trade and commerce. Commerce called for trading centers at strategic points along the water courses. As the trading centers grew into cities the inhabitants, to protect their wealth from the plundering tribes of the hinterland, erected heavy walls about their cities. Each city guarded and governed the district surrounding it. Thus developed the city-states, or city-kingdoms, of ancient Chaldea. Such a city-kingdom was Ur of the Chaldees.

Trade and commerce are always the advance agents of civilization. Civilization really began when man said to man, "This is mine and that is thine, and I will exchange part of what is mine for part of that which is thine." When commerce advanced beyond the barter stage it called for accounting and written records. Long before Abraham's day the Chaldeans had invented a method of writing. Like all primitive systems of writing, it was originally pictographic. The earliest examples of this system still in known existence—such as the Kish tablet in Oxford— had reached a stage where the pictographic symbols represented sounds, syllable sounds, not single letter sounds. Which branch of the human race first invented writing—the placing of connected thought into permanent record—is at present unknown. At the present time the writing of the Chaldeans is the oldest known.

---

*See *Ur of the Chaldees*, by C. L. Wooley, page 21ff.

As a material on which to inscribe their permanent records the Chaldeans had only one native substance, clay. Using a reed or bone stylus, they made markings on clay tablets, which were afterward baked. A sharp instrument used on clay makes a wedge-shaped mark. From this characteristic we have the word "cuneiform," "wedge-shaped," as applied to this ancient method of writing. All early systems of writing developed along lines governed by the nature of the materials on which the records were made. The Egyptians used the pith of the papyrus plant, which they pressed into thin sheets, then scraped with bone or shell to make an excellent writing surface. Using this medium, the Egyptians were able to make more realistic renderings of objects than was possible with wet clay. Both in Egypt and Mesopotamia, in later times, the picture symbols became so conventionalized that their original form was lost; but neither attained the stage of alphabetic writing.

Before Abraham's day the inhabitants of Ur had made excellent progress in mathematics and accounting. Elaborately ruled and accurately balanced business documents attest the business training and ability of merchants and record keepers. The variety of products handled indicates that merchants traded over a wide radius that extended far beyond the natural geographical boundaries of the kingdom of Ur.

Strange as it may seem in our day of mass production, Abraham's home town was a manufacturing city. The inventive genius and technical skill of the craftsmen and artisans of Ur gave the city the distinction of being one of the earliest of manufacturing towns. The principal manufactured products were in the lines of articles of personal adornment in gold and silver and of household utility in copper and bronze. Since the region had no native metals, all the raw materials for this extensive manufacturing had to be imported. This exchange of manufactured products of Ur for metals from other lands developed the commerce that made Ur a city of wealth and luxury.

The artistic development and creative ability of the craftsmen of Ur are well exemplified by the findings in the graves of "the Unknown Kings" in the Royal Cemetery.* The exact age of these tombs is difficult to determine. A rough estimate of their age might be said to be the third millennium B. C. It may be safely said that they were old when Abraham was young. The language on inscriptioned objects found is Sumerian. The Sumerians did not mummify their dead. They did, however, provide them with servants and with complete equipment for life and travel in another world.

The graves of the Unknown Kings had been very thoroughly despoiled by expert grave-robbers centuries ago, but fortunately one grave, that

*See *Ur Excavations*, Vol. II, by C. L. Wooley, page 33ff.

of Queen Shubad, remained intact. Thousands of years ago the remains of the young queen had been deposited in her stone-built vault. Her cold clay, dressed in royal robes, had been decorated with a mass of crown jewels, and surrounded with vessels of stone, copper, and precious metals. Outside the tomb proper, in the great "death pit" adjacent, the conveyance that brought her there, and the animals that drew it, with the groom at their heads, the armed dromos who acted as guards, and the brightly clad, jewel-bedecked young women of the queen's personal retinue were sepulchred to serve their sovereign in another world. The secret of how they met their deaths slumbers with them.

The architects and builders of Ur faced unusual handicaps in erecting their city. The country had no stone, no lime, no timber. A little stone was imported for the construction of royal tombs and other special purposes. The only native building materials were Mesopotamian clay and bitumen. The writer of *Genesis,* although he lived in a country where stone and mortar were used for building, shows by his circumstantial details that he was familiar with Chaldean building materials and methods when he says: "And they said one to another, Go to, let us make brick, and burn them thoroughly. And they had brick for stone, and slime" (*i.e.,* bitumen) "had they for mortar" (*Genesis* 11:3). The outstanding architectural feature of every Chaldean city was a great temple tower, usually referred to by the Assyrian name "ziggurat" (Hill of Heaven). These ziggurats are, in a way, prototypes of the "Tower of Babel." The Chaldeans made excellent brick. The usual size of these is something over twenty inches long, twelve inches wide, and four inches thick. With these brick and imported timber for roofing and trim, the builders of Ur reared imposing structures. Sometimes many of the bricks in a building were stamped with the name of the king who reigned when the structure was being erected. Naturally, the builders of Ur, using only brick, could never obtain the architectural effects possible to peoples who possessed unlimited stone for building purposes, but they developed all the basic architectural forms in use today. The great Greek builders of the fourth century B. C. borrowed all their basic architectural forms from ancient Chaldea.

When the coating of clay, the decomposed residue of bricks disintegrated by the wind and weather of centuries, was removed from the Mound of Pitch, the great ziggurat of Ur stood revealed. This ziggurat is the best preserved of any so far discovered. It forms a part of a great temple complex, and was built by King Ur-Nammu and his son Dungi during the Third Dynasty of Ur (B. C. 2300-2180). This tower measures more than two hundred feet in length by one hundred and fifty in width, and its original height was something over seventy feet. The outer walls are laid up in burnt brick and bitumen. The whole structure is one solid mass of brickwork without passages or chambers within. The building of the ziggurat was accomplished without a single straight line showing on its outer surfaces. Every surface conforms to carefully calculated curves, both longitudinally and vertically. The architect aimed at an optical illusion, which the Greek builders of the Parthenon were to achieve many centuries later. Three great stairways led to the top, which was staged off into a series of terraces, and crowning all was a small sanctuary surrounded by trees and flowers that ornamented the terraces.

Since the great ziggurat was in its glory in Abraham's day, he must have seen the great religious processions, bright with banners and gay with music, wending their way up the triple stairways of the structure toward the sanctuary on the summit, there to offer adoration to Nannar and Ningal, the Moon-god and Moon-goddess of ancient Ur. The ziggurat formed a part of the "Temenos," or sacred area, all of which was enclosed in a massive brick wall. Within the walls of the sacred area were the temples dedicated to the Moon-god and his consort. The Moon-god was regarded as the ruler of the city-kingdom, administering through the king. This type of national administration centered all the public offices of the realm in the sacred area. Here the neighbors of Abraham came to pay their tithes, their rent, and their taxes. Here all important documents had to be drawn in due legal form, signed, sealed, and properly attested by the contracting parties, the scribe, and the witnesses.

Abram, son of Terah, had the good fortune to be reared in the greatest center of culture and education in the then-known world. The youthful Abram strolling the narrow streets of ancient Ur must have been impressed by the busy scene about him. In his cosmopolitan city he must have known, or at least seen, men from varied walks of life, shepherds and agriculturists, craftsmen and merchants, priests, soldiers, and government officials, as well as semi-barbaric tribesmen from the hinterland. In his day the river followed its old course and flowed past the city. As he loitered, boy-fashion, on the wharves, he must have seen the slaves unloading from ships the raw materials so necessary for the life of the manufacturing city. The eager eyes of youth must have watched the fascinating processes with which the craftsmen molded and hammered, welded and soldered the gold from the rivers of many lands, the silver from southern Persia and the mountains of the north, the bronze from Oman, and the copper from foreign mines.

The lad must have been interested in the goods the merchants offered for sale in the bazaars. Here was pottery made from the native clay of the river banks, clothing made from native cloth, and the fruits of the soil from the fertile fields surrounding the city; but, here also were artistically shaped diorite cups, bowls and lamps of alabaster, household utensils in copper and bronze, articles of personal adornment in gold and silver, lapis-lazuli, carnelian and other semi-precious stones, and cunningly-shaped containers for cosmetics.

The streets of young Abram's town were very narrow. They were so narrow that at intersecting streets the outermost corners of the houses were rounded so as not to damage goods being transported on donkey back. There were no windows on the street front through which Abram's inquisitive young eyes could have caught a glimpse of his neighbors. The only opening to the street was a heavy door. The houses, mostly two stories in height, depended for light and air on the central court around which they were built. This paved courtyard was the principal feature of the house. Careful reconstructions made by Dr. C. L. Wooley, director of the expedition, enable us to visualize the domestic arrangement of the houses that were erected during the Larsa Period, about the time young Abram lived in Ur. Entering the house from the street, one came into a tiny lobby in which provision had been made for the washing of feet (Comp. *Genesis* 24:32). On the first floor was a kitchen provided with a fireplace, a large reception room for guests, servants' quarters, and a domestic chapel. The second floor of the house was reached by means of a brick stairway. Under the stairway, on the first floor, was a lavatory. The top of the stairway opened on a wooden gallery that ran around the courtyard at the second-floor level. The upper rooms were entered from this gallery.

Abram's neighbors wore brightly colored woolen outer garments. Those of the men were worn toga-fashion, over one shoulder and under the opposite arm. This was fastened in front with a long pin which was usually of copper, but might be of gold or silver with a highly ornamented head. Both sexes wore much jewelry. Presumably, the old folks worried then as now because the young women were going "modern." The girls fixed up their eyebrows, aided nature a bit with a touch of color on their cheeks, and added a dark green shadow under the eyes. When decked out for festive occasions they wore much false hair fashioned into place with ribbons of pure gold, gold so soft that it would wind easily tight to the head. Surmounting their dusky locks, those that nature gave them and those they had purchased, rose a broad pin of gold, like a Spanish comb, spreading into seven points connected with gold wire. Many of the ladies' "vanities" recovered still contained the cosmetics that were used to decorate complexions that passed into nothingness over four thousand years ago!

As young Abram grew to manhood he was constantly rubbing shoulders with men who could read and write, with artists and skilled craftsmen, with merchants and traders, and with men learned in the law. He lived in a city whose inhabitants had inherited a culture based on definite progress in almost every branch of science, and had already evolved that complex mode of life that is called civilization. Civilization is relative. As civilization advances more attention is paid to the higher branches of learning. Men have more leisure to think. Leisure to think and the ability to write are the parents of history. The rise and development of economic and political movements of yesteryear are the history of today: those of today are the history of tomorrow. History is the record of human achievement in the past: literature, our priceless inheritance from the great minds of the ages. Judging by the histories and the literature the inhabitants of Abram's home town left behind them they were a civilized people. Abram's youth must have been rich in life experiences.

Until comparatively recent years it has been commonly assumed that what we call "our western civilization" had its origins in the valley of the Nile. Ancient Egypt was commonly credited with being the cradle of civilization. This was but natural. Egypt has long been "the happy hunting ground" of the historian and the archæologist. Ever since the scientists who accompanied Napoleon on his invasion of Egypt in 1798 published their interesting reports, scientific investigators have flocked to the valley of the Nile. When, early in the eighteenth century, the French scholar, J. F. Champollion, found the linguistic key which unlocked the mystery of hieroglyphic writing, the history of a civilization many millenniums old was revealed.

The inscriptions and reliefs on the monumental architecture of ancient Egypt picture every phase of rural, urban, and commercial life through thousands of years of rising civilization. Here the scholar can trace the history of agriculture, of transportation by land and water, and of the development of trade and commerce.

Much of the history of Egypt can be definitely dated. Thousands of years ago the Egyptians recognized the value of exact chronologies. They worked out and elaborated an excellent calendar which served their needs for thousands of years. On stone and on papyri these ancients left behind them a remarkable record of intellectual achievement. It was natural that ancient Egypt should have been looked upon as the cradle of civilization.

Recent discoveries in ancient Chaldea have called for many modifications of initial conceptions of the rise of civilization. Many standard textbooks on the subject have been completely antiquated by information gleaned at the point of the spade by modern scientific investigators. The unearthing of the ruins of ancient Chaldean cities reveals that much of the civilization of ancient Egypt was borrowed from a much older and much broader civilization which flourished in the Tigris-Euphrates valley at a time when the Nile valley was inhabited by tribes of wandering nomads.

The Old Testament—greatest of our literary treasures—was produced by a cultured people, by a people who had made long strides toward civilization. With all due allowances for divine inspiration and for prophetic revelation, it must be admitted that such an outstanding literary production could only be the work of a cultured people. Hebraic civilization must have been of slow growth. The thought and life of the Israelites must have been greatly influenced by the many peoples with whom they mingled as they wound their tortuous trail along the paths of history. They borrowed much in the way of culture, but they must, also, have benefited from a rich cultural inheritance. Not in Palestine, nor in Egypt, but in Chaldea began the rise of Hebraic civilization.

It is not the purpose of the present writer to attempt to trace the beginnings of civilization. It would be interesting to speculate on wher primitive man first scratched seed into the soil and first began to herd the animals he formerly hunted, thus starting the twin industries of farming and stock raising. These industries form the economic basis of civilization. Food is the first instinctive need of man. In farming was found the means of meeting this need for settled populations. Farming also met, in part, man's second great need, clothing. Where farming first began is a matter of conjecture, but long before the Nile valley was extensively cultivated the Chaldean farmers were reaping rich harvests from the soil.

Next to food and clothing, shelter is the most pressing need of man. Where man constructed his first artificial shelter is not known, but the remains of the world's oldest known city were found at Tepe Gawra in northern Irak. All the basic architectural forms which enter into the construction of the modern "sky-scraper" were first worked out by the inhabitants of ancient Chaldea.

Weaving is supposed to have originated when some keen observer noted the pattern in wind-blown grass. Who was the first weaver? No one knows, but the earliest loom-weights so far discovered were found in Chaldea.

Probably the earliest scientists were astronomers. To gaze at the heavens is to ask questions. It is likely that the first astronomers were shepherds. Flocks had to be closely watched at night. Shepherds, perhaps, were the first to note the phases of the moon. Certain stars appeared at certain points in the heavens at certain seasons. This recurrence was regular. The stars were a surer guide of direction than the sun or the moon. The star is prominent among the earliest pictographs that man inscribed on clay. The first astronomical records of the ancients must have been extremely crude, but the modern astronomer, looking forward eagerly to the revealing of myriads of now unknown stars through the two-hundred-inch telescope now building in America, can check to a second the time of astronomical observations made in Chaldea thousands of years ago.

There is evidently a close connection between the work of the early astronomer and the first attempts at an orderly system of reckoning time in the form of an annual calendar. Early observers in many countries must have noted the regularity of the moon's revolutions and that a complete revolution (from new moon to new moon) occurred twelve times between seed time and seed time. Fitting the periods of the moon's revolutions (lunar months) which occupy a period of 29 days, 12 hours, 44 minutes, and 2.7 seconds, with the period of the earth's revolution around the sun (astronomical year) which covers 365 days, 5 hours, 48 minutes, and 45.51 seconds, must have caused early calendar makers many a headache. They never succeeded in solving this problem.

The ancient Egyptians based their calendar on the appearance of Sirius, the "dog star" of later day Greeks. The Egyptians noted that the rise of this star coincided with the annual rise of the Nile, which takes place in June. The rise of the Nile is the most important natural phenomenon which is peculiar to Egypt. On the annual overflow of the river depends the agricultural prosperity of the country. Since the star always appeared on the date which is now the 19th of June, the ancient Egyptians made this the opening date of their system of reckoning time. They called the star "Sothis" and their calendar is known as the "Sothic Calendar." This calendar covered only 365 days, taking no account of the odd hours and fractions of the hour needed to make their calendar year coincide with the astronomical year, thus their calendar gained a quarter of a day every year or a full day every four years. In each 1,460 (365x4) years their calendar gained a full year and the new year started on the original date, June 19th. These 1,460 years formed what is known as the "Sothic Cycle" which is commonly used in determining early Egyptian dates.

The calendar the Old Testament Hebrews used was derived from Sumerian and Babylonian sources. This was an agricultural calendar. The first definite date given in the Bible (*Genesis* 7:11) speaks of "the second month, the seventeenth day of the month." *Genesis* 8 speaks of the "seventh month" (v. 4), the "tenth month" (v. 5), and the "first month" (v. 13). The many mentions of the months with their numbers in the Old Testament indicates clearly that the Hebrews had a twelve-month calendar. There was a definite connection between the numbering of the months and the agricultural pursuits of the people. A fragment of a Hebrew calendar dating from the days of the Hebrew monarchy was found by R. A. S. Macalister during his excavations at Gezer.* This furnishes a clue to the numbering of the months. The "First Month" was the "Month of Ingathering," or October. *Exodus* 23:16 speaks of "the feast of ingathering, which is in the end of the year." This may have been a sort of new-year feast.

Even at the earliest date to which the writing of *Genesis* is ascribed there is nothing anachronistic in the giving of dates. The Chaldeans had a well defined system of reckoning time long before young Abram left Ur of the Chaldees. Dynastic tablets now in the University Museum in Philadelphia give dates for kings of Ur which are dependable for at least as early as B. C. 3000. Abram left Ur approximately one thousand years later.

As civilization advances increased leisure gives opportunity for the study and development of the arts—music, painting, sculpture, and literature.

Probably primitive man formed some crude conceptions of music through rhythmic drumming on a hollow log, or he may have found the forerunner of the harp in the musical vibration of his bowstring. Recent excavations in the Mesopotamian valley have added hundreds of years to the history of musical instruments. The Old Testament places the invention of musical instruments before the flood in the passage which says: "He was the father of all such as handle the harp and organ" (*Genesis* 4:21). In this connection it is interesting to note that the oldest known musical instrument yet recovered was recently found in Tepe Gawra by Dr. E. A. Speiser, Director of the joint expedition of the University Museum of Philadelphia and the American School of Oriental Research, Bagdad. This was a simple flute, found in the grave of a child who belonged to the last remnants of the Painted Pottery People.

No people of their day made such progress in music and the development of musical instruments as the Sumerians. The stela of Ur-Nammu, who built the ziggurat at Ur long before Abram lived there, shows a musical instrument in the form of a double pipe. Other earlier reliefs show the same instrument. The remains of many beautiful stringed instruments were at Ur of the Chaldees.† These were not the crude instruments of semi-barbarians. The sounding boxes were shaped and inlaid by expert craftsmen. On these harps and lyres the number of strings varies from four to eleven. The harps found in the tomb of Queen Shubad date to the third millennium B. C.

---

*See *Excavation of Gezer*, II, page 1ff, by R. A. S. Macalister.
†See *Ur Excavations*, by C. L. Wooley, Chapter XII, page 249.

THE ZIGGURAT AT UR

Built by King Ur Nammu during the Third Dynasty of Ur (B. C. 2300-2180). The Ziggurat (Hill of Heaven) was the outstanding architectural feature of all early Babylonian and Assyrian cities.

SCALE REPRESENTATION OF THE ZIGGURAT

This great structure, part of a temple complex, was in its glory when Abram lived at Ur.

All early peoples made extensive use of colors. Before man could write he was attempting to paint pictures, often with considerable success. In fact, his first writing was merely a series of pictures. In art the peoples of the Mesopotamian valley were early leaders. Mention was made in a previous chapter that the earliest known attempt at landscape painting was found at Tepe Gawra, the world's oldest known city.* The inhabitants of ancient Chaldea deserve little credit for their excellent sculptures. Necessity forced them to make articles from clay and modeling was but a natural development of the art.

The world of letters owes much to the Chaldeans for trail-breaking work in literature. The literary giants of the "Golden Age of Greece" borrowed many of their ideas from Chaldean and Babylonian sources. Many learned commentators on the Scriptures have assumed that Abram was an unlettered nomad when he left Ur of the Chaldees. There would seem to be little to support this view. It would seem passing strange if the great religious genius whose mental and spiritual stature has shadowed the centuries was unable to read and write. The *Genesis* narratives of Abram's later life picture him as a person who took advantage of every opportunity. In his native city he had ample opportunity to learn to read. The foundations of Abram's massive character were laid while he lived in Ur. From the city of his boyhood the ancestor of Israel must have taken much in the way of culture.

In the light of modern archæological research the *Genesis* narratives of Abram's later life become increasingly vital. There is a ring of reality about the great stories of the child of Chaldea who, as Abraham, became the "Father of the Faithful" and of whom it was said: "Abraham believed God, and it was imputed unto him for righteousness: and he was called the Friend of God"—*James* 2:23.

*See Chapter I, page 12.

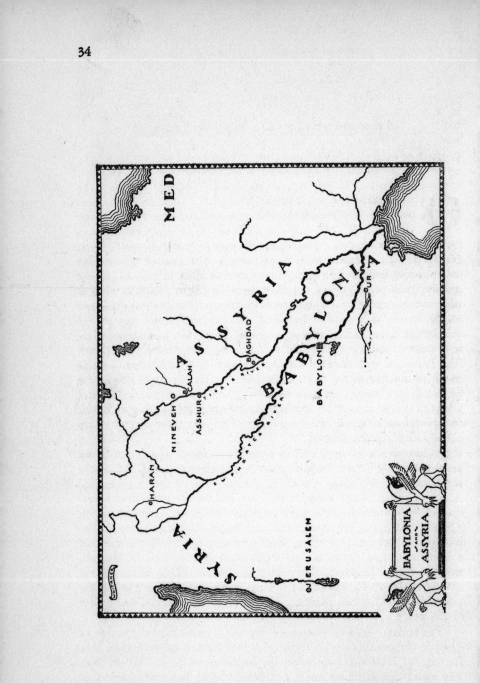

III

THE PATRIARCHS IN CANAAN

And the Canaanite was then in the land.—Genesis 12:6

ON the reason that the family of Terah left Ur the Bible is silent, other than the statement: "Your fathers dwelt on the other side of the Flood" (the Euphrates River) "in old time, even Terah, the father of Abraham . . . and they served other gods" (*Joshua* 24:2). Perhaps in this statement from *Joshua* and in the ruins of the temples of Ur may be found a clue to the reason for the family migration. Ur was an idolatrous city. Terah's neighbors were idolaters. Terah's relatives who remained in Chaldea remained idolatrous. According to *Genesis* 31 the household of Laban, Abraham's nephew, was thrown into an uproar by the disappearance of the household gods. Many of these household gods, or teraphim, are found in the ruins of cities all over the Near-East. Abraham was reared in idolatry. It may be that Abraham's ideals could not flourish in the pagan atmosphere of Ur. Perhaps, among the quiet hills of Haran, alone with the silence and his God, he could better prepare the message eternal that he was later to carry to a pagan world, and formulate the gospel that causes men of many faiths to reverence him as the "Father of the Faithful."

It may have been easy to err in some of our initial conceptions of the personality of Abraham. Probably most of us picture Abraham as a simple shepherd wandering about Canaan in the dim days of the Third Bronze Age with his flocks and herds, in the same manner as the Bedouin herdsmen of today drift over the same territory. When we study the city in which Abraham was raised and the cultural and educational opportunities which were open to him there, and note that he talked on terms of equality with the kings of his day and was received at court by Pharaoh, that his Hittite neighbors deferred to him as "a mighty prince among us" (*Genesis* 23:6), it becomes increasingly possible to picture the patriarch as a Chaldean patrician, an educated, cultured, civilized citizen of the world.

The known world of Abraham's day was a small world. Outside of Egypt it consisted mostly of territories which formed parts of what was, for us, the Turkish Empire before the beginning of the late World War. The world that Abraham knew was dominated by two rising centers of civilization, Mesopotamia and Egypt. Between these centers lay many mountains and much desert and semi-desert country, but the most important territory was the "fertile crescent" which rimmed the arid regions in a great arc reaching from the Euphrates to the Nile. Here lay what is now known as Palestine and Syria with Asia Minor in the background. Beyond these boundaries a semi-barbaric hinterland was slowly emerging into known history.

When the migrating family of Terah left Ur its immediate destination, according to *Genesis* 11:31, was Haran. When the family "came unto Haran, and dwelt there," they found the country occupied by the people known under the generic name of "Canaanites."

The Canaanites were not the original settlers. Far back in dim antiquity, so far back that no definite dates can be assigned to them, a semi-barbaric people occupied the fertile valleys of Palestine. These early settlers were but little better than cave-dwellers. For shelter they dug rectangular pits in the earth, walled them with unmortared masonry, roofing them, probably, with branches and clay.

Probably primitive man settled there because the red soil of the valleys yielded easily to his crude methods of agriculture, and the surrounding countrysides were well adapted to his pastoral pursuits. Behind him he left little but the crude walls of his miserable dwelling, flint tools, and many fragments of his hand-molded pottery. Since some of his pottery still shows a curious decoration in withered *red paint*, this primitive settler would seem to be definitely linked with the "Painted Pottery People" first discovered under the flood deposits at Ur of the Chaldees in 1928.

Long before B. C. 2000, the Amorites, a stronger and more advanced people, entered the country and crowded the original settlers from their poor fields and squalid villages. Since the Amorites were familiar with the Babylonian civilization, as is shown by their building methods and their religion, it is commonly assumed that they came from the northeast. With the coming of the Amorites a new day dawned for Palestine. With the beginnings of trade the cattle-paths grew to caravan trails, trails developed into highways, and market towns grew up at sites which are today familiar to us under their later Biblical names.

Just when the Amorites came into Palestine is not known. On Assyrian tablets dating earlier than B. C. 2000, the name "Amorite" signifies "inhabitant of the west," which would seem to indicate that at that time the Amorites held practically all the land west of Babylonia, including Palestine. Canaan is described as the "land of the Ammuru" (Amorites) on an inscription of Sargon I of Accad. This would indicate the presence of Amorites in Palestine as early as B. C. 2800. It seems clear that the Amorites were the first Semitic immigrants into Palestine.

At strategic points throughout Palestine the Amorites erected fortified cities, such as Megiddo, Taanach, Gezer, Lachish, Jericho, and many others. Each of these strongholds controlled a district with its lesser towns and villages. From their capital in the north, Kadesh, the Amorites governed the country systematically through commissioners, or governors. Each governor was held responsible for the security of his district and for the collection of the revenue. In the Old Testament these governors are referred to as "kings." This might lead us to assume that the city-kingdoms were more or less independent sovereignties, free to form alliances or make war independently. Such was not the case.

Amorite control of Palestine was rudely shaken when the warlike Hittites swept down from Cappadocia (the modern province of Angora) and, after conquering the Amorites, apparently amalgamated with them to form the people known as "Canaanites." The Hittites seem to have been a powerful, pioneering people. Excavators finds traces of their conquests and civilization over a wide area. They overran Syria and Palestine, and stretched their conquests to the Euphrates and over into Egypt, thus confirming the statement in *Joshua* 1:4, that the Hittites occupied the land from Lebanon to the Euphrates.

The amalgamation or merger of the Amorites and Hittites was a long process, apparently extending over centuries. From this merger of the Amorites and Hittites sprang many of the lesser city-kingdom peoples mentioned in the Old Testament. The Jebusites took their name from the little pagan city of Jebus. "Jebus" means "threshing-floor," and referred to the great threshing floor on the heights above the little town. Jebus stood on a portion of the present site of the city of Jerusalem. Ezekiel, upbraiding Jerusalem for her idolatry, exclaims: "Thy father was an Amorite, and thy mother an Hittite" (*Ezekiel* 16:3). This statement would have been true of many another city in Palestine.

Although the Hittites won the distinction of having a part of their history included in the world's greatest literature, the books of the Old Testament, practically all of our knowledge of this great people, outside that given in the Bible, has been brought to light within the memory of living men. Only within the last half century have scholars solved the problem of deciphering the written language of the Hittites. Even now knowledge of the language is extremely limited, but scholars are constantly throwing more and more light on the almost forgotten people who relinquished an empire to the descendants of Abraham.

The question as to where the Hittites originated has not been definitely settled. Archæological evidence seems to indicate that they were
Indo-Europeans. They first appear in written history as the *Khati*, or
Khatu, meaning "silver men," a name derived from the fact that at a
very early date they mined for silver in central Asia Minor. In the light
of such of their history as is now known, it is clear that they were the
dominating people in Asia Minor, Syria, and Palestine in the days when
Abraham was adventuring in Canaan. They were far from being alone
in these countries, however. The Amorites must still have constituted
a substantial minority of the population. It was a period of great unrest.
Mankind was on the move. Other peoples were attempting to penetrate
the land. According to *Genesis* 15:18-21 the lands occupied by ten peoples
were promised to Abraham. Most of these lands must have been occupied
by Amorite-Hittites or by some of their many offshoots.

Abraham was not adventuring in a wilderness as he wandered about
Canaan. He was not a pioneering pathfinder. A very ancient document,
which cannot be definitely dated, indicates that it was possible to drive a
wagon from Babylonia to the shores of the Mediterranean Sea.* The
country was already extensively cultivated. There were already many
cities. To Abraham, a native of the great Chaldean city of Ur, the cities
may have seemed insignificantly small. At this time Jericho covered less
than eight acres, and Jebus (later Jerusalem) less than twenty. The
existence of cities indicates that the country was so far settled that it could
support urban populations. Trade and commerce had long been flowing
more or less freely over the caravan routes between Babylonia and Egypt.
Judging by the *Genesis* narratives, Abraham did very well for himself
in Canaan.

The Amorite-Hittite, or Canaanite, civilization that Abraham knew
was probably strongly influenced by both Egyptian and Babylonian culture.
When the late Hugo Winckler, a German archæologist, working with an
expedition under the auspices of the Turkish Museum of Constantinople,
excavated the ancient Cappadocian capital of the Hittites at Boghaz Keui,
he found tablets written partly in Hittite and partly in Babylonian. These
tables were of great aid to the array of scholars engaged in deciphering
the inscriptions of the people who for centuries struggled with the Israelites for control of Canaan. The tablets found by Winckler proved to be
part of a correspondence between Hittite kings and the rulers of Egypt
and other countries. They belong to a period much later than Abraham,
but indicate clearly that the rising Hittite civilization had long been
influenced by Egyptian and Babylonian culture.

---

*See *Beiträge zur Assyriologie*, V, page 498.

Get thee out of thy country, and from thy kindred, and from thy father's house, unto a land that I will shew thee.—Genesis 12:1

During his long stay at Haran, Abraham must have altered with the passing years. The young man who had left Ur with his father's family was now a patriarch. According to *Genesis* 12:4 he "was seventy and five years old when he departed out of Haran." He was long past the age of craving for adventure. He was already a wealthy man, his whole life deep-rooted in the quiet countryside of Haran. Personally, one would think, Abraham had everything to lose and nothing to gain when he left the fertile, well-watered country about Haran to go into the unknown, "unto a land that I will shew thee." Small wonder the *Epistle to the Hebrews* calls this journey an act of faith.

What was the motivation behind this journey? Why should a settled, mature man, already wealthy, venture on a journey "not knowing whither he went" (*Hebrews* 11:8)? Why a Promised Land at all? As it was the mission of Israel to spread a gospel that would bring about the spiritual regeneration of mankind, this great movement must center itself somewhere on the great highways. At that early date, the highways were the great means of communication, and in Palestine the great intercontinental highways running east and west were intersected by the commercial highways running north and south. Although it seems to us today an out-of-the-way country, Palestine was really almost in the commercial center of the then-known world. Situated like a corridor opening on three continents, Palestine was the logical place to be the Promised Land.

And there was a famine in the land: and Abram went down into Egypt to sojourn there.—Genesis 12:10

After Abraham left Haran he apparently never again had a permanent home. Abraham had become a tent-dweller. His was a wandering clan-family. Moving about in the regions where his flocks and herds would best find pasturage, he marked his tenting places with altars to his God. There is nothing unusual in the rich herdsman and flockmaster moving his stock into the delta country of Egypt. Shortage of pasturage and fodder has always been common in Palestine, and migrating with flocks and herds is an age-old custom. The narrator in *Genesis,* however, handles this story with a master's touch. He is writing about the first of the great Hebrews, the outstanding religious genius of his race. With such a hero, a less able and less conscientious chronicler might have yielded to the common weakness of national historians and indulged in a bit of hero worship. The writer of *Genesis* was no mere teller of tales, no recreator of history from tradition. He was a faithful delineator of character, who scorned to throw a veil over human frailties, even the weak-

nesses of his mighty ancestors, Abraham and Sarai, the father and mother
of Israel. He might have given us a magnificent hero-tale of how a
Hebrew herdsman overawed a proud Pharaoh of Egypt, instead he gives
us a story with a distinctly human touch. He wrote of men as men, not
as demi-gods.

In connection with this story it must be remembered that Abraham's
visit took place during the "Hyksos Period" in Egyptian history. The
Hyksos or Shepherd Kings reigned in North Egypt from about B. C. 2180
to 1600. Long before Abraham's day the Hyksos had invaded Egypt,
overrun the delta, and were governing the country as far south as Thebes.
Most authorities are convinced that the Hyksos, like the Canaanites, were
of Amorite-Hittite racial descent. There is no doubt that the Hyksos
were of the same original stock as the Hittites, or were closely allied to
them. Abraham had lived long among the Hittites. Probably he had
spoken their language for years. He was visiting a Hyksos country. These
things made possible such a reception by the ruler as is recorded in the
narrative. It is unlikely that the family of Abraham would have received
such a reception from a purely Egyptian Pharaoh.

Abraham was evidently a bit uneasy "when he was come near to
enter into Egypt." He, himself, was well along in years, and Sarai was
probably well past her youthful blooming, but she was still "a fair woman
to look upon." Eastern potentates were always a trifle casual in acquiring
women. Perhaps the charming Chaldean would create a sensation in
Egyptian court circles. The husband of such a personage might find himself in an embarrassing position. Being a living brother would be better
than being a deceased husband. It was not exactly a lie to pass the fair
Sarai off as his sister. She really was his half-sister. However, this clever
bit of policy led to Abraham's abasement. In the language of the East,
he "lost face" before Pharaoh. He left the country, into which he had
been welcomed, under guard: "And they sent him away, and his wife,
and all that he had"—*Genesis* 12:20. It must have been a shamefaced
Abraham that journeyed back to Bethel.

And Abram was very rich in cattle, in silver, and in gold.—
Genesis 13:2

*And Lot also, which went with Abram, had flocks, and herds, and
tents.*—Genesis 13:5

After Abraham's return from Egypt there was a break in the clan-
family of which he was head. He himself was childless, but he had
reared his brother's son, Lot. In the old home in Haran, throughout the
migrations in Canaan, and during the sojourn in Egypt his nephew had
been ever at his side. Together they had prospered. Their livestock had

multiplied until no single grazing ground would support their combined flocks and herds. Perhaps the clan-family itself had grown a bit unwieldy. Only a little later than this Abraham was able to muster three hundred and eighteen able-bodied men among his own servants (See *Genesis* 14:14). With their women and children, and the aged and infirm, these alone would form a sizable tented colony. Trouble broke out among the herdsmen, the age-old strife over water-holes and pasturage. Wealth was breaking up a family. The parting hour had come. Magnanimously, Abraham waived his rights of seniority and told the lad he loved to choose which way he would go. Lot, unfortunately for his future welfare, chose "the cities of the plain," while Abraham "came and dwelt in the plain of Mamre." This parting of the kinsmen was a prelude to the dramatic events recorded in *Genesis* 14.

And it came to pass in the days of Amraphel king of Shinar, Arioch king of Ellasar, Chedorlaomer king of Elam, and Tidal king of nations; that these made war with Bera king of Sodom, and with Birsha king of Gomorrah, Shinab king of Admah, and Shemeber king of Zeboiim, and the king of Bela, which is Zoar.
—Genesis 14:1, 2

The fourteenth chapter of *Genesis* has all the earmarks of authentic history. Even the most drastic critics admit that this chapter has some historical validity. Many able writers still maintain that the first thirteen chapters of *Genesis* are merely a superb literary presentation of Oriental folk-lore, and that history really begins with the fourteenth chapter. The evidence, recovered at Ur, Kish, and other sites, that the flood is historical, renders this position untenable.

It would seem that the writer of this graphic chapter must have had original documents before him as he wrote. There is no logical reason why he should not have made use of such data. Abraham himself might have made notes on the subject. Abraham may have employed a scribe. A "mighty prince," whose establishment was so extensive that he could arm "his trained servants, born in his own house, three hundred and eighteen" (v. 14), might well have kept an accountant and recorder. Abraham was brought up in Ur, where the services of the scribe were well known. Since the art of writing was known in Babylonia, Syria, and Egypt long before the days of Abraham it would seem unsound to assume that the art was unknown in Palestine.

Although the writer uses the words "made war," the episode would be classed today as a military raid. This was a war of city-kingdoms rather than a war of nations. Some thirteen years before the recorded incident Chedorlaomer had led a raid down through the Jordan valley, subdued and levied tribute on five city-kingdoms in the vicinity of the Dead Sea. In the thirteenth year the "kings" (really governors) of the five Canaanite kingdoms—Sodom, Gomorrah, Admah, Zeboiim, and Bela—refused to pay the tribute. The following year Chedorlaomer decided to collect the tribute by force and, incidentally, lay some additional territory under tribute.

Raiding as they came, Chedorlaomer and his allies rode down through the trans-Jordan and around the southern end of the Dead Sea, subduing the country as far south as "Elparan, which is by the wilderness." On their way back, the victorious kings, laden with loot, were attacked by the five rebellious Canaanite kings. The engagement took place in the Vale of Siddim. This is described as a region "full of slime-pits; and the kings of Sodom and Gomorrah fled and fell there; and they that remained fled to the mountain." These slime-pits were the bitumen pits, such as are found at both ends of the Dead Sea to this day.

After Chedorlaomer's army had dispersed the forces of the rebellious Canaanite kings, and looted Sodom and Gomorrah, the way lay open for a military campaign against Jebus, or Salem (Jerusalem). This ambitious program was halted, not by an army in battle, but by a skillfully arranged ambush in the hill country carried out by a handful of herdsmen from the plain of Mamre, under the leadership of Abraham. Although Abraham's strategic attack had for its object the rescue of his nephew, Lot, its results were far-reaching. The campaign against Jerusalem was definitely halted. The forces of the four raiding kings from the north-east were forced to retreat, fighting a rearguard action against Abraham's forces and their allies who followed the fleeing enemy as far north as the neighborhood of Damascus. Abraham probably had plenty of help after the invaders were definitely defeated. The enemy was forced to retreat through hostile country and the Canaanites along the route would be only too glad to turn out and aid in the rout of a hated foe.

The retreating invaders must have fought a stern series of rearguard actions, since the forces of Abraham were forced to follow them the length of Palestine before they could recover the prisoners and the loot which the invaders had gathered in. Abraham's leadership was highly successful: "And he brought back all the goods, and also brought again his brother Lot, and his goods, and the women also."

Abraham's return southward was somewhat in the nature of a triumphal march. A grateful countryside turned out to greet a popular hero. The king of Sodom met him with offers of material reward which Abraham spurned. Abraham evidently had a low opinion of the king of Sodom. There is a hint of disdain, even scorn, in Abraham's refusal of reward: "That I will not take from a thread even to a shoelatchet, and that I will not take anything that is thine, lest thou shouldest say, I have made Abram rich." Abraham was willing that his neighbors from the vicinity of Mamre, who had aided him in the initial attack on the invaders, should be rewarded, but for his own household and servants he wanted nothing.

The writer of *Genesis* 14 had for his central theme an unusual incident in the life of Abraham. Abraham had always been a peaceful man. Here he is pictured as a shepherd warrior. The story becomes geographically clear if we accept Sir Flinders Petrie's conclusion that the "Dan" of *Genesis* 14 is the Dannah of *Joshua* 15:49 (between Socoh and Debir). Here in the broken, hilly country around Dannah, where horses would be useless, was the ideal place for a night ambush such as Abraham carried out. This story is so accurate in detail and so geographically correct that it is difficult to set it aside as mythical.

Many scholars identify Amraphel of *Genesis* 14 with Hammurabi, king of the Westland, who reigned over Babylon for forty-three years during the First Dynasty of Babylon, B. C. 2179-1870. Dr. T. G. Pinches, and Prof. A. H. Sayce, as well as many other authorities, after exhaustive study have come to this conclusion. As Pinches reads the Spartola tablets* (period B. C. 2000-1800) Babylon was overrun and conquered by a group of kings among whom were Tudhula (Tidal), Eri-Eku (Arioch), and Kuder-Lahamel (Chedorlaomer), all of whom are mentioned in *Genesis* 14. In the tablets Tidal is described as king of the Mandu (mercenary soldiers) who may have been from several nations, hence "king of nations" (v. 1). Other authorities hold that the connection between Amraphel and Hammurabi is open to doubt. More light on this subject is eagerly awaited.

This chapter introduces one of the most mysterious characters in Scripture, Melchizedek, king of Salem, and "priest of the most high God." Although some modern scholars interpret this chapter to mean that Melchizedek blessed Abraham in the name of El Elyon, the Amorite god of the heights of Salem (Jerusalem), the descendants of Abraham always regarded Melchizedek as an unparalleled figure in the realms of religion. Melchizedek means in Hebrew "Zedek (i. e., Righteousness) is my king." Who was he? Whoever he was, he made an indelible impression on the mind and thought of Israel. After the promulgation of "the Law" of the later day Hebrews by Moses, the priesthood of Israel was strictly confined to the Levitical order. Only those of unblemished blood and of unquestioned direct descent from Levi could ever aspire to the priesthood of Israel. (See *Numbers* 3:3-11), yet the great writers

---

*See *The Old Testament in the Light of Historical Research and Legends of Assyria and Babylonia*, by T. G. Pinches, page 222ff.

of the Bible, in fact, all Jews even to this day, recognize Melchizedek as
an outstanding priestly personality. Abraham, "the Friend of God," did
not hesitate to bow to the priestly grace of this man of unknown ancestry,
man of mystery, priest of the Living God. The Psalmist, catching a vision
of the coming Lord, cries: "Thou art a priest for ever after the order of
Melchizedek"—*Psalm* 110:4. St. Paul re-echoes these words in one of
his epistles (See *Hebrews* 5:6), and adds: "Without father, without
mother, without descent, having neither beginning of days, nor end of
life, but made like unto the Son of God; abideth a priest continually."
Over this strange figure, who lent his radiance to Hebrew history for but
a moment, later day Israel must have pondered much.

And Abraham sojourned in the Philistines' land many days.—
Genesis 21:34

Many years after Abraham's return from Egypt, he found it necessary
to travel again toward the south in search of richer pasturage. This time
he did not find it necessary to go as far as Egypt. He found supplies
sufficient for his needs at Gerar, "in the Philistines' land." This mention
of the Philistines is interesting. Archæological research has proved that
the Philistines entered Palestine for the purpose of growing grain for
export to their homeland, which was either Crete or some portion of the
mainland of Asia Minor subject to Crete. The Philistines confined themselves at first to the grain-growing sections of Palestine. Wherever the
Philistines settled they left behind them great quantities of sickles and
other evidences of a grain-growing people. The excavation of Gerar by
Sir Flinders Petrie proved that in Abraham's day, Gerar had become a
flourishing town in the center of a great grain-growing district. This
explains Abraham's long stay. Abraham's servants fought with the Philistines over control of the water-holes, but a day was to come when the
descendants of Abraham would fight to the death with the Philistines
for the control of Palestine itself.

*I will give thee money for the field; take it of me, and I will bury
my dead there.*—Genesis 23:13

In the light of modern archæological research we can read the twenty-
third chapter of *Genesis* with new interest. This chapter is a description
of a deal in real estate between two astute Orientals, and verses 16, 17 and
18 are evidently based on an actual deed of sale. Abraham had been
raised at Ur of the Chaldees where deeds of sale had to be drawn in
due legal form, signed, sealed, and properly attested by the contracting
parties, the scribe, and the witnesses. Naturally he would wish that the
field he expected to use as a family burial place should be properly and

legally conveyed. The writer of the narrative probably had an actual deed of sale before him as he wrote.

The traders met in the open space in front of the city gates. This was the customary place for bargaining and the settling of all matters of a legal nature. In fact, the space before the gates was frequently used as a sort of minor court for adjusting disputes and legal differences among the people. In *Deuteronomy* 21:19 we read: "Then shall his father and his mother lay hold on him, and bring him out unto the elders of his city, and unto the gate of his place." *Amos* 5:10 speaks of "him that rebuketh in the gate," while in the 15th verse of the same chapter we read, "and establish judgment in the gate."

Anyone who has lived among Oriental peoples will note the fidelity with which the writer describes the traders' approach to the matter in hand. After Abraham had mentioned the property he desired, Ephron, true to the customs of bargaining, offered Abraham the field as a gift, well knowing that his apparently generous offer would be refused. Abraham insisted on a price. There is only one departure from Oriental custom. Abraham did not haggle over the price. It is but natural that he would make the interview brief, since there had been a recent death in the family.

The price paid for the field,—"four hundred shekels of silver, current money with the merchant,"—may, at first glance, seem strange. These words imply a system of weights and measures as well as a standard of monetary values. Many students of the Bible, assuming that Abraham was an unlettered nomad, wandering about Canaan in the Middle Bronze Age, naturally concluded that there was something anachronistic about this description of the purchase price. Coined money was, of course, unknown until eleven hundred years after Abraham's day. It must be remembered, however, that long before Abraham's time a great civilization had developed along the lower reaches of the Tigris and the Euphrates. Simultaneously, a civilization was developing in the Valley of the Nile. The trade routes between these two early centers of culture and civilization traversed the land of Canaan. Since the exportable products of Mesopotamia were largely in the form of manufactured articles made up in gold and silver, precious and semi-precious stones, a unit of value for use as a commercial medium had to be established. The discovery of shekel weights, covering the shekel and fractions thereof, provides definite evidence of the unit of value adopted. The weight of the merchandise in shekels, with the type and fineness of the metals involved, furnished the "current money with the merchant." Viewed in this light, verses 15 and 16, instead of being anachronistic, merely reflect standard commercial practices of the day.

*But thou shalt go unto my country, and to my kindred, and take
a wife unto my son Isaac.*—Genesis 24:4

Abraham apparently never returned to Ur of the Chaldees, but, evidently, he still retained his love for the ancient city beside the Euphrates. We catch a glimpse of this natural love for his boyhood home in the world's oldest love story, the twenty-fourth chapter of *Genesis,* when Abraham, "well stricken in age," sought a wife for his son, and asked his servant to find a bride, not among the Canaanites, but among the people of "my country."

To the Occidental mind the choosing of the bride by parental authority may seem strange. This was, and still is, in many Asiatic countries, a customary method of arranging matrimonial alliances. Among the descendants of Abraham the exercise of parental authority in preliminary matrimonial matters was customary for many centuries. Old Testament narratives frequently reflect this custom. In *Judges* 14 we find Samson imploring his parents to procure him a Philistine woman he had seen in Timnath for a wife. We read of Saul, in the role of parental matchmaker, saying to David: "Behold my elder daughter Merab, her will I give thee to wife"—1 *Samuel* 18:17.

Abraham was too old to undertake the long journey to Mesopotamia, so he commissioned his trusted servant as his ambassador. This was no ordinary mission. Abraham's life was nearly over, but he must keep faith with the future. The future of his race; the future of the people to whom he must soon entrust the fulfilling of the covenants he had entered into with his Creator; the spiritual development of mankind throughout ages still unborn, was to be made or marred by the success or failure of this mission. Abraham was seeking a mother for Israel. Imponderable possibilities hung on the decision of Abraham's servant. With only the Unseen for witness, a faithful servant listened to the parting prayers and final instructions of his aged master, and, in time-honored custom, placed his hand under his patron's thigh as he pledged fidelity in a solemn oath of honor between man and man. Months will pass before they meet again. The trail lay long over plain and mountain pass, and weary leagues of shifting desert sand must be traversed before Abraham's servant could hope to sight the gray walls of Nahor rising above the Chaldean plain.

Many weeks later a camel train drew up at the watering-place outside the city wall of Nahor. It was eventide, that hour of cool that succeeds the heat of the Chaldean day. Perhaps a thoughtful caravan master had carefully planned the time of his arrival. His search for a suitable young woman might be simplified if he could, with apparent nonchalance, survey the young women of the city as they gathered at the well. The young women, emerging from the city gates, must have eagerly eyed the foreign entourage that had halted at the well. This was no ordinary caravan. A train of ten camels bearing the trappings of a Hebrew prince was something unusual. The young Rebekah must have been impressed with the size and apparent wealth of the caravan, since she addressed the leader as "my lord." On the other hand, Abraham's servant must have been impressed with a damsel who "was very fair to look upon," and yet had the physical vigor to draw water for ten camels. Camels drink mightily. By the time the "camels had done drinking" the servant knew that his quest was ended. He had met the Mother of Israel. "And the man bowed down his head, and worshipped the Lord"—*Genesis* 24:26.

An eye-arresting passage in this chapter is the verse which reads: "And it came to pass, as the camels had done drinking, that the man took a golden earring of half a shekel weight, and two bracelets for her hands of ten shekels weight of gold." This offering of gifts is an age-old custom, which even today sometimes proves embarrassing in dealing with the Oriental. Your Oriental friend is only too prone to offer as a gift some article from his person if you express admiration for it. Perhaps, the servant gave her the large earring he himself was wearing. It was the prevailing custom among men to wear a single earring. This may account for the expression, "the man took a golden earring," instead of pair of earrings as we might naturally expect. The definite weight given to the articles is not an anachronism, since we now know that the shekel was at that time a definite commercial unit of value.

In this chapter we see the beginning of the Jewish objection to marriage with Gentiles. A generation later we see this objection intensified when Isaac charged Jacob: "Thou shalt not take a wife of the daughters of Canaan. Arise, go to Padanaram, . . . and take thee a wife from thence of the daughters of Laban thy mother's brother"—*Genesis* 28:1, 2.

Probably the writer of the inimitable narratives that picture the patriarchs in Canaan never thought of himself as an historian. He was not interested in chronicling successions of kings or the barren details of the battles of the mighty. His was a nobler task. To him was given the glory of recording the rise and early developments of a religious movement immortal. His story of the betrothal of Isaac and Rebekah was told with a purpose. With the intense national pride of his race, he was tracing the selective continuity of the early fathers of his faith. To have pictured Abraham as a strict monogamist would have been unappropriate to Abraham's time and place. The writer makes it clear that the keeping of the covenants was committed to a pure racial strain. Not to the half-caste son of Hagar, nor to the doubtful issue of Keturah, but to the unblemished line of Isaac and Rebekah was entrusted the priceless heritage of the message eternal. As the curtains of time fell on the first great figure of the immortal drama, it was Isaac and his seed that took the center of the stage.

> *And it came to pass after the death of Abraham, that God blessed his son Isaac.*—Genesis 25:11

Sons of great men are likely to start life handicapped by the reputation of their sires. Isaac was one of those fated to follow in the footsteps of the great. He was the son of one of the world's immortals. In the reverence of the Hebrews, Abraham stands alone. Isaac, the son of Abraham's old age, was a man of lesser caliber. The *Genesis* narratives which center around this patriarch strongly suggest that he never reached the mental and spiritual stature of his father. Under the blessing of God he became a mighty patriarch.

> *And there was famine in the land, beside the first famine that was in the days of Abraham. And Isaac went unto Abimelech king of the Philistines unto Gerar.*—Genesis 26:1

Soon after Abraham's death his son, Isaac, was faced with the same problem that had troubled his father, famine. Isaac contemplated a visit to Egypt, but was directed to go to Gerar (*Genesis* 26).

There is a striking similarity between chapters 20 and 26. Conditions were similar. The scenes were laid in the same place. Even the Philistine administration at Gerar was the same. Abimelech was "king" or "governor" of the district. Many commentators have assumed that this was a "twice told tale," with the substitution of the name "Isaac" for "Abraham," and a slight variation of the details. The narrator, however, in *Genesis* 26:1, makes it clear that these were two different occasions, and relate to separate famine conditions.

There is a ring of reality in stories of struggle over the water supply. It was common practice to excavate cisterns in the soft native rock about Gerar for the storage of water. Isaac apparently followed his pastoral pursuits on the same lands on which Abraham had previously pastured his flocks and herds, and had cleared out the wells or cisterns which Abraham had used for the storage of rainwater, and which the Philistines had filled up when Abraham had abandoned the land. The finding of "a well of springing water" (v. 19) was naturally an important matter. Water always has been and still is a valuable commodity in Palestine, and the location of a spring might well cause serious trouble between rival groups of herdsmen.

HEADDRESS OF QUEEN SHUBAD
Modeled head wearing some of the crown jewels of Queen Shubad. The queen's jewels suggest the wealth of the ancient home of the patriarch Abraham.

NECKLACE OF QUEEN SHUBAD
Polished agate and gold necklace from the grave of Shubad.
By permission of The Museum of the University of Pennsylvania

And Jacob said, Sell me this day thy birthright.—Genesis 25:31

The narratives placed in the period of Isaac's later life deal largely with his children. Jacob really becomes the central figure of the narratives. This is natural, since, next to Abraham, Jacob is looked upon as the common father of Israel. Each of the twelve tribes of Israel was named after one of his sons.

Although destined for great things, Jacob began life under a handicap. Although a twin, a matter of minutes denied him the honor of being a first-born son. In the patriarchal period precedence of birth was an important matter. A first-born son, if he lived, usually became the head of the clan-family. In addition, Jacob seems to have been of retiring nature compared with his ruddy, robust brother: "Esau was a cunning hunter, a man of the field; and Jacob was a plain man dwelling in tents"— *Genesis* 25:27.

Aside from their sacred purpose, the stories that center around Jacob are well worthy of study as character portraitures. The writer of these narratives revered Jacob as one of the great fathers of Israel, yet he did not hesitate to turn every facet of Jacob's character to the pitiless light of publicity. Against a background of patriarchal life a master craftsman in letters sketches around the central figure of Jacob some of the intriguing figures who helped to shape the life of his hero. Without waste of words the writer pictures the household of the aged Isaac dominated by the imperious Rebekah who craves power for her favorite son, Jacob. He shows us Jacob as a young man not lacking in guile, shrewd to the point of sharpness. Not only did he trick his strong-bodied but clumsy-witted brother into trading his birthright for a meal, but, by means that savor strongly of fraud, he secured the paternal blessing that made him head of all Israel. His sharp practice brought him the headship of the clan-family, but it also brought down on him the hatred of his brother, who planned to kill him, and sent Jacob into years of semi-exile. During the years in exile the moral transformation of Jacob began. Through his spiritual experiences a rather unscrupulous youth grew into a great leader worthy to carry on the great religious ideals of his grandfather, Abraham. Having executed a covenant with his cunning father-in-law, Laban, and appeased the wrath of his brother Esau, Jacob returned to his homeland to become a real father of Israel.

And he said, Thy name shall be called no more Jacob, but Israel. —Genesis 32:28

Jacob, "the supplanter," became Israel, or "who prevails with God," and his descendants bore the honored name of "Children of Israel."

5

Although the name "Israel," as used to designate a people, is not known outside of the Bible earlier than the inscription of Merneptah,* it was used as a personal name in Babylonia before the days of Jacob. A seal, now in Paris, dating to B. C. 2600, bears the inscription, *"Israel, son of Rishzuni."* This, of course, has no bearing on the Old Testament. It is merely an interesting circumstance.

And they took him, and cast him into a pit.—Genesis 37:24

It was probably an anbandoned cistern, or water-pit, in the land of Dothan into which Joseph was thrust by his brothers. Storage pits, or chambers cut in the rock, are common throughout Palestine. Sometimes they were used for dry storage, but they were most commonly used to conserve the water supply. While some of these pits were meant for the storage of spring water, most frequently they were used as cisterns for the storage of rainfall and surface water, which was led into them by ditches.

Storage pits were convenient places for disposing of unwanted persons, living or dead. When Mizpah (Tell-en Nasbeh) was excavated by Professor F. W. Bade, the excavators found large rock-hewn pits, one of which contained a great number of skeletons that had rested there for at least 2,600 years. *Jeremiah* 41 gives a graphic description of this type of interment which took place in this same city of Mizpah, when Ishmael, conspiring against Gedaliah, governor of Judah, after slaying Gedaliah, lured the supporters of the dead governor into Mizpah, slew them, and cast them into the midst of the pit.

Jeremiah himself had a disagreeable experience in the rock-hewn dungeon of Malchiah while he was incarcerated there. The mention of mire in this pit would indicate that it was a surface water-pit: "And in the dungeon there was no water, but mire: so Jeremiah sunk in the mire" (*Jeremiah* 38:6). A knowledge of this cruel practice probably furnished the inspiration for the Psalmist when he wrote: "He brought me out of an horrible pit, out of the miry clay, and set my feet upon a rock, and established my goings" (*Psalm* 40:2).

There is nothing improbable in the story of Joseph being cast into a water-pit. "And the pit was empty, there was no water in it" (*Genesis* 27:4). The purchase of Joseph by the Midianite merchantmen, and his resale in Egypt to Potiphar as a bond servant, would, at that period, not be an unusual commercial transaction. Trafficking in human beings was common. Historically, the only importance of this incident is that the youth was the first of the descendants of Abraham to locate permanently in

---

*See Chapter IV, page 68.

Egypt, where later he was to become an important factor in the introduction of Israel into Egypt.

While shortage of grain and fodder was of fairly common occurrence in Palestine, Egypt was occasionally visited by famine, as early Egyptian records prove. The famine in the days of Jacob was evidently a major calamity, since *Genesis* 41:55 states that "the famine was over all the face of the earth." It is probable that by this time the patriarchal establishment of Jacob was so extensive that migrating with flocks and herds was not feasible, as famine conditions would not admit of pasturage along the way; so Jacob sent his sons to Egypt to purchase corn. Most movements in history are motivated by economic necessity. It is likely that promise of easier living conditions offered by the delta section of Egypt prompted the patriarchal movement of Jacob's family into Egypt quite as much as did the urging of Joseph.

The intrusion of a few Hebrew families was of little moment in the long history of Egypt, but it was a turning point in the history of Israel. The ideals of Abraham, kept alive by the religious experiences of his descendants, had become the star of destiny to the Israelites. Canaan was behind them, but, in the fullness of time, the Lord God of Israel would lead them back to the Promised Land.

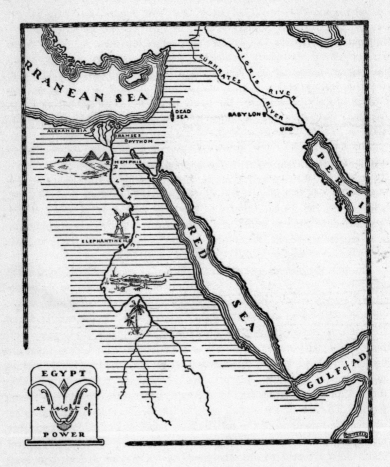

EGYPT
at height of
POWER

IV

ISRAEL IN EGYPT

I will go down with thee into Egypt, and I will also surely bring thee up again.—Genesis 46:4

THE writer of the *Genesis* narratives of the patriarchs of Israel evidently had a definite objective which he kept ever before him in his literary labors. His purpose was to record the rise of a great religious movement. Incidentally, in portraying the spiritual experiences of the patriarchs, he pictured the making of a people, the rise of a race. His matchless series of picture narratives of these early religious leaders form a fitting introduction to the great galaxy of Hebrew heroes whose lives furnished the inspiration for literary geniuses of succeeding centuries. To him was given the distinctive task of sketching the foreground and tracing the initial outlines of the great historical picture that later generations of literary artists would fill in with historical detail, illuminate with master strokes of philosophy, prophecy, and spiritual truth, and pass on to posterity as the Old Testament.

In this method of presentation the writer used rare discrimination. He wrote of men as men, not demi-gods. He hung no halos on his heroes, placed no man on a pedestal. He wrote of a primitive, virile people, imbued with deep spiritual insight, and of their never-ending search for a clearer understanding of the Unseen, and man's relationship with his Creator. His stories are timed to a period of great unsettlement and unrest. Mankind was on the move. Restless clan chieftains were seeking wider grazing grounds. A world with limitations unknown lay before them. Control of pasture lands and potable water were important economic factors. The law of the strong was the law of the grazing ground. Outwardly, the migration of the patriarchs of Israel was of minor importance, merely one of many clan movements; inwardly, its significance was unparalleled. Into a world whose inhabitants saw a god or a demon in every manifestation of nature, the patriarchs were bringing Abraham's inspired ideals of righteous living and his unique conception of man's spiritual fellowship with his God. The sacred writer was not chronicling secular history. His were not tales to amuse the idle. His task was to picture the motivation of the mightiest historical movement mankind has ever known.

The writer of the narratives of the patriarchs of Israel had a rich background for his stories. The scenes are laid in the regions that witnessed the beginnings of civilization and the dawnings of history. The series of stories forms a travelogue which covers practically all of the civilized world of the writer's day. It was a small world. Roughly speaking, it lay between the Tigris and the Nile. Between the Chaldean-Babylon country in the east and the Nile Valley in the west lay Mesopotamia, Canaan, and Syria; beyond these boundaries was semi-barbarism. The family which furnished the inspiration and material for the narratives originated in the cradle of civilization, the Tigris-Euphrates valley. The narrator follows this family in its meandering migrations around the "fertile crescent" that rims the desert, until famine finally forces the famous family to enter the other great center of rising civilization, the Nile valley. It was a small world that the patriarchs marked with their altars, but the writer pictures it faithfully in his annals of four generations of the patriarchal family.

Biblical scholars argue endlessly as to whether or not all the Children of Israel entered Egypt with Jacob. Such a detail would not have worried the writer of *Genesis* overmuch. The important fact, which he makes clear, and which is abundantly substantiated by archæological research, is that the most important and directive section of Israel entered Egypt. With his narratives of Joseph he describes the movement which introduced Israel into Egypt, where the birth of Hebrew nationalism took place.

The exact date of Israel's entrance into Egypt is unknown. The Joseph narratives (*Genesis* 37 and 39 to 50), while rich in local color and circumstantial detail, unfortunately carry nothing that permits of definite dating. The mode of life of the early Israelites adds to the difficulty of accurately dating events recorded in these chapters. The early Israelites built no cities for themselves, and apparently used little pottery. Footloose, they ranged the pasture lands, rearing their tent poles and spreading their camel-hair tents wherever their flocks and herds were likely to fare best. Outside their livestock, their wealth had to be kept in highly portable form, such as gold and silver which could be readily fashioned into articles of personal adornment. This migratory mode of life did not call for the building of walls, or contribute to the accumulation of material evidence in the form of heaps of potsherds and settlement debris.

To young Joseph the transition from the quiet, rural life in the "Vale of Hebron" to the home of "Potiphar, an officer of Pharaoh's, and captain of the guard," must have been bewildering. Judging from the evidence we have of the living conditions in the homes of minor nobility of that period, Joseph must have found himself domiciled in rather an extensive establishment. The house of that period would be built of sun-dried bricks and roofed with wood. Around Potiphar's house would be grouped the stables, granaries, workshops, and other essential buildings of the estate. Here would be the bakery and confectionery shop, the shops for spinning and weaving, the making of fishnets, and the weaving of reed mats for floors, as most domestic crafts were practiced on the premises.

The Egyptian man of means invested not so much in his house as in his garden, which always contained a fish-pool and many varieties of flowers, trees, and shrubs. He presumably spent most of his time in his garden, sparing neither labor nor expense to elaborate its development. Even the interior of the house was decorated to imitate a garden. Ponds and flowerbeds were painted on the floors, outdoor scenes upon the walls, the columns represented conventionalized papyrus plants, and the ceiling the star-dotted sky at night.

Animal and flower motifs adorned the furniture. Pets were common in Egyptian households. Little girls played with dolls, and boys spun tops. Dice were common. The familiar game of checkers was well known to the Egyptians. Guests were entertained with music, and with solo and group dancing. The Egyptians followed such outdoor sports as hunting, racing, and wrestling.

The Biblical narratives of Joseph present him to us as a man of the executive type. A victim of fraternal faithlessness, transported to a foreign land, introduced into an environment that was utterly alien to him, his native ability was such that he became the administrative head of his master's estate. Potiphar "made him overseer of his house, and all that he had he put into his hand"—*Genesis* 39:4.

Potiphar's position in the realm of Pharaoh was such that when Joseph became the victim of the thwarted amorous ambitions of his master's wife he was cast, not into a common prison, but into "a place where the king's prisoners were bound." Even in these doleful surroundings, Joseph's administrative abilities enabled him to dominate his unfortunate environment to such an extent that the "keeper of the prison committed to Joseph's hand all the prisoners that were in the prison, and whatever they did there, he was the doer of it"—*Genesis* 39:22.

Even his prison experience contributed to Joseph's ultimate advancement by bringing him to the attention of Pharaoh. The forty-first chapter of *Genesis* gives a graphic account of how Joseph was rescued from prison and ushered into the presence of Pharaoh. Here is an outstanding model for all "rags to riches" stories. The denizen of the dungeon becomes the prime minister of Egypt, second only to Pharaoh as a figure of national importance. Clad in "vestures of fine linen, and a gold chain put about his neck" (a ceremonial custom frequently illustrated in Egyptian reliefs), he rode in the second chariot, acquired a bride, and even had his name changed to Zaphnath-pa-a-neah, which means: "The one who furnishes the nourishment of life," i. e., "The Steward of the Realm."*

The narrative of Joseph's legislative provisions for a time of famine, and his administrative control of the country's stored resources during the period of the famine, have known parallels in Egyptian records. Thanks to the life-giving waters of the Nile, famines are rare in Egypt, but by no means unknown. Joseph was not the first to make provisions against such a calamity. Anememha, king of Egypt, as early as B. C. 2714, records a famine in Egypt, and tells of the provisions he took to feed the people of his country during that period. There are other later records of similar occurrences. An inscription found in the tomb of Baba at El-Kab, in Upper Egypt, states: "I collected corn, as a friend of the harvest god. I was watchful of the time of sowing, and when a famine arose, which lasted many years, I distributed corn to the city each year of famine." The fact that others took steps to prevent widespread starvation during times of famine does not detract from the Joseph narrative. It renders the story more logical and credible.

The great famine so frequently mentioned in *Genesis* was the means of bringing about the reunion of Joseph with his family. Joseph must have been startled when his brothers, who had "cast him into a pit," and sold him "to the Ishmaelites for twenty pieces of silver," "came and bowed down themselves before him with their faces to the earth." Here was a moment when a small-souled man might have been tempted to take revenge for long post, but never forgotten, indignities. With rare magnanimity, Joseph decided to forgive, but could not forego the opportunity to dramatize the situation by resorting to a subterfuge which brought his young brother, Benjamin, and eventually his aged father, into the country.

Under the benign auspices of Joseph, "governor over all the land of Egypt," the caravan of "the sons of Israel carried Jacob their father, and their little ones, and their wives" (*Genesis* 46:5) out of the land of Canaan into Egypt. The period of patriarchal pilgrimage was over. In a new land, the descendants of Abraham were opening a new chapter in the history of Israel.

And Joseph placed his father and his brethren, and gave them a possession in the land of Egypt, in the best of the land, in the land of Rameses, as Pharaoh had commanded.—Genesis 47:11

The entry into Egypt was an important turning point in the history of Israel. In the long history of Egypt, it was, at the time, an insignificant incident. The narratives of Israel's entrance into Egypt become more

---

*See M. G. Kyle: *The Deciding Voice of the Monuments in Biblical Criticism*, page 261.

intelligible, but lose nothing of their dramatic interest when the political status of Egypt at the time is considered.

Egypt had been for centuries a self-sufficient kingdom. It was then, as now, a one-dimension country, a land of length without breadth. The fertile flats that fringed the Nile reached ribbon-like from the First Cataract northward to the delta, where the river found its many-mouthed entrance to the sea. The rich alluvial soils along the river furnished the foundations for a rising civilization which was peculiarly insular and isolated. The ever-encroaching desert flanked the major portion of its longitudinal boundaries. Its limited northern sea-front brought only a meagre amount of water-borne commerce. This Nile-mothered civilization found its principal contact with the outside world over the isthmus that tied Egypt to Asia, and formed the western end of the great land bridge across Palestine which carried the caravan commerce from the lands beyond the Jordan. Egypt was a self-contained world.

About the time that Abraham first adventured westward, roughly B. C. 2000, Egypt began to expand commercially and territorially toward the north-east. Imperially-minded Pharaohs began to push their conquests into the territories their successors were to fight over for centuries.

Egyptian expansion on the Asiatic mainland was sharply halted by coming in contact with the advancing Semitic people who are known to us as the "Hyksos." The Hyksos not only halted the tide of Egyptian expansion eastward, but swept it backward. Early in the seventeenth century B. C., the Hyksos invaded Egypt, and forced the Pharaoh to flee for refuge far up the Nile to the shelter of the Theban hills. The hardy Hyksos seized the delta, and secured control of the country as far south as Thebes. It must be remembered that Joseph's entry into Egypt (*Genesis* 37:36), as well as the entrance of his father's family (*Genesis* 46:6), took place during the Hyksos period. This fact renders intelligible the Joseph narratives. It is unlikely that Joseph, even though a man of unusual mental capacity, would have risen so rapidly to power in the formal court of a purely Egyptian Pharaoh.

While the Egypt that Joseph knew was governed by the Hyksos, the country itself was essentially Egyptian. Joseph had been brought to a country where culture and civilization had been developing for centuries. This civilization was not so deep and broad as the Chaldean civilization that Joseph's great-grandfather, Abraham, had known at Ur of the Chaldees, but it was much superior to anything that Joseph could possibly have known during his boyhood in Canaan.

Rural life in "the land of Rameses," the section to which the immigrant clan-family was assigned, has altered little since the days when the sons of Jacob pastured their flocks and herds there. The Nile Valley, now as then, is chiefly agricultural. The annual inundation of the life-giving river insures the fertility of the soil. Dykes and canals control the surplus water. The primitive methods of raising water from one level to another are the same today as were used in the days of Joseph. Cattle raising was an important factor in the economic life of Egypt. Its importance was such that the cow was worshipped as sacred to Hathor, Egypt's foremost goddess.

As early as the sixteenth century B. C., the Egyptians began to depict a strange people on the walls of their funerary structures. These people are easily distinguishable from the Egyptians by their clothing, their beards, and, particularly, by their facial features. In their inscriptions the Egyptians always referred to these people as "Asiatics," or "Foreigners." The early reliefs show them entering the country as peaceful immigrants, and as shepherds.

Into an agricultural and cattle raising country came Israel, a part of the despised "Asiatics." Being mainly shepherds, they would naturally be unwelcome intruders in the cattle-raising sections of the delta, "for every shepherd is an abomination unto the Egyptians"—*Genesis* 46:34. Close-cropping sheep ruin grazing grounds for cattle. Here we catch a glimpse of the age-old feud that has always existed between cattlemen and sheep raisers. This story has had many counterparts on our own western plains.

In addition to difficulties over water and pasture lands, the intruding Israelites probably had other difficulties with their unwilling hosts in Goshen. Naturally, there would be the primitive feeling of simple hostility to the strangers. To race antipathy and race prejudice would be added the enmity engendered by deep-lying differences in religion. The Israelites might well have been welcomed by a Hyksos king of Egypt, whose prime minister was also an Israelite, but the native Egyptians probably hated them just as much as they hated the despised Hyksos.

The *Genesis* narratives of the patriarchs close on a note of comparative peace. The Israelites found the more or less friendly Hyksos dominating the portion of Egypt to which economic forces had led them. During the early part of the sojourn in Egypt, Israel was apparently free to come and go, and to visit the homeland of Canaan, at will. When Jacob died his remains were ceremoniously carried to Canaan, and laid to rest in the family burial place at Machpelah (See *Genesis* 50:13). Is there a sinister note of foreboding in the recording that the remains of Joseph were not immediately taken to Canaan for burial? Was the ominous shadow of servitude already settling over Israel? Was there a prophetic foreshowing of impending evil in the oath which Joseph took to the

Children of Israel, saying, "God will surely visit you, and ye shall carry up my bones from hence"?

Now there arose up a new king over Egypt, which knew not Joseph.—Exodus 1:8

The centuries between the time of the arrival of the clan-family of Jacob in Goshen and the great tribal movement out of Egypt under Moses witnessed profound changes in the political, economic, social, and cultural conditions of the peoples of the then-known world.

Israel entered Egypt at a time when the political fortunes of the Egyptians were at low ebb. The proud power of Egypt had been thrust backward up the Nile to the Theban hills. The great granary of Egypt, the fertile delta, lay under the heel of the Hyksos conqueror.

Between that time and the period when Moses found his place in history, Egypt reached and passed the flood-tide of its greatest imperial glory. Long before the days of Moses the Hyksos had been expelled from Egypt. The Egyptians not only recovered control over their own country but, under a number of warlike and ambitious Pharaohs, had established military and commercial control over the group of rising civilizations clustering in and about the eastern end of the Mediterranean Sea. The military campaigns of the Egyptian monarchs centered largely in Canaan, the Promised Land, the country we know today under its Phoenician name, Palestine.

The geographical location of Palestine, a small buffer state between ambitious empires, made it for centuries a common fighting ground. Over the great intercontinental highways flowed not only the currents of commerce, but also succeeding waves of conquest. Much in the same manner that geographical location has made the low plains of Belgium "the cockpit of Europe," Palestine became the scene of frequent arbitrament by force of arms. Throughout the ages the foot of the foreign foe has fallen frequently on Palestine.

The writers of the early books of the Old Testament, telling the story of a great religious movement, reflect, rather than relate, secular history. The Pharaoh who was contemporary with Moses, the "new king over Egypt, who knew not Joseph," is not identified. Centuries had elapsed between the historical periods marked by the closing chapters of *Genesis* and the opening chapters of *Exodus*. Meanwhile, the descendants of the clan-family of Jacob had become so numerous that "the land was filled with them."

To bridge the time-distance between *Genesis* and *Exodus* we must turn to known Egyptian history, to the inscriptions and bas-reliefs on Egyptian temples and tomb structures, and to the vast number of contemporary portrait statues which illustrate every phase of life in Egypt during the centuries when the Children of Israel served in bondage there.

Long before the coming of the Hebrews the Egyptians had advanced far toward the mode of life that is called civilization. They had invented a method of writing, had a very definite knowledge of art and science, and stood pre-eminent in certain types of architecture. This type of architecture is evidenced most strongly by the marvelous tomb structures known as the pyramids. Each year, thousands of tourists clamber over the limestone blocks of the Great Pyramids, and gaze with awe at the time-mocking, inscrutable countenance of the Sphinx. These pyramids, one of the "Seven Wonders of the World," were old when Joseph first saw them, yet today they would be as perfect as when the workmen left them five thousand years ago were it not for man's depredations. The exquisitely fitted limestone facing blocks were almost all removed by the Mohammedan conquerors of Egypt for their buildings in Cairo, and only the bare rough blocks of the core were left. While some people profess to see in these sentinels of the centuries some astronomical or mysterious significance, archæology finds them only an architectural development from earlier forms of tombs.

More lavishly than any other people, the ancient Egyptians entombed with the remains of their dead material objects for the comfort and entertainment of the departed as they journeyed through another world. As the wealth of the nation grew, and private fortunes increased, tomb structures and tomb furnishings varied accordingly. The prehistoric tomb was merely a square pit sunk in the ground, roofed with poles and brushwood. Later a wooden lining was developed. Next came a wooden chamber free-standing in the pit. The First Dynasty kings (about B. C. 3400) built brick tombs at Abydos. The sixth king (Den) introduced a stone floor. About B. C. 3200, Kha-sekhemui built a tomb chamber of hewn blocks of limestone—the oldest stone building in Egypt. After centuries of gradual architectural development, Seneferu (about B. C. 2900), built the first true pyramid to mark his tomb.

Seneferu's successor, Khufu (Cheops), built the largest of the great pyramids. Composed of about 2,300,000 limestone blocks, each weighing about two and one-half tons, it measures 755 feet 8 inches on each side. Despite its great size, the maximum deviation from perfect symmetry is less than one inch.

Biblical scholars differ widely in their conclusions as to the probable date of the Exodus. Brugsch and others place the date as early as the 15th century B. C. They suggest that the birth of Moses may have occurred as early as during the reign of Thutmose I (B. C. 1545-1514), and identify the daughter of Thutmose, the famous Queen Hatshepsut, as rescuing the infant Moses from the flags in the river brink where his mother had left him. In the tomb that was prepared for Hatshepsut, but in which she was not buried, an inscription describes her as "king's daughter, king's sister, wife of the god, great wife of the king, Hatshepsut." Definite evidence is lacking to connect the great queen, who influenced the history of Egypt throughout the reigns of three successive Pharaohs, with the "Pharaoh's daughter" who is mentioned in *Exodus* 2. Moses seems to have belonged to a much later date. However, Hatshepsut was evidently the leading feminine figure in the famous family of "Thutmose" that drove the Hyksos out of Egypt.

When Thutmose III defeated the tribes on the plain of Megiddo, in B. C. 1479, he seized the important stronghold of Megiddo. The strategic location of Megiddo made it the indispensable military key to the highway from Egypt between the two Lebanons to the Euphrates. Migiddo dominates the plain which as "Armageddon" has become the historic battlefield of the ages from the time of Thutmose to the days of the World War. On this plain, which John the revelator visions as the scene of world catastrophe (See *Revelation* 16), Allenby, in 1918, waged the climactic campaign that shattered Turkish resistance, and won for him his title, "Viscount Allenby of Megiddo."

Under Thutmose, Egypt became the political arbiter and economic center of the then-known world. Over Egyptian coastal waters, and through the canal that ran from the Nile to the Bitter Lakes, waterborne commerce found an outlet under Egyptian control. Located astride intercontinental waterways and highways, Egypt made a determined bid for world empire.

Of the many great obelisks that Thutmose erected to commemorate his military campaigns, but one remains in the country he ruled. Of the largest pair, which once graced the approach to the Sun-temple at Heliopolis, one decorates the Thames Embankment in London, while in Central Park, New York, children play around the base of the other. Such is worldly fame.

Thutmose III was succeeded by Amenophis II, and he in turn by Thutmose IV. Under the next ruler, Amenophis III (Amenophis the Magnificent), Egyptian power reached its zenith. With his passing, the high tide of Egyptian political power began to ebb.

Amenophis IV (B. C. 1375-1358), while not a great emperor, is one of the most amazing characters known to history. Ascending the throne as a mere boy, probably not more than nineteen years of age, he attempted to alter completely the age-old religious beliefs of Egypt. Egypt was a land of many local gods. Among the local deities was the Sun-god, Amon. Amenophis sensed the folly of the many cult worships of his

people and conceived the idea of a single, universal god. Since all life
came from the sun, he concluded that the sun must be the only god. He
named his god "Aton." Spurred by religious fervor, Amenophis inaugurated a campaign to make the worship of Aton the national religion
of Egypt. He ordered all references to the old Sun-god, Amon, removed
from the multitudinous monuments of Egypt. Outside of the Bible, this
is the earliest known movement toward a monotheistic religion. While
some have attempted to trace a connection between this movement and
the great religious movement which originated with the Hebrews, there
can be no possible connection. The conceptions of Amenophis are purely
pagan. He had no ideas as to an Unseen God.

The unique religion of Amenophis immediately brought him into
conflict with the priesthood of the many cult worships of Egypt. The
power of this priesthood centered in Thebes, the national capital. To forward his movement, Amenophis decided to move the seat of government.
He founded a new capital city, Akhetaton, near the Nile about two hundred miles south of Cairo. This site is now known as Tell el-Amarna.
He also changed his name to "Ikhnaton," which means "He in whom
Aton is satisfied."

At Tell el-Amarna, in 1887, was found the first of the remarkable
collection of cuneiform tablets that are known as the "Tell el-Amarna
letters." These letters are perhaps the most interesting mass of documents
surviving from the early East. They began to come to light when an old
peasant woman, digging in the garden back of her little hut, found a
strange "stone" which she sold for the equivalent of fifty cents, little
dreaming that a fortune lay under her feet. The recovered documents,
now numbering nearly four hundred, consisted largely of a series of state
dispatches between the rulers of Egypt and the rulers of Asiatic countries, and throw much light on political conditions of that period. The
letters mention more than twenty cities and towns that are mentioned
in the Old Testament and speak of Jerusalem and its king, who was a
vassal of Egypt.

In his zeal for the new religious cult, Ikhnaton neglected his empire.
Intrigue and rebellion were rife in the Asiatic provinces. Failing to use
the suppressive forces his forefathers would have employed, his Asiatic
colonies slipped from his fingers. Only an energetic ruler, backed by a
strong government, could control Palestine and Syria during those ancient
days.

Ikhnaton had no sons. His kingdom was inherited by two sons-in-
law in succession. The second of these was Tutenkhaton, who married
Ikhnaton's third daughter. With the death of Ikhnaton, the religious
cult he sponsored died with him. Tutenkhaton moved the seat of gov-

ernment back to Thebes, and changed his name to Tutenkhamon. Tutenkhamon's rule was short, less than seven years. Although unimportant in history, his name is better known than any other Pharaoh, since in October, 1922, he crashed the front pages of the daily press when his tomb and its magnificent equipment were discovered by the Earl of Carnarvon's expedition, under the leadership of Mr. Howard Carter.

Most of the great tombs of Egypt were rifled by expert grave-robbers centuries ago. During the days of Egyptian decadence, grave robbing became an established industry. How Tutenkhamon's tomb escaped is a mystery. The treasures recovered from the tomb of this rather insignificant Pharaoh give some idea of the historical treasure trove that may be recovered if ever the tomb of one of the great Pharaohs is found undisturbed.

With the death of Tutenkhamon a great period in the history of Egypt came to an end. With him vanished the last of the illustrious Theban family that had driven out the Hyksos and built up the nearest approach to empire the East had seen up to then. Egypt's greatest day was done. The internal government of Egypt and the administration of colonial affairs became a welter of chaos.

Into the political arena now came Harmhab, a wily politician and able organizer, who had formerly been attached to the court of Ikhnaton. Though not of royal blood, he strove to inaugurate a new imperial dynasty. It is impossible to trace any connection between Harmhab and Rameses I, who succeeded him in B. C. 1315.

Rameses I was a feeble old man when he came to the throne. His son, who had been co-regent, soon succeeded him as Seti I. Seti I attempted to recover the lost Asiatic empire. He did recover a considerable part of northern Palestine. When Seti died in 1292, his son, Rameses, successfully usurped the throne from his eldest brother, and began his long reign of sixty-seven years as Rameses II.

During the early years of his reign, Rameses II contemplated nothing less than the complete recovery of the Asiatic provinces his predecessors had ruled. Times had changed, however, since the days when Thutmose III had built up his great empire. In his first campaign against his Asiatic neighbors, Rameses encountered the tribes well organized under the leadership of the Hittite king, Mutallu. After a great, but indecisive battle, he returned to Egypt to erect monumental boasts of his personal prowess in battle. Later he carried on a series of intermittent campaigns against Mutallu for some fifteen years. Then Mutallu died, and was succeeded by his brother Hatusil. Hatusil concluded a treaty of peace with Rameses II. A copy of this treaty was recovered by archæologists at Boghaz Keui, the ancient capital of the Hittites.

Although Rameses II was unable to extend his empire beyond north-ern Palestine, he held firmly the line of fortified cities that stretched across the country from the Mediterranean to the Jordan. Although these cities remained essentially Canaanite in population, Egyptian palaces and temples loomed above the city walls. Among the temples reared during the reign of Rameses II were "the house of Ashtaroth" (1 *Samuel* 31:10) and the "temple of Dagon" (1 *Chronicles* 10:10) the temples to which at a later date the victorious Philistines carried the body of king Saul for defilement after his disastrous defeat on the slopes of Mt. Gilboa.*

During the reign of Rameses II the importance of Egypt's interests in Asia caused the center of Egyptian power to shift from Thebes to the eastern portion of the Delta. The turbulent Hittites and their allies were a constant threat. Only the sword could control. The Wadi Tumilat, along which ran the fresh-water canal from the Bitter Lakes to the Nile, formed a natural gateway from Asia to Egypt. Rameses barred this gate-way with a line of military outposts from the Mediterranean to Lake Timsah, and, according to his records, built store-cities with forced labor as military depots for his forces operating in Asia and also to form a secondary line of defense.

While *Exodus* fails to give dates, it states very definitely: "And they built for Pharaoh treasure cities, Pithom and Raamses" (*Exodus* 1:11). In the annals of Rameses II he mentions using forced Asiatic labor, and the building of Pithom and Per-Ramses (Raamses). For this reason he is commonly identified as the Pharaoh of the oppression.

Pithom (Tell el Maskhutah) was excavated by Naville.† The city was dedicated to the god "Tum." Its name is derived from "Pi Tum," the city, or abode, of Tum. Inscriptions describe the place as "the city that is at the eastern door."

Raamses (Tell el Ratabeh) was excavated by Sir Flinders Petrie.‡ This city contained many monuments of Rameses II, and since it con-tained nothing more ancient than these monuments, it would seem to be fairly well established that Rameses II was the Pharaoh of the oppres-sion.

Raamses, like Pithom, was built as a storage city, a place for the assembling of supplies for military campaigns. The ruins of the storage rooms remain in evidence to this day. *Exodus* 1:11 refers to them as "treasure cities," which is quite consistent. The discovery by Naville of buildings in which the lower courses of the brickwork were laid up with bricks made with straw in the usual manner, with higher courses

*See Chapter VIII, page 122.
†See Naville: *The Store City and the Route of the Exodus.*
‡See Petrie: *Egypt and Israel.*

ANCIENT EGYPTIAN BOAT MODEL

The boats that Joseph saw on the Nile differed little from some of the craft which ply the ancient river today.

ANCIENT EGYPTIAN GRANARY MODEL

By permission of The Museum of the University of Pennsylvania

of bricks mixed with stubble and grain roots, and the building finished with bricks made without straw, exemplifies the striking material confirmation of Old Testament narrative that archæology frequently reveals.

Rameses II was the greatest builder of all Egyptian Pharaohs. Besides many other extensive works, he completed the largest building in the ancient world—the Hypostyle Hall at Karnak. Throughout his realm he erected innumerable statues of himself. Some of these were colossal, weighing a thousand tons or more. These building operations called for a vast army of "forced labourers," and of these the Israelites must have been forced to furnish a quota. The tent-dwelling, nomadic Israelites must have found it exceedingly irksome "to serve with rigour," and to be housed in the huts of a construction camp.

The extensive military operations of Egypt and the monumental building campaign constantly in progress doubtless occasioned a shortage of man-power in the country. The strategic military strongholds of Syria and Palestine had to be garrisoned by mercenary troops imported from the countries bordering the northern shores of the Mediterranean. In the ruins of Palestinian cities archæologists have found innumerable evidences of the long stay of these mercenary troops during the time that Egypt was in political control of Palestine. The Biblical account that "the Egyptians made the children of Israel to serve with rigour" (*Exodus* 1:13), and the Rameses annals which state that Pithom and Per-Ramses were built "with forced Asiatic labor," are quite in keeping with known facts of history.

War times make work. Labor was needed in all lines of endeavor. Foreign labor was used in the mines in the Sinai Peninsula. That Israel, along with other immigrants, or captive foreigners, was pressed into service by the Egyptians was quite consistent with the traditions of the country. Tomb reliefs show the labors in the fields to which the "Asiatics" were condemned—plowing and sowing, reaping and threshing (See *Exodus* 1:14), and making sun-dried bricks in moulds (See *Exodus* 5:6-19). Probably it paid to keep busy. A favorite outdoor sport of Egyptian Pharaohs and their court followers was hunting Asiatic captives with trained leopards. *Exodus* opens with a faithful pen-picture of the times.

And there arose not a prophet since in Israel like unto Moses.— Deuteronomy 34:10

Hebrew nationality was born in Egypt. Hebrew history really begins with Moses. Moses laid the foundations on which was reared the national life of Israel. Abraham founded a faith. Moses founded a nation. With rare prophetic insight, Moses sensed that nationalism was but a thing

6

of Time, but that faith, founded on truth, was of things Eternal. Even as he built a nation from a horde of slaves, Moses foresaw a time when his people would be "removed into all the kingdoms of the earth" (*Deuteronomy* 28:25). Men like Moses cannot be measured in terms of time; they are citizens of the ages.

Moses seems to have been singularly well fitted for his great life-work. Reared in the court of Pharaoh, the beloved foster son of Pharaoh's daughter, he doubtless learned the court etiquette and acquired the court manners, which would stand him in good stead years later when he appeared before the rulers of Egypt to plead the cause of Israel. Although reared in the royal family, he remained so essentially a Hebrew that when "he spied an Egyptian smiting a Hebrew, one of his brethren . . . he slew the Egyptian, and hid him in the sand" (*Exodus* 2:11,12).

When his impulsive action provoked the wrath of Pharaoh, Moses fled from impending vengeance into the country of the Midianites, a semi-nomadic, pastoral people, whose grazing grounds bordered the desert near the eastern arm of the Red Sea. Here, as he ranged far and wide over the countryside, tending his father-in-law's flocks, he came to know the landmarks of a part of the country though which he was later to lead his people. This knowledge would some day be invaluable. He also acquired knowledge and wisdom of still greater value. Here in the loneliness of the waste lands, praying to the "Lord God of the Hebrews" as only the lonely can pray, he underwent the great spiritual experiences that laid the foundations for his massive character. Brooding over the degrading bondage of his people back in Egypt, he visioned a day when Israel would drop its shackles, renounce its allegiance to Egypt, and, guided by Jehovah, would achieve independent nationality in the Promised Land.

What manner of man was this Moses who returned to Egypt, burning with patriotic zeal, armed with Jehovah's assurance, to arouse a people drugged dormant by the degradation of forced labor to a consciousness of national unity and to lead them to liberty? From the Biblical portraiture of Moses as a personality, we gather that he was a man of astounding mental and physical vigor. In *Exodus* 11:3, we read: "Moreover the man Moses was very great in the land of Egypt, in the sight of Pharaoh's servants, and in the sight of the people." Here was a diplomat, a man who could "walk with kings, nor lose the common touch," a man whose faith in his God was such that he could withstand the magicians of Pharaoh with such assurance that the results caused the magicians to say "unto Pharaoh, This is the finger of God"—*Exodus* 8:19.

Although late investigations (1934-1935) in the Trans-Jordan regions, through which Moses led Israel *en route* to the Jordan, support strongly those who hold that the Exodus took place in the thirteenth century, the date of the Exodus can not as yet be fixed from external evidence. Regardless of when the Exodus took place, Moses was faced with a stupendous task. The real marvel of the Exodus was not the famous water-passage out of Egypt, but that Moses, regardless of how able or talented he may have been, was able to organize a horde of semi-slaves and successfully lead them out of Egypt without disaster. Here, indeed, is an historical marvel.

Although the Pharaoh of the oppression cannot be definitely identified, there can be no doubt that the lot of the Israelites, during the late years of their stay in Egypt, was exceedingly unhappy. All aliens in Egypt lived under the threat of an iron hand. Tomb reliefs show "Asiatics" pleading before the rulers of Egypt. It is not strange that a downtrodden Israel should greet with welcoming wonder the returning Moses bringing a burning message direct from God: "And God said unto Moses, I AM THAT I AM; and he said, Thus shalt thou say unto the children of Israel, I AM hath sent me unto you"—*Exodus* 3:14.

And the Lord spake unto Moses, Go unto Pharaoh.—Exodus 8:1.

Abraham had been the guest of a Pharaoh. Joseph had been summoned to appear before a Pharaoh. These meetings, however, had taken place when the more or less friendly Hyksos or Shepherd Kings had governed the land in a now far distant day. Times had changed. A formal and unfriendly Pharaoh sat enthroned in the seat of the mighty when Moses and Aaron were ushered into the august presence. They came not as Princes of Israel, nor as interpreters of regal dreams. They came to plead for a people. They were asking Pharaoh to give up a great national asset, the unpaid labor of a multitude of slaves. They could anticipate little more than a curt refusal from Pharaoh. Nevertheless the representatives of the slaves regarded themselves as the ambassadors of Jehovah. They could not be overawed by any earthly king.

Most authorities on the subject are convinced that Rameses II was the Pharaoh of the oppression. It may be that the Exodus took place during the latter years of his reign, or, still more likely, shortly after his death, when Merenptah occupied the throne of Egypt. The negotiations of Moses, looking to the release of Israel, may have been with one or the other, or perhaps both, of these monarchs.

Unfortunately for his country, Rameses II lived too long. With his physical decay came the beginning of the disintegration of his empire. The Philistines, long resident in the agricultural districts of Palestine, were beginning to intrigue with the mercenary troops who held the Palestinian cities for Egypt. The scenes on the stage of international politics were shifting rapidly. Storm clouds were gathering in the north and west. The Libyans, and the maritime peoples allied with them, began to invade the western Delta. Aegean peoples, dislodged from the regions that were later the Greek world by the southward movement of the Hellenic tribes, began the first historic intrusion of hostile European forces into the Near-Eastern arena. Egypt's imperial day was drawing to a close. A decrepit Pharaoh ruled a ramshackle empire.

Rameses II outlived most of his family. At his death there was no stalwart young son to succeed him. His thirteenth son, Merenptah, B. C. 1225-1215, was already a senile old man when he came to the throne. The death of Rameses was the occasion for widespread revolt in the Asiatic provinces. In the third year of his reign, Merenptah, despite his advanced years, led a successful expedition into Palestine and crushed the revolters. In his record of this triumph the name of "Israel" makes its first appearance in secular history as the name of a people. The inscription reads:

The kings are overthrown, saying: "Salaam!"
Not one holds up his head among the Nine
Nations of the Bow.
Wasted is Tehenue,
The Hittite land is pacified,
Plundered is the Canaan, with every evil.
Carried off is Ashkalon,
Seized upon is Gezer,
Venoam is made a thing not existing,
Israel is desolated, her seed is not,
Kharu (South Palestine) has become a widow for Egypt.
All lands are united, they are pacified;
Every one that is turbulent is bound by King Merenptah.

If, as many scholars believe, the Exodus took place during the reign of Merenptah, it is probable that the dramatic interviews between Moses and the Pharaoh took place in the great palace of Merenptah at Memphis. In the years 1915-1920, the Coxe Egyptian Expedition of the University Museum uncovered this mighty palace.*

As one stands by the great portal pillars that once graced the entrance to this palace, or amid the great limestone columns that supported its roof, it is possible to picture a pair of lone Israelites pleading before Pharaoh and competing with the court magicians in the halls of this mighty structure. In such an awe-inspiring atmosphere, Moses and Aaron needed more than common courage to face a hostile Pharaoh.

---

*See *University Museum Journal,* Vol. VIII, Num. 4.

As Moses and Aaron approached the royal precinct they must have felt themselves dwarfed by the mere size of the place. It covered approximately thirteen acres of ground. A great wall, twenty-one feet thick, shut out the world. Perhaps many man-hours of Israelitish labor had been sweated into that wall's construction. As the brothers awaited admittance at the great gateway, which towered above their heads to a height of twenty-six feet, the reliefs on the portal pillars, picturing Merenptah slaying Syrian captives, must have been a grim reminder of the type of tyrant with whom they had to deal. Only men armed with righteousness would undertake such a mission as theirs. No wave of welcome awaited them with the opening of the gates. Probably the palace guards would greet with ill-disguised disdain the representatives of the hated Hebrews. One can imagine the simple shepherds praying for Jehovah's guidance as they were conducted through the architectural splendors of the great colonnaded court and ushered into the throne room. They were now in a magnificent room, where Egyptian decorative art had reached its highest perfection. The massive, monolithic columns were elaborately carved, painted and gilded with figures of the Pharaoh before the gods of Memphis. The stuccoed walls and floors gleamed with brilliantly painted scenes. Shafts of sunlight, streaming down from slotted openings high on the walls, blended the glitter and gleam of the room into a scene of awe-inspiring beauty.

At the end of the room most distant from the entrance, the throne of the Pharaoh rested on a raised platform. The entire surface of this platform was covered with reliefs of bound figures, representing the ten nations Merenptah claimed to have conquered. Perhaps the eyes of Moses and Aaron fell on these very figures as they bowed down before Pharaoh.

The dramatic interviews between the leaders of Israel and the Pharaoh may, or may not, have taken place in the palace of Merenptah. One thing, however, is certain, it was in some such place and in some such surroundings that "Moses and Aaron came in unto Pharaoh, and said unto him, Thus saith the Lord God of the Hebrews, How long wilt thou refuse to humble thyself before me? let my people go that they may serve me"—*Exodus* 10:3.

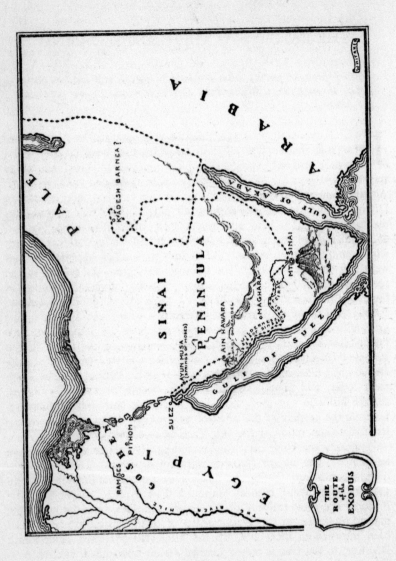

THE ROUTE of the EXODUS

V

THE RETURN TO THE PROMISED LAND

Also I brought you up from the land of Egypt, and led you forty years through the wilderness, to possess the land of the Amorite.
—*Amos* 2:10

FOUR thousand years ago Palestine was promised to Abraham for an inheritance: "For all the land which thou seest, to thee will I give it, and to thy seed forever"—*Genesis* 13:15. From that day to this the life story of Israel has always been associated with Palestine. Abraham entered into a solemn compact with his God, and accepted a Divine mandate for himself and for his people. This was a provisional mandate. It was, in part, a prophetical covenant. So long as the seed of Abraham kept this covenant and observed the Divine ordinances, they would enjoy a priceless legacy. The rewards for keeping the covenant were only in part material. The ultimate objectives—the essence of the covenant—reached far beyond all geographical boundaries. The Promised Land was not bounded by land and sea, or measured by time and space. Israel inherited spiritual resources unknown to lesser breeds of men. The great gift of God to Israel was a penetrating insight into the sublime intangibles that exist in the realms of the spirit and the mind. If the Promised Land had meant only a tiny territory in western Asia, or even all the great places of the earth, we would not be reading the Old Testament today, and Israel's stay in Palestine would be merely something for the historian and the archæologist to ponder over. The supreme reward for the keeping of the covenant was that Israel's spiritual idealism—its sublime conception of the One True God—should never perish.

Humanly speaking, man's understanding of the Unseen must always be limited. The ancient Hebrews were not supermen. They were ordinary human beings, sharing the timeless life experiences that are the common lot of mankind, even as you and I share them in our world today. Probably the great majority of the ancient Israelites never fathomed the underlying values of the great treasure of divine instruction which had been intrusted to their race. To the many, the Promised Land meant Palestine; to the few, it meant spiritual realms unbounded, endless, eternal. To the materially minded, Palestine may have seemed reward sufficient; to the spiritually minded men to whom we owe the Old Testament it was but a symbol of things to come. The inspired writers realized

[71]

that Hebrew nationalism could not long endure. Nations rise and fall
within man's measurements of time; noble ideals endure through God's
eternal years. "If these ordinances depart from before me, saith the Lord,
then the seed of Israel also shall cease from being a nation"—*Jeremiah*
31:36.

Israel lived out its little day of national glory. In its brief era of empire it saw the heights of Jerusalem crowned with a Hebrew metropolis.
Today, "the stranger that shall come from a far land" (*Deuteronomy*
29:22) rules in Palestine. Israel is scattered "among all the people, from
one end of the earth even unto the other" (*Deuteronomy* 28:64), but
Palestine is still the homeland to the heart of the Hebrew. Throughout
the crushing cruelties of the centuries the soul of Israel has clung to
Jerusalem.

The Jew is a hardy perennial. The peoples who were contemporary
with the Chosen People during Old Testament days have largely disappeared. No recognizable descendant of the Amorites, the Hittites, the
Assyrians, or the Babylonians can be found today, yet there are three
times as many Hebrews in the world today as there were in "the Gold-
en Age of Israel" when Solomon reigned in Jerusalem. New York has a
greater Jewish population than Jerusalem ever had. Even in its most
productive days, Palestine could never have supported the present Jewish
population of the world. To the great majority of Jews, Zionism—the
restoration of Jewish nationalism in Palestine—can never be more than
a dream. Sixteen million Jews could never find sustenance in Palestine,
but to the Jewish world it will always be the Promised Land.

The racial history of the Hebrews has been more accurately kept
than that of any other ancient people. The history of the Hebrews is
largely a tragic tale of woe. Their national home was built on one of the
historic battle grounds of the ages. Jerusalem has been more frequently
destroyed and rebuilt than any other city ever reared by man. Before
the dawn of written history, primitive man fought over its limestone
caves. The Amorites and the Hittites battled for its possession. The arms
of Egypt reduced it to vassalage. As the little pagan city of Jebus, it was
frequently the scene of inter-tribal warfare, until it fell before the Hebrews
in the days of David. For nearly five hundred years Jerusalem was the
sacred capital of Hebrew nationalism. Then succeeding waves of invasion swept over it. Assyria ravished the city. Babylonia destroyed it.
After the restoration by Nehemiah, Jerusalem was once more a Hebrew
city. Then came European invasion. Hellenic (or Greek) culture was introduced into Jerusalem by force of arms. With the legions of Rome
came the darkest of days for Jerusalem and the Jews. Although the earthly
lifetime of Our Lord began and ended during the Roman Period,

although He walked the city's streets and taught in the great temple, the city knew no peace. Patriotic Hebrews were constantly plotting against their Roman overlords. Finally, in 70 A. D., the exasperated Romans determined to annihilate the Jews. Jerusalem was destroyed. Over a million Jews fell during the fighting in Palestine. Survivors were sold into slavery by tens of thousands. So many Jews were offered for sale in the slave-marts of the world that the markets became glutted, and Jews could not be sold at any price. "Ye shall be sold unto your enemies for bondmen and bondwomen, and no man shall buy you"—*Deuteronomy* 28:68.

No race blood has ever remained so pure and distinct as that of the Hebrew. With his rare gifts of business acumen and genius for statecraft, the Hebrew has contributed greatly to the economic and political history of many modern countries, yet his racial history remains distinct. Ever the alien, he mingles with many peoples but mixes with none. Without a country, wandering where "among these nations thou shalt find no ease" (*Deuteronomy* 28:65) the Hebrew cherishes the history and traditions of his people in Palestine with a love that will not die. Nationless, he is the world's most passionate nationalist.

Hebrew nationalism was born in Egypt, born after agonizing travail in the dark days of semi-slavery. The Hebrew annalists make no attempt to conceal their lowly ancestry. They picture a noble nation sired by shepherds and slaves. The boastfulness of secular history is missing from their writings. They looked on life through religious lenses, and interpreted the current events of their day in terms of their faith in the Lord God of Israel. Are their measurements of the human dimensions of the mighty Moses overdrawn? Think of the pæans of praise any modern people would pour into their word-pictures of any national hero who rescued them from slavery. Think! Think, and remember that the sacred writers, who were depicting the birth of a nation, were Orientals, writing with the vivid imagery and word-picture forms of the ancient East. The arrival of Moses from Midian awakened Israel from a nightmare of slavery to a dawn bright with the promise of freedom. Bearing a mandate from Israel's God, the long-prayed-for Emancipator had come to lead the Chosen People back to the land of their ancestors.

And it came to pass the self-same day, that the Lord did bring the children of Israel out of the land of Egypt.—Exodus 12:51

The date of the Exodus is unknown. However, scientific investigators are convinced that the great folk-migration actually took place. The event, rather than the date, is the important matter; although it would be gratifying if the date could be definitely placed. There is no longer any logical reason to doubt the historicity of the Exodus.

The estimate of the number of people who moved out of Egypt as given in *Exodus* 12:37, and reiterated in *Numbers* 1:46; 26:51—upwards of six hundred thousand adults—indicates one of the greatest folk-migrations in history. Such a movement would call for almost military organization, as is indicated by the words, "and the children of Israel went up harnessed out of the land of Egypt." (*Exodus* 13:18, "by five in a rank," margin.)

Moses had little choice in the matter of routes. The three great caravan trade routes were guarded by the armies of Egypt and her allies. The route "through the way of the land of the Philistines" (*Exodus* 13:17) held a double threat of disaster. In the improbable event of the tribes successfully passing the military outposts of the Egyptians, they would certainly "see war" if they attempted to pass through the grain-growing districts of the Philistines. Moving out of Egypt successfully over any of the ordinary routes would have been a greater miracle than any water-passage through the waters at the head of the Red Sea possibly could have been.

When the time of departure arrived, only "the way of the wilderness of the Red Sea" (*Exodus* 13:18) lay open to Moses. This meant that he must travel to the south of the usual trade routes. However, he must not go too far south, or he and his followers would perish in the waterless desert. His expedition, carrying women and children as well as livestock, must be kept close to potable water. His logical route would be down the Wadi Tumilat, following the fresh-water canal as far as practicable, then skirting to the southward of the line of garrisoned outposts that guarded the gateway to Asia between the Mediterranean and Lake Timsah. Even this route presented great difficulties, since it would inevitably lead to a water front. A water-passage of some sort would be unavoidable.

Moses must have known well the route to the frontier. He was headed toward his old home in Midian. He was familiar with the waterways that lay before him. Naturally, he would direct his march toward some place where the waters were both shallow and narrow. To march to the shores of the Red Sea proper would be to travel weary leagues out of his way, over a burning desert, to no purpose. Time was precious. Over a million souls were intrusted to his care. Naturally he would make for the lake-like arms that fringed the northern end of the Red Sea. To cross anywhere, under any conditions, would be miracle enough for Moses. While depending on divine guidance, he would doubtless take every precaution his mature judgment would dictate. He was carrying out a project he had planned for, and prayed over, for years.

And Moses stretched out his hand over the sea; and the Lord caused the sea to go back by a strong east wind all that night, and made the sea dry land, and the waters were divided.—Exodus 14:21

The site of this crossing is unknown. It will probably never be definitely identified. Shorelines shift with the passing centuries. The topography of those regions alters rapidly. Artistic conceptions of the events usually picture the Hebrews marching between vertical walls of water. Actuality probably presented a more prosaic picture, but nonetheless miraculous. *The Journal of the Transactions of the Victorian Institute** relates that a group of British officers, stationed in this region, saw the sands at the bottom of the lake laid bare for a great distance by a strong wind that blew for hours, making a crossing possible. This condition may, or may not, have been paralleled at the time of the migration of Israel. "And the people feared the Lord, and believed the Lord, and his servant Moses" (*Exodus* 14:31). Regardless of the manner or method of the crossing, the sacred writer was describing a miracle. Well might the people believe in Moses and the God of Moses. Jehovah had delivered his people. The Israelites were eye-witnesses of awe-inspiring and soul-moving events. As they watched the returning waters engulf the hosts of Pharaoh, and realized that at last they were free, it was natural that Israel should burst into song and Miriam compose her exultant hymn of praise to the Lord God of Israel.

So Moses brought Israel from the Red Sea, and they went out into the wilderness of Shur.—Exodus 15:22

When Israel had passed the great barrier to freedom, the waters at the northern end of the Red Sea, the difficulties of the great enterprise that Moses had undertaken were merely begun. Moses had on his hands a loosely organized horde of ex-slaves, many of whom were still slaves in spirit. The songs of praise to Jehovah for the wonderful manifestation of His presence that had led them out of Egypt died out within three days in murmuring against Moses, even before he could lead them to "Elim, where there were twelve wells of water, and threescore and ten palm trees" (*Exodus* 15:27).

It is altogether likely that the Israelites were more than dissatisfied. Probably many of them were terrified. This was a strangely forbidding land. Reared in Egypt they knew the sand desert and its terrors, but

*See *Transactions*, Vols. XXIV and XXVI.

this was infinitely worse. Behind the sand belt which the tourist of today sights from the rail of his steamer on his Red Sea tour lies a most fantastic land. The Israelites were entering a sea of stone, a land of great granite barriers denuded of almost every green thing. To penetrate this broken country their only roadways were the wadies. A wadi is a dry water-course. If rain fell, which was unlikely, it would rush down the wadi with great speed and be gone.

After leaving Ayun Musa (Springs of Moses) the Israelites could find no water until they came to Ain Hawara (supposed to be the "waters of Marah"). The camel, who likes brackish water, will drink the water of these springs but it is not palatable for human beings. The sight of this water must have almost maddened the hot and dusty foot-travelers who followed Moses. Probably the sacred writer was putting it mildly when he said "the people murmured against Moses" before they reached Elim.

Where was Elim? It must have been either Wadi Taiyibeh, which the Arabs of today call "The Goodly Valley," or Wadi Gharandel, which, strangely enough, has about threescore and ten palm trees scattered around its springs today.

Naturally, we marvel much at the roundabout route that Moses took to reach Mt. Sinai. *Exodus* 16:1 indicates that he swung toward the coast line about midway between the present-day port of Suez and the little seaport town of Tor, some one hundred and forty miles south, to enter the "wilderness of Sin." Why did he not travel directly overland? Moses evidently knew what he was doing. He was out of Egypt, but the Sinai Peninsula was under the control of Egypt. The direct route to Mt. Sinai would have brought him too close to Maghara, where the Egyptians had extensive turquoise mines. There would be a strong military guard at Maghara, where mining operations were carried on with forced labor. The Nakb el-Budra (Nakb means "defile") must have been tempting to Moses, but, probably to avoid bloodshed, he chose to travel south until he could pick up the Wadi Feiran and swing westward toward Mt. Sinai.

Moses had consecrated his life and invested his future in a determined effort to lead his people to national independence in Palestine. Throughout the remainder of his days he was to be their religious leader, the codifier of their laws, and the organizer of their national life, as he led them toward a passable gateway to the Promised Land.

If Moses had been able to travel directly eastward from Egypt into the Promised Land, avoiding the water-passage and the long trek through the wilderness, it would have profited Israel but little without divine aid. An unorganized horde of ex-slaves could not have wrested the strongly fortified cities of Canaan from a people well skilled in warfare, if they were dependent on their own resources. Numbers alone would not suffice. Organization was essential. Military leadership must be developed. Israel must become accustomed to the use of arms, for the Promised Land would not now fall at their feet like manna.

If, as seems reasonably clear, Moses traveled up the Wadi Feiran, it is easy to see why the Amalekites "fought with Israel in Rephidim" (*Exodus* 17:8). Passing up the wadi the Israelites would finally sight fertile soil, green shrubs would appear, then the welcome sight of water, as they broke into field-floored, palm-decked Oasis of Feiran, the "Pearl of Sinai." Any people holding such a place would hold scant welcome for a horde of hungry Hebrews pouring out of the defile. The Hebrews could not go back. Advance meant fight. Moses called on his military leader, Joshua, "and Joshua discomfited Amelek and his people with the edge of the sword" (*Exodus* 17:13).

Wresting a scanty livelihood from the wastelands as they wandered in search of a passable gateway, fighting the foes in front, repelling the desert nomads whose lands they were invading, and living again the semi-nomadic life of their forefathers, reawakened the sturdy, enduring qualities that have always distinguished the Hebrews. Fighting nature and fighting their neighbors turned ex-serfs into soldiers. The almost constant warfare developed the necessary military leadership. Joshua and his fellow military leaders were products of the wilderness. The wilderness years were not wasted years.

And there Israel camped before the mount.—Exodus 19:2

Sinai is the most famous mountain mentioned in the Old Testament. It was made famous by Moses. The rugged mass of granite which rises 7,519 feet above sea level has been called by many names—Sinai, Mount of the Decalogue, Mount of the Law, Mount of the Commandments— but is known locally as Jebel Musa, meaning in Arabic "Mount Moses." To the north-west of the mountain lies the traditional "Plain of the Tribes," where the famous pilgrimage halted "in the third month, when the children of Israel were gone forth out of the land of Egypt."

The centuries have dimmed the trail of Israel through the wilderness. At this late date it is impossible to follow completely, geographically, the detailed itinerary outlined in *Numbers* 33. Many of the places mentioned have not as yet been located by geographers or archæologists. Doubtless time and nature have obliterated some of them. There is, however, no logical reason to doubt the accuracy of the outline. The tribes wandered widely but were never lost. They had a definite objective in view. Theirs was not a military movement clearing the way for a civil population. It was a folk-movement rounding the desert rim of a country held by strong, warlike peoples who were potential enemies of the migrating multitude from Egypt. The gateways to Canaan were guarded by the iron hand of military might. Israel was seeking an unguarded, or weakly held, entrance to the Promised Land.

That the search for an available point of entry into Canaan was intensive is indicated by the story of espionage related in *Numbers* 13. It is evident from the text that the spies sent out by Moses conducted an intensive survey of the borderlands. There is an interesting touch of local color in verse 23: "And they came unto the brook of Eshcol, and cut down from thence a branch with one cluster of grapes, and they bare it between two upon a staff." The implied size of the cluster of grapes may seem astounding to those of us who pluck grapes from a trellis in the garden or buy them by the pound in the market. It should be remembered, however, that the wine grapes of Canaan were the Syrian grapes, *vitis vinifera,* which, if not carefully husbanded, will produce clusters of grapes between twenty and thirty inches long, a size that is not suitable for marketing.

The many mentions in the Bible of the vineyard and the vine indicate that then as now the grape was an important factor in the economic life of the peoples of Palestine. Our Lord mentions the vine frequently in his teachings and uses it as an illustration in the great sermon contained in *John* 15. Jesus was talking of what is still the most advanced method of cultivating the Syrian grape. Every autumn the good husbandman carefully examines every vine. The branches that do not bear are cut off. The productive branches are pruned back to the heavy wood. If this is not done the vine will bear a few bunches of grapes of unmarketable size. The Israelitish spies evidently plucked their cluster of grapes from the vineyard of a poor husbandman or found a vine which had run wild.

And the people abode in Kadesh.—Numbers 20:1

Next to the Mount of the Decalogue, the most important place of encampment of the Israelites was Kadesh, or Kadesh-Barnea. From the economic standpoint it was probably the most important, since it was evidently the headquarters of the expedition for a very long period. *Deuteronomy* 2:14 suggests that Israel may have been at Kadesh for thirty-eight years. The many Biblical mentions of the place indicate that it was the most important base of Israel between the time they left Egypt and the time when they found an entrance to Canaan through the lower East-Jordan country. Where was Kadesh? This is a question not yet answered to the satisfaction of all authorities. The two possible sites which are most often discussed, and seem the most likely, are Ayn

Qadees and Ayn el-Waybeh. Ayn, or "ain," means "spring" in Arabic. The late Dr. H. Clay Trumbull in his excellent book *"Kadesh-Barnea"* presents interesting arguments in favor of Ayn Qadees. On the other hand such well-known explorers as Dr. C. Leonard Wooley and the late Colonel T. E. Lawrence decided that the more fertile district of Kossima must have been the site of the famous encampment.

And the Lord said unto Moses, Write this for a memorial in a book.
—Exodus 17:14

Although the Old Testament, in its present form, is regarded by most scholars as the work of redactors of a later age, most of the data must have come from original documents written at about the time the recorded events took place. In the light of recent discoveries, one can no longer lightly assume that the earlier books of the immortal classic are merely a national epic of poetical tradition. In view of the many documents, written centuries before the days of Moses, which have been found at many sites in Babylonia and Egypt, it is logical to assume that writing was in vogue among the Israelites long before they entered Canaan.

Moses may have had an official recorder. Although the first mention of the professional writer (or scribe) is found in *Judges* 5:14, there were evidently writers among the Israelites at a much earlier date. *Numbers* 5:23 mentions a priest writing in a book, while *Numbers* 11:26 speaks of "them that were written." In *Deuteronomy* 31:9-11, Moses is represented as writing the law. Someone must have kept the "book of the wars of the Lord" mentioned in *Numbers* 21:14. There is certainly nothing anachronistic in the early indications of a knowledge of the art of writing among the Hebrews.

Thus Edom refused to give Israel passage through his border: wherefore Israel turned away from him—Numbers 20:21.

The Israelites were not the only people migrating about this time. An advanced civilization was centered in the lower Tigris-Euphrates Valley. Another advanced civilization was centered on the Nile. Between these settled centers of power the ancient world was in an age of political unsettlement. Egypt, itself threatened with foreign invasion, was being forced to loosen its grip on northern Palestine. The rich grain-growing regions of Philistia were held by the Philistines. The Amorites and the Hittites, although weakened by their long warfare with Egypt, still clung to most of Canaan. There were, however, other lesser semi-nomadic peoples seeking new environments in which to establish their national homes. Some time, but not long, before the Israelites began their famous migrational movement, one of the semi-nomadic peoples had settled in the high lands that stretch between the Gulf of Akabah and the lower end of the Dead Sea. These were the Edomites. Soon afterward, the Moabites settled in the country just to the north of Edom. Much of this land was, and still is, well watered and fertile.

Even to this day there are no accurate maps of some of the regions the wandering Israelites traversed. Israel evidently made several attempts to invade Canaan from the south (See *Numbers* 13; *Deuteronomy* 1). Repeated failure to force an entrance from the south finally forced them to attempt negotiations with the Edomites for peaceful passage through their country. The recently discovered (1933-1934) strongly fortified boundaries of the Edomite kingdom * indicate that any passage other than a peaceful one was impossible. In the 13th century B. C., the Edomites had erected an intricate system of border fortifications. These fortresses, placed in strategic positions, each within sight of another, formed an impassable barrier. Israel must make a circuit of Edom when negotiations for peaceful transit failed.

Evidently Israel could successfully cope with wandering tribes and indifferently established kingdoms, as witness the campaigns described in *Numbers* 21:21-35, but had not sufficient military power to force a passage through Edom. Rebuffed by Edom, Israel now gave up its long established headquarters at Kadesh, and "journeyed from Kadesh, and came unto Mt. Hor" (*Numbers* 20:22). This was a decisive move. Moses evidently decided to march around Edom and reach the caravan highway that ran northward on the eastern side of the Seir range of mountains. Incidentally, it might be mentioned that the discovery recently of rich but long-disused copper mines in the vicinity of Mt. Hor might suggest where Moses could have secured the ores to make his "serpent of brass" (*Numbers* 21:9).

And Moab was sore afraid of the people, because they were many: and Moab was distressed because of the children of Israel.—Numbers 22:3

Once east of the Seir range, the character of the Exodus apparently changed completely. The weary pilgrimage was nearly over. Israel was now entering a decisive military campaign to secure an entrance into the Promised Land. A vulnerable spot had been found. The goal was not far distant. Israel was ready to write new pages in "the book of the wars of the Lord" (*Numbers* 21:14). After establishing a new headquarters on the banks of the Arnon, Israel sent messengers to the Amorite king of Sihon to negotiate for peaceful passage along the borders of his country to the lower Jordan. When permission to pass peacefully

---

* See Bulletin 51 of the American School of Oriental Research, 1934.

PALACE OF MERENPTAH

Scale model reproduction of the palace of Merenptah. In some such surroundings Moses and
Aaron appeared before Pharaoh to appeal for Israel.

By permission of The Museum of the University of Pennsylvania

was refused, Israel took to the sword. After a decisive battle at Jahaz, Israel pushed on to Heshbon, which they soon captured. Heshbon, high in a beautiful hill country, became the first capital of a Hebrew state. The country of king Og of Bashan next fell a victim to the Hebrew hosts. The pathway to the Jordan was now clear.

The Moabites, lacking the bristling armed frontier of the Edomites, naturally were alarmed over the advance of this militant horde of new-comers. Here were hosts of determined desert warriors, fresh from an-nihilating the forces of the king of Sihon and the king of Bashan, en-camped on their borders. Sensing the futility of armed resistance the Moabites invoked the powers of Oriental magic, but Israel was not to be stayed. The gateway to the Promised Land lay open.

The initial campaign for the conquest of Canaan really opened in the Trans-Jordan country. Before the death of Moses a great section of fer-tile country east of the Jordan had been consolidated and transferred to the children of Reuben and the children of Gad for an inheritance. When Moses stood on Mt. Nebo and gazed westward on the Promised Land he was never to enter, he already stood in a blessed land that was firmly in the possession of Israel. Israel now held a firm base for future mili-tary operations. Although the Reubenites and the Gadites were allotted this land, they were not released from military duty in the coming con-quest of Canaan (See *Numbers* 32:17, 18; *Joshua* 1:12-18).

And the Lord said unto Moses, Thus shalt thou say unto the chil-dren of Israel, Ye have seen that I have talked with you from heaven.—Exodus 20:22

Although it is not the purpose of these pages to invade the province of the pulpit by attempting to interpret the spiritual growth of Israel during the wandering in the wilderness, it must be stated that, from a religious viewpoint, this is the most important period in Old Testament history. Into a world steeped in paganism Moses brought an authoritative disclosure of the intervention of a personal God into human affairs.

The religion of Israel must have been more or less crude at this period. How easily they could lapse into idolatry is illustrated by many Old Testament narratives. Although the Israelites worshipped Jehovah, they were far from the enlightened monotheism which distinguished the later Hebrews. Abraham's conception of Deity, the One True God, kept alive by the religious experiences of his descendants, apparently was but dimly understood by many of the primitive-minded followers of Moses.

All primitive peoples seem to have found it imperative to have some emblem they could use in the rituals of worship. The Canaanites wor-shipped the sacred stone and the sacred tree. The early Egyptians could

7

not visualize a god in any other form than a man or an animal. Abraham's kinsmen in Ur used little figurines, usually made of baked clay, in their devotions. These figurines were of such importance that a domestic storm was raised in the family of Laban, when his daughter Rachel purloined the household gods (*Genesis* 31). The use of these teraphim is also indicated in *Genesis* 35, when "Jacob said unto his household, and to all that were with him, Put away the strange gods that are among you . . . And they gave unto Jacob all the strange gods which were in their hand." To replace forever man-made idols, Moses brought down from the cloud-enshrouded summit of Mt. Sinai "two tables of testimony, tables of stone, written with the finger of God" (*Exodus* 31:18).

Here was a great turning point in the history of Israel. The Ten Commandments became the foundation for all the basic laws of the Hebrew race and a priceless legacy to Christendom.

Moses was not the first great giver of laws. Laws, crude at first, followed man's first feeble steps toward civilization. As culture and civilization developed laws became more definite and refined and were formulated into tribal, and finally national, codes. Israel had always lived under some system of law. Abraham was raised at Ur of the Chaldees, a city-state that had long before his day formulated and codified a system of civil and criminal laws. Out in the quiet hills of Haran, Abraham had come to know a higher law than the law of man—the law of Jehovah. The law of the Lord God of Israel was the law of the Patriarchs. Even when Israel was submerged in slavery under the laws of Egypt, the law of Jehovah was still the cardinal guide of the Chosen People. Sinai saw this law resanctified and interpreted into the great code of moral law which forms the foundation for the law codes of all civilized peoples.

Since several codes of laws more ancient than the Laws of Moses have been discovered, some scholars have suggested that perhaps Moses may have founded his code to some extent on these earlier codes. There are, however, no logical grounds for such an assumption. The codes most frequently used for comparison are the Code of Hammurabi, king of the Westland, and the Hittite Codes found on tablets excavated at Boghaz Keui, ancient capital of the Hittites.

The Code of Hammurabi is one of the great Law Codes of the world's history. In 1901 the French excavator, De Morgan, while working at Susa, discovered a great stela (or obelisk) of black diorite on which this famous code is inscribed. On this block of stone, which stands about eight feet high, and is now in the Louvre, Hammurabi, the well-known king of the First Dynasty of Babylon (19th Century B. C.), had caused to be inscribed the basic laws of his country. These laws were not originated by Hammurabi. They are simply improvements on earlier laws, which mostly stem back to the Sumerians. Sumeria was the cradle of law. Sumeria furnished the earliest international compacts, such as the treaty between Elam and a Sumerian king. It also furnished the earliest attempts to settle international disputes by arbitration instead of war. Mesilim, an early king of Kish, acted as mediator in a boundary dispute between the kings of Umma and Lagash. On the stela, Hammurabi is shown in an attitude of adoration before Shamash, the Sun-god of Law and Justice. The great engraved stone was originally erected in the temple of Marduk at Babylon, and stood there until some Elamite conqueror carried it off as a trophy to Susa.

Naturally, there are some striking parallels between some of the laws of the Hammurabi Code and some of the laws and ordinances of Moses. Since right is right and wrong is wrong any fairly complete codes of civil and criminal laws must bear some resemblance to one another, regardless of the dates of the institution of the codes. As peoples progress toward civilization, their national codes of law come nearer to being parallel. The principles underlying codes of law are the same, although details may vary with their local application.

It would be interesting to compare the Laws of Moses with the Code of Hammurabi. Similarly, it would be interesting to compare both with the Hittite Code. A detailed comparison of parallel parts of these codes is too technical for these pages.

The code of Hammurabi is a code of the laws of a highly organized commercial people. It reflects hundreds of years of business practices which through custom became law. It contains laws covering banking and brokerage, leasing and sale of real estate, slavery and bond service, bankruptcy, traveling salesmen, minimum wages, price regulation and taxation. The problems that perplex the businessman of today were not unknown to the Babylonian businessman of four thousand years ago.

The Hittite Codes antedate the Mosaic Codes by less than two hundred years. They contain many amendments to earlier laws. The Hittite laws reflect the customs of an agricultural people only a few centuries removed from semi-barbarism. The Hittite laws are feudal in character, since the state owned all the land. While the laws indicate a very definite advance toward civilization, they reflect a shockingly low conception of moral living.

The laws and ordinances of Moses owe nothing to previously existing codes of law. The existing codes were purely civil codes, while the laws of Moses were both ethical and spiritual. With penetrating judgment Moses legislated not only for the Israel of his own day, but for the Israel of the future. With rare insight, he perceived the social problems that would await his people when they had "come into the land of your habitations" (*Numbers* 15:2), "even the land of Canaan with the coasts thereof" (*Numbers* 34:2).

Making laws for a simple people, the majority of whom had been born during the years of wilderness wandering, and the remainder cradled in serfdom, Moses provided for conditions they would encounter as they settled in the cities and the agricultural districts of Canaan. The nomadic life was largely over. Israel was approaching maturity. Provisions were made for community life and co-operative action such as nomadic Israel had never known. The laws, founded on the direct commands and promises of Jehovah, were such that Israel could understand and obey. Moses was but the humble instrument for the transmission and codifying of the laws. Nearly half the chapters of the Book of *Numbers* open with the words: "And the Lord spake unto Moses."

Some of the fundamental truths underlying the Ten Commandments must have been perceived by spiritually-minded individuals in other ages, in other lands and climes. Truth is eternal. The laws of God are eternal, unmeasured by time or circumstance. To Moses, however, belongs the undying distinction of being the messenger who brought them direct from God to a waiting world.

Nine of the Ten Commandments are so fundamental that they have become the basis of the laws of all civilized peoples. Only one, that beginning "Remember the Sabbath day to keep it holy," has attracted attention of the critical commentator. Efforts have been made to link this commandment with the date of the Feast of Marduk and Ishtar, the great god and goddess of ancient Babylon, which fell, according to tablets translated by Rawlinson,* on the seventh day of the month. Since only the governmental classes of the Babylonians celebrated this day as a holiday, comparisons would seem to be extremely far fetched. There is no logical reason for assuming any connection.

Since the fifteenth day of the Babylonian lunar month was called *Shebatum*, some commentators have suggested that this had some connection with "the Sabbath day." While the word *Shebatum* is etymologically the same as the Hebrew word "Sabbath," there is certainly no connection between the name of the Babylonian monthly date and the weekly day of rest and consecration of the Hebrews.

On the Laws of Moses was built the great prophetic idealism which later distinguished God's Chosen People.

When the Israelites became the custodians of the "two tables of testimony," writ with the very finger of God, divine command impelled them to enthrone them fittingly in a sanctuary. This is specified as being "an ark of shittim wood; two cubits and a half shall be the length thereof,

---

*See Rawlinson: *Cuneiform Inscriptions of Western Asia.*

and a cubit and a half the breadth thereof, and a cubit and a half the height thereof" (*Exodus* 25:10). In our measurements, this would be approximately four and a half feet long, two feet three inches wide, and two feet three inches high. Since it had to be portable, it was not impressive as to size, but the Biblical descriptions of its embellishment indicate that the "ark of the testimony" was a craftsman's masterpiece of rare art and beauty.

To house the ark a tented tabernacle was constructed. The specifications for the construction of the tabernacle and the fabrication of its hangings and furnishings are amazing in their details. Aside from its deep religious significance, the tabernacle with its consecrated contents must have been an awe-inspiring product of super-craftsmanship. Many learned commentators on the Scriptures maintain that the elaborately detailed descriptions of the ark of the covenant and the tabernacle that enclosed it are due to historic idealization. Where, they ask, could Israel obtain the extraordinary amounts of precious metals indicated? How could skilled weavers of fine fabrics and artistic artisans in wood and metal be found among tribes of wilderness wanderers? These are pertinent questions.

The recent discoveries at various sites in the Mesopotamian Valley, particularly at Ur of the Chaldees, of vast quantities of precious metals possessed by peoples living in regions that had no native metals, indicate that Israel might well have possessed a considerable quantity of gold and silver.

Gold is nearly indestructible. Acquisitiveness is a characteristic of the Hebrews. When they left Egypt, they had recompensed themselves for their forced labor in jewels of gold and gems (*Exodus* 12:35, 36). Necessity urged the Israelites to carry their wealth on their persons. Well might a people in a mood of soul-stirring emotion and spiritual exaltation, bring "the Lord's offering to the work of the tabernacle of the congregation, and for all his service, and for the holy garments"—*Exodus* 35:21. "And they came, both men and women, as many as were willing-hearted, and brought bracelets, and earrings, and rings, and tablets, all jewels of gold: and every man that offered, offered an offering of gold unto the Lord"—*Exodus* 35:22.

The fine linens of ancient Egypt are, even today, wonderful examples of the weaver's art. The Israelites had left that country comparatively recently. They did not leave their knowledge of industrial skills behind them. The same would be true of craftsmen in other lines. That they had the wherewithal, as well as the ability, to build the ark and the tabernacle is not impossible, or even improbable.

While the tabernacle was constructed for religious purposes, it became the center of the social and political life of Israel. On the tabernacle and its consecrated contents was polarized all the idealism of Israel. Where moved the tabernacle, there moved the government of Israel. Around it an infant nation grew to maturity. For seven centuries the religious thought of Israel centered around the Ark of the Covenant and the codes of law which carried divine sanction. Before the Ark the waters of Jordan were cut off when Israel entered the Promised Land (See *Joshua* 4:7). Its presence comforted and sustained them during the long struggle for the cities and valleys of Canaan. The first city built by the Israelites after entering Canaan was built to protect the tabernacle that housed the ark. This was at Shiloh.* The most famous of all temples, the mighty sanctuary reared by king Solomon on the holy heights of Mt. Moriah was built to house the Ark of the Covenant.

"Moses was very great in the land of Egypt" (*Exodus* 11:3). Moses was very great in the wilderness, as he led his people toward the gateway of the Promised Land. Who knows but what his mightiest moments were those when he stood alone with his God on the summit of Nebo? As he looked out on the land which had been promised to the seed of Abraham for an inheritance, he could look back over a life of remarkable achievement. Ever urged by the impelling promises of Jehovah, he had brought his people out of slavery, welded the disjointed tribes into a strong confederation, and imparted to them a course of religious instruction which would remain unparalleled until the coming of the Messiah. Somewhere on the silent slopes "over against Beth-peor," Israel's most distinguished son sleeps in a grave unmarked, but the Mighty Man of Israel will remain monumented in the memory of mankind as long as time shall last.

----

*See Chapter VI, page 99f.

VI

THE CONQUEST OF CANAAN

*Be strong and of a good courage: for unto this people shalt thou
divide for an inheritance the land, which I sware unto their fathers
to give them.*—Joshua 1:6

THE Israelites had arrived at the gateway of the Promised Land.
They had reached the long-sought end of the tortuous trail they
had been following for forty years. Jordan lay in front. Beyond
it lay the country that was to become the homeland of Israel. Destiny
beckoned. The Ark of the Covenant was brought up. At a respectful
distance behind it, some "two thousand cubits by measure" (*Joshua* 3:4),
the fighting men of Israel rallied around their tribal standards. Time and
place considered, they were a formidable fighting force. On "dress
parade" the arms of Israel awaited the command of Joshua to advance.
The watchword was: "Be strong and of a good courage." The day of
Israel was at hand.

This was an auspicious occasion. Israel was about to pass one of the
great milestones of her history. Israel was moving from adolescence
toward maturity. Although Israel had been fostering and developing for
centuries Abraham's inspired conceptions of the One True God and had
kept alive the sacred flame that was later to illuminate the world, the
secular history of Israel was far from glorious. The wide-horizoned freedom of the Patriarchal Period had been submerged in semi-slavery in
Egypt. Since the emergence from Egypt, Israel had been the recipient of
outstanding revelations of the powers of Jehovah and His care for His
Chosen People; but Israel had yet to prove herself worthy of a place in
the family of nations. Beyond the Jordan lay the testing ground.

Israel was about to thrust herself into the arena where for centuries
the rising civilizations of the East had striven for supremacy. She was
preparing to seize the strategic center of the ancient world. Canaan, the
corridor to three continents, was traversed by the great intercontinental
highways over which passed a large portion of the world's commerce
between east and west. This was no virgin country awaiting the settler.
It was already occupied by peoples highly proficient in the arts of war.
The Canaanites were a highly organized people. Many Egyptian and
Babylonian records attest the considerable degree of civilization the inhabitants of Canaan had attained. The military engineering skill of the

Hittites had been utilized in constructing the defenses of strategically located cities. The conquest of Canaan would be no triumphal parade.

Hebrew writers and scholars loved to look back upon the crossing of the Jordan. To them the event was more important than the crossing of the waters of the Red Sea. This is easy to understand. Egypt was associated with remembrances of slavery, Palestine with the achievement of true nationality. One marked the beginning, the other the end, of the weary wilderness wanderings.

The writer of the Book of *Joshua* dwells on the crossing of the Jordan in great detail. Some modern scholars ascribe the fact that "the waters which came down from above stood and rose up upon an heap very far from the city Adam" (*Joshua* 3:16), to some phenomenon of nature. The explanations most commonly offered are an earthquake, or a landslide, far up the Jordan, such as is described by an Arabian historian, who records that in the twelfth century A. D. the engineers sent to repair a bridge over the Jordan, so that a retreating army could cross, found the bed of the Jordan dry, owing to such a landslide. However, all Jews, and most Christians, ascribe the crossing of the Jordan, as described in *Joshua*, to direct intervention of Providence. Without the intervention of Jehovah, there might have occurred such a bloody shambles at the Jordan as took place at Tussam in Egypt, when the Turks gallantly attempted to cut the Suez Canal during the progress of the late World War. Had the Turks succeeded in cutting the canal, the Allied victory would have been long delayed. Had Israel been held up at the Jordan until the Canaanite tribes had had time to rally on the west bank, the conquest of Canaan might have been definitely delayed.

Fortunately for the Israelites they arrived in the east Jordan country at an opportune time. While some of the cities of northern Palestine were still in the hands of the Egyptians, Egypt itself was governed by a weak line of Pharaohs, the feeble Ramesids. The Assyrians were keeping to their own country. The Philistines, who occupied the coastal grain-growing districts, were not yet strong enough to attempt to seize control of the country. The Canaanites, weakened by their long struggles with Egypt and shattered by devastating wars that foreign nations had waged on their soil, were seriously handicapped in presenting military resistance to the invaders. Time and the tides of political fortune favored Israel.

Palestine had long been in a state of political turmoil. With the breaking up of the Hittite empire, and the gradual withdrawal of Egypt from the Palestinian provinces, Canaan had become a common fighting ground. From the days of Amenophis IV of Egypt (B. C. 1375-1358) until the establishment of the Hebrew kingdom under David, there was apparently no stable government in Palestine. Various tribal peoples were carrying on almost constant warfare over the ruins of ancient empires. Among the Tell el-Amarna letters are several sent to Amenophis IV by his viceroy at Jerusalem, one Ebed-Hepa. In these letters Ebed-Hepa complains that invaders, whom he describes as the "Habiri," are overrunning the land, and frantically petitions the Pharaoh to send him mercenary soldiers to protect the cities and towns from the advancing enemy.

The letters of Rib-Adda to Amenophis IV reflect similar conditions in Phoenicia. Rib-Adda wrote that the "sons of Ebed-Ashera" were taking possession of all "the land of the Amurru," or, "land of the Amorites." He, too, petitions for military aid.

The chaotic conditions indicated in the Tell el-Amarna letters, and in other later letters from western Asia, are reflected strongly in *Joshua*. Although the exact date of Israel's arrival at the gateway of the Promised Land cannot as yet be determined from external evidence, there can be no doubt that the *Joshua* narratives are framed into the correct historical setting.

> *From the wilderness and this Lebanon even unto the great river, the river Euphrates, all the land of the Hittites, and unto the great sea toward the going down of the sun, shall be your coast.*— Joshua 1:4

Palestine, or even "all the land of the Hittites," is but a tiny territory resting on the western rim of the great continent of Asia, yet on this tiny stage was played the most appealing historical drama of the ages. Egypt and the Wilderness furnished the pre-curtain preface and prologue for the spectacular pageant of Israel in Palestine. The pages of the Old Testament picture the continuous unrolling of the profound panorama of man's spiritual progress along the trail of time, until the action reaches its dramatic climax with the coming of Jesus of Nazareth, the Redeemer of Mankind. Palestine furnished the setting; Israel, and the peoples of the ancient East, the characters; the impelling promises of Jehovah, the motivation, for the sublime scenario that swung through the most pregnant centuries of history.

The Promised Land was the ideal setting for the great drama. Nowhere else on earth can so many varieties of scenery and climate be found in so small a compass. The proverbial "from Dan to Beersheba" is but little more than one hundred and fifty miles. From the shores of the Mediterranean to the Jordan, the country has an average breadth of a trifle over forty miles. In this limited land of broken hill and valley, the climate ranges from north temperate to torrid. Mt. Hermon, where the Jordan finds its source, is snow-capped eight months of the year, while the Dead Sea, into which the Jordan empties, burns under almost unbearable heat.

Ages ago, some cataclysmic convulsion of nature broke the earth's crust with such violence that it piled up the parallel mountain ridges that lie between the Jordan and the Mediterranean Sea, and left the deep depression which forms the valley of the Jordan and the bed of the Dead Sea. Rising from springs on the slopes of Mt. Hermon, the Jordan finds its way to shallow, reed-grown Lake Huleh. Leaving Lake Huleh, it dashes swiftly down a distance of some ten miles to the calm waters of the Sea of Galilee. Leaving Galilee, it twists and turns through such a tortuous course that it travels two hundred miles in making a direct line distance of sixty-five miles. Finally, it loses itself in the Dead Sea, the "Sea of Salt." For countless centuries the river has been bringing down mineral salts leached from the soil and depositing them in the Dead Sea. Today the solution of salts is so strong in the sea that the non-swimmer can sit at ease on the water's surface, half submerged in a briny bath. Here is one of the great treasure houses of the world. The value of the chemical and mineral wealth in the Dead Sea exceeds the wealth of any gold or diamond mine in the world. Plans are under way to recover these vast treasures of chemical wealth. Soon they will be used to cure the ills of mankind.

Parts of Palestine are sterile and barren. This has always been so, but when Israel entered the country the productive areas were much larger and much richer than they are today. Medieval poets and scholars speak of the great fertility of the soil and the fine quality of the country's products. Esthori Ben Mosche Hap-parchi describes it as "a blessed and beautiful land, bearing fruit like the garden of God." This description, and many another, matches well with the description of the Promised Land given in *Deuteronomy* 8:7-9.

Since it was the mission of Israel to give to the world the enlightened monotheism which had been revealed to Abraham and driven home to the hearts of the Chosen People by the teachings of Moses during the dark days in the wilderness, Palestine offered the ideal environment for the carrying out of the mandates of Jehovah. Here the wandering people could settle down in a land of cities and towns, of fertile valleys and green countrysides rich with olive groves and vineyards. The seed of Abraham could take root in the center of the then-known world. Israel would be in touch with world affairs. The highways that carried the commerce between the two great centers of rising civilization passed through Palestine. Lesser highways radiated in every direction. Israel might develop the Promised Land: the Promised Land would certainly develop Israel. The highways that carried commerce would carry Israel's God-given message to the world.

When Israel entered Palestine the country was capable of sustaining a much larger population than it can properly support today. Years of Arab neglect; primitive, fertility-destroying methods of farming; over-crowding with close-cropping flocks around the watering places in time of drouth—all have helped to diminish the population carrying powers of this once glorious land.

Under the rule of Great Britain, which now governs the country under a mandate, Palestine is recovering some of her former productivity. The Zionist movement has brought thousands of enterprising Jews into Palestine. Intensively cultivated wheat fields are rapidly stretching out over the plains of Esdraelon, where Israel under David fought the Philistines. Orange groves dot the plain of Sharon. Near Joppa rises the modern Jewish commercial city of Tel-aviv. The sacred waters of the Jordan turn the dynamos of a modern electric power plant, sending illumination to ancient cities once lighted with the torches and clay lamps of the Canaanites. The shores of the Sea of Galilee are becoming a health resort. Jerusalem, for the first time in centuries, has an adequate water supply. Ribbons of concrete are replacing time-worn trails. From wells in distant Mesopotamia petroleum pulses through a pipeline to tank vessels at Haifa, which has been converted into a modern seaport. Science is altering "all the land of the Hittites." Is an ancient prophecy finding fulfillment? "And I will bring again the captivity of my people of Israel, and they shall build the waste cities, and inhabit them; and they shall plant vineyards, and drink the wine thereof; they shall also make gardens, and eat the fruit of them"—*Amos* 9:14.

This recrudescence of Palestine is not without attendant troubles. There is a dark side to the picture. The present population of Palestine, seven hundred thousand Arabs and four hundred thousand Jews, cannot be indefinitely increased without provoking serious trouble. The influx of Jewish immigrants is creating consternation among the Arabs. Behind the Arabs may lie the power of Islam. Jerusalem, the sacred city of Jew and Christian, is also a sacred city of the Moslem. Into a world still dazed with horror from the World War comes the spectre of a Holy War in the East. Here smolders a spark that may set the world aflame.

More than thirty centuries ago, a horde of hardy Hebrews poured into Palestine under the leadership of Joshua. They came to build an empire over the dust of empires. With them they brought a power stronger than a multitude of marching armies. The nation they created went the way of all things created with human hands; their God-given idealism will endure forever.

Now Jericho was straitly shut up because of the children of Israel: none went out, and none came in.—Joshua 6:1

Jordan passed, Jericho loomed in front. Jericho was a small city. It covered less than ten acres. Unlike most Palestinian cities, it was not a "city that is set upon an hill" (*Matthew* 5:14). The "Mound of Jericho" owes its height to the building up of the city inside the walls. Just outside the eastern wall was a spring, later called "Elisha's Fountain" (See 2 *Kings* 2:19-22).

Joshua, a prudent military commander, realized that once the hosts of Israel had passed the Jordan, the city of Jericho must be captured or destroyed. Any military force, particularly if hampered by a large number of tent-sheltered non-combatants, must be able to operate over a wide base. Joshua faced problems that still stand unique in the annals of military maneuvers. Joshua was not merely clearing the way for a civilian population, he was carrying that population with him. The position of the invaders was precarious with a river in the rear and the walled city of Jericho on its flank. Jericho must be promptly and effectively reduced.

That Joshua appreciated the difficulties of his problem is evidenced by the account of careful espionage recorded in the second chapter of *Joshua.* Two men, probably able but inconspicuous individuals, were sent out "to spy secretly." Theirs was a dark and dangerous mission. Avoiding the open, they "came into an harlot's house, named Rahab, and lodged there." Their choice of headquarters was a fortunate one. An honest landlady would have turned them over to the king's guard forthwith, instead of hiding them under the flax she was curing on her houseroof. It was fortunate that Rahab's house was so located that she was able to "let them down by a cord through the window: for her house was upon the town wall." This would indicate a very heavy wall, or, more likely, that debris had accumulated during previous centuries inside the wall to such an extent that the ground inside the wall was flush with the top of the wall, a condition fairly common in ancient Biblical cities. Evidently the outer wall of Rahab's house rested on the city wall and was faced flush with the same.

Since the excavators of ancient Jericho, Dr. Sellin, with a German expedition* in 1907-1909, and Dr. Garstang with an English expedition in 1930-1931, found three city walls, the question naturally arises, which was the wall of *Joshua* 2:15? This, of course, is the same wall mentioned in *Joshua* 6:5, "and the wall of the city shall fall down flat."

---

*Deutsche Orient-Gesellschaft.

The ruins of Jericho, as viewed today, show three sets of defensive walls, each dating from different periods. The inner wall, some thirteen feet in thickness and built entirely of brick, seems to have outlived its usefulness long before Joshua saw Jericho. Outside of this wall, later inhabitants had constructed a defensive fortification system composed of two brick walls, spaced about twenty-five feet apart. Similar defensive military engineering work is indicated at a later period in Jerusalem in the passage of Scripture which says: "Ye made also a ditch between the two walls"—*Isaiah* 22:11. In 2 *Kings* 25:4 we find the statement: "All the men of war fled by night by way of the gate between two walls." The double walls of brick had also outlived their usefulness before Joshua's day. Outside of the old double wall, Hittite military engineers had constructed a more effective barrier. This was a heavy stone wall, about ten feet thick, surmounted by a brick parapet wall six and a half feet thick. This wall was comparatively new when the armies of Israel faced Jericho. It was sufficiently strong to carry the outer walls of dwellings on its top. Against this stronghold Joshua could bring only such offensive military equipment as was easily transported by foot soldiers. Engines of war, such as are mentioned in 2 *Chronicles* 26:15, had not as yet been invented. To take Jericho, Joshua was faced with a formidable military problem.

Despite the popular conception of the incidents that occurred in connection with the fall of Jericho, the careful reader will note that the writer of *Joshua* makes no statement that all the walls of Jericho fell. He always speaks of "the wall of the city." He also states that "the wall fell down flat." In the original Hebrew the words used for this expression literally mean "the wall fell under itself." This would indicate that it was the stone wall (*khomah*) that was destroyed. In simple words, "*qir khomah*" (the wall on the wall) fell flat. Much has been made by some commentators of the fact that part of the walls of Jericho still stand. Investigations at site, however, prove that an extensive portion of the wall did "fall flat," and was extensively repaired at a much later date, probably by Hiel (See 1 *Kings* 16:34).

After Jericho had been destroyed, Joshua uttered a terrifying malediction against the future rebuilder of the city: "Cursed be the man before the Lord, that riseth up and buildeth this city Jericho: he shall lay the foundation thereof in his firstborn, and in his youngest son shall he set up the gates of it." Here we find reference to a custom prevalent among many ancient peoples, that of infant sacrifice. The custom of sacrificing young children in connection with the building or the dedication of a city, or even a temple or other important building, was common among the Canaanites, the ancient Egyptians, and the ancient Babylonians. It was not practiced by the Chosen People. With prophetic vision, Joshua intimates that the rebuilder of the city will either be a Canaanite, or some apostate Israelite who has reverted to heathen customs (See 1 *Kings* 16).

> *O Lord, what shall I say, when Israel turneth their backs before their enemies!*—Joshua 7:8

Israel received a sharp set-back at Ai. Evidently the expeditionary force sent against the little city, "about three thousand men," succeeded in penetrating the town since the unlawfully acquisitive Achan was able to appropriate for himself considerable loot. This light-fingered lad gathered in a "goodly Babylonish garment, and two hundred shekels of silver, and a wedge of gold of fifty shekels weight" (*Joshua* 7:21), which he later hid under his tent. Probably looting interfered with warfare, since "the men of Ai smote of them about thirty and six men: for they chased them from before the gate even unto Shebarim, and smote them in the going down" (*Joshua* 7:5).

This reverse brought dismay to Joshua. If Israel could be turned back by a tiny town like Ai, what could they hope to do against the great Canaanite strongholds farther north? The triumph at Jericho was dimmed by defeat at Ai. A discouraged commander "fell to the earth upon his face before the ark of the Lord." Here Joshua found faith, the antidote for despair. With faith renewed, Joshua started an intensive hunt for the culprit who had brought disgrace to the arms of Israel. This was not a mere case of larceny. It was a case for court martial, a military offense that had brought about defeat. The gravity of the offense is indicated by the stern sentence meted out to the ill-fated Achan when his guilt is discovered. This sentence illustrates the extremely severe punishments inflicted on transgressors at that period (See *Joshua* 7:24-25). The custom of punishing entire families for the sins of individual members seems to have persisted until the days when Amaziah reigned in Jerusalem (See 2 *Chronicles* 25:4).

Joshua, himself, led the next expedition against Ai. This time he resorts to stratagem. After carefully concealing a strong force in ambush on the west side of the city, he lured the inhabitants to battle on the plain east of the city. When the troops on the west entered and fired the little city, the defeated inhabitants of Ai had no avenue of retreat, no refuge from annihilation. Victory was complete. Here was a record that the scribes could exultantly enter in the "book of Jasher" (See *Joshua* 10:13).

The site of Ai (Et-Tell) was partially investigated by Dr. Garstang in 1928. He located the old city walls. The city was destroyed by fire about the fourteenth century B. C.*

---

*Garstang: *Foundations of Bible History.*

So Joshua smote all the country of the hills, and of the south, and of the vale, and of the springs, and all their kings: he left none remaining, but utterly destroyed all that breathed, as the Lord God of Israel commanded.—Joshua 10:40

Israel entered Canaan in an iron time. Defeat in battle usually meant death. Mercy to the fallen foe was practically unknown. The cardinal rule of warfare was: Slay or be slain. There has never been such a thing as "civilized warfare." Joshua was soon drawn into a major military campaign against five allied kings through the guile of the Gibeonites. The desert-reared Joshua was taught a sharp lesson in the devious diplomacy of the East by the crafty citizens of Gibeon. The inhabitants of cities in the path of the advancing horde of Israelites were naturally alarmed. These wild men from the wilderness had just obliterated Jericho and Ai. What city would be next? The jackal cannot fight the lion, so the craven Gibeonites, through a rather shabby ruse, inveigled the unsuspecting Joshua into a treaty of alliance. This sharp practice of the Gibeonites saved their city, but Joshua reduced them to "hewers of wood and drawers of water for the congregation" (*Joshua* 9:27). Nevertheless, Joshua found himself called upon to defend the Gibeonites and their city, "a great city, as one of the royal cities" (*Joshua* 10:2) from the wrath of the five kings who had been angered by the servile submission of the Gibeonites.

The miraculous defeat of the five kings at Bethhoron (*Joshua* 10:1-27) gave Joshua control of southern Palestine, but the military strength of Palestine lay in the fortified cities of the north, which were to defy the Israelites for centuries. In fact, Gezer, the last city in Palestine to pass into Hebrew control, was never captured by the Israelites. This city resisted Israel until the days of Solomon, when it was captured by the Pharaoh of Egypt and given as a present to his daughter, Solomon's wife (See 1 *Kings* 9:16).

And the Lord said unto Joshua, Be not afraid because of them: for tomorrow about this time will I deliver them up all slain before Israel: thou shalt hough their horses, and burn their chariots with fire.—Joshua 11:6

In the battle fought at "the waters of Merom" (*Joshua* 11:5) between Israel and a coalition of kings under Jabin, Israel seems to have come in contact with the use of horses in warfare. In the hill country of the south horses would be of little use in battle, but as they reached the plains farther north, where cavalry and chariots could operate freely, the Israelites must have found themselves at a great disadvantage. We catch an echo of this in the plaint of the Children of Joseph, "all the

Canaanites that dwell in the land of the valley have chariots of iron"
(*Joshua* 17:16).

Joshua 11:6 mentions the unique method the Israelites used to disable
the horses of their adversaries: "thou shalt hough their horses."
This was a method of disabling animals used by primitive hunters, who
could capture or bring down an animal by severing the tarsal, or heel,
tendon by a skillfully thrown spear. The Hebrews must have become
exceedingly skillful in the use of the javelin and the arrow at close range.

We find another mention of houghing of horses in 2 *Samuel* 8:4.
After David had defeated Hadadezer "David houghed all the chariot
horses, but reserved of them for an hundred chariots." This would indicate that even as late as the time of David the Israelites had little use
for horses. In the latter years of Solomon's reign, however, horses were
of such value that Solomon imported them from Egypt (See 1 *Kings*
10:28).

*And all the cities of those kings, and all the kings of them, did
Joshua take.*—Joshua 11:12

The number of Canaanite kings mentioned in the Book of *Joshua*,
particularly the long list given in the 11th chapter, might easily lead us
to assume that Canaan was cut up into a number of small independent
kingdoms, free to form alliances and to make war at will. Such was not
the case.

When the Amorites took the country from the original primitive settlers, they built a series of fortified cities from which they governed the
country. The smaller cities, with the district around each of them, were
placed under the control of governors, whose duty it was to administer
the laws and collect the revenue which they forwarded to the central
government.

Under the Hittite-Amorite (or Canaanite) administration, the country became more completely organized politically. That the Hittites had
a highly centralized form of government is shown by the results of Winckler's excavations at Boghaz-Keui, the ancient capital city of the Hittites.*
The "kings" of the Book of *Joshua* were really governors representing
the state, rather than independent sovereigns.

During the long period that Egypt controlled Canaan the same system
was used. This is clearly evidenced by the Tell el-Amarna letters.

The Philistines, who controlled large areas of the grain-growing dis-
tricts of the country in the time of Joshua, also used the same system.
Abimelech, the Philistine district governor at Gerar, who centuries before
Joshua's day had extensive tribal troubles with Abraham (See *Genesis*

*See Winckler: *Boghaskoi die Bauwerke.*

CANAANITE TEMPLE

The ruins of four purely Canaanite Temples were unearthed at Beisan, the Biblical Beth-shan.

By permission of The Museum of the University of Pennsylvania

21), and later had similar difficulties with Isaac (See *Genesis* 26), is referred to as "king of Gerar," and as "king of the Philistines."

Later, when Solomon "was king over all Israel," he employed a modification of this system for the civil administration of his kingdom. His administrative organization with its twelve district officers is outlined in 1 *Kings* 4.

The "kings" whom Joshua defeated were really governors of "city-kingdoms." From many a high place in Canaan, Joshua could have covered with a glance several of the city-kingdoms he conquered.

As for the Jebusites the inhabitants of Jerusalem, the children of Judah could not drive them out.—Joshua 15:63

And they drave not out the Canaanites that dwelt in Gezer.—Joshua 16:10

Although the keen military strategy and brilliant leadership of Joshua enabled Israel to gain a firm foothold in southern Canaan, there were apparently two cities in the south, Jerusalem and Gezer, that the Israelites were unable to capture during Joshua's day. The campaign south of these cities, that is described in *Joshua* 10:31-43, evidently was highly successful, since the stronghold of Lachish fell into the hands of the Israelites after a siege that lasted less than two days. The excavation at Lachish (Tell-el-Hesy) by Sir Flinders Petrie, and later by Dr. Bliss, seems to confirm this account, since the ruins of the city were occupied between B. C. 1400 and 1000 by a nomadic people who built no fortifications.

The little Jebusite city of Jerusalem was admirably situated for defense. It could only be attacked from the north. The free-cutting limestone of the district would provide walls amply strong to defy an army so poorly equipped with siege appliances as the early Israelites must have been. Even at a later period, when "the children of Judah had fought against Jerusalem, and had taken it, and smitten it with the edge of the sword, and set the city on fire" (*Judges* 1:8), they could not hold it. About B. C. 1050, David captured the city and made it his capital.

. . . Beth-shean and her towns, and Ibleam and her towns . . . Dor and her towns . . . Taanach and her towns . . . Megiddo and her towns, even three countries. Yet the children of Manasseh could not drive out the inhabitants of those cities, but the Canaanites would dwell in that land.—Joshua 17:11, 12

While Jerusalem and Gezer in the south defied the military efforts of Israel, the five cities mentioned in *Joshua* 17:11 offered a still more difficult problem. These cities lay on the great land bridge over which from time immemorial the currents of commerce had passed between the

8

two most ancient civilizations in the world. Over this same land bridge succeeding waves of conquest have swept throughout the centuries. Almost every acre of the terrain has been fertilized by the blood of the brave. Amorites, Hittites, Egyptians, Hebrews, Assyrians, Babylonians, Persians, Greeks, Romans, Arabs, Crusaders, and the contending forces in the late World War have fought over this tragic territory, which St. John the Divine visioned as the final fighting field of Armageddon.

Dor was located on the coast, while Beth-shean, located four miles west of the Jordan, guarded the gateway to the lands beyond the Jordan. Between these cities stretched the fertile plain of Esdraelon, guarded by the other cities mentioned.

When Joshua led his people into Canaan, these cities, while Canaanite in population and customs, were ruled by the Egyptians. They had been captured by the Egyptians under Thutmose III about B. C. 1479, and remained under Egyptian control until the reign of Amenophis IV. Recaptured by Seti I, they remained in Egyptian possession until the reign of Rameses III (B. C. 1198-1167). Both Megiddo and Beth-shean are being excavated and scientifically investigated at the present time. At Beisan (the ancient Beth-shean) the Palestinian Expedition of the University Museum has uncovered, in material evidence, the complete history of the city during the Egyptian Period.* Step by step, level by level, the history of this period has been followed and definitely dated.

Shortly after the death of Rameses III, mercenary troops from the northern shores of the Mediterranean, whom the Egyptians had employed to garrison these cities, seem to have taken the cities for themselves. Later, about B. C. 1080, they joined forces with the Philistines against whom they had formerly fought. It was against the Philistines that Saul campaigned for control of northern Palestine (See 1 *Samuel* 31; 1 *Chronicles* 10).

And these are the countries which the children of Israel inherited in the land of Canaan, which Eleazar the priest, and Joshua, the son of Nun, and the heads of the fathers of the tribes of the children of Israel, distributed for inheritance to them.—Joshua 14:1 . . . and there remaineth yet very much land to be possessed.— Joshua 13:1

It is clear, both from the Joshua narratives and archæological investigation, that the Promised Land that Israel occupied during the day of Joshua was divided into three parts, namely: The portion south of the Jerusalem-Gezer section; the portion between these cities and the northern fortified cities; and the portion north of these latter cities. Evidently Israel held the hills and valleys close to the uncaptured cities, since Joshua

---

*See Chapter XIX, page 273ff.

did not hesitate to apportion the entire country among the tribes. *Joshua* 13:2-6 lists the portions of the country yet to be possessed by Israel, but closes with the promise that the inhabitants will be driven out "from before the children of Israel."

If among the successors of Joshua there had been such another warrior as he, the final campaigns for the conquest of Canaan might not have been delayed until the days of David.

And the land had rest from war.—Joshua 14:15

The Hebrew conquest of Canaan was a long and painful process. It was accomplished partly by force of arms, and partly by infiltration and peaceful penetration. This is reflected in the Books of *Joshua, Judges,* and *Samuel.* The writers of the Old Testament looked upon Joshua as their greatest military leader, the God-chosen champion of a God-chosen people. Naturally, their writings stress the military might of the great leader. Joshua had many non-military problems with which to wrestle. A restless, nomadic race was settling down in the agricultural regions, and organizing community life in urban centers in the midst of a culture such as Israel had not seen since leaving Egypt. The simple tribal institutions of nomadic life were being replaced by the complicated and complex political and social organizations essential to the growth and development of municipal and national life. Most of the Hebrews were wilderness born and desert bred. From such crude metal a nation was being forged.

And the whole congregation of the children of Israel assembled together at Shiloh, and set up the tabernacle of the congregation there.—Joshua 18:1

Immediately after entering the Promised Land, Israel established a sacred center at Gilgal (See *Joshua* 5:9). Here the Passover was celebrated with due ceremony, and the site consecrated as holy ground. Gilgal remained a sacred center for many centuries. Long after the days of Joshua, Israel brought Saul to Gilgal to be confirmed as Israel's first king (See 1 *Samuel* 11:15).

After Joshua had subdued and pacified most of Palestine, the need arose for a new sanctuary to house the Ark of the Covenant. Shiloh, high in the hill country of Ephraim, was selected as the site. Here Israel reared its sanctuary and around it built a town for the Ark's protection. Shiloh became a center of religious culture and education. Here Eli lived and taught. The saintly Samuel was one of his pupils. Devout Hebrews pilgrimaged to Shiloh for prayer and sacrifice.

Shiloh was the first city the Hebrews ever built for themselves, the first purely Hebrew town. They knew little about the arts of building. Their initial effort at town planning and building offers a striking contrast to the one purely Jewish city of the present century, the modern commercial metropolis of Tel-aviv.

The site of Shiloh (Tell Seilum) was investigated by Danish expeditions in 1922, in 1926, and again in 1931, under the direction of Hans Kjaer. Excavation revealed a striking corroboration of the Biblical history of Shiloh. Old Israelite (iron age) pottery proves that the little town was built by Hebrews at about the time of Joshua. The houses were built of stones crudely laid up without mortar.

After the Ark of the Covenant was captured by the Philistines (See 1 *Samuel* 4:11) it never returned to Shiloh. The town sank to insignificance. Finally fire reduced it to the scene of desolation pictured by Jeremiah six hundred years later (See *Jeremiah* 7:12, 14; 26:6).

After the beginning of the Christian Era the town was reoccupied. In the remains of an old Christian church, built over the ruins about 500 A. D., was found a mosaic depicting two harts, one on each side of a tree, doubtless symbolical of the passage: "As the hart panteth after the water brooks, so panteth my soul after thee, O God" (*Psalm* 42:1).

And I have given you a land for which ye did not labour.—Joshua 24:13

Israel's accomplishments under Joshua were truly remarkable. A nomadic people had taken possession of a country which the powerful Egyptian empire could not hold. They had vanquished the Amorites and the warlike Hittites in battle. Israel had come to maturity. No people in history had ever risen so rapidly as the Israelites under Joshua. Joshua claimed no credit. Throughout a trying time he had felt that Jehovah was ever at hand to aid. When he had "waxed old and stricken in age," he knew that another must soon take up the burden of completing the conquest and bringing Israel to true nationalism. The hour of parting was approaching. Joshua had one last duty to perform. "Joshua called for all Israel" to assemble in solemn conclave to hear his parting exhortation, and a restatement of the law of the Lord.

Standing in sacred Shechem, a place hallowed as the resting place of Jacob, Joshua reviewed for Israel the historical trail over which the hand of Jehovah had led His Chosen People. Warning them of the dangers inherent to their changed mode of life, visualizing the disasters that will certainly befall if they return to the idol worship their ancestors knew "on the other side of the flood," or turn to "the gods of the Amorites," Joshua reached the sublime peroration: "Behold, this stone shall be a witness unto us; for it hath heard all the words of the Lord which he spake unto us: it shall be therefore a witness unto you, lest ye deny your God"—*Joshua* 24:27.

VII

ISRAEL UNDER THE JUDGES

Nevertheless the Lord raised up judges which delivered them out of the hand of those that spoiled them.—Judges 2:16

JOSHUA, the conqueror of Canaan, was dead. He had left no worthy successor. The Israelites were still far from their ultimate goal, the subjection and pacification of Palestine. They were still strangers in a strange land. The intrepid Joshua had won for them most of the country they had been promised for an inheritance, but Israel's position was far from secure. Some of the cities which kept the keys of empire were still in the hands of their enemies. With the death of Joshua, Israel's glorious march toward nationalism dropped to the dull monotony of marking time. A nomadic, desert-bred people faced the social and political problems incidental to settling down in an agricultural country without distinguished leadership.

The time-tried leaders who had brought them out of Egypt and into the Promised Land were gone. A new day brought new conditions, but brought no great leader worthy of the Hebrew traditions of leadership. Israel's nomadic days were done. Israel had brought flocks and herds, but the far-flung areas of grazing lands that had been open to the patriarchal forefathers of Israel were closed by the advance of civilization. Vineyards, olive groves, date orchards, and grain fields dotted the valleys and hillsides where Abraham and his immediate descendants had moved freely with their flocks. Several centuries had set their mark on Canaan since the days of Abraham. Cities the patriarchs had never known had come into being. New conditions brought new problems and dangers. Joshua, who knew his people, had warned Israel of the difficulties which would daily beset them: "And I have given you a land for which ye did not labour, and cities which ye built not, and ye dwell in them; of the vineyards and olive yards which ye planted not do ye eat. Now, therefore, fear the Lord, and serve him in sincerity and in truth" (*Joshua* 24:13, 14).

Nomads no longer, Israel became a nation of urban dwellers and small farmers. The barter of the desert gave way to trade in the bazaars of the alley-like streets of the cities and towns. Israel must learn new trades and acquire new skills. Utensils which would have been impracticable to carry about during nomadic days now became household necessities.

Pottery was now an essential. The crude pottery of the Hebrew settlers in Palestine, when compared with the fine, hard pottery of the Canaanites of the same age, illustrates one of the many problems the Hebrews were called upon to face.

The Israelites had much to learn from their Canaanite and Philistine neighbors. The Canaanites were city builders, husbandmen, vine-growers, and small farmers, while the Philistines grew grain on a large scale.

Farming meant much hard labor. The early Israelites made little, if any, use of the horse. They had asses, but these were of comparatively little use in agriculture except for carrying. Breaking the soil, sowing the seed, reaping the grain, and winnowing was all hand labor, although, in threshing, cattle were sometimes used to tread out the corn.

Israel entered Canaan during what is commonly called the Third Bronze Age, but it is unlikely that they ever made much use of bronze for agricultural implements. Until the coming of the Iron Age cutting tools were usually made of flint. Wherever flint was available, primitive man made flint knives from time immemorial. Fortunately flint was plentiful in Palestine. The great number of flint sickles found in Palestine indicates the extensive use of this material in agriculture.

Regardless of when, or by whom, it was written, the Book of *Ruth* probably presents a faithful picture of agricultural conditions during the early days of Israel in Canaan. The scene is laid near Bethlehem "in the days when the judges ruled." The writer sketches a realistic picture of the reaping of the barley and of the mid-day meal of the reapers and gleaners. Besides barley, wheat and corn are mentioned. "Corn," as used in the Old Testament, usually means wheat. When Dr. R. A. Stewart Macalister explored the ruins of Gezer he found granaries in which barley, beans, oats, and wheat were still in the bins.

Grinding the grain to meal and flour was a household task for the women. Before the introduction of the hand mill with its upper and lower stones, the grain was usually reduced to powder through rubbing between stones.

Palestine was a fruit country. The many varieties of climate led to the introduction and cultivation of many small fruits. The remains of ancient wine-vats and olive-presses indicate that wine and olive oil were in common use in Palestine even before the coming of the Amorite-Hittites. The fig was also a common fruit.

While it is probable that a considerable portion of the Hebrews still lived in tents, the bulk of the population must have occupied the cities, towns, villages and hamlets, and lived in the houses built by the Canaanites. The Hittites were excellent builders and the country had plenty of free-working stone, so the house-dwelling Hebrews must have lived with a considerable degree of comfort. The detailed story of the slaying of Eglon by Ehud (*Judges* 3:15-25) conveys the idea of a house with a porch and several rooms: "Then Ehud went forth through the porch, and shut the doors of the parlour upon him, and locked them" (v. 23). Not only is there mention of locks, but in verse 25 we read: "Therefore they took a key, and opened them." The scene of this story is laid in Moab, but crude types of wooden locks were in use in Palestine at a very early date.

Ehud used a "dagger which had two edges, of a cubit length." This must have been of bronze. Iron was not yet in use for weapons, although the use of iron was introduced into Palestine during the days of the judges, most probably by the Philistines (See 1 *Samuel* 13:19). The hammer with which Jael killed Sisera (*Judges* 4:21) was probably a stone lashed to a handle with rawhide. An early type of sickle used in Palestine was the jawbone of an animal with flints inserted in the tooth sockets. Probably Samson's famous weapon (See *Judges* 15:15) was the flint-armored jawbone of an ass fastened to a heavy handle. In the days when stature and muscle counted heavily in warfare, this would make a formidable weapon.

Judges presents a picture of Israel in a trying period of transition. A nation was finding itself. Setbacks were many, but the general trend was upward. It was unfortunate for Israel that Joshua died before the conquest of Canaan had been completed. The enemies of Israel still held the strategic keys to the military and commercial control of Palestine.

In the south, the Canaanites still clung to the district dominated by the cities of Jerusalem and Gezer. In the north five fortified cities frowned down on Israel. The Philistines were ready to fight for their fertile fields. Hostile tribes, many of whom had felt the sting of Joshua's military might, awaited the day when Israel could be successfully attacked. The dawning day of Hebrew nationalism was marred by ominous clouds. Threatened by foes from within and without, standing in danger of reversion to tribalism, Israel's political position was precarious. In Israel's darkest days "the Lord raised up judges, which delivered them out of the hand of those that spoiled them."

Of some of the judges we know nothing other than their names. Others, either through military exploits or spiritual leadership, added bright pages to the history of the Hebrew race.

It is unlikely that the jurisdiction of any of the judges extended over all of Canaan. Difficulties of communication, intensified through a portion of the country still being in the hands of enemies, would preclude the extension of the authority of any one judge throughout the land.

Since several of the judges climbed to eminence through their ability as military leaders, it would seem that they were chosen more frequently

for military might than for legal acumen or spiritual insight. Their
duties were not merely judicial, they were the defenders of Israel. Some
few, such as Eli and Samuel, gained power through religious leadership.
Samson, best remembered of the judges, earned prominence by personal
prowess in battle.

With the exception of that of Samuel, the work of the judges seems
to have been largely local, almost tribal in character. Barak, inspired by
Deborah, who herself "judged Israel at that time" (*Judges* 4:4), seems
to have confined his operations to the north. When a portion of the
Israelites were reduced to vassalage by the "king of Mesopotamia,"
Othniel was the man of the day, "and he judged Israel, and went out
to war" (*Judges* 3:10). When "the children of Israel served Eglon the
king of Moab eighteen years" (*Judges* 3:14) the Lord raised them up a
deliverer, Ehud the son of Gera. Jephthah's military operations took
place east of the Jordan, and it is unlikely that his authority extended
west of the river. Gideon's campaigns were aimed at the conquest of
Midian. When emergencies arose, "the Lord raised up judges" to meet
them. These leaders, while frequently extremely effective locally, failed
to reach the mental and spiritual stature necessary to weld a people, still
essentially tribal in outlook, into effective national unity.

*And the children of Israel dwelt among the Canaanites, Hittites,
and Amorites, and Perizzites, and Hivites, and Jebusites.*—Judges
3:5

The scenes of the great adventure stories depicted in *Judges* are laid
in a land that lacked any form of universal national government. Important remnants of once powerful peoples still populated parts of Palestine. The Amorite-Hittites were eager to regain the territories they had
lost. The little pagan city of Jebus (Jerusalem) had long been a thorn
in the side of Israel. The advance of civilization and science had brought
the Perizzites into prominence. Iron, the most useful of metals, was coming into use in Palestine. The Perizzites were iron workers. The Hittite
word for iron is *parzi-ili*. The importance of iron and of workers in iron
is emphasized in 1 *Samuel* 13:19-22, where Israel's lack of iron workers
is lamented. After the death of Joshua, the Israelites apparently lacked
military leadership strong enough to drive out the Amorite-Hittite peoples—"and the children of Israel dwelt among the Canaanites."

The earlier narratives of *Judges* picture a period of sporadic and
desultory warfare between the Israelites and the unconquered remnants
of the Canaanites. Joshua's campaign of conquest degenerated into grim
guerrilla warfare. Israel was surrounded by predatory peoples always
ready to plunder and pillage the territories taken by the unwelcome

Hebrew invaders. The Israelites could not be driven out, but in some sections they were forced to pay tribute to neighboring nations. When a leader arose who could free a portion of the people from oppression he was promptly proclaimed a judge. Othniel conquered the "king of Mesopotamia." Ehud deftly disposed of Eglon, king of Moab, with a dagger (See *Judges* 3:15-35), and roused his people to a successful fight for liberty. Gideon's destruction of the Midianitish marauders established his place in the annals of Israel forever.

Gideon's preeminence among his people was such that they offered him a kingship. This is the earliest movement among the Israelites toward monarchy. The government of Israel had always been a theocracy—a direct government by Jehovah administering through His chosen leaders—but this movement contemplated hereditary monarchy: "Rule thou over us, both thou, and thy son, and thy son's son also" (*Judges* 8:22).

Although Gideon at first demurred at monarchy, the lure of regal honors seems to have overcome his scruples. Establishing his capital at Ophrah, he inaugurated the short-lived dynasty which ended when his successor, Abimelech, perished beside a besieged tower at Thebez, when a woman dropped a "piece of a millstone" on his head (See *Judges* 9). The resourceful woman in the tower probably lifted the loose upper stone from her little handmill, and with it ended the life of a king.

And the children of Israel did evil again in the sight of the Lord; and the Lord delivered them into the hand of the Philistines forty years.—Judges 13:1

The political picture in Palestine altered greatly toward the end of the era of the Judges. The Philistines became the principal opponents of Israel's nationalistic ambitions. Evidently they had acquired a great deal of additional territory since Joshua first led his forces into the Promised Land. In *Joshua* 13 we learn that Joshua left the five lords of the Philistines in possession of five cities only, namely: Gaza, Gath, Ashdod, Ashkelon, and Ekron. In other words, Joshua had left them in possession of only a limited area in the coastal plain of southern Judea. Excavations at Bethshemish,* Gaza,† Ashkelon,‡ and other sites in this area, indicate clearly that the Philistines occupied this territory in the time of Joshua. Five fortified cities in the north, mentioned in *Joshua* 17:11 as defying the military efforts of Israel, Beth-shean, Ibleam, Dor, Taanach, and Megiddo, were Canaanite cities under the administration of Egypt. When Egypt was forced to withdraw from Palestine these cities came into the

*See *Annual of the Palestine Exploration Fund*, Vol. 1 and 2.
†See *Quarterly of the Palestine Exploration Fund*, Jan. 1923.
‡See *Quarterly of the Palestine Exploration Fund*, Oct. 1921.

hands of the Philistines, and Israel's campaigns for the conquest of Palestine were against the Philistines rather than the Canaanites.

After the death of Rameses III in B. C. 1167, Egypt could no longer control the fortified cities that guarded the plains of Esdraelon. Control of these cities meant control of Palestine. Egypt, threatened with invasion from Libyia and from countries on the northern shores of the Mediterranean, was forced to withdraw within her own borders. The military keys to control of Palestine were left in the hands of the mercenary troops who had formerly garrisoned these cities for Egypt. The resulting political chaos offered a splendid opportunity for the Philistines to seize control of the cities that dominated northern Palestine.

That the Philistines were temporarily successful in this daring enterprise is indicated by the Old Testament records. 1 *Samuel* 31 places the Philistines in Beth-shean, which is located only four miles west of the Jordan, and is the easternmost of the key cities. Excavations now being carried on by the University Museum at Beth-shean indicate that the city was in the hands of the Philistines until about B. C. 1130.

Interesting sidelights on political conditions in Palestine during the days of the Judges are to be found in the Report of Wenamon.* Wenamon, an Egyptian, according to the interesting account he left behind him, was engaged in conveying timber from the famous forests of Lebanon to Egypt. While *en route* to Syrian ports to obtain timber for a royal barge for the rulers of Egypt, the vessel on which he had engaged passage entered the harbor of Dor, which Wenamon describes as a "city of Thekal." The "Thekal" was one branch of the Philistines. Bedel, whom he calls the "king" of the city, sent him "much bread, a jar of wine, and a joint of beef." His trip, however, was ruined when a thief stole a goodly part of his treasure in the form of gold and silver vessels and a sack of silver.

Wenamon went to "the king of this land," and complained that he had been robbed in the harbor, and asked the king to search for his money. The king made reply that the thief belonged to the ship, and not among the residents of the city, and added that had the thief belonged to the city he would repay Wenamon from the city treasury. Wenamon failed to recover his treasure, and had great difficulty in getting away from the city. When Wenamon arrived at Byblos (also a city of the Thekal) he laid hands on an amount of treasure approximately equal in value to that which had been stolen from him, and hid it to hold until he had been reimbursed by the Thekal. This elementary method of obtaining justice led him into a series of adventures that are not germane to this story. The important point is that the coast cities of Palestine and Syria were

*See Breasted's *Ancient Records, Egypt*, IV.

evidently in the hands of the Philistines at the time of Wenamon's chronicle, about B. C. 1100. The city-kingdoms of northern Palestine had apparently passed into the hands of the Philistines about the time indicated in the closing chapters of *Judges* and the opening chapters of 1 *Samuel*. The narratives are placed in the proper historical framework.

Samson is probably the most widely remembered of the judges, since admiration for physical strength is inherent in mankind. A consecrated Nazarite, reared in ceremonial purity, there was little that was saintly about Samson. Here was a burly, overgrown young Hercules, bubbling with good humor, eager to test his prodigious physical strength against the hated Philistines, now the foremost foe of Israel, since "the Lord delivered them into the hand of the Philistines forty years" (*Judges* 13:1).

Then the Lords of the Philistines gathered them together for to offer a great sacrifice unto Dagon their God, and to rejoice: for they said, Our god hath delivered Samson our enemy into our hand.—Judges 16:23

In the sixteenth chapter, the writer of *Judges* has a tragic story to tell. Samson's colorful career culminates in a dramatic setting. Dagon is apparently triumphant. Flushed with victory, the populace pours into the courtyard of the temple. Points of vantage are at a premium. The lords and ladies crowd the floor, so eager onlookers swarm to the roof, while others cling to the balconies. What does it matter if toes are trampled, or elbows injured? This is the Day of Dagon. Soon a blinded behemoth of a man, the mutilated hulk of their arch enemy, will roll in agony about the courtyard. On with the festivities!

The roof is strong. It is made of logs split in half, and covered deep with well-tramped clay baked brick-like by the sun. It is a very heavy roof. The span is too great for single timbers to reach from outer wall to outer wall, so the roof timbers meet in a longitudinal line throughout the center of the roof structure. This is the point of weakness. The builders have met this problem by placing wooden columns upright in pairs in the center of the building. The bases of the columns rest on low brick pedestals. The outer walls of the building are only a few feet high. On these walls rest the bases of tall wooden columns carrying the curtain walls of the building and supporting the outer edges of the heavy roof. The paired columns in the center of the building carry half the weight of the roof and its deckload of humanity. Compared with its ground area, the temple is very tall.

A child leads in the haltered hulk of the mighty man of Israel, the sightless wreck of the man who, in his heyday, had wrought disaster on the hosts of the Philistines. Let him rest a moment in the shade: he will suffer soon enough. A blind man in agony of soul and body winds his gorilla-like arms around a pair of the center columns and prays to his God while awaiting the coming tortures. His mighty hands tighten around the columns as a flicker of grim hope reaches his mind and calls up every last reserve of nerve and sinew. Better sudden death than to be baited like a bull in a pit. Some of his enemies may take the last journey with him. A fervent prayer—then a mighty pull. The bottoms of the columns slip slightly on their pedestals and move toward him. Another short breath of prayer—another mighty heave on the columns. Crash! Death shrieks mingle with the thudding crashing of the heavy roof and the shattering sound of splintering timbers. The tall temple of Dagon is turned into a charnal house. Samson enters eternity escorted by his enemies.

While the wooden superstructures of such ruins of Philistine temples as have been discovered in Palestine have long since vanished, the layouts of the foundations and lower walls indicate clearly the details of their construction. In the light of modern investigation, the narrative of Samson's spectacular death can no longer be regarded as pure legend. It is well within the realms of possibility.

In those days there was no king in Israel.—Judges 18:1

During the incumbency of the judges the political fortunes of Israel rose and fell, but the general trend was upward. Judges, major and minor, were "raised up" to conquer the Canaanites, and repel the outland invader. Gideon could crush the Midianites and Jephthah conquer the Ammonites, but during the latter days of the judges a stronger foe had arisen within the confines of Palestine itself. Holding the strategic military centers, superior in military equipment to the Israelites (See 1 *Samuel* 13:19), the Philistines were ready for a conflict which was to decide the destinies of Palestine. The times demanded a leader who could unite all Israel under the banners of Jehovah.

In these dire days Israel was under the administration of the aged priest-judge Eli. This saintly old man, unable to control his own family (See 1 *Samuel* 2:22-25), evidently lacked the physical force and mental ability to enable him to unite Israel in the face of the Philistine menace. When a messenger arrived from the stricken field of Aphek, where "the Philistines put themselves in array against Israel," with news of national calamity in battle and the capture of the Ark of the Covenant by the Philistines, the tragic tidings were too much for him: "And it came to pass, when he made mention of the ark of God, that he fell off the seat backward by the side of the gate, and his neck brake, and he died"— 1 *Samuel* 4:18.

The death of Eli brought to the front a worthy leader in the person of Samuel. Consecrated from birth to the service of the Lord, he emerged from cloistered Shiloh, the religious capital of Israel, to lead his people in a fresh and vigorous start toward national unity.

And Samuel spake unto all the house of Israel, saying, If ye do return unto the Lord with all your hearts, then put away the strange gods and Ashtaroth from among you, and prepare your hearts unto the Lord, and serve him only: and he will deliver you out of the hand of the Philistines.—1 Samuel 7:3

Samuel sensed one important weakness in Israel's political position. In the days of Israel's advancing military glory they had been inspired by their abiding faith in Jehovah. With their victories over the Canaanites their dependence on Jehovah had lessened; their faith had waned; and they had begun to follow after strange gods. Samuel strove to unite the social, political, and religious aims of Israel in one mighty movement.

The religious life of Israel was frequently profoundly affected by the pagan cult-worship of the peoples with whom they came into contact. All through Old Testament history we find the religious leaders of Israel inveighing against the cult practices of pagan worship. Despite preaching and prophecy, Israel was ever prone to turn to the worship of the sacred stone and the sacred tree of the Canaanites, or to the more widespread cult of Ashtoreth, until some dire calamity turned them again to the worship of the Lord God of Israel.

Ashtoroth is the plural form of the name Ashtoreth. In one form or another, the worship of Ashtoreth spread throughout all the rising civilizations of the ancient East. Originally the great nature-goddess of the Sidonians, she became, under various names, the goddess of love and productivity to all peoples from the Tiber to the Euphrates. The rituals of the worship of Ashtoreth were far from elevating. From them developed the "mystery religions" of the Romans and the Greeks.

During the days of the judges Israel frequently suffered from mediocre leadership. Many of her most excellent leaders had been tribalists, rather than nationalists. The centuries had seen no religious leader like Moses, no military leader like Joshua. In Samuel, Israel finally found a leader capable of fulfilling the ancient ideals of religious leadership. Samuel discerned that before Israel could present a united front to the Philistine foe, the nation must return to its fundamental faith in Jehovah. After persuading his people to "put away the strange gods and Ashtaroth," he summoned all Israel to prayer at Mizpeh. When the Philistines decided that the assembly at Mizpeh offered opportunity for an annihilating attack, Samuel's prayers were answered and his faith vindicated when "the Lord thundered with a great thunder on that day upon the Philistines, and dis-comfited them; and they were smitten before Israel" (1 *Samuel* 7:10).

The subsequent campaign against the Philistines, detailed in 1 *Samuel* 7, while highly successful to the arms of Israel, was not the decisive campaign of the war. The climactic campaign against the Philistines was not to come until the days of David, when the period of the judges was past. Nevertheless, the leadership of Samuel was highly constructive. He was able to effect a strong national union of the tribes of Israel, a union that was both political and spiritual. Samuel, prophet, priest, and kingmaker, paved the way for Israel's national glory.

And the Lord said to Samuel, Hearken unto their voice, and make them a king.—1 Samuel 8:22

The eagerness of Israel for a king is easily understandable. Sporadic warfare, such as Israel had been waging against the Canaanites, might well prove unavailing against the Philistines. The Philistines could base their military campaigns on a strong line of fortified cities. They could bring unlimited food supplies from the rich farming districts they held. Israel must co-ordinate its efforts. Intertribal strife must cease, and a united front be presented to the common enemy. A leadership worthy of the best traditions of Israel must be found. Political conditions de-manded a king.

The task of choosing a king was not one that could be lightly under-taken. Samuel must find a rare individual, a man outstanding physically, mentally, morally, and spiritually. Not only must the candidate for king-ship be capable of leading Israel in war and in the establishment of national government, but he must also be a man of deep spiritual insight, capable of interpreting the will of Jehovah, since the underlying basis of Israel's morale was reliance on Jehovah's might.

In Saul, Samuel seemed to have found a man who would justify his choice. Here was "a choice young man, and a goodly: and there was not among the children of Israel a goodlier person than he: from his shoulders and upward he was higher than any of the people" (1 *Samuel* 9:2). Saul's spiritual fitness seemed to have been demonstrated when, at Bethel, "the spirit of God came upon him, and he prophesied among them"— 1 *Samuel* 10:10.

While the history of the period of the judges, as recorded in *Judges* and *Samuel,* is largely a story of conflict and strife, the story of a sturdy people fighting for a homeland, winning when they were loyal to Jehovah, losing when they left their ancient faith to wander after strange gods, yet it reflects advancement toward a higher degree of civilization. Israel was settling down in the Promised Land. During the periods of peace education was advancing. Evidently knowledge of the art of writing was becoming more widespread. We find mention of the professional scribe in *Judges* 5:14: "Out of Zebulun they that handle the pen of the writer." Samuel must have been a man of considerable educational attainment, since he "told the people the manner of the kingdom, and wrote it in a book" (See 1 *Samuel* 10:25). *The Book of Jasher*, mentioned as being in existence as early as the days of Joshua (See *Joshua* 10:13), must have been kept throughout all the period of the judges, since we find it mentioned in 2 *Samuel* 1:18.

Samuel, the greatest of the judges, must be counted among the great leaders of Israel. He saw Israel through a great national crisis. Although his selection of Saul was unfortunate, his selection of David, the shepherd lad of Bethlehem, opened the way to Israel's greatest days of glory.

MOUND OF BETH-SHAN

Buried beneath the dust and debris of the "Mound of the Fortress" were twenty-one distinct city levels dating from the days of the Crusaders back through the ages to the time of the Painted Pottery People.

ARAB AND BYZANTINE RUINS AT BETH-SHAN

Many waves of conquest, Amonite, Hittite, Egyptian, Philistine, Hebrew, Assyrian, Babylonian, Persian, Greek, Arab and Crusader swept over Beth-shan. Each of these peoples left material evidence of their stay buried in the dust and debris of the famous "Tell."

By permission of The Museum of the University of Pennsylvania

VIII

THE COMING OF THE KINGS

Give us a king to judge us.—1 Samuel 8:6

DURING the latter days of the judges there was evidently a strong political movement throughout Israel looking toward the establishment of a constitutional monarchy. This was a natural trend in national growth. The march of civilization was ending the days of tribalism throughout the entire East. Twelve petty tribal states would lack the political power of one national union. Israel was no longer a nomadic people. They were an agricultural people in a country where agriculture was the principal industry. Among the elders of Israel there were many who supported the new political movement. Samuel, after sturdy opposition, had finally bowed to the will of the majority, and anointed Saul as king of Israel.

The rule of Samuel, the last of the judges who really governed, witnessed a great transition period in the political life of the Hebrew people. Samuel was the kingmaker. The two books of the Old Testament which are dedicated to him (1, 2 *Samuel*) appear in the Septuagint and Vulgate versions as the "First and Second Books of Kings," *Kings* being in four books. These books tell the dramatic story of the rise and fall of the Hebrew kingdom. They picture the rise of the Hebrews, as a people, to political power and prominence in Palestine, and show them sinking, after four centuries of glory, into political oblivion.

The annalists who kept the original records of the Hebrew kingdom interpreted life and the current events of their day in the light of Israelitish idealism. They strove to articulate the religious aspirations of a people. They looked upon the Chosen People as an instrument of Jehovah. In telling the story of a great religious movement, they pictured patriotism in action. They measured men with an iron rule. The leader who faltered or failed in the keeping of the Covenant was viewed with stern displeasure. They countenanced no compromise with evil. Israel's failures were attributed to Israel's sins. Although these writers interpreted history in terms of Jehovah, the spade of the archæologist and the notebook of the scientist are today proving that the sacred writers were excellent historians, as far as outstanding historical events are concerned.

The change to constitutional monarchy was a gradual movement. While Saul's kingship was appropriate to the times and the conditions

9

of the country, his monarchy was not at all comparable to that later established by David and Solomon. No regal palace housed him. No crown adorned his head. His sceptre was a warrior's spear. His family servants constituted his royal retinue. "Now Saul abode in Gibeah under a tree in Ramah, having his spear in his hand, and all his servants were standing about him" (1 *Samuel* 22:6). His primitive methods of summoning his armies were more akin to the methods of the tribal chieftain than to those of a reigning sovereign (See 1 *Samuel* 11:7).

Although Samuel had abdicated his political office, he did not resign his duties as a priest and prophet of Israel. He was still the religious leader of the Chosen People. Saul had yet to prove himself. Political opinion as to the desirability of a king was not unanimous. Probably there were many minor leaders who were loath to surrender their freedom of independent tribal action (See 1 *Samuel* 10:27). In the early days of Saul's reign, the new king recognized his dependence on Samuel. His earliest proclamation contains the words: "Whosoever cometh not after Saul and after Samuel." So long as Saul kept the confidence of Samuel his reign was a success.

> *Then Nahash the Ammonite came up, and encamped against Jabesh-gilead: and all the men of Jabesh said unto Nahash, Make a covenant with us, and we will serve thee.*
>
> *And Nahash the Ammonite answered them, On this condition will I make a covenant with you, that I may thrust out all your right eyes, and lay it for a reproach upon all Israel.*—1 Samuel 11:1, 2

Saul did not have long to wait for an opportunity to justify Samuel's choice of a king of Israel. No sooner had he assumed leadership than messengers arrived at his headquarters in Gibeah, bringing news of the dire plight of the inhabitants of Jabesh-gilead, a little town east of the Jordan, who were not only threatened with the loss of liberty, but also with degrading mutilation. Summoning Israel to rally to his standard, Saul made a forced march to the relief of Jabesh, and, by strategic maneuvering of his troops, completely routed the Ammonites. That Saul's gallant action was gratefully remembered by the inhabitants of Jabesh is attested by 1 *Samuel* 31:11-13; 1 *Chronicles* 10:11, 12.

Saul's brilliant victory over the Ammonites aroused great enthusiasm among the Israelites. Some over-zealous patriots were in favor of putting to death the political opponents of Saul. Saul, however, was not in favor of such drastic measures: "And Saul said, There shall not a man be put to death this day: for to day the Lord hath wrought salvation in Israel" (1 *Samuel* 11:13). At the call of Samuel, a triumphant Israel gathered at Gilgal, "and there they made Saul king before the Lord."

Now there was no smith found throughout all the land of Israel: for the Philistines said, Lest the Hebrews make them swords or spears. But all the Israelites went down to the Philistines, to sharpen every man his share, and his coulter, and his ax, and his mattock.—1 Samuel 13:19, 20

This statement is interesting. It indicates the use of weapons, tools, and agricultural implements made of iron, during the reign of Saul— roughly, the middle of the eleventh century B. C. The Old Testament speaks of the use of iron even earlier than this. Moses mentions "any iron tool" (*Deuteronomy* 27:5). Og, king of Bashan, is represented as having a "bedstead of iron" (*Deuteronomy* 3:11). The children of Joseph found "chariots of iron" in the valley of Jezreel (See *Joshua* 17:16). These passages speak of the use of iron in the thirteenth and twelfth centuries B. C.

Some commentators on the Old Testament, pointing out that Israel entered Canaan in the Third Bronze Age, have suggested that these early mentions of the use of iron were anachronistic, since it has been commonly assumed that iron was not in use in Palestine until about B. C. 1000. However, excavations at the sites of ancient Philistine cities, notably Gerar, prove that iron was in fairly common use among the Philistines as early as the thirteenth century B. C.

Mention of the share and the coulter (parts of a plough) indicate that the Israelites had adopted some of the agricultural methods of the Philistines who had been farming in Palestine for centuries. Ploughs had been used in Babylonia at a much earlier date, but a wooden plough that would furrow the alluvial soils of lower Mesopotamia would be useless in some of the rocky soils of Palestine. The finding of Philistine plough points made of iron, and dating from about B. C. 1170, indicates that the writer of 1 *Samuel* 13:19-22 is quite correct as to his facts.

So it came to pass in the day of the battle, that there was neither sword nor spear found in the hand of any of the people that were with Saul and Jonathan.—1 Samuel 13:22

Saul was severely handicapped in his campaigns against the Philistines in northern Palestine. The Philistines not only had strongly fortified natural lines of defense, but, also, a very definite advantage in offensive armament. The finding of furnaces for the smelting of iron and tools for the making of swords and spears, among the ruins of Philistine cities of the eleventh century B. C., indicates that the Philistines had "smiths" of no mean ability. The Philistine superiority in arms is denoted in 1 *Samuel* 13, and abundantly proved by archæological discovery.

So Saul took the kingdom over Israel and fought against all his enemies on every side, against Moab, and against the children of Ammon, and against Edom, and against the kings of Zobah, and against the Philistines: and whithersoever he turned himself, he vexed them.—1 Samuel 14:47

But the spirit of the Lord departed from Saul.—1 Samuel 16:14

In the early part of his reign Saul seems to have been highly successful against the enemies of Israel. The Philistines were held in check. Aggressive, warlike neighbors were driven from Hebrew territory. Unfortunately, these military successes turned Saul's head, and caused him to suffer from delusions of grandeur. When he attempted to usurp the priestly prerogatives of Samuel and failed to carry out the commands of Jehovah, he not only incurred the wrath of Samuel, but also lost divine guidance for his administration. "And Samuel said unto Saul, I will not return with thee: for thou hast rejected the word of the Lord, and the Lord hath rejected thee from being king over Israel" (1 *Samuel* 15:26). Saul was suffering from one of mankind's most common complaints, an exaggerated ego.

With the loss of Samuel's support, Saul's days were filled with gloom. The populace, which had so proudly proclaimed him king at Gilgal, now began to center its devotion on a new national hero, the rising young David. David had won popular acclaim by his deft disposal of the gigantic Goliath in personal combat. The dramatic ending of the spectacular duel between the stripling shepherd boy, armed with a sling and five pebbles, and the colossal champion of the Philistines, the staff of whose spear "was like a weaver's beam," had turned the Israelites, who "were dismayed and greatly afraid," into a triumphant host which realized that the "Lord saveth not with sword and spear: for the battle is the Lord's" (1 *Samuel* 17:47). Saul's star was setting.

At first Saul seems to have welcomed the promising young Bethlehemite to his court. Not only did David win the favor of Saul, but he also gained the undying devotion of the noble-hearted Jonathan, with whom he established a friendship which stands to this day as the proverbial example of unselfish comradeship between man and man. "The soul of Jonathan was knit with the soul of David, and Jonathan loved him as his own soul"—1 *Samuel* 18:1.

David's popularity with the people aroused the jealousy of Saul. Suspicion darkened his mind, and when he heard the women singing, "Saul has slain his thousands, and David his ten thousands," his anger knew no bounds, "and Saul was very wroth, and the saying displeased him" (1 *Samuel* 18:8). "And Saul eyed David from that day and forward"—1 *Samuel* 18:9.

When Saul failed to dispose of David by pinning him to the wall with a javelin, he resorted to guile. Strong men have often succumbed to the wiles of women. Samson was the historic Hebraic example. David, too, might be vulnerable. Saul determined to use his daughter Michal as a lure: "that she may be a snare to him, and the hand of the Philistines may be against him" (1 *Samuel* 18:21). Saul realized that his strategem had failed when he "saw and knew that the Lord was with David, and that Michal Saul's daughter loved him" (1 *Samuel* 18:28). "And Saul was yet more afraid of David."

Saul's gloom and terror were bringing him to the verge of mental and moral collapse. The destruction of David became his dominating obsession, hovering like an evil spirit over his apprehensive mind. In his mental distress he attempted to inveigle Jonathan, who "delighted much in David," into a conspiracy for the assassination of his rival. The fidelity of Jonathan, his friend, and the love of Michal, his wife, enabled David to evade the cunning clutch of Saul, "so David fled, and escaped, and came to Samuel to Ramah, and told him all that Saul had done to him" (1 *Samuel* 19:18).

Wherefore they say, Is Saul also among the prophets?—1 Samuel 19:24

David had found refuge with Samuel at Naioth. "And Saul sent messengers to take David: and when they saw the company of the prophets prophesying, and Samuel standing as appointed over them, the Spirit of God was upon the messengers of Saul, and they also prophesied" (1 *Samuel* 19:20). A second and a third set of messengers underwent the same experience. Finally Saul set out himself for Naioth, where he, too, prophesied, "and lay down naked all that day and all that night." Was this practice of exposing the person to the elements a common practice among prophets? While the prophets of Israel are not to be compared with the pagan prophets so often mentioned in the Old Testament in connection with the worship of Baal, Ashtoreth, and other false gods, an interesting incident is recorded in the Report of Wenamon.* Wenamon writes:

> "Now, when he sacrificed to his gods . . . the god seized one of his noble youths, making him frenzied. . . . Now, while the frenzied youth continued in frenzy during this night, I found a ship bound for Egypt, and I loaded all my belongings into it."†

---

*See Chapter VII, page 106.

†See *Ancient Records, Egypt, IV*, Breasted.

Wenamon is describing the customs of the Philistines, whose religious practices are frequently referred to in the Old Testament, either directly or by inference. Many customs of the Hebrews were common to other peoples with whom the Israelites came in contact. The above offers an interesting parallel.

Saul's implacable hatred of David involved him in such a relentless pursuit that David became, to all intents and purposes, a sort of outlaw, roving through southern Judea. Adroitly dodging his arch enemy, Saul, sparing the king's life when he had him in his power at Engedi (See 1 Samuel 24:4), David was constantly gathering unto himself an effective fighting force (See 1 Samuel 22:1, 2; 23:13; 27:2).

Saul's demoniacal obsessions in regard to David were not only slowly destroying Saul, they were also disrupting Israel. The reign that had started so gloriously at Gilgal was torn by factional feud. The better minds of Israel were alienated by Saul's perverse actions and turned to David as the coming king. Abigail recognized this when she said: "And it came to pass, when the Lord shall have done to my lord according to all the good that he hath spoken concerning thee, and shall have appointed thee ruler over Israel" (1 Samuel 25:30). Even Jonathan, the king's son, assures David with the words: "Fear not: for the hand of Saul my father shall not find thee; and thou shalt be king over Israel" (1 Samuel 23:17). David, however, found the situation disheartening. In his despair he turns to Achish, king of Gath, one of the hated Philistines, in search of a peaceful haven, pleading: "Let them give me a place in some town in the country, that I may dwell there" (1 Samuel 27:5). "Then Achish gave him Ziklag that day."

David's acceptance of the hospitality of Achish of Gath brought him face to face with a dilemma. As a potential ally of Achish he might be constrained into bearing arms against Saul in the battle that was brewing in the neighborhood of Beth-shan. Fortunately, the jealousy of the princes of the Philistines extricated him from an awkward position, and left him free to pursue and punish the Amalekite marauders who had despoiled Ziklag. David thus missed participation in the dark drama that took place on the slopes of Mt. Gilboa.

The smooth-flowing narratives of 1 Samuel conclude with a magnificent account of a battle fought on the slopes of Mt. Gilboa between the army of Saul and the hosts of the Philistines. Recent archæological discoveries have proved that the Biblical account is historical.

Saul's day was done. A kingdom was slipping from his hands. His dream of empire was ending in a nightmare of doom. The hated Philistines, whom he had hoped to conquer, were gathering for decisive conflict. Deprived of the divine support which had sustained him in his earlier years, he vainly sought solace in the realms of wizardry. Although nothing could be done to redeem the misspent years, he could still fight and die like a soldier. Gallantly he gathered his forces to face the coming storm.

> *And it came to pass on the morrow, when the Philistines came to strip the slain, that they found Saul and his three sons fallen in Mount Gilboa. And they cut off his head, and stripped off his armour . . . And they put his armour in the house of Ashtaroth; and they fastened his body to the wall of Beth-shan.*—1 Samuel 31:8-10

In the *Chronicles* account of the same events, the passage reads:

> *And they put his armour in the house of their gods, and fastened his head in the temple of Dagon.*—1 Chronicles 10:10

The student of the Scriptures, in comparing the *Samuel* version of the dramatic events that took place around Beth-shan with the account given in *Chronicles,* might well wonder if there were not some "slip of the pen" in the apparent variation in these details concerning the temples. The actual discovery of these two temples and the "wall of Beth-shan" on which the body of Saul was fastened, not only clears up all doubt, but also adds a brilliant chapter to the long story of archæological discoveries that supplement Old Testament narratives.

Long before these temples were built it had become the custom for pagan peoples to build their temples in pairs, one for the male deity and one for his female counterpart. "Ashtoroth" is the plural form of "Ashtoreth," the "Queen of Heaven," the great Eastern goddess of love and fertility, so the words "house of Ashtoroth" really mean "house of the Ashtoreths," or the "house of the goddesses."

Ashtoreth, or Astarte, seems to have been a sort of universal goddess. The Ashtoreth of Palestine, in the days of Saul and David, seems to have been a curious combination of the Babylonian goddess Ishtar and the Egyptian goddess Hathor. Excavation in Palestine has revealed countless numbers of figurines representing this goddess. The Amorites and Hittites used a crude figure of a similar goddess in Palestine before the days of Abraham. From time immemorial down to about B. C. 100, Ashtoreth had many devotees in Palestine. Even the intelligent Greeks left behind them ivory plaques representing Astarte.

Ashtoreth was extensively worshipped throughout Palestine during all the days of the Hebrew kingdom. Even Israel was not immune to the lure of the bounteous goddess of love and fertility. Again and again they bowed down and offered sacrifice to the Queen of Heaven (See *Jeremiah* 7:17-19; 44:16-18). Excavation proves that the Hebrews made

many a figurine and fashioned many a jug bearing the form of Ashtoreth.
The thundered warnings of Israel's prophets were certainly needed.

Evidently the battle on the slopes of Mt. Gilboa ended in the night.
With the coming of the dawn, "when the Philistines came to strip the
slain," they came upon the body of the fallen king of Israel. Here was
a find, indeed! One can imagine the ghoulish glee of the conquerors as
they form a triumphal procession to convey their ghastly trophies to the
temples in nearby Beth-shan. On to the House of Ashtoreth! On to
the Temple of Dagon! The procession swings down the slopes of Mt.
Gilboa into the valley of Jezreel, while messengers rush to carry the glad
tidings to the Philistine cities. A king of Israel has fallen.

Carry the cursed carrion high, so that those who crowd the walls
of Beth-shan may see all that remains of the hated Hebrew king. Swing
wide the citadel gates; clear the way to the temples. This is the day of
Ashtoreth and Dagon! What glory it would have been if, instead of this
cold clay, the Queen of Heaven could have been presented with a still-
living king of Israel. Torture of the living would have brought her
greater glory than the defilement of the dead.

When, at last, the long day of Philistine rejoicing comes to an end,
and the people of Beth-shan, wearied with the orgies in honor of Ashtoreth and Dagon seek surcease in slumber, the armor of Saul adorns
the House of Ashtoreth; his head hangs, ignominiously upside down,
in the Temple of Dagon; and the mutilated body of Israel's first king
makes a grim embellishment to the wall of Beth-shan. "How are the
mighty fallen!" Israel was shattered by an overwhelming disaster. "They
forsook the cities and fled."

. "And when the inhabitants of Jabesh-gilead heard of that which the
Philistines had done to Saul," they remembered how, in their hour of
peril, Saul had gallantly come to their aid and delivered them from
Nahash, king of the Ammonites (See 1 *Samuel* 11). There is only one
thing left that they can do for their benefactor—they can make decent
disposal of his remains. He saved their right eyes; they will salvage his
headless corpse. "All the valiant men" of Jabesh silently cross the Jordan, move stealthily along the banks of the little river Jalud, and under
cover of night rescue the body of Saul. In grateful remembrance of
Saul's deliverance of their little city, they "took the body of Saul and
the bodies of his sons from the wall of Beth-shan, and came to Jabesh,
and burnt them there." "And they took their bones, and buried them
under a tree at Jabesh."

Israel was stunned. The decisive defeat on the slopes of Gilboa was
the greatest military disaster that had ever overtaken the Chosen People.
Israel had not only been defeated, but also humiliated and disgraced.

The mutilated corpse of Israel's king, the Lord's anointed, hanging on the wall of Beth-shan, had proclaimed the shame of the seed of Abraham. The future of Palestine was balanced on the edge of the sword. Centuries of glorious Hebrew history might be blotted out in blood. Israel's only hope lay in the redoubtable David. News of the national calamity was carried to David's camp at Ziklag. Overwhelmed by the magnitude of the military disaster, stricken with grief for the fallen king, mourning his bosom friend Jonathan, David found temporary relief in writing the immortal lament which begins:

> *The beauty of Israel is slain upon thy high places!*
> *How are the mighty fallen!*
> *Tell it not in Gath,*
> *Publish it not in the streets of Ashkelon;*
> *Lest the daughters of the Philistines rejoice,*
> *Lest the daughters of the uncircumcised triumph.*
> —2 Samuel 1:19-20

Israel's hour was striking! This was not the time for poetry and repining. The great poet of Israel was also a well-tried warrior. Lay aside the pen; pick up the sword! David rallied his forces to wreak vengeance on the Philistines and destroy their cities.

Among the cities that David destroyed was Beth-shan. How thoroughly the work of vengeance was carried out the mute walls of Beth-shan bear witness to this day. In places the gray brick walls were burned bright red by the heat of the conflagration. The holocaust that swept the city destroyed the wooden superstructures of the "house of Ashtoreth," and the "temple of Dagon," where the Philistines had desecrated the dead body of Saul. Fortunately, in addition to the brick walls with their foundation deposits, there were many articles in the temples which would not burn. The cult objects found around the altars definitely mark these two buildings as being those designated by the passages in 1 *Samuel* 31 and 1 *Chronicles* 10.

It should be remembered that northern Palestine was under Egyptian domination for nearly three hundred years. During the days when Egypt held sway they built and rebuilt the fortifications of strategic military centers. Beth-shan had been a strategic military center from time immemorial. Located just where the valley of Jezreel drops down to meet the valley of the Jordan, it controlled the military and commercial highway leading from the Mediterranean to the Jordan. It also controlled the junction of this highway with the north and south highway running along the banks of the Jordan. Beth-shan was the indispensable military key to military and commercial operations in northern Palestine. It was the easternmost of the cities mentioned in *Judges* 17:11, 12 as being those that Israel was unable to capture during the days of Joshua. The conquest of Canaan could never be complete as long as Beth-shan, the guardian of the gateway to the lands beyond the Jordan, remained uncaptured.

The Palestinian Expedition of the University Museum, Philadelphia, now operating at Beth-shan, on City Level V of the site, uncovered the ruins of the "house of Ashtoreth," and the "temple of Dagon." It was discovered that Rameses II of Egypt, in the ninth year of his reign (B. C. 1283), had rebuilt the citadel at Beth-shan, and enclosed two temples within the walls. The southern temple, the smaller of the two, is the temple of Dagon mentioned in 1 *Chronicles* 10:10 as being the building in which Saul's head was fastened. The northern temple is the "house of Ashtoreth" where Saul's armour was placed, according to 1 *Samuel* 31:10. The temples stood side by side with only a narrow corridor between them.

Foundation deposits of Rameses II definitely date the temples. In the northern temple was found a monument showing the figure of the Canaanite warrior-goddess Antit. The goddess is dressed as Ashtoreth, with whom she must therefore be identified. Before the crown of the goddess are two lines of text which read: "Antit, the Queen of Heaven, the mistress of all the gods" (Compare *Jeremiah* 44:19). Numerous cult objects found around the altar indicate clearly that this was a temple of Ashtoreth.

On the shattered lintel of the Temple of Dagon was found the name, titles, and portrait of the builder of the temple. The temple was erected under the direction of an Egyptian named Rameses-wesr-Knepesh, who identifies himself as "an overseer of soldiers, commander of the bowmen of the Lord of the Two Lands (*i. e.,* Pharaoh), royal scribe, and great steward." He was the son of one Thotmes, "a fanbearer at the right hand of the king, chief of the bowmen, and overseer of foreign lands."

Among the cult objects used in the rituals of worship of Ashtoreth was a curious clay object closely resembling a doll's house, frequently with human figures, doves, and snakes, peeping from the windows. Another common cult object was a vase-like stand, open top and bottom, with apertures in the sides. These were filled with rich earth. Seeds were planted in them, frequently watered, and exposed to the sun. The forced growth seemed a simple magic to primitive-minded peoples. Evidently the Israelites frequently indulged in this symbolic ceremony. "Because thou hast forgotten the God of thy salvation, and hast not been mindful of the rock of thy strength, therefore shalt thou plant pleasant plants, and shalt set it with strange slips."—*Isaiah* 17:10. A. R. V., margin: "vine slips of a strange god."

Shortly after the death of Rameses III in B. C. 1167, Beth-shan passed out of the control of Egypt. The Egyptians had garrisoned the cities of northern Palestine with mercenary troops imported from countries bordering the northern shores of the Mediterranean. When the Egyptians, threatened with invasion of their own country, were forced to withdraw from Palestine, they left Beth-shan in control of these mercenaries. Later (about B. C. 1080) these mercenaries seem to have amalgamated with the Philistines against whom they had formerly fought. Thus the two famous temples, which were still standing, became Philistine temples — the "house of Ashtoreth" and the "temple of Dagon." The Old Testament narratives of the end of Saul's reign are placed in the correct historical setting.

The neighborhood of Beth-shan was a logical location for the climactic campaign for the control of Palestine. This is an age-old fighting ground. Many a wave of invasion has swept over Tell-al-Hosn (meaning, "the Mound of the Fortress"), but Beth-shan probably has never witnessed a more dramatic day than that described in 1 *Samuel* 31.

To the recorders who wrote the annals of the kings, Saul was a sore disappointment. Despite the promise of his youth, he never measured up to the high standards set by historic Hebrew leadership. The reign that began in glory ended in shame. Saul's reign, however, was not devoid of accomplishment. The Canaanites were conquered; Israel's boundaries greatly extended; the way was paved for the coming of Israel's greatest kings, David and Solomon.

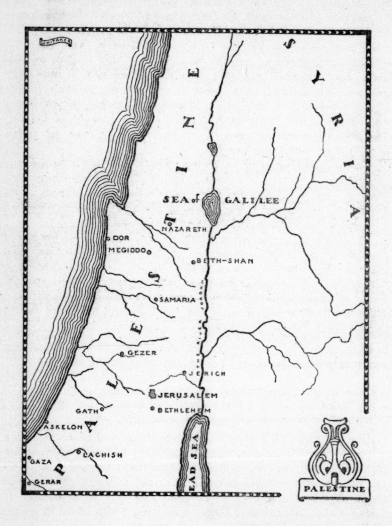

IX

ISRAEL UNDER DAVID

And the men of Judah came, and there they anointed David king over the house of Judah.—2 Samuel 2:4

DAVID was the natural successor of Saul as the anointed king of Israel. Long before the death of Saul, David had been selected by Samuel as the coming king (See I *Samuel* 16). However, the disaster on Mt. Gilboa and the death of Saul definitely divided the tribes into two factions. There was a tendency on the part of some local leaders to return to the outmoded methods of tribal government. While Judah, in the south, proclaimed David king, his authority was not unquestioned in the north. Abner, an able military leader who had served under Saul, brought Ishboseth (Ishbaal) to Mahanaim, "and made him king over Gilead, and over the Ashurites, and over Jezreel, and over Ephraim, and over Benjamin, and over all Israel" (2 *Samuel* 2:9).

This cleavage of the country naturally brought about civil strife. According to 2 *Samuel* 2, the losses in battle were trifling during this civil conflict. Although the breach was later healed, there always remained a smoldering spark of jealousy between the north and the south. A day was to come, long later, when this spark would burst into the flame that was to help break the power of the Hebrew kingdom in Palestine.

Now there was long war between the house of Saul and the house of David; but David waxed stronger and stronger, and the house of Saul waxed weaker and weaker.—2 Samuel 3:1

The end of the civil war was hastened by the revolt of Abner against Ishboseth. Smarting under an unjust accusation by Ishboseth, whom he had placed in power over the northern kingdom, Abner threatened to "translate the kingdom from the house of Saul, and to set up the throne of David over Israel and over Judah, from Dan even to Beersheba" (2 *Samuel* 3:10). Abner visited David, and arranged with David to "gather all Israel unto my lord the king" (2 *Samuel* 3:21).

Unfortunately, David's dealings with Abner brought the latter to an untimely death at the hands of Joab, David's military leader. Fearing that he might be supplanted by Abner, Joab first tried to influence the mind of David against the northern general. Failing in this, he lured

Abner to the city gate, "and smote him there under the fifth rib." David promptly rebuked Joab for his precipitate action, and ordered his people into a period of mourning for Abner, "and king David himself followed the bier."

Ishboseth would now probably have surrendered to David had not the sons of Rimmon, hoping to be rewarded by David, murdered him as he lay in his bed and brought his severed head to David. This cold-blooded murder enraged David, and the sons of Rimmon paid for their folly with their lives. With the death of Ishboseth, the short-lived northern kingdom came to an end. The ill-fated "House of Saul" had perished. The elders of Israel gathered at Hebron, "and they anointed David king over Israel."

With the collapse of the northern kingdom, all opposition to David seems to have crumbled. All Israel was united. When David was anointed king of all Israel, a real Hebrew nation came into being. Behind the new nation lay a thousand years of history. Slowly, but surely, the material portions of the promises of Jehovah were being fulfilled. The Chosen People had inherited the Promised Land. The conquest of Canaan was complete, save for two sore spots, the Philistine stronghold of Gezer and the little pagan city of Jebus.

And David and all Israel went to Jerusalem, which is Jebus; where the Jebusites were, the inhabitants of the land. And the inhabitants of Jebus said to David, Thou shalt not come hither. Nevertheless David took the castle of Zion, which is the city of David.—1 Chronicles 11:4, 5

Jerusalem had long defied Israel. "The children of Judah had fought against Jerusalem, and had taken it, and smitten it with the edge of the sword" (*Judges* 1:8), but they could not hold it (See *Judges* 1:21).

The city that David captured about B. C. 1050 was not such a city as Allenby entered on foot in 1918, reverently saying that he "walked where One had walked before." It was a little city that stood on the long spur of rock that is today known as Ophel. While all Christendom was thrilled when Allenby wrested Jerusalem from Islam, this was, historically considered, a minor episode when compared with the results of David's capture of the little pagan city three thousand years ago.

Even at that early date it may have been a Holy City to the Israelites. Centuries earlier Abraham, the "Father of the Faithful," after his dramatic rescue of Lot, had here met Melchizedek, king of Salem and priest of the Most High God, and had been blessed by that dignitary (See *Genesis* 14). On Mt. Moriah, Abraham, about to sacrifice his son, was enabled to substitute the "ram caught in a thicket by his horns." Here the Divine promises had been renewed: "And in thy seed shall all the nations of the earth be blessed."

The little town of Jebus, the "Salem" of *Genesis* 14, and the "Urusalim" (City of Peace) of the letters of Ebed-Hapi, its governor, to his overlord, Amenophis IV, Pharaoh of Egypt, which were found among the Tell-el-Amarna tablets,* had been a military stronghold from time immemorial. Manetho, the Egyptian priest-historian, who lived in the third century B. C., claimed that Jebus was founded by the Hyksos when they were driven out of Egypt. Excavations at Jerusalem, however, prove Manetho in error, as there was evidently a town there as early as B. C. 2000, or at least four hundred years before the Hyksos were driven out of Egypt. Even before the coming of the Jebusites, the original settlers in Palestine (probably some branch of the semi-barbaric Painted Pottery People) had chosen the limestone caves of the place for a habitation. Isaiah, prophesying the desolation the Assyrians may bring, warns the inhabitants of Jerusalem that "the forts and towers shall be dens (caves) for ever" (See *Isaiah* 32:14). The Jebusites were of Amorite-Hittite extraction, taking their name from the "jebus" (threshing floor) that loomed above their tiny town. Ezekiel, upbraiding Jerusalem, tells her: "Thy father was an Amorite, and thy mother an Hittite" (See *Ezekiel* 16:3).

Jebus, perched on an arm of rock, with the deep Kidron Valley on one side and the Tyropœan Valley on the other, was easily approachable only from the north. The Hittites, who were excellent fortification builders, with an abundance of free-working limestone at hand for a building material, heavily walled this northern approach to render the little city almost impregnable.

Jebus, in addition to its easily defended position, possessed the other great essential necessary to a military stronghold of that day, a readily available water supply in time of siege. In the Kidron Valley is a never-failing spring, which was known in Old Testament days as "Gihon." It was beside this spring that David's son, Solomon, was later anointed king of Israel (See 1 *Kings* 1:45). This spring is mentioned in connection with the building operations of Manasseh in 2 *Chronicles* 33:14. In New Testament days, this spring was known as "Bethesda," and it was by this pool that Our Saviour healed the man "which had an infirmity thirty and eight years" (*John* 5:5). Today this spring is known as the Virgin's Fountain. Until the Romans came to Jerusalem, this spring, and another (the Biblical En-rogel) farther down the valley, furnished most of the water supply of Jerusalem.

*See Chapter IV, page 62.

Without Gihon, there would have been no city of Jebus. Prehistoric man here found a dependable water supply with habitable caves adjacent. The water supply would naturally attract the early Amorites, so here sprang up a settlement, so long ago that its date cannot be definitely determined. Before the beginnings of written history, crude settlers were building primitive walls to control the water of Gihon.

Gihon (meaning "gusher") is an intermittent spring. Somewhere on the underground course of the water before it issues from the spring, there is a cavern which traps the water like a cistern. When this underground reservoir is filled to overflowing its narrow outlet acts as a siphon, and all the water in the cavern emerges from the outlet with a rush.

The annual output of the spring varies with the seasonal rainfall. The annual rainfall of Palestine varies greatly. During the winter months the winds from the west bring water-laden clouds from the Mediterranean. When the clouds meet the stratum of cold air over the uplands of Palestine, rain falls. Plentiful winter rains mean abundant crops the following autumn. Light rains mean lesser crops, and in ancient days frequently meant famine. In dry periods the waters of Gihon may erupt but once or twice a day, but in wet periods as many as five times. The spring, however, never fails.

The water of Gihon fed the Pool of Siloam, and, since it was to this pool that Jesus sent the blind man (See *John* 9:7) it is not strange that healing properties have been ascribed to its waters.

Although Gihon lay outside the city walls, the Jebusites made the waters available in time of siege by cutting a tunnel from the spring to a natural cavern under the city. From the top of the cavern they cut a perpendicular shaft for some forty-five feet upward, and then cut a long sloping passage connecting the top of the shaft with the surface of the ground in the upper part of the city. In order to secure water the inhabitants had only to walk down the sloping passage to the top of the vertical shaft and lower their goatskin water-carriers to the pool below. This ingenious engineering work of the Jebusites is now known as "Warren's Shaft," after its discoverer, Sir Charles Warren.

In the time of David, only a small part of the waters of Gihon were required for the needs of the city. The remainder formed the "brook Kidron" of 2 *Samuel* 15:23 and 2 *Chronicles* 29:16 Three hundred years later, when Hezekiah was carrying out his extensive building operations at Jerusalem, more of the water was diverted into the city, and the brook was probably dry, excepting after heavy rains, just as it is today.

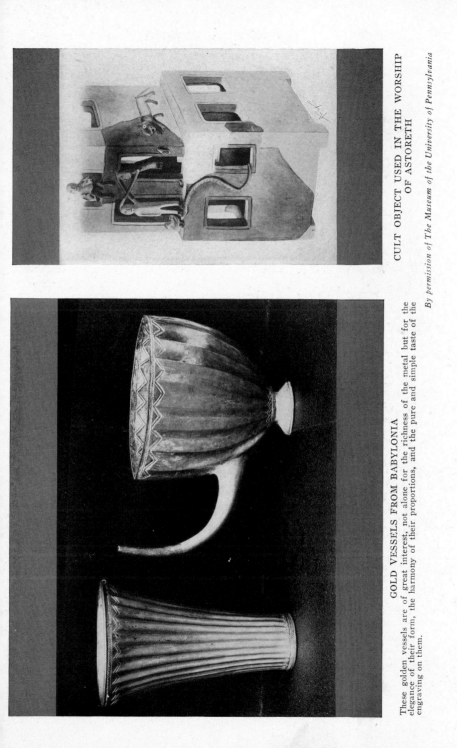

GOLD VESSELS FROM BABYLONIA

These golden vessels are of great interest, not alone for the richness of the metal but for the elegance of their form, the harmony of their proportions, and the pure and simple taste of the engraving on them.

CULT OBJECT USED IN THE WORSHIP OF ASTORETH

By permission of The Museum of the University of Pennsylvania

Israel had found a warrior worthy to wear the military mantle of the mighty Joshua. The sceptre that slipped from the death-shaken hand of Saul was clenched in the iron hand of his illustrious successor. The rock-kept key to political and commercial power in central and southern Palestine was now entrusted to the keeping of the Chosen People. "David dwelt in the fort" which dominated a town which was itself a fortress. The City of David was now a truly national capital of the Hebrew kingdom. With the taking of the city, the seal of Israel was set for coming centuries on Palestine. The site of the city had originally been determined by a living spring, Gihon. The hill above the spring became the most significant hill in spiritual history. From it flowed the stream of spiritual truth which has shaped the religious thought of a large proportion of mankind. The holy heights of Jerusalem are sacred to Christian, Jew, and Moslem.

The taking of a tiny town on a rocky ridge established David in prominent place in Hebrew history forever. He holds high honor as a political and military leader. It is doubtful if David, despite his classical contributions to Old Testament literature, merits enrollment among the great religious leaders of Israel. His life story, more completely told in Holy Writ than that of any other Old Testament character, reveals a many-sided man, capable of answering Israel's crying need for a creative national organizer, but religious in character rather than spiritual in nature.

The thrilling series of historical narratives that picture the rise of a shepherd lad to a throne is marred by shadowy sidelights which the annalists of Israel were too candid to conceal. Endowed by nature with capacity for physical prowess, granted the God-given leadership of the Chosen People, gifted with grace to sing the songs of Israel with the soul-touch of a poetical musician, David sometimes sank to superstitious crudities unworthy of an anointed king of Israel and of the high standards of Hebrew spiritual leadership. The heart that could pour itself out in loving lament over Saul and his sons fallen on Mt. Gilboa (2 *Samuel* 1:17-27) could harden to have other sons of Saul hanged high on the hill of Gibeah (2 *Samuel* 21:1-14) to appease the wrath of the servile Gibeonites over the nonfulfillment of a covenant which dated back to the days of Joshua (See *Joshua* 9). The lofty soul that scorned the curses of Shimei (2 *Samuel* 16) could work vindictive vengeance against the aged Joab, who had served him on the fields of battle all his life (See 1 *Kings* 2:5). The religious idealism which animated the soul of Abraham and motivated the mighty mind of Moses was seldom shown in the career of the king who carried Israel to complete national establishment in Palestine.

The name of David will always be associated with the hallowed hills of Jerusalem. The tiny town taken from the pagans has grown to the most inspiring city mankind has ever known. Jerusalem is today held sacred by the adherents of the three great living religions that worship only one God. Even today, as modernism overtakes the ancient city, the name of David still clings. A great modern hotel of two hundred rooms, named the "King David Hotel," now overlooks the scene of David's famous victory.

And David built round about from Millo and inward.—2 Samuel 5:9

Jerusalem, the "City of Peace," has a history far from peaceful. Its history is a story of mingled glory and tragedy. The City of Altars has, itself, been frequently sacrificed on the altar of war. Armies unnumbered have marched on Jerusalem, unnumbered multitudes have died to defend the ancient city, or lived in exile to deplore its fate. The earliest mention we have of the city outside the Bible (in the El-Amarna letters) is part of a plea for aid in defending the city from invaders. Here the Jebusites prayed to pagan gods for power to repel the Hebrews. The Hebrews, in turn, implored Jehovah for aid against the Assyrians, the Egyptians, and the Babylonians. Greeks and Romans bowed to strange gods before the walls of Jerusalem. Here came Crusades of Christian knights asking God to give them Jerusalem; while the Saracens, setting their lances to drive them back, invoked the aid of Allah to enable them to hold the Holy City. In our day, the streets of Jerusalem rang to the tread of military feet as the armies of the Allies under Allenby entered the city. Deep under the dust of the ages, successive sieges of the city are monumented in massive masonry, shattered almost to shapelessness by the tides of battle that tell the story of an often war-torn town. Here are reminders of Titus, of Nehemiah, of Nebuchadnezzar, of Hezekiah, of Solomon, and of David and of the Jebusites.

Parts of the northern wall must have been destroyed by the Hebrews. Since David built "from Millo and inward," it would seem that the Millo or citadel must have formed a part of, or been adjacent to, the northern defense system. Evidently it was a defensive feature of outstanding importance. 2 *Chronicles* 32 in describing the preparations made by Hezekiah to repel an expected assault on Jerusalem by the Assyrians states that he "repaired Millo in the city of David." Nehemiah in his excellent account of the rebuilding of Jerusalem after the return of the Hebrews from exile makes no mention of the Millo. Nehemiah, however, speaks of the "tower which lieth out" (See *Nehemiah* 3:25-28).

The exact meaning of the word *Millo* as used in the Old Testament is by no means clear. Evidently Millo is a Hittite word that crept into the Hebrew language. The literal meaning is "a filling between two walls." As used in connection with David's repairs to Jerusalem, the word undoubtedly meant a citadel, or tower.

The siege of Titus in 70 A. D. so completely altered the appearance of Jerusalem that it has been difficult to prove to the satisfaction of all authorities just where or what the Millo was. The work of Dr. Macalister,* who excavated at Jerusalem in 1923-1924, and his successor, J. G. Duncan,† has done much to clear up this difficulty. According to their deductions, based on scientific examination of the massive walls and foundations they uncovered, the Millo was located just above and just north of Gihon. The remains of the ancient tower are now being preserved as a national monument.

In the north wall of the City of David, Dr. Macalister believes that he has discovered "the breaches of the city of David," and the repairs made by Solomon (1 *Kings* 11:27). The discovery at the site of Jebusite, Davidic and Solomonic masonry indicates clearly that the historical narratives of events at Jerusalem in connection with David's capture of the city are placed in the correct historical framework.

David must have carried out other extensive building operations in addition to his repairs of the old city. The little fifteen-acre town of the Jebusites would not long accommodate the influx of population which would result from the establishment of the capital of the Hebrew kingdom at Jerusalem. Jerusalem was now the center of the social, political and religious life of Israel. Expansion was imperative. The city could only expand northward or by building on the western hill. Probably extensive suburbs sprang up around Jerusalem during the reign of David. David contemplated the erection of a temple (2 *Samuel* 7), and it is unlikely that he would consider placing such an edifice north of the old city unless there was adequate walled protection for it.

So David reigned over all Israel, and executed judgment and justice among all his people.—1 Chronicles 18:14

The capture of Jerusalem practically climaxed the conquest of Canaan. Israel's ancient enemies, the Amorite-Hittites, had been shattered and subdued. Only one powerful people, the Philistines, remained to challenge Hebrew control of Palestine. The day of decision was not long delayed. Twice, in the valley of Rephaim, the Philistines challenged Israel to combat, only to be slaughtered from "Geba until thou come to

---

*See *Quarterly Statement of the Palestine Exploration Fund,* Vol. IV.
†See *The Accuracy of the Old Testament,* by J. Garrow Duncan.

Gazer" (See 2 *Samuel* 5). The ending of the major campaign against the Philistines seems to be summed up in 2 *Samuel* 8:1—"David smote the Philistines and subdued them."

With the Philistine menace removed, David was free to devote his attention to international affairs. These were days when international treaties were largely written in blood. National boundaries were set by the sword. Fight or pay tribute was the order of the day. During the days when Israel was struggling for a foothold in Palestine arrogant neighbors had often collected tribute from the tribes. Times had changed. Israel was now the dominant power in western Asia. The day of reckoning had arrived for the nations which were left "to prove Israel" (See *Judges* 3:1). One by one, ancient enemies were brought to heel. The yoke of servitude was set on Moab, Ammon, Zobath and Edom. Even the powerful Syrian city of Damascus was garrisoned with Israelites (2 *Samuel* 8:6). The tiny territory which David originally governed grew to a small empire, stretching from Egypt to the Euphrates.

The City of David now became the cultural center of Israelitish idealism. The Ark of the Covenant now had a national home. It was natural that David should wish to rear a mighty sanctuary to house the symbol of the Lord God of Israel's protecting presence with His Chosen People. This privilege was denied him. However, when "David built an altar unto the Lord" on the famous field he purchased "for fifty shekels of silver," he sanctified the site on which his illustrious son raised the mighty temple which glorified the holy heights of Mt. Moriah for four hundred years.

During the reign of David the political power of Israel in Palestine was consolidated. Saul had governed Israel from under the greenwood tree (See 1 *Samuel* 22:6); David ruled Israel from "the king's high house." The finding of Hebrew pottery mingled with Canaanite pottery, dating from about B. C. 1000 onward, indicates that, with the exception of Gezer, all the Palestinian strongholds were in the hands of the Israelites.

Now the acts of David the king, first and last, behold, they are written in the book of Samuel the seer, and in the book of Nathan the prophet, and in the book of Gad the seer.—1 Chronicles 29:29

Of all the remarkable personal portraitures presented in the Old Testament, that of David is the most complete. While the completeness of the records of his reign is doubtless largely due to his importance in Hebrew history, some small part of their comprehensiveness must be due to the fact that the art of writing and the custom of keeping records had become more common by B. C. 1000 than was possible at earlier dates.

So far as is now known, the earliest system of writing originated in ancient Chaldea. At first this system was purely pictographic. Men were attempting to place connected thought in permanent record through realistic drawings on common clay. It is difficult to make realistic drawings on clay with a pointed reed or a sharpened bone. Lines on clay were naturally wedge-shaped. Gradually characteristic combinations of wedge-shaped markings took the place of the more difficult drawings, and thus was evolved the method of writing which today is called cuneiform, meaning "wedge-shaped."

The ancient Egyptians were more fortunate in finding a workable material for their records. The pith of the papyrus plant properly pressed and dressed made a paperlike substance on which realistic drawings were readily rendered. Necessity simplified this system. As the art of writing developed, characteristic drawings came to represent syllabic sounds. To this system modern scholars gave the name "hieroglyph," meaning "sacred carving," on the assumption that the writing was originally the work of priests.

During the days when cuneiform, hieroglyphic, and other forms derived from the pictographic were the only methods of writing known, correspondence and the keeping of official records must have been largely in the hands of professional scribes. Before the days of David, even before the Israelites under Joshua invaded Palestine, the art of writing had been much simplified. With advancement in methods, knowledge of the art became more widely disseminated. The archæological work of Schaeffer and Chenet at Ras Shamra, in northern Syria, has opened new chapters in the history of the art of writing.

When the Egyptians held sway in western Asia, they developed extensive copper mines on the Island of Cyprus. The crude ore was conveyed in sailing vessels to Ras Shamra, about a hundred miles due east of Cyprus, for smelting. The industrial town which grew up around the smelting works evidently became a great center of culture and education. In addition to many other important discoveries, the excavators uncovered a school for scribes where eight different languages were taught.*

Knowledge is never static. Initial conceptions on any subject must frequently be modified in the light of later information. Educators have long taught that our alphabet was originally devised by the Phoenicians. Probably the pedagogues are in error. The inhabitants of ancient Ras

---

*See *Secrets from the Syrian Hills*, by Claude F. A. Schaeffer, *National Geographic*.

Shamra used a finished alphabet containing only twenty-eight letters.*
They were using this before the days of David.

Modern scholarship in commenting on the Old Testament has always
assumed a lamentable lack of scholarship on the part of the early religious
leaders of Israel. However, if the inhabitants of Ras Shamra, during the
days of the Israelitish conquest of Canaan, were writing great epics and
odes in praise of pagan gods, is it not logical to assume, by inference,
that the highly intelligent Israelites were capable of producing profound
writings in praise of the Lord God of Israel?

The writings of the Ras Shamrites bespeak a people well advanced
in literature. They had dictionaries. These clay slate dictionaries listed
words of about the same meaning. They were real dictionaries of syno-
nyms. Since this people had made such strides along the royal road of
learning, it would seem passing strange if contemporary Hebrews in
nearby Palestine had not made similar progress. The Hebrews have always
been leaders in learning and literature. No people, past or present, has
produced prose or poetry surpassing that of ancient Israel. The wondrous
word-weaving and thought-rhythm which distinguish the work of a
later age of writing prophets was not a spontaneous product of their day.
The pathway for Isaiah, Jeremiah, and Ezekiel was prepared by generations of lofty-minded writers who preceded them. The glorious days of
Hebrew literature were dawning during the days of David.

David kept a court recorder, as well as an official scribe (See 2
Samuel 8:16, 17). The appointment of such officers in David's original
cabinet at Jerusalem indicates that David sensed the importance of accurate official records. David himself was a man of letters, one of the
great writers of his era.

The name of David is always associated with the *Psalms*. Most of
the contents of this great Book of Praise is dedicated to his name. Higher
literary honor would be difficult to attain. Few works in all literature
are more frequently quoted. Selections from this work are household
words throughout the civilized world. The great poems of praise and
prayer are taught to children at mother's knee; chanted in church and
synagogue; intoned in solemn cadence beside the tomb when loved ones
are laid to rest—ever an enduring literary monument to Israel's poet-king.

Although parts of the collected work, as it appears in the Old Testament, are ascribed by modern scholarship to authors other than David,
the *Psalms* are indelibly linked in the minds of mankind with "The Sweet
Singer of Israel." The poems admitted to be the work of David are un-
surpassable. Probably some of the *Psalms* are ancient songs of Israel

*See *A New Alphabet of the Ancients Unearthed,* by Claude F. A. Schaeffer,
National Geographic, Oct. 1930.

which David collected and polished with poetical phrase. Additions may have been made after his day. In the Septuagint, the Arabic, and the Ethiopic Versions of the *Psalms*, an extra poem, the 151st *Psalm*, appears. In our versions of the *Psalms* this poem is omitted, as it is undoubtedly spurious. It purports to tell the story of David's conflict with Goliath. The Psalms, David's song of praise for deliverance (2 *Samuel* 22), and his elegy over the death of Saul and Jonathan (2 *Samuel* 1:19-27) are outstanding poetical productions.

In reading Old Testament poetry, one should remember that songs like the *Psalms* are intended to be chanted by a double choir. One choir chanted a reading and the other chanted the response. Much Oriental poetry, ancient and modern, is written with this purpose in view. Even today, around Oriental campfires in the eventide, sometimes someone will suddenly quote or chant a part of a verse and another promptly furnish the finishing part. Occasionally this grows into a sort of "question and answer" game.

In the titles of some of the *Psalms*, as we read them, some guide-words, untranslated from the original, appear, like *Maschil*, instruction, or homily; *Michtam*, memorial; *Eduth*, testimony. *Gittith, Neginoth,* and *Nehiloth* are names of musical instruments.

In the Old Testament there are many words of no known derivation. Many of them are evidently words that crept into the Hebrew language from the tongues of peoples the Israelites met and mingled with. They are words borrowed from neighboring nations. In *Psalm* 74:14 we read: "Thou brakest the heads of the leviathan in pieces." Among the many epics found at Ras Shamra* is one describing a battle between Baal and a seven-headed serpent. "Leviathan" is the name used in the Ras Shamra text. The Ras Shamra text and *Isaiah* 27:1 both give realistic descriptions of this famous serpent. The sacred writers are using a creation of the pagan mind as a symbol of the evils the God of Israel would crush.

Evidently from the time of David onward, a record was kept of the "acts" of the kings. Although there is no mention of any book of the acts of Saul, we read that when Saul was anointed king, "Samuel told the people the manner of the kingdom, and wrote it in a book" (1 *Samuel* 10:25). In other words, Samuel wrote the original constitution of the Hebrew kingdom. The many references to the "Book of the Chronicles of the Kings of Israel" and the "Book of the Chronicles of the Kings of Judah" indicate that very complete records of the acts of the kings were kept in some type of book form. Perhaps they were kept in the form of a roll, as many ancient Egyptian manuscripts were kept. By the time of Jeremiah (about B. C. 600) documents were apparently

*See *Secrets from the Syrian Hills*, Schaeffer, *National Geographic.*

kept in the form of a roll. "And it came to pass, that when Jehudi had read three or four leaves, he cut it with the penknife, and cast it into the fire that was on the hearth, until all the roll was consumed in the fire"—*Jeremiah* 36:23.

In 1 *Chronicles* 29:29 we have an early instance of the prophets acting as national historians. Samuel had been David's spiritual advisor during the earlier years of the latter's reign. Nathan served in a similar capacity during the latter part of David's reign, and also carried on as recorder during a part of the reign of Solomon (See 2 *Chronicles* 9:29). Many of the original documents referred to in the Books of the *Kings* were probably official records kept by prophets. Isaiah acted as recorder for Uzziah (2 *Chronicles* 26:22) and also performed a similar service for Hezekiah.

Probably prophet recorders kept the annals of David's declining days. The narratives show the fiery-hearted hero of the Philistine campaigns shrinking toward the shadows of senility. The career that carried Israel to the completed conquest of Canaan, that crowned the conquest with the glory of a national capital at Jerusalem, that gave to Israel its long-sought place in the family of nations, was wrecked on the rocks of illicit love and domestic difficulty. No hero worshipper was the man who entered these narratives in the annals of Israel. The writer recognized a moral law that transcended the "divine rights" of kings. The ancient dictum, "My king can do no wrong," had no place in the minds of the prophets of Israel. Nathan's parable of the man rich in flocks and herds and of the poor man who had nothing "save one little ewe lamb," while meant to mirror the enormity of David's sin, reveals that at this early age the Israelites had a high conception of moral obligations. Israel was far in advance of any other people of that day in righteous living and religious thought.

The reign of David opened the era of Israel's greatest glory. His creative nationalizing work placed Israel in position to carry out its great mission. Over the ruins of the empire of the Hittites he reared the Hebrew kingdom. The city he selected for the capital of the kingdom became the world's most sacred city. His name and his deeds will never be forgotten as long as Jerusalem stands.

X

THE GOLDEN AGE OF ISRAEL

Then sat Solomon upon the throne of David his father; and his kingdom was established greatly.—1 Kings 2:12

THE reign of Solomon was the Golden Age of Israel. This was Israel's imperial day. Political power in Palestine rested in the hands of the Hebrews. The rise of this race to political power and prominence is without parallel in history. A nation of nomads, motivated by an amazing mixture of political purpose and spiritual idealism, climbed to world eminence over the ruins of other early rising civilizations. The story of this rise is one of the most romantic records in all the annals of time.

The rise of races and the development of nations have generally been governed by geographical location and certain economic factors. Food and the means for its distribution have always been prime factors in racial and national development. Our modern world is governed, and long will be governed, by the powers which control four great staples: grain, cotton, iron, and coal—food for man and food for man's machines. These are the keys of modern empire. Modern agricultural methods may increase indefinitely the production of grain. The same is true, in lesser degree, of cotton. Iron is widely distributed throughout the earth's crust. Iron deposits may be almost useless unless abundant fuel for smelting is readily available. The coal measures of the world are very closely delimited. Wherever coal and iron are found in close proximity, there great industrial centers inevitably arise. Modern empire rests on natural resources and national ability to protect them. When, at the close of the Russo-Japanese War, the former "Hermit Kingdom" suddenly found itself a world power, the sagacious Japanese realized that if they were long to remain a first-class power they must secure plentiful supplies of the great essentials—coal and iron. Their own country was poor in these raw materials. Over on the Asiatic mainland lay vast unworked deposits of both. The eyes and the arms of Japan turned toward China. Minerals were the magnet that drew Italy into Ethiopia. The hands which hold the earth's resources pave the paths of modern empire.

In the early Old Testament days, agricultural areas and pasture lands were the great economic factors which shaped the history of rising civilizations. The earliest civilizations arose on the rich alluvial soils of the river valleys. When these sections became crowded, ambitious rulers invaded the territories of their lesser neighbors to plunder, pillage, and collect tribute. Such was the history of all the ancient empires of the east. The history of the Hebrews, however, was largely shaped by an intangible factor hitherto unknown in the annals of national growth. This was the religious psychology peculiar to the Chosen People. This factor must be noted if the history of the Hebrews is to appear in proper perspective. The all-pervading influence of religious idealism was woven into the warp and woof of political expediency. The rise of the Hebrews sometimes ran contrary to accepted rules of national growth. Hebrew nationalism was founded on and built by religious idealism. The Old Testament writers recognized this factor. It was the dominant factor in their recording of history. They interpreted the current historical events in accordance with their conception of Jehovah's covenant with his Chosen People. For cherishing the God-given ideals of Abraham and faithfully keeping the covenants concerning them, "the seed of Abraham" were promised certain rewards. While, in the larger sense, these rewards were to be reaped in the realm of the spirit, there were also promises of material gain; not for Abraham but for his descendants: "And I will make of thee a great nation" (*Genesis* 12:2).

Hebrew nationalism was of slow and painful birth. Only a people endowed with exceptional spiritual fortitude could have constantly kept on persevering toward such a distant goal. To a people sunk in slavery for centuries, nationalism must have seemed a dream of a far, faint future. The weary wandering through the wilderness must have tried the stoutest hearts. The dark days of the Judges had seen the national aspirations of Israel crushed again and again. The national spirit, which soared when Saul was anointed king at Gilgal, sank when he was slain on the slopes of Mt. Gilboa. Finally, the intrepid David had crushed the enemies of Israel. Independent Hebrew nationalism had been achieved. The banners of Israel floated over Jerusalem, the capital of the kingdom. Kingdoms rise and fall: righteous idealism endures eternally. Time took the Hebrew kingdom as it takes all kingdoms reared by man. The spiritual idealism of Israel still endures; is still paramount in the Jewish world; is still the firm foundation of Christianity.

David, the first of his regal line, was not of royal birth. Life had led him from a sheep-cote to a throne. His illustrious son, Solomon, was born to the purple. The anointing of Solomon as king of Israel marked a day of fulfillment. A royal king ruled the Chosen People. Well might an exultant Israel greet the new king with shouts of "God save king Solomon."

Solomon had inherited a well organized kingdom. Ambition urged him to develop the kingdom into a great empire. Early in his reign he selected a cabinet and divided the kingdom into twelve administrative districts. The same form of administration had been used by the Canaanites and by the Egyptians, as is amply proved by Hittite and Egyptian inscriptions. Solomon, however, made one important change. Instead of the numerous city-kingdoms of the Hittites were the limited number of districts, each governed by an officer whose duty it was to administer the laws and collect the revenue. It was also the duty of the twelve regional officers to provide the food for the royal table: "Each man his month in a year made provision" (1 *Kings* 4:7).

In addition to organizing his court and the internal affairs of his kingdom, Solomon entered into treaties of alliance with the rulers of surrounding countries. Diplomacy was superseding the sword in the arrangement of international affairs. Solomon sealed several of these political treaties with matrimonial alliances. The most noteworthy of these was his early marriage with the daughter of the Pharaoh of Egypt. Solomon did not originate this custom of uniting royal households through marriage. It was already an old one.

In the early years of his reign Solomon's administration brought peace and plenty to a country that for centuries had been an almost constant theatre of war. That "his kingdom was established greatly" is summed up in the words: "And Judah and Israel dwelt safely, every man under his vine and under his fig tree, from Dan even to Beersheba" (1 *Kings* 4:25).

And the Lord gave Solomon wisdom, as he promised him: and there was peace between Hiram and Solomon; and they two made a league together.—1 Kings 5:12

Jerusalem (in David's day) had been but little more than a fortress. The imperially-minded Solomon visioned the rebuilding of the city of such size and beauty as would be worthy of an Oriental potentate. Here he would rear a mighty walled city suitable for the contemplated splendor of his court and kingdom. He would extend the city walls to enclose the suburbs on the western hill. On the eastern hill to the north of the city of David, on the old threshing floor of the Jebusites, he would erect a great temple complex, and crown the holy height with a glittering gem of architecture to house the Holy of Holies in which would be enshrined the Ark of the Covenant.

Solomon's contemplated building program included not only the capital city of Jerusalem, but many other cities which had been Canaanite strongholds before the Israelitish conquest. Such a building program would be utterly beyond the artistic and architectural skill of Hebrew artisans of that period. The pre-Solomonic Hebrews had little experience in building. The ruins of the sacred city of Shiloh, long the sanctuary of the Ark of the Covenant, show that the early Israelites knew practically nothing of the art of building. They had no need to build cities. They took them. "And I have given you a land for which ye did not labor, and cities which ye built not" (*Joshua* 24:13). Both brains and brawn must be imported to carry out Solomon's ambitious plans.

Facing such a dilemma, Solomon must turn to some country with which he had a treaty of alliance. The Assyrians were great city builders, but most of their cities were built with clay products. The Egyptians had built monumental structures in stone, but the great building age of Egypt was past. Tyre, a near neighbor, possessed men with building skills acquired through the building of their own magnificent capital. Here was the logical solution of Solomon's problem.

Long before Jerusalem became the capital city of the Hebrews and for four hundred years afterward, Tyre was one of the wonder cities of the world. It was a great maritime city, the Mistress of the Mediterranean, gathering wealth from the water-borne commerce of every land. The faultless phrases of the scholarly Ezekiel tell of the beauty and riches of the maritime metropolis in the twenty-seventh chapter of the book that bears his name. Although all that remains of ancient Tyre lies under the blue waters of the Mediterranean, its history is well known.

Ezekiel prophesied that Tyre would be destroyed by Nebuchadnezzar (See *Ezekiel* 26:7). He also foretold the fate of Tyre for hundreds of years after both he and Nebuchadnezzar had joined their fathers in dust. His malediction against Tyre included not only the city itself, but also its ruins and the very earth that covered the rocks on which the ancient city stood:—"And I will make thee like the top of a rock: thou shalt be a place to spread nets upon" (*Ezekiel* 26:14).

When Alexander the Great was sweeping over the Near East, his armies, in B. C. 332, arrived at the site where ancient Tyre had stood and found that a new city had been erected on an island and was protected from invasion by a strip of water half a mile wide. A less determined man might have been deterred from attack by such an obstacle, but not Alexander. He set his legions at work hurling the massive ruins left by Nebuchadnezzar into the sea to form a causeway from the mainland to the island. When the great mass of ruins proved insufficient for his purpose, he ordered the dust and debris scraped from the site of the ancient city, leaving it bare rock which fishermen have since found an admirable place for drying nets. Such was the fate of Tyre.

In Solomon's day Tyre was still rising in magnificence. Here were skilled workers in wood and stone and clever craftsmen capable of converting Solomon's dream city into a masterpiece of enduring stone. Solomon naturally turned to his revered father's friend, "for Hiram was ever a lover of David" (1 *Kings* 5:1), when in need of engineering and architectural assistance.

And, behold, I purpose to build an house unto the name of the Lord my God, as the Lord spake unto David my father.—1 Kings 5:5

During the Old Testament period the building of a temple did not consist of the erection of a single great sanctuary, as was common in later ages. The Oriental custom was to dedicate a sacred area for purposes of worship. This holy ground was protected from profanation by a heavy wall. Within the walls would be the temple, or temples, proper; the headquarters of the religious administration; the residential quarters for the priesthood, and, in pagan cities, where the gods of the city were looked upon as rulers administering through the king, it was the custom to include the official residence of the ruler.

Jerusalem was the capital of a religious people. Israel predicated all its national success on the sustaining power of the Lord God of the Hebrews. The great temple, looming above the walls, would be a constantly visible reminder of Israel's dependence on Jehovah. In addition to the temple the sacred area would contain the Hall of Pillars, the House of the Forest of Lebanon, the Throne Hall, the Royal Palace, the Palace for the Daughter of Pharaoh, and other necessary buildings. Surrounded by proper planting would be an artistic architectural creation worthy of king Solomon's splendor.

The site for the temple had been selected by David. Here he had "built there an altar unto the Lord" (2 *Samuel* 24:25). The site had been sacred long before David's day. Probably primitive man came from his caves under the hill to implore his strange gods for aid to repel the invaders who brought to the country the first crude traces of rising civilization. Here on the hill the Amorite and the Hittite worshipped. Cup marks the Canaanites cut on their altars show on the rocks today. Abraham offered sacrifice here. Solomon's sanctuary set the seal of sacredness on the site for all time, made it the most significant spot of religious history. This hill of history is holy to the Jewish world and to all the hosts of Christendom, and is second only to Mecca in the mind of the Moslem.

Solomon started the erection of the temple about B. C. 977. After four hundred years of glory this temple was destroyed by Nebuchadnezzar. It is ironic that of the two greatest builders of the Old Testament period, the one should have destroyed the masterpiece of the other.

In B. C. 516, Israel, returning from Babylonian captivity, reared a second temple on the site. This second temple, smaller and less glorious than the first, rose, stark and alone, above the blackened ruins of the city that had once been the pride and glory of the Hebrew kingdom. Aged men, who remembered the glory of king Solomon's temple, wept when they beheld its successor.

About eighteen years before the birth of Our Lord the second temple was removed and replaced by the third temple. When Herod the Great became ruler of Jerusalem in B. C. 37, another great builder appeared upon the scene. Herod had an inordinate ambition to rebuild all the cities of Palestine. The fortifications of Jerusalem were entirely rebuilt. Beautiful buildings arose within the walls. These included a great palace for Herod. Compared with the great structures erected by Herod, the five-century-old second temple must have seemed a shabby old edifice. Herod determined to replace it with a larger and more modern structure.* The proposal to tamper with the temple aroused the indignation and fears of the Jews. Herod finally won them over by allowing the Jews to perform the work themselves, under the supervision of the priests. The Jews would not permit any departure from the ground dimensions of the old temple, but the height was greatly increased.

The third temple was the temple Our Saviour knew. Although this sanctuary was in use throughout the earthly lifetime of Our Lord it was never entirely completed until long after He had died on the cross. The walls were erected in eighteen months, but work on the decorations dragged slowly. When Jesus drove the money changers from the temple it had been forty-six years in building (See *John* 2:20). The final embellishments of the temple were not added until 64 A. D., and six years later this temple was destroyed by Titus.

About 130 A. D., Hadrian, emperor of Rome, attempted to end Jewish influence forever by ordering the sacred area cleared and the site sown with salt. To complete his work he had a temple of Jupiter erected on the holy hill. In 277 A. D. the ruins of this temple were removed and a great Temple of Bacchus was reared on the site. This was converted into a Christian church by the Byzantine emperor Justinian in 534 A. D.

In the seventh century A. D. a wave of Moslem invasion swept over the Near-East. Jerusalem fell. The Crescent supplanted the Cross. The enclosing walls of the sacred area were entirely rebuilt. The ruins of Justinian's church were swept away to make room for beautiful Saracenic structures. Over the rock where Abraham offered sacrifice arose the magnificent mosque often erroneously called the Mosque of Omar. The Caliph Abd el-Malek was the real builder.

---

*See Josephus, *Antiquities of the Jews,* Book XV, Chap. XI.

ARAB WORKMEN REMOVING COLUMN

By permission of The Museum of the University of Pennsylvania

The beautiful building, which is known to "the Faithful" as "Haram esh Sherif" (meaning in Arabic "The Noble Sanctuary"), covers the rock that is sacred to the Moslems. From it the Mohammedans believe the Prophet ascended to heaven mounted on his human-faced steed. From the Arabic "Kubbet es-Sakhra" comes the well-known name, "The Dome of the Rock."

During the days of the Christian Crusades (1096 to 1271 A. D.) the knights held the city for about a hundred years. The Cross surmounted the famous mosque. Then the gallant Saladin drove the Crusaders from the holy hill and out of Palestine. Once more the Crescent supplanted the Cross. The only memento of the Crusades still in the building is an iron grill erected by the knights to guard the rock which has been worn smooth by the kisses of millions of pilgrims.

The site selected for king Solomon's temple stood apart from the other portions of the site of ancient Jerusalem. Its commanding position marked it as a logical site for a fortress, since it could be defended apart from the city. Unfortunately, the tides of war have rolled so frequently over the temple site that not a single stone remains that may definitely be identified as having been a part of the famous temple. The exquisite masonry cut by Hiram's workmen has undoubtedly been used and reused in the frequent rebuilding of Jerusalem. Of the outer enclosing walls of the sacred area it is probable that some portions of the lower foundation walls remain *in situ*. Sir Charles Warren, in his extensive excavations at Jerusalem, discovered twenty-one courses of masonry bearing workmen's markings in Phoenician characters. This he identifies as Solomonic masonry.*

Authorities on the subject of king Solomon's temple describe the details of the temple according to their varying predilections. Some scholars follow the specifications given by Josephus in Book VIII, Chapter III, of his *Antiquities of the Jews,* while others base their reconstructions on the works of still later historians. While the writings of Josephus give a much more detailed account of the building of the temple than is found in 1 *Kings* 6 and 2 *Chronicles* 3, it must be remembered that Josephus knew Jerusalem long after Solomon's temple had been destroyed. The Herodian, or third, temple was standing in the days of Josephus. On the other hand, the annalists who compiled the original documents of *Kings* and *Chronicles* actually saw and knew the original temple. Since Josephus differs from the Old Testament annalists on important points, on which *Kings* and *Chronicles* agree, it would seem the safer course to accept the Biblical accounts as written.

*See *Jerusalem,* by Warren and Condor, page 148.

11

It seems clear that the sacred area lay just to the north of the City of David, on the site of the old Jebusite threshing floor, with the temple occupying the highest point of the hill. Ezekiel, who knew the temple well, having served there as a priest before the captivity, indicates that the temple faced toward the east (See *Ezekiel* 8:14).

As a building, the temple was impressive for its ornate beauty and the splendor of its setting and surroundings, rather than for its size. It was not intended as a gathering place for common worship. Congregational worship, as we understand it today, did not come into common practice until the time of Nebuchadnezzar. The primary purpose of the temple was to house suitably the Ark of the Covenant. Here in glory and majesty would be enshrined the visible symbol of the protecting presence of Jehovah. To the devout Hebrew, this would be truly the dwelling-place of the Lord God of Israel. Only the sanctified and purified priesthood could enter its sacred precincts. Beyond the outer courts of the temple complex the populace could not penetrate.

The style of the building would seem to indicate that David, in preparing the plans he later gave to Solomon (See 1 *Chronicles* 28:11), was influenced somewhat by Egyptian architecture. This would be quite natural, since impressive Egyptian architecture was still standing in the cities of northern Palestine. The ground dimensions of the temple proper, according to commonly accepted measurements, were 124 feet long by 50 feet wide. The main part of the building, about 104½ by 34½ feet, rose to a height of 55 feet. On both sides and the western end of the building were ranged the three stories of chambers described in 1 *Kings* 6:5, 6. The bearing walls, on which the floor beams rested, varied in thickness with each floor level, thus giving varying dimensions to the superimposed chambers, as is indicated in verse 6. The pillared porch on the eastern end was evidently the outstanding external architectural feature of the building (See 1 *Kings* 6:3). In addition to the main entrance on the eastern front, there was evidently an entrance door on the northern side. 1 *Kings* 6:8 states this was "in the right side," while Ezekiel describes it as looking toward the north, which agrees with the statement in *Kings*.

The three-storied chambers built "against the house round about" would confine the admission of daylight to a limited area high up on the outer walls of "the house." "And for the house he made windows of narrow lights" (1 *Kings* 6:4). This would suggest the Egyptian method of lighting large structures. This consisted of cutting rows of long narrow slits in thin sheets of stone, and inserting these sheets, with the slits vertical, at regular intervals in the outer walls. The slanting shafts of light, striking down on the gleaming gold of the temple furnishings, must have lighted up a scene of awe-inspiring majesty.

If we could, on some mental "magic carpet," project ourselves backward through time-space some three thousand years, and vision ourselves as tourists in "the little city of David," we might gaze northward and upward at the greatest architectural glory of the ancient East. If we could forget our unworthy lives and imagine ourselves clothed with sufficient priestly grace to be deemed worthy of admission to the sacred precincts, we might dream of some goodly guide leading us on a personally-conducted tour through the breath-taking beauty and glory of the holy heights.

Ascending the hill and passing through the great gates, we would find ourselves in the great court before the "house of the forest of Lebanon" (1 *Kings* 7:2). This "house of the forest" is evidently an artistic conception of a proper method of tying the entire architectural plan down to its site—an appropriate link between nature and art. This motif is stressed in the "four rows of cedar pillars" of the lower floor, and the "forty-five pillars, fifteen in a row," of the upper floor. The lighting of the great building, which is 174 feet long by 80 feet wide, "light . . . against light in three ranks," suggests the forest from which the giant cedars came, with leaf-filtered light striking against the trunks of the dark-crowned cedars. The living green of the surrounding landscaping completes the picture.

Passing through "the house of the forest" we come to the "porch of pillars" leading to the throne room and the administrative headquarters of the king. Here, seated in majesty on an ivory throne, Israel's mightiest monarch judged his people. Since we are but humble tourists, we will not intrude to the inner court where stands the king's "own house" and the "house for Pharaoh's daughter, whom he had taken to wife." Rather than disturb the regal residences, we move along the passage to the eastward and enter the court which surrounds the temple. This is the "inner court," enclosed "with three rows of hewed stone and a row of cedar beams" (1 *Kings* 6:36).

Approaching the great eastern entrance to the temple, we pass on the left the great bronze laver described in 1 *Kings* 7:23-26. The rim of the great bowl, "wrought like the brim of a cup with flowers of lilies," looms far above our heads. The Palestinian sun glows on its glittering surface and lights up the lines of the twelve great brazen oxen which, oriented by threes to the cardinal points of the compass, bear on their backs the "molten sea."

Directly before the temple stands a great bronze altar. This is the altar on which king Solomon placed "a thousand burnt offerings" (2 *Chronicles* 1:5, 6). This is the altar that Ahaz later profaned with his idolatry (See 2 *Kings* 16:14).

Crossing the temple porch, with its monumental portal pillars, Jachin and Boaz, we enter the heavy hush of the Holy Place. This is a great room seventy feet long. Through "the windows of narrow lights" shoot shafts of sunlight, dimly illumining walls of polished cedar decorated with glittering gold, and bringing out the design of cherubim wrought on the near side of "the vail of blue, and crimson, and fine linen" (2 *Chronicles* 3:14) which shrouds the inner end of the room. Beyond that veil we may not pass. Behind it is the "holy of holies, in which is enshrined the Ark of the Covenant." This "most holy house," from which even sunlight is excluded, is not for our eyes.

And all the cities of store that Solomon had, and cities for his chariots, and cities for his horsemen, and that which Solomon desired to build in Jerusalem, and in Lebanon, and all the land of his dominion.—1 Kings 9:19

No small part of Solomon's fame rests on his reputation as a builder. Although his greatest building campaign centered upon the building of the temple and the beautification of Jerusalem, the rest of the kingdom was not overlooked in Solomon's plans for reconstruction.

From the standpoint of national security, the rebuilding and fortifying of some of the cities mentioned in 1 *Kings* 9 were even more important than the rebuilding of Jerusalem. Some of these cities guarded the life lines of the kingdom. International trade was an important factor in the economic life of the Hebrew kingdom. The annalists, in 1 *Kings* 10 and 2 *Chronicles* 9, indicate that international trade was centering in Jerusalem. Wealth was flowing toward Jerusalem from all points of the compass. While part of this wealth was undoubtedly tribute from subjugated neighboring nations, the great bulk of it was the harvest of international trade. Regardless of source of origin, this wealth had to be protected in transit. While Solomon possessed a navy, the major portion of commerce still followed the ancient trade routes, the international highways. The envious eyes of the foreigner would not long overlook the golden stream flowing into the coffers of the Hebrew kingdom.

David had conquered all of Palestine with the exception of the city of Gezer. Gezer was an important stronghold guarding the mouth of the valley of Ajalon. For centuries this city had defied the Israelites. Finally it fell to the Egyptians, and was handed over by the Pharaoh "for a present unto his daughter, Solomon's wife" (1 *Kings* 9:16). This addition to the queen's dowry must have been welcomed by the Hebrews. The conquest of Canaan was now complete. Naturally a city which had just been damaged by siege and fire would call for extensive rebuilding.

The site of Gezer has been very extensively explored by Dr. Macalister.*
Like the ancient city of Jebus (Jerusalem), Gezer had a rock-cut tunnel
leading to an underground spring which served as a water supply in
times of siege. The city was guarded with a heavy wall. About the time
of Solomon, a series of towers was added to this wall. Dr. Macalister
believes these to have been part of the work mentioned in 1 *Kings* 9:15.

Megiddo has always been a strategic key to military and commercial
operations in northern Palestine. The city guarded the old trade route
from Egypt between the Lebanons to the east. Megiddo was first explored
by the Deutscher Palastina-Verein (German Palestine Society) in 1903.
The latest exploration at this site was inaugurated by the Oriental Institute
of the University of Chicago in 1925. This work is still being carried
on. Among the more important finds were extensive stables erected by
king Solomon. These buildings were erected of excellently cut stone. The
roofs, now gone, were supported by stone columns, which also served as
hitching posts. Between the columns were mangers. The floors were of
lime mortar. These stables would provide accommodation for three hundred horses. Living quarters for grooms were provided, as well as storage
space for chariots and harness.†

Before the reign of Solomon the Hebrews apparently made little use
of horses, either for war purposes or as beasts of burden. Joshua had
ruthlessly destroyed horses by "houghing" them (See *Joshua* 11:9).
David employed the same practice against most of the horses captured from
Hadadezer (See 2 *Samuel* 8:4). Solomon, however, seems to have made
extensive use of horses. 1 *Kings* 10:28 mentions that Solomon imported
horses from Egypt, while verse 26 of the same chapter states: "And
Solomon gathered together chariots and horsemen: and had a thousand
and four hundred chariots, and twelve thousand horsemen, whom he
bestowed in the cities for chariots." Evidently Megiddo was one of "the
cities for chariots," and the building of the stables was part of the work
indicated in 1 *Kings* 9:15.

Hazor, another city mentioned in connection with Solomon's rebuilding
work, was an ancient Canaanite concentration camp, west of the Jordan
near Lake Huleh. It was near Lake Huleh (the waters of Merom) that
Joshua met and defeated a coalition of kings under "Jabin king of Hazor"
(See *Joshua* 11). The site of Hazor was located by Dr. John Garstang,
and explored by him in 1926 and 1928. The site had been protected by a
moat about one hundred feet wide and an earth embankment about sixty
feet high.‡

---

*See *The Excavation of Gezer*, by R. A. S. Macalister.
†See *New Light from Armageddon*, by P. L. O. Guy.
‡See *Annals of Archæology of the University of Liverpool*, Vol. XIV.

"Tadmor in the wilderness" (1 *Kings* 9:18) guarded the gateway to Hebron. This town would be an important factor in preventing invasion from the desert tribes.

Although Taanach is not mentioned by name in this connection, it must have been one of the cities that Solomon rebuilt "in all the land of his dominion." The north fort at Taanach and its outlying tower are the best preserved specimens of Solomon's building work extant.

Israel's national growth and development in Palestine are reflected in the records of their religious centers or capitals. The Hebrews were still a tribal people when they first penetrated Palestine. The crossing of the Jordan was a landmark in their history. Such an important event should be properly marked and monumented. The spot where the tribes first gathered to praise their God and observe the Passover in the Promised Land would ever after be sacred soil. A crude people, without tools, could erect only a crude memorial. "And those twelve stones, which they took out of Jordan, did Joshua pitch in Gilgal" (*Joshua* 4:20). "Wherefore the name of the place is called Gilgal unto this day" (*Joshua* 5:9). A "gilgal" is an arrangement of unhewn stones set up in a circle. Primitive men, in many lands, had used this type of monumentation from time immemorial. Gilgals are found today in many widely scattered places. The Israelites did the best they could with the materials at hand. Gilgal long remained a sacred center of the Hebrews. Here "they made Saul king before the Lord" (1 *Samuel* 11:15).

When advancing Israel found it necessary to build a town to protect the Ark of the Covenant, a site was selected high in the hill country of Ephraim. This was Shiloh. Here rose the first purely Israelitish city. The ruins of this remarkable town show that Israel had advanced far from tribalism, but still knew little of architecture or of building.

It was a far cry from primitive Gilgal and crudely constructed Shiloh to the polished perfection of Solomon's temple-crowned capital at Jerusalem. Israel had traveled far along a tortuous trail. The tented tribes of nomads, who had gathered around a circle of unhewn stones to hymn their praises to Jehovah by the light of the smoking torch, had been followed by a posterity which now magnified the glory of the Most High in a sublime sanctuary set in solemn splendor on the holy heights of Jerusalem. The tented tabernacle made of ram skins and badger skins had been succeeded by a glittering gem of polished stone and gold-encrusted cedar. The altar-enshrined glory of Jerusalem reflected the rise of a truly religious people to nationalism. Israel had arrived at a long-sought goal.

And king Solomon raised a levy out of all Israel.—1 Kings 5:13
But of the children of Israel did Solomon make no bondmen.—
1 Kings 9:22

Solomon's building program called for technical skill, treasure, and man-power. Hiram of Tyre supplied the technically trained workmen under treaty and contract. Part of the treasure for the construction of the temple had been collected by David and turned over to Solomon (See 1 *Chronicles* 29:1-9). However, treasure far beyond anything David could possibly have contemplated was urgently needed. Tribute and trade turned in treasure almost untold (See 1 *Kings* 10:27-29; 2 *Chronicles* 9:10-28). When funds from tribute and trade proved insufficient the king resorted to exhaustive taxation. This policy was provocative of much future trouble (See 1 *Kings* 12; 2 *Chronicles* 10). The solution of the labor problem was more easily found. Solomon simply resorted to a labor levy. Forced labor had long been used in the East. The ancient Egyptians built many of their great public works through the use of this system. The working of the system is depicted on many Egyptian monuments. Under it Israel had formerly suffered (See *Exodus* 1 and 5). The Turks made use of this system in Palestine up to the time of the late World War. The levies were called up monthly between seed time and harvest. Solomon had a ready reservoir of such labor. The Canaanite tribes still living in Palestine must have furnished an almost unlimited supply (See 1 *Kings* 9:20, 21).

Solomon possessed real genius for government. Under his rule Israel rose to its greatest national glory. Palestine progressed as it never had before. Peace and plenty blessed the age-old fighting ground. Domestic and international trade was promoted and protected. Diplomatic relations with powerful empires east and west were maintained. Local peoples who had long plagued Israel were effectively subdued (See 1 *Kings* 9:20). Solomon's "kingdom was established greatly."

And he spake three thousand proverbs: and his songs were a thousand and five.—1 Kings 4:32

The establishment of Jerusalem as the capital of the Hebrew kingdom opened an epoch of great literary production. Jerusalem became a seat of ecclesiastical learning. This city cradled the greatest writers of all time. Here the soul-songs of Israel found expression in the *Psalms;* distilled wisdom and profound philosophical thought were shaped into the pungent paragraphs of the *Proverbs;* the great school of prophetic writers thundered warnings to a people ever prone to turn from the Lord their God; history and religious teaching were woven into the immortal classic we know as the Old Testament.

Although the greatest of the inspired writers of the Old Testament belong to a later period, there can be little doubt that the Golden Age of Israel witnessed a great period of literary production. The great religious appeals of the writing prophets derive from the days when the Hebrew kingdom was disintegrating. The fall of Jerusalem inspired Jeremiah's poetical *Lamentations*. Only a soul sunk deep in disillusionment could sense the sorrow shown in *Ecclesiastes;* only a sublime soul could have preached the majestic measures portraying old age found in the twelfth chapter of the book. The decline of the Hebrew kingdom inspired the greatest writing of any age, but the rise of the Hebrew kingdom opened the great literary era.

Although modern scholarship may assign a date as late as B. C. 350 to the compilation of the *Proverbs,* they will always be associated with the name of Solomon. Who can say with safety when they were written? Probably many of the *Proverbs* are much older than Solomon. The Oriental loves to lard his speech with proverbs. All Asiatic peoples make extensive use of them. The present writer has listened to glittering gems of wisdom drop from the lips of Chinese children, only to read them later in the works of Confucius. In Solomon's day there was many a writer who could have recorded the *Proverbs*. There would seem to be nothing anachronistic in assuming that Solomon may have been the original compiler.

Critical comment on *The Song of Solomon* runs the range from the ridiculous to the sublime. To add to it would be useless labor. Ancient Oriental poetry may have many a hidden meaning. "The song of songs" might have been written in any age. There is no reason to doubt that it is the song "which is Solomon's."

Now that it is known that the art of writing was invented long before even the oldest book of the Bible purports to have been written, and since it was in use in Palestine before the Israelites began their famous conquest, it seems idle to assume that the Hebrews could not have kept accurate historical records long before they ever had a king.

The reign of Solomon marked the zenith of Hebrew nationalism in Palestine. After his death came disruption and decline. No people known to history ever rose to political power so rapidly; no people ever had a more dismal or more dramatic downfall. In secular history, the founding of the Hebrew kingdom would have been an insignificant event but for the fact that the spiritual idealism of Israel altered the currents of religious thought throughout almost the entire world.

XI

THE DIVISION OF THE KINGDOM

Wherefore the Lord said unto Solomon, Forasmuch as this is done of thee, and thou hast not kept my covenant and my statutes, which I have commanded thee, I will surely rend the kingdom from thee.
—1 Kings 11:11

THE Hebrew kingdom was a wonder-child in the family of nations. The rise of the Hebrews to political power and prominence in Palestine was phenomenal. Israel reared a kingdom over the great battlefields of the ages. Across its territory stretched the great land bridge over which the currents of international conflict had intermittently risen and receded for centuries. In the land where all the rising civilizations of the ancient East had struggled for supremacy, an inspired people had created a kingdom. Serving an unseen God, relying on His assurances, they had dedicated that kingdom to the service of the Most High.

Under David the great forces which created the Hebrew kingdom, religious idealism and political purpose, had been properly co-ordinated. The conquest of Canaan had been completed. The confederated tribes of Israel were knit into national unity. Jerusalem became the national capital of an independent people. David left a settled kingdom to his distinguished son.

Israel grew to its greatest national glory under Solomon: "And he reigned over all the kings from the river" (i. e., the Euphrates) "even unto the land of the Philistines, and to the border of Egypt" (2 *Chronicles* 9:26). Into this empire poured the portable wealth of the world (See 2 *Chronicles* 9:13-28). Jerusalem became a world capital. Above the city's enlarged walls loomed the great sanctuary, a solemn sentinel of Jehovah's guardianship over His Chosen People.

In the days of Solomon's greatest glory, destructive trends began to appear in the internal organization of Israel's national life. Troubles were brewing in the religious, political, social, and economic structure. The deepening shadow of coming national eclipse was already discernible to the prophetic-eyed scholars who were recording the annals of Israel's imperial day.

Solomon's ambitious building program had brought about a great period of prosperity. Palestine enjoyed a building boom. Solomon's far-reaching plans called for national expenditure that outran the financial resources of a country like Palestine. Excessive taxation bled the country white. The pocket nerve is extremely sensitive. Discontent was rampant.

While Solomon lived it was unlikely that smoldering discontent would flame into active rebellion. The dominant Solomon overawed his subjects, but the signs of the times augured ill for his successor. Ancient enemies nursed undying hatred of the Hebrews for ousting them from their lands. Hadad was stirring up trouble in Edom (See 1 *Kings* 11:14). At Damascus, the Syrians, under Rezon, were actively hostile (See 1 *Kings* 11:23). Nearer to the capital, Jeroboam, "a mighty man of valor," who had been a district governor under Solomon, entered the political picture to such an extent that Solomon sought his life.

Farther afield, the scenes on the stage of international politics were shifting. Assyria was again in the ascendant. Egypt was looking eagerly eastward toward Palestinian provinces that had once been hers. Neighboring nations bided their time. Coming events were casting ominous shadows before them.

The royal recorders were religious men. Naturally, they viewed with alarm the rapidly multiplying signs of coming national disintegration. Imbued with a consciousness that the Hebrew kingdom had been established only through the intervention and sustaining power of Jehovah, they ascribed the degenerative forces at work in the kingdom to decadence in the spiritual life of Israel and its king. To hold the country for which the nation's bravest and best had worked and prayed, fought and fell, Israel must preserve the idealism of Abraham and observe the laws of Moses.

The annalists attribute the beginning of the downfall of the kingdom to the infiltration of pagan forms of worship into the religious life of Israel. They charge the foreign wives of Solomon with being the medium through which the abhorrent worship of Ashtoreth and Milcom had been introduced.

For it came to pass, when Solomon was old, that his wives turned away his heart after other gods: and his heart was not perfect with the Lord his God.—1 Kings 11:4

The better minds among the Israelites attributed the great national development to the working out of the covenant with Jehovah. To them the keeping of the covenant meant the keeping of the kingdom. Naturally they viewed with horror the spectacle of their great king, Solomon, making concessions to idolatry. With Solomon erecting altars to pagan gods, religious unity in Israel was impossible. The covenant and the kingdom were both in danger.

Solomon's passion for imperialism found expression in many ways. Apparently he set out to overshadow all the Oriental monarchs of his day. History shows that Oriental monarchs have always been extremely casual in acquiring women in their royal households. Probably a large proportion of Solomon's matrimonial alliances were not the result of amorous adventure. They were merely a part of the increment accruing to Solomon from international and intertribal treaties.

Solomon was now old. Perhaps incipient senility was sapping the strength of his once mighty mind. Swayed by the counsel of his wives, "Solomon went after Ashtoreth the goddess of the Zidonians, and after Milcom." The intelligence and ability which formerly found expression in erecting sacred structures to glorify the name of the Lord God of Israel were now devoted to erecting altars to pagan gods.

The writers whose annalistic notes have come down to us in *Kings* and *Chronicles* were primarily interested in religion. They interpreted history in the light of their faith. Their records and their editorial surveys reflect this tendency. This is particularly true of the recorders of the Davidic Dynasty. Prophets of Israel kept the records of "the acts of Solomon" (See 2 *Chronicles* 9:29). These writers attributed the dissension and division that threatened the existence of the Hebrew kingdom to spiritual decadence.

And Solomon slept with his fathers, . . . and Rehoboam his son reigned in his stead.—1 Kings 11:43

When the new sovereign ascended the throne, internal troubles which had long been fomenting in Palestine broke out in open revolt. During the days of David, the necessities of completing the conquest of Canaan had firmly united Israel and Judah. Local jealousies and rivalries had been submerged. Later, the northern tribes suspected that Solomon had taxed them unduly for the glorification of the cities of Judah. The malcontents in the north under the leadership of Jeroboam had threatened rebellion. Solomon was too strong for such a movement to succeed. Jeroboam fled to Egypt, and sought refuge with Pharaoh Shishak (See 1 *Kings* 11:28-40). Now Solomon was dead. A new king was about to ascend the throne. The time had come to right ancient wrongs. Before the national assembly, gathered at Shechem to confirm Rehoboam as king, Jeroboam, representing the north, made an impassioned plea for reform and relief in taxation (See 2 *Chronicles* 10:1-4). Rehoboam's undiplomatic reply to the petition of the north brought about the severance of the Hebrew kingdom into the Kingdom of Israel and the Kingdom of Judah.

Israel's imperial day was over. Much of the constructive legislative work of David and Solomon had come to naught. A hot-headed, impulsive young king undid much of the creative national labor of his illustrious ancestors. Palestine was divided into two rather insignificant kingdoms. To a certain extent the two new nations neutralized each other. Each offered a tempting prey to ambitious neighboring nations.

> *And it came to pass, that in the fifth year of king Rehoboam Shishak king of Egypt came up against Jerusalem.*—2 Chronicles 12:2
>
> *And he took the fenced cities which pertained to Judah, and came to Jerusalem.*—2 Chronicles 12:4

During the lifetime of Solomon, Palestine had been free from foreign invasion. The death of Solomon in B. C. 937 altered the political picture. Palestine had formerly been under the control of Egypt for three hundred years. Now an ambitious Pharaoh sat on the Egyptian throne. Under Solomon Palestine had waxed fat. Here was excellent ground for plunder and pillage. Solomon had been too strong for open attack, but Shishak probably abetted Jeroboam's early attempts to stir up trouble. At any rate, he had given asylum to Jeroboam when he was forced to flee from Palestine. The time was ripe for Egyptian military adventure.

Shishak of the Biblical narratives is the well-known Sheshonk, founder of the Twenty-second Dynasty of Egypt, who ruled from B. C. 945 to 924. In B. C. 932, Shishak staged an extensive military raid against Judah. Shishak probably felt that Jeroboam would not interfere with Egyptian military operation against Rehoboam of Judah.

The laconic chronicler states that Shishak "took the fenced cities" when he raided to Jerusalem. Shishak is more explicit in his account. On the second pylon of the southern wall of the Amen Temple at Karnak, Shishak caused the record of his Palestinian campaign to be inscribed. This inscription contains the names of many Palestinian places well known to readers of the Bible. It is noteworthy that the name of Jerusalem does not appear in the list of 133 towns and cities Shishak claims to have captured.

In the great raid of Judah, Shishak and his allies did not entirely spare the northern kingdom. Cities well within the boundaries of Israel appear in the Karnak list.

Evidently Jerusalem was not sacked by the invaders. The tribute levied on the city, however, was so heavy that the temple treasury had to be ransacked. The enemy "carried away also the shields of gold which Solomon had made" (2 *Chronicles* 12:9).

Old Testament writers minimized material losses. Religious history was their particular province. Shishak's raid ravished Judah, swept over much of Israel, and even collected tribute from cities east of the Jordan, yet the annalists devote more space to the losses of the temple treasury than to the fate of the fenced cities. The Biblical records and the Egyptian records, however, supplement and confirm one another.

> *And Jeroboam said in his heart, Now shall the kingdom return to the house of David: If this people go up to do sacrifice in the house of the Lord at Jerusalem, then shall the heart of this people turn again unto their lord, even unto Rehoboam king of Judah.*— 1 Kings 12:26, 27

The disruption of the kingdom left Judah with certain important advantages over Israel. Although the territory of Judah was the smaller, it was more easily defended. The most important advantage was, however, that Judah possessed Jerusalem, the religious capital of the Hebrews.

Jeroboam realized that if his people went to worship at Jerusalem they might be drawn back toward political reunion with Judah. To forestall such a movement he decided to establish two national sanctuaries, one at Bethel in the south and the other at Dan in the north. In each of these religious centers he set up a golden calf, and proclaimed to his people: "It is too much for you to go up to Jerusalem: Behold thy gods, O Israel, which brought thee up out of the land of Egypt." (1 *Kings* 12:28). Here we catch a glimpse of how the mind and thought of the Israelites were influenced by the various peoples with whom they came into contact. The ancient Egyptians regarded the cow as sacred to Hathor, Egypt's foremost goddess.

> *And there was war between Rehoboam and Jeroboam all the days of his life.*—1 Kings 15:6

The division of the kingdom ushered in half a century of great political and social unrest. Smoldering jealousy and rivalry frequently flared into open conflict. The government of the southern kingdom was fairly stable, but changes in kings and dynasties were frequent in Israel.

Since most of us are armchair students of the Bible, we may find the brief notations of the annalists on the history of this period a bit confusing. Perhaps it would clarify matters if we arranged the rulers of Israel and Judah in order of succession:

Israel		*Judah*	
Jeroboam I	937-915	Rehoboam	937-920
Nadab	915-913	Abijam	920-917
Baasha	913-889	Asa	917-876
Elah	889-887	Note: The reader should bear in	
Zimri	887	mind that regnal dates in some	
Omri	887-875	cases can only be approximated.	

Jeroboam was a practical politician. To him religion meant little. The founding of religious centers at Bethel and Dan was purely a political movement, an effort to win the religionists away from Jerusalem. Lacking in religious insight, he failed to understand the religious psychology of his people. A crass materialist, he failed to fathom the depths of religious idealism which underlay all the purposes of a spiritually inspired people. Without religion the Hebrew nation would have been as nothing. Without religion the Hebrews would have been a people politically unimportant. The meager kingdom they founded would merit insignificant mention in world history. In a strictly secular sense the migrations and movements of the Israelites may seem insignificant; in the realms of religion, and in the broader aspects of world history, the reactions of this movement are of supreme significance. The spiritual idealism of Israel gave a new meaning to the life of mankind. The "seed of Abraham" introduced spiritual and cultural influences which shaped the rise of civilization and altered all the currents of history. The idealism of Israel helped to shape the destiny of proud peoples who, today, deign to despise the Jew. The better minds among the Israelites had always been anchored to religion. This Jeroboam failed to understand. The attempt to lead his people away from the worship of Jehovah was an act of impiety which the sacred writers could never overlook. A later writer refers to him as "Jeroboam the son of Nebat, which made Israel to sin" (2 *Kings* 3:3).

Rehoboam, the southern contemporary of Jeroboam, was a weakling monarch, an unworthy scion of an illustrious sire. An abler, more mentally mature man could have kept intact the kingdom he had inherited. His lack of diplomacy had split the kingdom in twain. Religiously, he was little better than Jeroboam. However, the unifying influence of Jerusalem kept his kingdom intact and gave it underlying strength. Only time could completely undo the work of David and Solomon. Jerusalem gave Judah a power which the northern kingdom of Israel never possessed. The religious life of Judah was never so severely shaken as that of Israel.

Despite its weakness, the Davidic Dynasty seemed settled and secure in Judah. On the other hand, the story of the rulers of Israel, immediately after the death of Jeroboam, is a tragic tale of bloody intrigue. The reigns of the kings of Israel were dramatically brief. Death ended three of them suddenly. Two of the kings, Nadab and Elah, were murdered, while a third, Zimri, after a reign of only a week, committed suicide (See 1 *Kings* 15:28; 16:10; 16:18).

Nadab, who succeeded Jeroboam, reigned only two years before he was slain by Baasha, who then took over the throne of Israel. Two years later, Asa succeeded to the throne of Judah:

And there was war between Asa and Baasha king of Israel all their days.—1 Kings 15:16

The war between the northern and southern kingdoms was fought with all the ferocity which usually characterizes a civil war. Although separated nationally, these were peoples of the same blood. The historical highlight in the conflict was the blockading of the commercial trading of Judah by Baasha. The energetic Baasha cleverly cut the northern trade route of Judah by building fortifications at Ramah. Judah would soon be commercially crippled. Asa countered this move by bribing Benhadad of Damascus to attack the northern territories of Israel. This invasion of Israel by Benhadad forced Baasha to abandon Ramah, which was subsequently destroyed by Asa (See 1 *Kings* 15:17-22).

While the alliance with Benhadad afforded Judah temporary relief, it was probably a great political mistake. This invasion from the north was the forerunner of many invasions which later plundered both Israel and Judah.

The historical trustworthiness of Biblical annalists is exemplified in this incidental mention of Benhadad. Benhadad is well known to us through the records of contemporary kings of Assyria. The inscriptions of Shalmaneser III mention him frequently.

Asa's long reign of forty-one years as king of Judah found him contemporary with Baasha, Elah, Zimri, and Omri as kings of Israel. Elah was a worthless drunkard. Zimrı ruled only a week before he purposely ended his life by burning the king's palace down over his head. Omri, however, was a personage of considerable historical importance. The writer in *Kings,* owing to Omri's lack of religion, covers his reign with a few disparaging remarks. From external sources, however, we learn much that supplements the Biblical narratives.

On Assyrian inscriptions the kingdom of Israel is referred to as "the land of Omri." An inscription of Adadnarari IV of Assyria, 810-782, states that he "conquered from the Euphrates, the Hittite country, the Amorite land in its entirety; Tyre, Sidon, the land of Omri, Edom, Palastu, to the coast of the great sea.* This was written long after the death of Omri, but his name was still prominently identified with the country he ruled. The famous Black Obelisk of Shalmaneser III contains a curious mention of Omri.† The Moabite stone testifies to Omri's ability as a warrior. The memorial stone of Mesha, commonly known as the "Moabite Stone," was discovered by a Prussian missionary, the Rev. F. A. Klein, in 1868. It had been erected by Mesha, king of Moab,

*See *Cuneiform Inscriptions of Western Asia,* Vol. I, Rawlinson.
†See Chapter XII, page 170.

a contemporary of Ahab, king of Israel (875-853), near Dibon, about fifteen miles east of the Dead Sea. The top of the stone was protruding from the surrounding soil when discovered. Since one face of the stone bore an inscription in Phoenician characters it was evidently of historical value, so Klein started negotiations for its purchase from the Arabs. All Arabs are born bargainers. Negotiations dragged on for a year, when a purchase price of about $400 was reached. Meanwhile news of the existence of the stone reached Jerusalem, and the noted French scholar, Clermont-Ganneau, made a bid for it. The wily Arabs worked the price up to about $1500. Then they decided that the stone must have magic properties. If one large charm was worth that much money to these crazy Europeans, why not have a lot of charms? After heating it red hot with a wood fire, they poured cold water on the stone and shattered it to pieces. After considerable difficulty, French scholars were able to purchase most of the fragments. Fortunately enough of it had been preserved so that it could be fitted together and the inscription read.

The stone, which stands about four feet high, is about two feet wide and fourteen inches thick. It is now in the Louvre at Paris. Mesha, the author of the inscription on the stone, is mentioned (2 *Kings* 3:4) as "Mesha king of Moab." The entire inscription is too lengthy for these pages. In regard to Omri, Mesha says:

Omri, king of Israel, he oppressed Moab many days, because Chemosh was angry with his land. His son succeeded him, and he also said, I will oppress Moab. In my day he spoke according to this word, but I saw (my desire) upon him and his house, and Israel utterly perished forever. And Omri took possession of the land of Medeba, and dwelt there all his days, and half the days of his son, forty years.

The external and extra-Biblical evidence would seem to indicate that Omri was a soldier of no mean ability.

And he bought the hill Samaria of Shemer for two talents of silver, and built on the hill, and called the name of the city which he built . . . Samaria.—1 Kings 16:24

One outstanding accomplishment of Omri was the building of Samaria. Before his day the cities of Shechem and Tirzah had served as capitals of Israel. The soldierly Omri sensed the importance of a strongly fortified capital in an easily defended position. He selected a splendid site on the hill Samaria. High on a spur of rock, which on three sides drops precipitously down into a deep and fertile valley, the location was ideal for defensive purposes. Almost impregnable, the city withstood all

ASSYRIAN TROOPS BESIEGING A CITY
Date about B. C. 690

EARLIEST REPRESENTATION OF THE WHEEL
From a fragment of limestone, one of the earliest sculptures known. The wheel, a great human
discovery, was in use in Babylonia fifteen hundred years before it was introduced into Egypt.

By permission of The Museum of the University of Pennsylvania

military attack until the end of the kingdom in **B. C. 722**, when it fell before the Assyrians after a siege of three years.

During the century and a half that Samaria remained the capital of the kingdom of Israel it became a great city, rivaling Jerusalem in military and commercial importance. Frequently rebuilt, Samaria retained its importance down to the days when the Romans ruled Palestine. The Biblical statement that Samaria was built by Hebrews has been confirmed by archæological investigation. The work of exploration was originally carried out by Harvard University in 1908, 1909, and 1910.* In 1931, further investigations were started, with the British School of Archæology, the Palestine Exploration Fund, and the Hebrew University of Jerusalem, co-operating with Harvard. Pottery and other evidence marked the city as having been originally settled by Hebrews. No evidence of settlement earlier than the time of Omri was found. The remains of a large palace, built directly on native rock, were discovered. This is believed to be the palace of Omri.

> *But Omri wrought evil in the eyes of the Lord, and did worse than all that were before him.*—1 Kings 16:25

The annalists wrote bitterly of Omri. In fact they found little in the early history of the kingdom of Israel which merited their approval. Viewing the dismal aftermath of the glorious reigns of David and Solomon, they recorded the passing scene with the bitterness of disappointment. Their pens dripped acid. No great spiritual leader, worthy of the religious traditions of the Hebrews, had appeared to gladden their hearts.

The unsettled political conditions in Israel are reflected in the dramatic downfalls of ruling dynasties. That established by Omri was the fourth in fifty years. These were dark and bloody days for the infant kingdom of Israel. In Judah political conditions were more stable. The Davidic Dynasty still endured. After the unworthy Rehoboam and the ineffective Abijam, Judah found in Asa a sovereign of whose religious principles they could fully approve. Asa was a sincere religionist. He promptly suppressed the idolatrous practices which had crept into the kingdom. The adoration of the sacred stone and the sacred tree of the Canaanites was replaced by the time-honored worship of Jehovah.

> *And there was no more war unto the five and thirtieth year of the reign of Asa.*—2 Chronicles 15:19

Under Asa, Judah prospered. The little southern nation was at peace, but peace had been purchased at a dangerous price. The alliance with Benhadad of Syria was the result of short-sighted statesmanship. It

*See *Harvard Excavations at Samaria,* by Reisner, Fisher, and Lyon.

12

merely brought a lull that presaged a storm. The far-sighted prophet, Hanani, pointed out to Asa the evil portent of this purchased peace. In his hour of need, Asa had sought succor at the wrong source: "Because thou hast relied on the king of Syria, and not relied on the Lord thy God" (2 *Chronicles* 16:7), "therefore from henceforth thou shalt have wars" (2 *Chronicles* 16:9). Asa cast the bold prophet into prison, but this action could not halt the iron march of prophetic history. Two tiny Hebrew kingdoms rested on the rim of a volcano of war; time would swing them into its swirling vortex.

Beyond the confines of the little kingdoms, there was little in the international political picture that was reassuring. The political projects of Assyria were deeply disturbing the East. The military raids of the great Assyrian monarch Ashurnasirpal were spreading terror throughout western Asia. So far the Aramean kingdom of Damascus, under the able Benhadad, had stemmed the tide of invasion before it reached Palestine. How long would the northern dyke hold?

The division of the kingdom was the great political blunder of the Hebrews. The solid empire of Solomon was replaced by tiny twin kingdoms toddling in the path over which mighty peoples were already on the march to empire. The days of Israel and Judah were definitely numbered on the day when Rehoboam and Jeroboam found it impossible to compose their political difficulties.

Politically, the shadows of national oblivion were stretching out toward the Chosen People; religiously, their greatest days were at the dawning. Nationalism was dying, but the great Prophetic Age of Israel was being born.

XII

ISRAEL AND JUDAH

And in the thirty and eighth year of Asa king of Judah began Ahab the son of Omri to reign over Israel.—1 Kings 16:29
And Jehoshaphat the son of Asa began to reign over Judah in the fourth year of Ahab king of Israel.—1 Kings 22:41

WITH the coming of Ahab to the throne of Israel and Jehoshaphat to the throne of Judah came cessation to the long strife between Israel and Judah. Although the two kings were unlike in character and mentality, both displayed sterling qualities in the fields of national and international statesmanship. Each in his own way worked for the good of his kingdom. When danger threatened from without, the kings rallied their forces for joint defense. To guard against the ever-present threat of invasion from the north, the kings negotiated a treaty of peace between their respective kingdoms: "And Jehoshaphat made peace with the king of Israel"—1 *Kings* 22:44.

Peace was the counsel of wisdom. Compared with the rising empires of the east, neither Israel nor Judah was strong in a military sense. Mutual peace delayed the evil and inevitable day when each must resort to arms to repel powerful invaders. For a long time Benhadad of Damascus and his northern allies had had their hands full with the warlike Assyrians who were raiding the northern territories from the Euphrates to the Mediterranean, coming as far south as the Lebanon Mountains. Temporarily, the Assyrians had retired to their own land. Benhadad concluded that this lull in the almost constant warfare offered opportunity to snatch some valuable territory from Israel:

And Benhadad the king of Syria gathered all his host together: and there were thirty and two kings with him, and horses, and chariots: and he went up and besieged Samaria, and warred against it.—1 Kings 20:1

This invasion by a coalition of thirty-three kings was no mere raid for purposes of loot. This was a major military movement. It is remarkable that Ahab was able not only to force Benhadad to raise the siege of Samaria and retreat in disorder, but also to defeat completely Benhadad in a second campaign the following year (See 1 *Kings* 20:21-34). That Ahab was able to defeat the warrior who had held the famous Ashurnasirpal at bay speaks volumes for the military ability of Ahab. After

[163]

crushing Benhadad, Ahab concluded a treaty of peace with him. Ahab evidently concluded that Benhadad's kingdom would form an effective barrier to the Assyrians.

And they continued three years without war between Syria and Israel.—1 Kings 22:1

Not only was there peace between Israel and Syria but also at times an active military alliance. From Assyrian sources we learn that Ahab contributed troops to a northern confederation of kings under Benhadad, who fought against the Assyrians at the Battle of Qarqar.

The dreaded Ashurnasirpal, king of Assyria, was succeeded by his son, Shalmanesir III, in B. C. 859. Shalmanesir, like his father, was determined to conquer the lands to the west of his kingdom. In B. C. 854 he staged his first invasion of the west, and met the northern coalition of kings at Qarqar. Of this campaign he says, in part:

I departed from the city of Nineveh; I crossed the river Tigris . . . to the city of Qarqar I approached. Qarqar, his royal city, I destroyed, I devastated, I burned with fire. 1,200 chariots, 1,200 horsemen, 20,000 men of Hadadidri (Benhadad) of Damascus; 700 chariots, 700 horsemen, 10,000 men of Irhulina, the Hamathite; 2,000 chariots, 10,000 men of Ahab, the Israelite; 500 men of Que; 1,000 men of the Musraen; 10,000 chariots, 10,000 men of the Irqantaen; 200 men of Matinu-bali; 200 men of the Usantaean; 30 chariots, 10,000 men of the Adunubali, the Shianian; 1,000 camels of Gindibu, the Arabian; 1,000 men of Basa, the Amonite— these 12 kings he took as his helpers and they came to make battle against me.*

Shalmanesir boastfully claims to have completely overthrown the thirteen kings. His statements were evidently overdrawn, since he did not follow up his campaign, but withdrew. The battle must have been indecisive. To the student of the Old Testament, the important part of the inscription is the mention of "Ahab, the Israelite."

And Ahab the son of Omri did evil in the sight of the Lord above all that were before him.—1 Kings 16:30

The annalists of Israel found little to approve of in the life and character of Ahab. From the religious viewpoint, all his acts were abhorrent to them. Ahab might be a military genius, but to the prophets and recorders his name was anathema. During his reign, idolatry flourished in Israel as never before. Israel departed from the worship of Jehovah to bow down before the sacred tree and the sacred stone of the Canaanites.

---

*See Rawlinson's *Cuneiform Inscriptions of Western Asia.*

Israel's religious degeneration is illustrated in the description of the rebuilding of Jericho by Hiel of Bethel. Centuries earlier, Joshua, standing over the ruins of Jericho, had uttered dire malediction against the man who would rebuild that city: "And Joshua adjured them at that time, saying, Cursed be the man before the Lord, that riseth and buildeth this city Jericho: he shall lay the foundation thereof in his firstborn, and in his youngest son he shall set up the gates." The custom of infant sacrifice in connection with building projects was fairly common in early Egypt, Babylonia, and Palestine. The frequent findings of tiny remains in foundation deposits in the ruins of ancient cities tell of the prevalence of the practice. The foundation deposits, however, never tell who furnished the victims. This story of Hiel supplies the information. "In his (Ahab's) days did Hiel the Bethelite build Jericho: he laid the foundation thereof in Abiram his firstborn, and set up the gates thereof in his youngest son Segub, according to the word of the Lord, which he spake by Joshua the son of Nun" (1 *Kings* 16:34). Infant sacrifice was forbidden to the Hebrews. Only a pagan or an apostate Israelite would defy the curse. Only a religious renegade would sink to such depths of idolatry and superstition.

Ahab's life was greatly influenced by his queen, Jezebel, the daughter of the king of Sidon. Jezebel brought to the court of Ahab the religious customs of her native land. Probably no one objected to her personal worship of whatever gods she pleased, but when she started a nation-wide propaganda to introduce the worship of Baal into Israel she encountered vigorous opposition from the worshippers of Jehovah. Jezebel thrived on opposition. She was a powerful personality, who stopped at nothing, even bloodshed (See 1 *Kings* 18:13), to attain her ends. Nothing overawed her. Ahab, although a king, was completely under her thumb. Her name, Jezebel, has become proverbial as a symbol of strong-minded, strong-tongued, vindictive womanhood.

Jezebel's attempt to alter the ancient forms of worship could not go unchallenged. Out of the desert came Elijah, the Tishbite, to recall Israel to loyalty to the Lord God of the Hebrews. The desert-bred ascetic did not hesitate to appear at the royal court to vision to Ahab a vengeful God. To the unmoved Ahab he predicted a drought of unusual severity. Then he disappeared into the wastelands to await the day when, on the summit of Mt. Carmel, he would confound the "prophets of Baal" and the "prophets of the groves," and vindicate Jehovah before all Israel.

Elijah's wonder-working on Mt. Carmel, which heralded the coming of a great rain to the parched plains of Palestine, might convince Ahab, but Jezebel was made of sterner stuff. Loosing the vials of her wrath against Elijah, she caused him to flee for his life to the southern desert by way of Beersheba (See 1 *Kings* 19:1-4). Here on Mt. Horeb, Elijah received the three-fold divine commission—"Go, return on thy way to the wilderness of Damascus; and when thou comest, anoint Hazael to be king over Syria: and Jehu the son of Nimshi shalt thou anoint to be king over Israel: and Elisha the son of Shaphat of Abelmeholah shalt thou anoint to be prophet in thy room" (1 *Kings* 19:15, 16).

Jezebel's evil inspiration of her husband to plunder and murder, in the matter of Naboth's vineyard, brought Elijah hurrying to Samaria, to hurl at Ahab the soul-searing prophecies recorded in 1 *Kings* 21:20-26. The grim prophet predicted an awful end for the proud Jezebel: "The dogs shall eat Jezebel by the wall of Jezreel." This prophecy later found fulfillment when, at the command of Jehu, Jezebel was hurled from the city wall, and dog-gnawed fragments of her bones rotted on the red soil of Jezreel (See 2 *Kings* 9:30-37).

And the Lord was with Jehoshaphat, because he walked in the first ways of his father David, and sought not unto Baalim.— 2 Chronicles 17:3.

From the religious viewpoint, the reign of Jehoshaphat of Judah stood out in shining contrast with that of his northern contemporary, Ahab. Materially, the kingdom of Judah prospered greatly also. The *Chronicles* gleam with approval of Jehoshaphat's upright life and able administration of his kingdom. Baalism was banished. Education was encouraged. Domestic and international trade revived. Judah flourished.

In the field of international politics, Jehoshaphat proved his worth. Keeping his own boundaries intact, he collected tribute from neighboring nations (See 2 *Chronicles* 17:10, 11).

This period of nearly a quarter century, during which Ahab and Jehoshaphat reigned contemporaneously in their respective kingdoms, compares more than favorably with the tempestuous times immediately following the division of the Hebrew kingdom. The little kingdoms had settled down in peace with each other, and each made considerable political progress.

With his country at peace with Judah, Ahab of Israel turned his eyes northward. The town of Ramoth-gilead, formerly a part of Israel, was in the hands of the Syrians. Ahab proposed to Jehoshaphat that the latter lend aid in recapturing the place:

And he said unto Jehoshaphat, Wilt thou go with me to battle to Ramoth-gilead? And Jehoshaphat said to the king of Israel, I am as thou art, my people as thy people, my horses as thy horses.—1 Kings 22:4

The religiously inclined Jehoshaphat suggested that they enquire "at the word of the Lord." Ahab immediately summoned his retinue of would-be prophets. These advised advance against Ramoth-gilead. Jehoshaphat, distrusting Ahab's prophets, asked: "Is there not here a prophet of the Lord besides, that we might enquire of him?" (1 *Kings* 22:7). The "prophet of the Lord," Micaiah son of Imlah, not only advised against the adventure, but prophesied that it would end in disaster and in the death of Ahab. Proclaiming this prophecy put Micaiah in prison; failure to heed the warning sent Ahab to his death, when "a certain man drew a bow at a venture, and smote the king of Israel between the joints of the harness." Next day, as "one washed the chariot in the pool of Samaria," the dogs licked up the blood of Ahab, thus dramatically fulfilling a prophecy of Elijah (See 1 *Kings* 21:24).

Now the rest of the acts of Ahab, and all that he did, and the ivory house which he made, and all the cities that he built, are they not written in the book of the chronicles of the kings of Israel?—1 Kings 22:39

The writer of *Kings*, in his final summation of the life of Ahab, makes incidental mention of an "ivory house." The expedition of Harvard University, under the direction of Professor Reisner, operating at Samaria, discovered in 1910 the remains of a large palace which is believed to be "the palace of Omri," the founder of Samaria. At a later date this palace had been considerably enlarged. The new walls were faced with white marble. This would immediately suggest the "ivory house" of Ahab. The finding in the palace of a vase bearing an inscription of Osorkon II of the Twenty-second Dynasty of Egypt would seem to definitely date the palace. Osorkon II was a contemporary of Ahab. There would seem to be little doubt that this was the ivory house.

The immediate successors of Ahab of Israel and Jehoshaphat of Judah had confusingly similar names. The succession was in this order:

Israel		*Judah*	
Ahab	875-853	Jehoshaphat	876-851
Ahaziah	853-851	Jehoram	851-843
Jehoram	851-842	Ahaziah	843-842

Ahaziah of Israel was a weakling of little historical importance. The same might be said of his brother, Jehoram, who succeeded him. The annalists strongly condemn these rulers for their irreligious lives.

The 8th, 9th and 10th chapters of 2 *Kings* tell a dramatic story packed with thrilling circumstantial details. Among the persons presented in this story are Benhadad, king of Syria; Hazael, who succeeded him;

Jehoram, king of Israel; Ahaziah, king of Judah; Jehu, a military leader of Israel; and the prophet Elisha.

The story opens with a visit of Elisha to Damascus. The fame of Elisha as a prophet had spread far beyond the confines of Israel and Judah. When Benhadad learned that such a noted religious leader was approaching his royal city, he sent out his Prime Minister, Hazael, to meet him with a worthy present "of every good thing of Damascus, forty camels burden" (2 *Kings* 8:9).

Part of Benhadad's solicitude was due to the fact that he was ill and worried about his recovery. Hazael made this known to Elisha, saying: "Thy son Benhadad king of Syria hath sent me to thee, saying, Shall I recover of this disease?" Elisha, in tears as he visioned the ultimate outcome of his fateful answer, made this cryptic reply: "Go, say unto him, Thou mayest certainly recover: howbeit the Lord hath showed me that he shall surely die."

Hazael, noting the tears of Elisha, inquired, "Why weepeth my lord?" Elisha answered, "Because I know the evil that thou wilt do unto the children of Israel: their strongholds wilt thou set on fire, and their young men wilt thou slay with the sword, and wilt dash their children." "But what," exclaimed the astonished Hazael, "is thy servant a dog, that he should do this great thing?" And Elisha answered, "The Lord hath showed me that thou shalt be king over Syria."

Hazael conveyed only a part of the prophet's information to Benhadad, the part about recovery. Next morning, a young diplomat looked long at his sleeping sovereign and pondered the words of the prophet. A prophet of Israel had spoken. Surely his word was true. Why wait? There was no one about. It would all be over in a few moments. Stealthily Hazael "took a thick cloth, and dipped it in water, and spread it on his face." A short, sharp struggle as suffocation snuffed out the life of the sovereign of Syria, and a regicide rose to a throne. Benhadad, the mighty, was dead, "and Hazael reigned in his stead."

That Hazael was not of royal blood or in the royal line of succession is confirmed by an inscription of Shalmaneser III of Assyria, which states: "Hazael, son of nobody, seized the throne. He summoned his numerous soldiers and came to make war and battle with me."

Now, with the dread Benhadad gone and Hazael on the throne of Syria, Ahaziah, the stripling king of Judah, decided that the time was ripe to help his cousin, Jehoram of Israel, recover Ramoth-gilead from the Syrians, a task that had proved too much for Ahab and Jehoshaphat. Evidently they succeeded in entering the town (See 2 *Kings* 9:14), but Jehoram was wounded in the battle and retired to Jezreel to recover.

While he was recovering, his fellow sovereign, Ahaziah, decided to pay the convalescent a visit.

With both young kings at Jezreel, Elisha concluded that the time had come for the completion of the three-fold commission which had been intrusted to Elijah (See 1 *Kings* 19:15, 16). Elisha dispatched "one of the children of the prophets" to Ramoth to anoint Jehu "king over the people of the Lord, even over Israel." Jehu was also given the fearful command: "And thou shalt smite the house of Ahab thy master, that I may avenge the blood of my servants the prophets, and the blood of all the servants of the Lord, at the hand of Jezebel" (2 *Kings* 9:7).

The impetuous Jehu lost no time in exterminating the House of Ahab and all its important adherents. He, himself, sent an arrow through the heart of Jehoram, and cast his carcass, as a grim reminder, into the vineyard of Naboth, which Ahab and Jezebel had obtained by plunder and murder. Ahaziah, the king of Judah, fled wounded to Megiddo, where he died.

Jehu had yet to see how a queen could die. Jezebel was within the walls of Jezreel. Hiding? Not she. Jezebel was every inch a queen. Defiantly she had lived; defiantly she would die. At Jehu's approach "she painted her face, and tired her head, and looked out at a window" (2 *Kings* 9:30) and scorned her executioner as he stood under the wall. Finally her own servants hurled her from the tower. For a moment her blood brightened the wall of Jezreel as her body was trodden into the red clay of the valley; then the flesh that once had held the hellish heart of an evil queen was torn by the fangs of the pariah dogs that haunted the dark ways of the city. The grim and grisly prophecy of Elijah had come true: "The dogs shall eat Jezebel by the wall of Jezreel" (1 *Kings* 21:23). The blood of the prophets had been avenged.

Jehu wound up his bloody campaign with the wholesale destruction of the prophets and priesthood of Baal. Thoughtful Hebrew writers of later periods seem to question the wisdom of this reign of terror (See *Hosea* 1:4).

And the time that Jehu reigned over Israel in Samaria was twenty and eight years.—2 Kings 10:36

The royal historiographers tell us little of the reign of Jehu. External supplementary evidence, however, throws much light on this period. In the first year of Jehu's reign, B. C. 842, Shalmaneser III waged his fourth campaign against the confederation of western Asiatic kings, now led by Hazael of Syria. Instead of lending aid to the neighboring northern nations to resist the Assyrians, as had Ahab, Jehu weakly sent rich tribute to the invader. In the inscription of Shalmaneser describing his victories over Hazael at Mt. Hermon and Damascus, this statement appears:

At that time the tribute of the Tyrian, the Sidonian, and of Jehu, son of Omri, I received.

In connection with the apparent error of Shalmaneser in referring to Jehu as "the son of Omri," it must be remembered that Omri made such an impression on the kings of Assyria that the land of Israel was commonly referred to in Assyrian inscriptions as "the land of Omri."

The Black Obelisk of Shalmaneser, found at Nimroud, the site of Calah (*Genesis* 10:11), by Sir Austin Layard, and now in the British Museum, is inscribed with a record of the principal historical events of the thirty-one years of Shalmaneser's reign. On five tiers of bas-reliefs is shown the tribute received from subjugated nations. The second tier shows the tribute paid by Israel. Bowing before Shalmaneser, a prince of Israel offers the tribute which is carried by attendants. The tribute paid is recorded as follows:

Tribute of Jehu, son of Omri, silver, gold, a golden bowl, golden goblets, golden pitchers, lead, a staff for the hand of the king, shafts of spears I received.

Jehu's craven policy, in refusing to assist in the anti-Assyrian campaign and in paying tribute to Shalmaneser, kept Assyria from invading Israel. It was, however, a short-sighted policy. It marked Israel as a future field of tribute by the Assyrians and roused the wrath of Hazael of Damascus, who took terrible revenge in the days of Jehu and Jehu's successors. "In those days the Lord began to cut Israel short: and Hazael smote them in all the coasts of Israel" (2 *Kings* 10:32). Israel lost much of its northern territory.

The years immediately following the death of Jehu were full of trouble for both Israel and Judah. Israel was ravished by the Syrians under Hazael. Civil war over the succession to the throne was rampant in Judah. The killing of the kings of Judah and Israel by Jehu in B. C. 842 had broken the lines of regnal succession in both countries. The order of succession was now:

Israel		Judah	
Jehu	842-814	Athaliah	841-836
Jehoahaz	814-797	Joash	836-796
Jehoash	797-781	Amaziah	796-782
Jeroboam II	781-740	Uzziah	782-740

Some of the dates are difficult to follow. For the dates of many events mentioned in *Kings* and *Chronicles* we are indebted to the Assyrian records. The Assyrians kept records which are known as the "Eponym Lists" because each year was named after some king or important officer. These records were kept carefully and are exact. Astronomical data given in the lists have been verified by modern astronomers.

Israel and Judah frequently came into contact with Assyria. At first this contact was mostly on the battlefield. From the records of the Assyrians it is possible to ascribe dates to some of these contacts. Shalmaneser III dates his fourth invasion of the west as the eighteenth year of his reign. This would be B. C. 842. He states that he warred against Hazael of Damascus and received tribute from Jehu. In the fourteenth year of his reign, he had campaigned against Benhadad. The records of Shishak of Egypt establish that the division of the Hebrew kingdom took place in B. C. 937. From Old Testament chronology we gather that there were ninety-five years between the division of the kingdom and the ascension of Jehu to the throne of Israel. This would be B. C. 842, which is the date of Shalmaneser's fourth western campaign. This gives an important point of departure for checking the dates of historical events mentioned in the Old Testament.

The slaying of Jehoram of Israel cleared the pathway for Jehu to the throne of Israel. The slaying of Ahaziah at the same time left Judah without a king.

And when Athaliah the mother of Ahaziah saw that her son was dead, she arose and destroyed all the seed royal. . . . And Athaliah did reign over the land.—2 Kings 11:1, 3

Jehu had destroyed Baalism in Israel. Its roots still clung to Judah. Athaliah was a daughter of Ahab and Jezebel. Athaliah had inherited some of the ruthlessness of her infamous mother. It was an evil day for the Hebrews when Ahab introduced Jezebel to the courts of Israel. Then began the great battle between paganism and the prophets.

With the coming of Jezebel came a challenge to the time-honored religion of the Chosen People. Out of obscurity came powerful personalities to champion the cause of the Lord God of Israel. The greatest of these was the desert-bred Elijah. "He was an hairy man, and girt with a girdle of leather about his loins" (2 *Kings* 1:8). Beneath this rugged exterior was a courage capable of carrying battle into the courts of kings. Here was a hermit of the wastelands who could rally a people to loyalty to Jehovah, or hurl curses in the teeth of scornful sovereigns.

Elijah's successor, Elisha, was a different type of personality. Here was one at once a prophet and a statesman. Deeply consecrated to the service of Jehovah, he was equally interested in the every-day affairs of his fellow men. With the coming of Elisha the prophets took new place in political and social life. Although relentlessly determined to destroy the evil influence of the House of Ahab and banish Baalism beyond the boundaries of Israel and Judah, the gracious and sagacious Elisha attracted the attention of the leading minds of his day. When the king of Israel and the king of Judah came to grief in their campaign against Moab, they looked to Elisha to lead them out of difficulty (See 2 *Kings* 3). Naaman, a Syrian nobleman, traveled far to seek Elisha's help and healing. In carrying out the commission he had inherited from Elijah (1 *Kings* 19:15, 16) Elisha settled the succession to the thrones of three countries, Israel, Judah, and Syria.

The sweeping sword of Jehu had left only a single survivor of the hated House of Ahab, Athaliah, the queen mother of Ahaziah of Judah. Jehu had slain her son. This disaster did not shatter her proud Syrian spirit. Once a queen; she would again be a queen. She could be as ruthless as Jehu. "The seed royal," every last remnant of the old Davidic line, must be destroyed. All the seed royal perished by the sword; all, save one. The infant Joash, a future king of Judah, was rescued by his aunt, and hidden in the confines of the temple. Here the child would find sanctuary. The priesthood would never permit the pagan Athaliah to enter "the house of the Lord."

In Judah, these were days of the strong arm and unsparing bloodshed. Athaliah controlled the country for six years. Finally, Jehoiada, the high priest of the temple where Joash had been kept in hiding, rallied the populace to successful revolution. The seven-year-old Joash was crowned king in the temple amid popular acclaim. When Athaliah, attracted by the coronation ceremonies, attempted to invade the temple she was driven out, "and they slew Athaliah with the sword beside the king's house" (2 *Kings* 11:20).

When the boy king, Joash, came to the throne of Judah, Jehu was king over Israel. During his minority, Joash was ably aided by Jehoiada, the high priest of the temple, who acted as counselor, friend, and guide to the young monarch. Probably it was the influence of the priest which prompted the king to repair the temple, which had been his home during the years he was hidden from Athaliah.

And Joash did that which was right in the sight of the Lord all the days of Jehoiada the priest.—2 Chronicles 24:2

Joash (or Jehoash) was truly a child of the temple. To save him from death at the hands of Athaliah, his aunt had taken him as an infant to the House of the Lord and confided him to the care of the priesthood. Here, in cloistered seclusion, he had been trained as a future king of Judah. At the early age of seven, he had been crowned king. While the old priest lived, the young king prospered. After the death of Jehoiada the king seems to have deteriorated spiritually, mentally, and physically. Led astray by the "princes of Judah," the king embraced idolatry. When Zechariah, the son and successor of Jehoiada, expostulated with him over his departure from the worship of Jehovah, the king caused him to be stoned to death. "And when he died, he said, The Lord look upon it and require it" (2 *Chronicles* 24:22). The day of retribution soon arrived.

> *And it came to pass at the end of the year, that the host of Syria came up against him: and they came to Judah and Jerusalem.*— 2 Chronicles 24:23

> *Then Hazael king of Syria went up, and fought against Gath, and took it: and Hazael set his face to go up to Jerusalem.*—2 Kings 12:17

Hazael of Damascus, whom we know from Assyrian and Old Testament records to have been an able and active monarch, was wreaking dire vengeance on Israel for the failure of Jehu to support him and his allies in their anti-Assyrian campaigns. Israel had long been a bulwark protecting Judah from the power of northern invaders. Now Israel was so weakened that Hazael could march through that country at will to attack Judah. From Damascus to Gath is a long march. Evidently the Syrians were swarming over Judah like a plague of locusts. They "destroyed all the princes of the people from among the people, and sent all the spoil of them unto the king of Damascus." Rather than risk a siege of Jerusalem by the Syrians, the king decided to purchase immunity by paying tribute. The national treasury and the temple were ransacked to meet Hazael's demands, "and he went away from Jerusalem."

Hazael, as predicted by Elisha (See 2 *Kings* 8:12) had become the scourge of Israel. Militarily Israel was impotent before the power of Syria. When Jehu died he left but a vassal country to his son, Jehoahaz.

> *And the anger of the Lord was kindled against Israel, and he delivered them into the hand of Hazael king of Syria, and into the hand of Benhadad (Benhadad III) the son of Hazael, all their days. And Jehoahaz besought the Lord, and the Lord hearkened unto him . . . And the Lord gave Israel a saviour, so that they went out from under the hand of the Syrians: and the children of Israel dwelt in their tents, as before time.*—2 Kings 13:3-5

The annalists, surveying the passing scene from a religious viewpoint, fail to indicate who was the "saviour" of Israel, or what historical episode so definitely altered the political outlook of Israel. A people who had been ground under the heel of Syrian militarism suddenly return to their tents as before time. What happened? For answer we must look to external sources. The Assyrians were again marching westward. Syria itself was being invaded. Inscriptions of Adad-Nirari IV king of Assyria, tell of a great military expedition he led into the "Westland." Adad-Nirari reigned from B. C. 810 to 782. He was therefore contemporary with Jehoahaz of Israel. The inscription reads in part:*

> *The king of Damascus, in Damascus his royal city I besieged. The fear of the luster of Ashur my lord overwhelmed him and he seized my feet and became subject.*

The king of Assyria was the "saviour" of hard-pressed Israel. Invasion enfeebled Syria. Israel was temporarily saved.

The military movements of the Assyrians also relieved Judah from danger of invasion, but failed to bring tranquillity to Judah's king. In revenge for the brutal murder of Zechariah, Joash was murdered by his own servants. A reign that began auspiciously with a coronation in the temple ended in such ignominy that the remains of the king were denied burial in the royal sepulchres (See 2 *Chronicles* 24:25). Amaziah succeeded him.

> *Now it came to pass, when the kingdom was established to him, that he slew his servants that had killed the king his father. But he slew not their children, but did as it is written in the law in the book of Moses, where the Lord commanded, saying, The fathers shall not die for the children, neither shall the children die for the fathers.*—2 Chronicles 25:3, 4

These passages indicate that Amaziah was making a radical departure from a long-standing custom. Instead of exterminating the entire families of wrongdoers, Amaziah was invoking the law of Moses which declared that the innocent should not suffer for the guilty. This marks a definite step upward ethically and socially.

Amaziah's reign over Judah began auspiciously. He conducted a successful war against Edom. Perhaps he became puffed up with his own military importance. At any rate he issued a seemingly senseless challenge to Jehoash, then ruling Israel, to a trial of military might. The ensuing war ended disastrously for Judah. "And Judah was put to the worse before Israel, and they fled every man to his tent" (2 *Chronicles* 25:22).

Amaziah was taken prisoner at Bethshemish and led back to Jerusalem, where the king of Israel "brake down the wall of Jerusalem from

---

*Rawlinson's *Inscriptions of Western Asia*, Vol. I, page 35.

the gate of Ephraim to the corner gate, four hundred cubits." Jerusalem was sacked. Loaded with loot from the temple and the king's house, Jehoash marched triumphantly back to Samaria.

Probably it was the looting of Jerusalem which led to conspiracy against Amaziah, forcing him to flee to Lachish, whither he was pursued and slain. The death of Amaziah, and the death of Jehoash about the same time ushered in a long period of prosperity for both Israel and Judah.

Jeroboam the son of Joash king of Israel began to reign in Samaria, and reigned forty and one years.—2 Kings 14:23

Then all the people of Judah took Uzziah, who was sixteen years old, and made him king in the room of his father Amaziah.— 2 Chronicles 26:1

Now began an important period in the history of Israel and Judah. Under Jeroboam, Israel flourished. The writer in 2 *Kings,* disapproving of Jeroboam's religious life, dismisses him with scant mention. He does state, however, that Jeroboam delivered Israel from the domination of Syria. This would seem to be a natural development, since Syria had been greatly weakened by repeated invasions from Assyria. Jeroboam carried his conquests from Damascus clear down to Hamath. The long-lost East-Jordan provinces were restored to Israel, and the northern kingdom enjoyed a prosperity it had not known since it ceased to be a part of the realm of king Solomon.

In contrast with the scant notice given Jeroboam II, the chroniclers give space and praise to Uzziah's reign over Judah. 2 *Chronicles* 26:2-15 contributes an interesting description of how he extended the boundaries of Judah, forcefully quelled the remnants of the Philistines who were giving trouble, and forced neighboring nations to pay tribute. Uzziah also encouraged rural life by digging wells in semi-arid regions to increase the area of the grazing grounds, and by supervising the extension of the vine-raising districts in the mountains.

Uzziah equipped a great army and strengthened the fortifications of Jerusalem. "And he made in Jerusalem engines, invented by cunning men, to be on the towers and upon the bulwarks, to shoot arrows and great stones withal" (2 *Chronicles* 26:15). Here is incidental mention of an instrument of warfare that continued in use for many centuries, in fact, down to the time that the Chinese invented gunpowder. Similar "engines" were used against Jerusalem more than once. Around the walls of Jerusalem have been found many stones and ballista balls that were hurled from the engines of war by the troops of Titus, when the Romans besieged Jerusalem in 70 A. D.

During the reign of Jeroboam II, Israel had a chance to recuperate from the exhausting wars with Syria. Samaria and other cities grew in wealth and commercial importance. Incidentally, it might be mentioned that Dr. Schumacher, excavating for the German Oriental Society at Megiddo, found a seal bearing the inscription: "Belonging to Shema, servant of Jeroboam." There is no means of knowing whether the inscription refers to Jeroboam I or Jeroboam II.

The reign of Uzziah saw similar prosperity in Judah. Jerusalem flourished, increasing greatly in wealth and population. Probably the great increase in wealth allowed the leisure that is always essential for distinctive advances in art and literature. Doubtless there was a great increase in literary production. Some of the greatest writers of all time came to light about this period. Some of their works have survived in the Old Testament. Many a grand writer of this period must have been muted by the centuries.

Outwardly all was well with Israel and Judah; inwardly there was much to be desired. As wealth increased, an ever-increasing proportion of the population lived in luxury. Time has produced few peoples who could long survive great wealth. Lust for luxury was dimming the sensitiveness of the Hebrews to moral distinctions. The Children of Israel were in danger of losing the religious idealism which had been their greatest national asset. The great increase in vice and violence which accompanied the increase of wealth in the twin kingdoms alarmed religious leaders of the day. Inspired men were preaching and writing against the evils which were polluting the minds and morals of the Hebraic peoples. Prominent among these writers were Amos and Hosea.

Amos was a son of the soil, brought up among the herdsmen of Tekoa. Although Tekoa was in Judah, only a scant twelve miles from Jerusalem, Amos traveled to Israel to deliver most of his great messages. Proudly proclaiming his humble origin in the saying: "I was no prophet, neither was I a prophet's son; but I was an herdsman" (*Amos* 7:14), Amos dauntlessly carried his message to the court of Jeroboam, and to the precincts of the priesthood at Samaria. Accused of treason, threatened with expulsion from the country, Amos thundered his denunciations of the wickedness of Israel, and implored an erring people to return to the Lord their God.

The cultured Hosea was a finely-fibred, sensitive soul. The domestic tragedy which had darkened his outlook in life is reflected in his writings. A sorrow-stricken poet looked on life with the vision of a prophet. As he sorrowed over a wanton woman, he saw Jehovah sorrowing over a wayward people. Moved by patriotic love of his land and his people, he poured out passionate pleas for national repentance and painted prophetic pictures of the impending doom of an impious and idolatrous people.

At the time of their deaths in B. C. 740, Jeroboam and Uzziah left their respective kingdoms apparently prosperous. Beneath the surface, however, the social structure was rotten to the core. Luxury had lured to moral decadence. Hebrew nationalism was dying. Within twoscore years Assyria would sweep the northern kingdom into national oblivion. Sore wounded, the southern kingdom would stagger on for many a day, but Hebraic nationalism was moving toward its inevitable end.

Out of death comes resurrection. Nations die. Spiritual idealism endures eternally. Nationalism was but a parenthesis in the history of the Hebrews. The dramatic decline of political power brought into prominence the phenomenal power of the Chosen People in the realms of religion. The shattering of the shell of nationalism released the tide of moral and religious reform. Nationalism's era was ending: Israel's greatest religious era was but beginning. The horizons of religious thought were immeasurably broadened. Enlightened minds received more perfect revelation of the spiritual relationship between man and his Creator. The Lord God of Israel was visioned as the Lord God of mankind. The greater meaning of the promises of Jehovah were revealed. God was in His heaven. God would send a Messiah to redeem His world. The hearts of the Chosen People yearned for the coming of the Christ. The signs of the times heralded a brighter future. "For unto us a child is born, unto us a son is given: and the government shall be upon his shoulder: and his name shall be called Wonderful, Counsellor, The mighty God, The everlasting Father, The Prince of Peace" (*Isaiah* 9:6).

The crumbling of the Hebrew kingdoms ushered in an era of great religious thought which found expression in sublime Hebraic literature. Toward the close of Uzziah's reign, Isaiah, the greatest of the prophets, began his ministry. Isaiah lived in Jerusalem, and was probably born there. His early writings reflect his pride in, and love for, Jerusalem. His greatest writings date to the days when the Hebrews were under the heel of the Assyrians. The revolt of the Hebrews in B. C. 703 moved the mighty Isaiah to the majestic prophecies which established his name as the greatest in all literature. The pangs of national dissolution produced the great prophetic age.

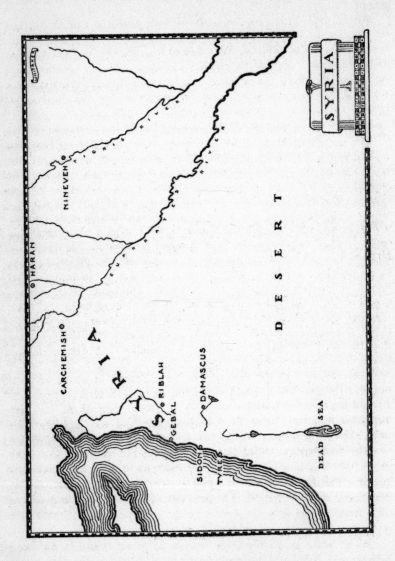

XIII

THE HEEL OF THE CONQUEROR

O Assyrian, the rod of mine anger, and the staff in their hand is mine indignation.—Isaiah 10:5

THE portions of the Old Testament which deal with the years between B. C. 750 and 600 indicate that the political fortunes of Israel and Judah were profoundly influenced by the policies and projects of the kings of Assyria. This period, so fateful for the Chosen People, happens to have been the most brilliant in the history of Assyria. Assyrian armies frequently swept through western Asia, ruthlessly exacting rich tribute from the countries they subdued.

The Assyrians were an extremely ancient people. Tradition links the Assyrians with Asshur: "Out of that land went forth Asshur, and builded Nineveh, and the city Rehoboth, and Calah" (*Genesis* 10:11). Asshur, Calah, and Nineveh were, at various periods, important capitals of Assyria. The Assyrians were an important people long before Abraham left his boyhood home at Ur of the Chaldees.

In the study of ancient history it is common practice to study Assyria and Babylonia together. The countries were adjacent to each other, and frequently during the long march of history they have been linked politically as well as economically. When these countries emerged from the mists of the past into the light of known history, Assyria was but a province in the hilly hinterland of the rich agricultural country of Babylonia. Babylonia was then one of the richest agricultural countries of the world, and Assyria a country of negligible economic and commercial importance.

The Babylonians, inhabiting the rich country between the "twin rivers," the Tigris and the Euphrates, became agricultural and commercial people. The Assyrians, in their rough, unfertile country, were hunters, herdsmen, and warriors. At that time much of Assyria was still covered with forest. Judging by the records of the kings of Assyria, these forests were abundantly supplied with wild game.

Along about B. C. 1400, the balance of power passed to the hardy hillmen and Babylonia became a province of Assyria. With the wealth of Babylonia behind them the Assyrians built up a great war machine. Assyria was ready for a place in the family of nations. The name of Ashur-uballit, king of Assyria, appears in the Tell-el-Amarna letters.

Under various warlike monarchs, Assyria frequently attempted to carry her conquests westward to the Mediterranean. The first of these invasions which directly affected the Hebrew kingdoms was that of Shalmaneser III (B. C. 860-824). In B. C. 854, Shalmaneser met and defeated a confederation of kings at the battle of Qarqar in Syria. Ahab of Israel contributed troops to resist this invasion.* On Shalmaneser's fourth invasion of the "westland," Jehu of Israel paid tribute to secure peace.†

And Pul the king of Assyria came against the land (Israel): and Menahem gave Pul a thousand talents of silver, that his hand might be with him to confirm the kingdom in his hand.—2 Kings 15:19

In the eighteen years immediately following the death of Jeroboam II Israel had six sovereigns. Only one of these, Menahem, died a natural death. Zechariah reigned but half a year before he was murdered by Shallum. Only a month passed before Shallum was in turn murdered by Menahem, who succeeded him on the throne. Menahem's reign saw the re-establishment of Assyrian domination over western Asia.

For a long time Assyria had been inactive in international affairs. With the coming of Pul to the throne of Assyria the pattern of international politics in the Near-East was suddenly and drastically altered. Pul was a usurper. In B. C. 745 he took forcible possession of the throne of Assyria and assumed the distinguished name of Tiglath-pileser, reigning as the third sovereign of that name. The Babylonians, whose country he despoiled, always refer to him as "Pul," the name given in 2 *Kings*.

Menahem evidently kept his kingdom from being overrun by the payment of tribute. To meet the demands of the Assyrians Menahem found it necessary to resort to a capital levy: "And Menahem exacted the money of Israel, even of all the mighty men of wealth, of each man fifty shekels of silver, to give to the king of Assyria" (2 *Kings* 15:20). In B. C. 738, according to the records of Tiglath-pileser, Assyria waged a military campaign against the western kingdoms, but did not penetrate Palestine. The following year he invaded Syria and Palestine. In his palace at Nineveh he caused to be placed on the wall a plaque commemorating this expedition. Although the inscription was defaced by some later reconstructor, enough remains to bear eloquent testimony to the trustworthiness of Old Testament recorders. Tiglath-pileser states that he received tribute from "Menahem, the Samaritan."‡ He also states that he was paid tribute by "Rezin, the Damascene," who is mentioned in 2 *Kings* 16:5, and *Isaiah* 7:1.

---

*See Chapter XII, page 164.
†Ibid, page 170.
‡See Rawlinson, *Cuneiform Inscriptions of Western Asia*, Vol. III.

Menahem was succeeded by his son, Pekahiah, who reigned for two years before he met a violent death at the hands of Pekah, who succeeded him on the throne of Israel.

During the reign of Pekah the Assyrians again invaded Palestine. Evidently at this time there was not sufficient portable treasure in Israel to satisfy Tiglath-pileser, so he annexed the east-Jordan country and all of Galilee (See 2 *Kings* 15:29). This reduced the kingdom of Israel to that portion of central Palestine directly dominated by the city of Samaria.

Israel was open to attack. Judah, on the other hand, was saved from invasion by Israel, which acted as a buffer state.

In the southern kingdom, Uzziah had been succeeded by his son Jotham, who had been co-regent during the years that his father had been ill with leprosy. After a short and fruitful reign, Jotham was succeeded by his son, Ahaz.

And it came to pass in the days of Ahaz . . . that Rezin the king of Syria, and Pekah the son of Ramaliah, king of Israel, went up toward Jerusalem to war against it, but could not prevail against it.—Isaiah 7:1

Rezin and Pekah were attempting to form a coalition of the small countries and had asked Ahaz to join them. When Ahaz refused, they invaded Judah with the intention of placing a new king on the throne at Jerusalem (See *Isaiah* 7:6). The invading allies, Rezin and Pekah, laid waste the country from the borders of Judah to Jerusalem and laid siege to the capital. With the foe before Jerusalem, Ahaz sought advice from the rising young Isaiah, who was a statesman and man of affairs as well as a prophet. Isaiah assured Ahaz that Jerusalem would not fall. Isaiah foretold the downfall of Syria and Israel and the death of Rezin at the hands of the Assyrians.

Ahaz purchased aid from Assyria at a terrible price. "And Ahaz took the silver and gold that was found in the house of the Lord, and in the treasures of the king's house, and sent it for a present to the king of Assyria. And the king of Assyria hearkened unto him: for the king of Assyria went up against Damascus, and took it, and carried the people of it captive to Kir, and slew Rezin" (2 *Kings* 16:8, 9).

A prophet of Israel had foretold the doom of Damascus; a king of Israel had paid for it with the gold of the great temple; a king of Assyria had the record written high on the walls of his palace in Nineveh. The story is tersely told in the Assyrian record.* Tiglath-pileser tells that "sixteen districts of Damascus like a deluge heap I destroyed." Rezin

---

* See *Inscriptions in Cuneiform Character,* by Sir Austin Layard.

was slain. The Assyrian invaders swept over Syria, northern Israel, Edom and Moab in a deluge of death. Over five hundred cities perished or paid tribute. Captives by the thousands were carried away to Assyria. The Assyrian monarch knew no mercy: "His captains alive on stakes I hung them and exhibited them to his land." The treasures of many lands were taken to Assyria to decorate the palaces of the king of Assyria and the mighty temples of his gods.

Jerusalem and Judah were saved for a time, but the payment of tribute reduced Judah to the status of a vassal of Assyria. Ahaz seems to have been carried away by all things Assyrian, even their strange religion. When he visited Tiglath-pileser at Damascus an elaborate altar attracted his attention. Ahaz had a copy of the altar made and installed before the temple at Jerusalem to supersede the great altar erected by king Solomon. This act of arch-impiety probably served to introduce the pagan religious practices which were later abolished by Hezekiah.

Judah was reduced to vassalage but its territory remained intact. Israel, however, was in a precarious position. The sword of Assyria hung in heavy threat over the remnants of the northern kingdom. These were dark days for Israel. King Pekah, who had won his crown with the regicide's sword, perished the same way. He was slain by Hoshea, who was fated to be the last king of Israel.

Against him came up Shalmaneser king of Assyria; and Hoshea became his servant, and gave him presents.—2 Kings 17:3

Assyrian greed for gold was rapidly reducing Israel to serfdom. In a vain effort to escape the heavy hand of Assyria, Hoshea conspired with king So of Egypt, and withheld the annual tribute to Assyria. This gave Shalmaneser V, who had succeeded Tiglath-pileser on the throne of Assyria, an excuse for the crushing and annexation of Israel. Shalmaneser overran Israel and laid siege to Samaria.

The superb location of Samaria, high on a hill which drops sharply down on three sides into a level plain, rendered it practically impregnable against the offensive weapons of that day. The Assyrians surrounded the city and cut off supplies from the outside. After three years, the inhabitants of Samaria surrendered to avoid starvation. The kingdom of Israel had come to an end.

From the account given in 2 *Kings* 17 we might gather that the fall of Samaria took place in the reign of Shalmaneser. It so happens that Shalmaneser died before the fall of Samaria, and the carrying on of the campaign fell to the lot of his successor, Sargon II. Sargon II is mentioned only once in the Old Testament. This is in connection with the siege of Ashdod (See *Isaiah* 20:1). Until the spade of the archæologist revealed his remarkable history, the name of Sargon was unknown to history and to literature, save for this incidental mention in the writings of Isaiah.

It should be remembered that less than a century ago practically nothing was known of the history of Assyria outside of what is written in the Old Testament. Her cities and her kings were frequently mentioned in the Bible, but beyond that there was nothing. The kings of Assyria, who once had terrorized the Near-East, were forgotten, their names unknown outside the pages of the Great Book. Their cities, great and glorious though they had been, lay under shapeless mounds in a country that was no longer of commercial or political importance.

In 1842 the French government created a vice-consulate at Mosul. Mosul is a modern city on the Tigris and today is a great center of the oil producing industry. The commercial uses of petroleum were unknown, and Mosul was merely a little trading town when Paul Botta was appointed vice-consul there. Botta's consular duties were so light that the young man had time to investigate the great mound of Kouyunjik, which lies across the river from Mosul. This mighty mound covered the ruins of Nineveh, one of the great capital cities of the ancient Assyrians.

Finding little near the surface, Botta soon tired of Nineveh, and, on the advice of natives, transferred his attention to Khorsabad, some fourteen miles away. Here he discovered the walls of an ancient city and the ruins of a great palace literally packed with interesting historical records inscribed on alabaster. Under the corners of the palace, and beneath the city gates, were found deposits of clay cylinders and clay tablets inscribed in cuneiform characters. These cylinders and tablets contained a complete record of the building of the city and a dated, detailed history of the reign of the king who built it. The city and the palace were built by Sargon, who ruled Assyria from B. C. 722 to 705.

Fortunately for the world's scholars, the work of Henry Rawlinson had furnished a key to unlock the mysteries of cuneiform writing shortly before this great discovery. In 1835, Rawlinson, a young British officer then stationed in Persia, had discovered a great inscription carved high on the face of a precipitous rock which towered above the little village of Behiston. Five hundred feet up from the base of the rock, king Darius I of Persia had caused to be carved a monumental relief commemorating his victory over Gaumata, a usurper who had attempted to seize control of the country. The relief depicts the triumphant Darius with his foot resting on the body of his fallen foe. A large inscription tells the story in the Babylonian language, and beneath this the story is repeated in eight columns, five in the Persian language and three in the Susian.

Rawlinson decided to copy the inscription. All his spare time for four years were spent on this work. Beneath the inscription there was a shelving ledge of rock, scarcely more than a foot wide, and badly broken in places. Standing on this precarious footing, Rawlinson copied what he could reach of the lower portions of the inscription. Then, standing on ladders held in place by natives, he worked higher. To copy the upper portions, Rawlinson found it necessary to have himself lowered with ropes from the top of the cliff. The copying completed, his work was but begun. Using the Persian language, with which he was familiar, as a key, he spent years deciphering the Susian and Babylonian inscriptions, before presenting to the world a key to Assyrian and Babylonian writings.

The records from Sargon's palace threw new and interesting light on 2 *Kings* 17. From them it was learned that the fall of Samaria was the first great event of Sargon's reign. 2 *Kings* 17:24 states that: "The king of Assyria brought men from Babylon, and from Cuthath, and from Ava, and from Hamath, and from Sepharvaim, and placed them in the city of Samaria." The wholesale interchange of the inhabitants of conquered countries was an established administrative policy of the Assyrians. It is frequently referred to in the Old Testament, and in official Assyrian records. Probably this had a pacifying effect in that those classes most likely to be ringleaders in rebellion would find themselves in an environment where they could cause little trouble. Sargon's inscriptions state that he was responsible for the deportations mentioned in 2 *Kings* 17. The inscription reads: "Peoples from all lands, my captives, I settled there." He mentions the number of captives he took from Samaria as 29,290. The number of inhabitants taken from Israel at this time was small when compared with the total population.

With the fall of Samaria the kingdom of Israel came to an end. As a kingdom, Israel had endured but little over two hundred years. The iron heel of the Assyrian conqueror had been heavy on western Asia. Solomon's empire was shrunken to the single state of Judah, and that lay under tribute to Assyria.

Hezekiah began to reign when he was five and twenty years old, and he reigned nine and twenty years in Jerusalem . . . And he did that which was right in the sight of the Lord.—2 Chronicles 29:1, 2

Ahaz was king of Judah when Samaria fell and the kingdom of Israel came to an end. Ahaz was succeeded by his son Hezekiah. The coming of Hezekiah ushered in a period of social and religious reform in Judah. One of the earliest acts of Hezekiah's reign was the cleansing and repairing of the temple. The filth and the profane gods were taken from the temple and hurled into the brook Kidron. The long-neglected Passover was reinstituted. Judah returned to the worship of Jehovah (See 2 *Chronicles* 29 to 31).

Hezekiah was a great builder. He rebuilt the old defensive walls of Jerusalem, which were sadly in need of repair. He also added an outer wall, part of which still stands today. Hezekiah was preparing for the inevitable coming of the Assyrians. With Samaria before him as an object lesson, a prudent king could do no less. "Also he strengthened himself, and built up all the wall that was broken, and raised it up to the towers, and another wall without, and repaired Millo in the city of David, and made darts and shields in abundance (2 *Chronicles* 32:5). In connection with the "wall without," it might be noted that Isaiah also indicates that at this time there were two city walls at Jerusalem (See *Isaiah* 22:11).

And ye gathered together the waters of the lower pool.—Isaiah 22:9

Isaiah is here referring to Hezekiah's remarkable engineering work in connection with the water supply of Jerusalem. 2 *Kings* 20:20 states that "he made a pool, and a conduit, and brought water into the city." Jerusalem had grown with the centuries. The water supply system, however, was essentially the same as it had been in the old days of the Jebusites, when Jerusalem was little more than a fortress on a hill. Hezekiah knew that some day he would be forced to defend Jerusalem. The old water system constituted a double danger to the successful defense of the city. The resourceful Assyrians might cut off the city from the Gihon spring, or they might find entrance into the city through the old Jebusite water tunnel. According to 2 *Chronicles* 32:30, "Hezekiah also stopped the upper watercourse of Gihon, and brought it straight down to the west side of the city of David." There would be no more waste water. Perhaps the spring was built over and concealed, after the manner later employed by Manasseh (See 2 *Chronicles* 33:14). To eliminate the double danger, Hezekiah caused to be constructed the rock-cut aqueduct that is now known as the "Siloam Tunnel." Hezekiah continued the old Jebusite tunnel through the solid rock for a distance of between 1,700 and 1,800 feet to the south end of Ophel, where he constructed a new pool, or reservoir, to receive the overflow waters of Gihon.

Hezekiah's engineers, working from both ends of the tunnel, almost missed each other at the proposed meeting place in the center. The story of how narrowly they escaped such an untoward happening is told in the "Siloam Inscription," now preserved in the Imperial Museum in

Constantinople. The story was carved in Hebrew by one of the workmen. It reads:

The boring through. . . . And this is the story of the boring through: while yet . . . the drill, each toward his fellow, and while there were yet three cubits to be bored through, there was heard the voice of one calling unto another, for there was a crevice in the rock on the right hand. On the day of the boring through the stone-cutters struck, each to meet his fellow, drill upon drill; and the waters flowed from the source to the pool for a thousand and two hundred cubits, and a hundred cubits was the height of the rock above the heads of the stone-cutters.

Hezekiah was fortunate in having the advice and counsel of Isaiah, who was a wise and far-sighted statesman. It is probable that no small part of Hezekiah's administrative success was due to the friendly guidance of Isaiah.

Now in the fourteenth year of king Hezekiah did Sennacherib king of Assyria come up against all the fenced cities of Judah, and took them.—2 Kings 18:13

Sennacherib had come to the throne of Assyria on the death of Sargon II. The coming of the new monarch was greeted with the widespread revolt of all the dependent countries of western Asia. In this rebellion they were encouraged by Egypt. Lured by promised aid from Egypt, Judah, against the advice of Isaiah, joined the revolt. The astute Isaiah sensed that the Pharaoh of Egypt was merely saving his own land at the expense of his little neighbors. Egypt was the great lure that ever led the Assyrian sovereigns westward. The fat lands of the Nile Valley offered a tempting field for loot. So far each Assyrian invasion had halted at the Syrian dyke. Egypt was eager to repair the broken barrier without loss to herself.

The revolt of the vassal kingdoms against Assyria brought such a dramatic chain of events to Judah that the annalists broke their rule of brevity to devote almost two entire chapters of 2 *Kings* to Sennacherib's invasion. Isaiah also contributes interesting historical notes on this campaign in the 36th and 37th chapters of his writings. Herodotus, the Greek historian, also offers interesting evidence. Sennacherib, himself, furnishes supplementary and confirming evidence in his records on what is now known as the "Taylor Cylinder," after its discoverer, J. E. Taylor. This cylinder is now in the British Museum. The events covered in 2 *Kings* 18 and 19 were not those of a campaign of a few months. They took place during a war which raged intermittently for several years.

In B. C. 701, Sennacherib swept westward with a great army, crushing Phoenicia and Philistia, and defeating Egypt. Then he swung around to take care of Judah. Laying waste the countryside of Judah, he established military headquarters at Lachish. Lachish is now known to have been a strongly fortified city which would make an ideal center for military operations. Sennacherib had a relief made showing the tribute received at Lachish, with the scribes entering up the quantities. With Jerusalem threatened with destruction, Hezekiah hastened to send tribute to Sennacherib at Lachish. To make up the necessary amount of treasure Hezekiah stripped the temple, even cutting off the gold with which the doors and pillars were overlaid (See 2 *Kings* 18:15, 16).

The paying of tribute did not long postpone the evil day. From his headquarters at Lachish, Sennacherib sent a strong detachment of troops to demand the outright surrender of Jerusalem. Standing in the Kidron Valley, the leaders of this expedition insolently harrangued the defenders of Jerusalem in the Hebrew tongue. Alarmed by the threats of the Assyrians, Hezekiah sent to Isaiah for advice. Isaiah sent back this comforting message: "Thus saith the Lord, Be not afraid of the words that thou hast heard, wherewith the servants of the king of Assyria have blasphemed me. Behold, I will send a blast upon him, and he shall hear a rumour, and return to his own land; and I will cause him to fall by the sword in his own land" (*Isaiah* 37:6, 7).

In his account of the expedition of B. C. 701, Sennacherib pictures the precarious position of Hezekiah beleaguered in Jerusalem in these words, inscribed on the Taylor Cylinder:

And as to Hezekiah, the Judean, who had not submitted to my yoke, 46 of his strongholds, fortified cities, and smaller cities of their environs without number . . . I besieged, I captured. 200,150 people, small and great, male and female, horses, mules, asses, camels, oxen, and sheep without number I brought out of their midst and counted as booty. He himself I shut up like a caged bird in Jerusalem, his capital city . . . The cities, which I captured, from his country I cut off and gave them to Mitinti, king of Ashdod, Padi, king of Ekron, and Sillibaal, king of Gaza, and diminished his land. In addition to the former tribute, their yearly tax, I added a tax as the impost of my overlordship and laid it upon them. As to Hezekiah himself, the fear of the lustre of my lordship overcame him and the Urbi and his favorite soldiers, whom he had brought to strengthen Jerusalem, his capital city, deserted.

Jerusalem was in sore straits. The surrounding countryside had been ravished. With much of its territory gone, Judah faced the fate that had overtaken Israel. Jerusalem was about to fall into the hands of the

Assyrians. Still stood the promise of the prophet with the cryptic words, "he shall hear a rumour." Perhaps we catch an echo of this rumour in the words: "And when he heard say of Tirhakah king of Ethiopia, Behold, he is come out to fight against thee" (2 *Kings* 19:9). This Tirhakah is undoubtedly "Tarku, king of Egypt and Kush" (Ethiopia), mentioned in an inscription of Esarhaddon, the successor of Sennacherib. Sennacherib might have heard many rumours. His empire, particularly Babylonia, was seething with rebellion. Something seriously interfered with his siege of Jerusalem. Of his later attempt to capture Jerusalem, that covered by 2 *Kings* 19:9-36, Sennacherib says nothing. Assyrian monarchs never recorded defeats or failures.

The great disaster which caused the withdrawal of the remnants of Sennacherib's mighty army from before the walls of Jerusalem, leaving "an hundred and fourscore and five thousand" (2 *Kings* 19:35) dead upon the field, must have filled the watchers on the walls with awe. Jehovah had intervened to save Jerusalem. An act of God had caused the proud Assyrian conqueror, just as Jerusalem was about to fall into his hands like a ripe plum, to beat a hasty retreat. "So he returned with shame of face to his own land" (2 *Chronicles* 32:21).

The writer gives us a ghastly glimpse of mysterious death destroying an army overnight, but he omits details. As the shades of night had fallen over Jerusalem a formidable fighting force faced the city with hope high in their hearts for its early capture, but, "when they arose early in the morning, behold, they were all dead corpses." Although the annalists' description of the angel of death destroying an army overnight is startling, it is well within the realms of the possible. Herodotus gives a graphic description of the destruction by bubonic plague of an Assyrian army commanded by Sennacherib. The historian was writing of Egypt, but it must be remembered that during the reign of Sennacherib the Egyptians were allied with the enemies of Assyria. Speaking of Sethos, priest-king of Egypt, Herodotus says:

And afterward Sennacherib, king of the Arabians and Assyrians, marched a great army into Egypt. Then the soldiers of Egypt would not help him; whereupon the priest went into the inner sanctuary to the image of the god and bewailed the things which he was in danger of suffering. As he wept he fell asleep, and there appeared to him in a vision the god standing over him to encourage him, saying that when he went forth to meet the Arabian army he would suffer no harm, for he himself would send him helpers. Trusting to this dream he collected those Egyptians who were willing to follow him and marched to Pelusium, where the entrance to his country was. None of the warriors followed him, but traders, artisans and market men. There as the two armies lay opposite to each other, there came in the night a multitude of field mice, which ate up all the bowstrings and quivers of the enemy and the thongs of their shields. In consequence, on the next day they fled, and being deprived of their arms, many of them fell. And there stands now in the temple of Hephaistos a stone statue of this king holding a mouse in his hand, bearing an inscription which says: "Let any who look on me reverence the gods."

It is well known that rats and mice are the carriers of the plague which has often ruined armies and even destroyed the populations of great cities. An influx of diseased rodents has often been the harbinger of the "black death." Probably there is no connection between the story of Herodotus and the Old Testament narratives, but each renders the other more logical and credible.

At that time Berodach-baladan, the son of Baladan, king of Babylon, sent letters and a present unto Hezekiah: for he had heard that Hezekiah had been sick.—2 Kings 20:12

If this Berodach-baladan (or Merodach-baladan) were unknown outside of Old Testament records, we might assume that the above passage merely recorded the friendly solicitude of the king of Babylon for a fellow monarch who had been gravely ill. Much may have been behind this little visit. Babylon, although among the richest of countries in material wealth and in culture and education, had long been a vassal of Assyria. Assyria drew much of its wealth from the fertile lands between the lower reaches of the Euphrates and the Tigris. Sometimes the Babylonians rebelled. Members of the House of Baladan had long been ringleaders in rebellion. As early as B. C. 851, Shalmaneser III had found it necessary to march to "the country of the sea," and force the House of Yakin, of which Merodach-baladan was a descendant, to pay tribute. Shalmaneser III recorded this in an inscription on the gates of Balawat. During the reign of Sargon II, Merodach-baladan set up an independent government in Babylon and maintained it for twelve years. Sargon defeated him; seized Babylon, and drove Merodach-baladan into the marshes around the head of the Persian Gulf. Merodach-baladan was again active during the reign of Hezekiah. Perhaps his present to Hezekiah was an entering wedge for a little bit of intrigue looking toward upsetting the plans of Sennacherib.

In B. C. 703, while Sennacherib was fully occupied with the countries to the west, Merodach-baladan staged a rebellion. Rebellion in Babylonia was a serious matter. Affairs in the west must wait until Merodach-baladan was put in his place. Sennacherib marched to the south.

Sennacherib's record of the putting down of this rebellion reads, in part, as follows:

> *I accomplished the defeat of Merodach-baladan, king of Babylon, together with the forces of Elam, his ally, in the environs of the city of Kish. In the midst of the battle he fled alone; he saved his life. The chariots, wagons, horses and mules, which at the onset of the battle he had left, my hands captured. I entered joyfully into his palace which was in Babylon. I opened his treasure house; gold, silver, gold and silver utensils, precious stones of all kinds, his untold treasured possessions, a great booty; the women of his palace, princes, his body guards, male and female musicians, the rest of his troops as many as there were, and the servants of his palace I brought out and counted as spoil.**

Almost constant rebellion in Babylonia was seriously interfering with the military plans of Sennacherib. Finally, in exasperation, he laid the country waste, burned and levelled the city of Babylon, and turned the irrigation canals through the site of the city, converting it into a marsh.

After his last appearance before Jerusalem, from which he departed leaving an army silent in death behind him, Sennacherib seems to have become singularly silent. There are no boastful records of the last few years of his reign. The prophecy of Isaiah, "I will cause him to fall by the sword in his own land," was finally fulfilled when Sennacherib was stabbed to death by his own sons.

The records of the reign of Sennacherib were largely revealed through the labors of Sir Austin Layard, the great English archæologist. When the news of Botta's great discoveries at Khorsabad reached Europe it aroused great interest in scientific circles. An expedition was fitted out in England, largely on money furnished by a newspaper. Layard was appointed director. Work was begun at Nimroud, the site of the ancient Biblical city of Calah (See *Genesis* 10). Operations were later transferred to Nineveh, where Layard unearthed a great palace which had been built by Sennacherib, and later remodeled by his son and successor, Esarhaddon.

It is to the German Orient Society, however, that we owe most of our knowledge of how the ancient Assyrian cities looked when they were in their glory. Through the painstaking efforts of the scientists of this society, which began work around the turn of the present century, in making scale models of ancient buildings and cities, it is possible to form a correct conception of how these cities appeared to the Hebrew captives who were transported to Assyria when the shadows of political oblivion were creeping over Israel and Judah.

*See Abel and Winckler's *Keilschrifttexte*.

French, English, German, and last, but not least, American archæologists and scientists have given, and are giving, much authentic information on the historical backgrounds of the Old Testament narratives of the Assyrian Period.

Little is known of the latter days of Hezekiah. During his reign Judah had lived in constant danger. The heavy tribute paid to Assyria was sapping the economic life blood of a stricken kingdom. Still Judah lived on, and Jerusalem was saved from disaster. The prophecy of Isaiah that Jerusalem would not fall was vindicated. About B. C. 702 Isaiah disappeared from history. Perhaps he retired. He had lived long, and had served four sovereigns of Judah. Greatest of the prophets, Isaiah was more than a prophet. His was one of the mighty intellects which shine above the shadows of history like snow-capped mountain crags rising above rain-laden clouds. Of his end nothing is known. Doubtless he died as nobly as he had lived. For the rabbinical tradition that he was placed between two pieces of wood and sawn asunder during the reign of Manasseh there seems to be no foundation.

Sennacherib was succeeded on the throne of Assyria by his son Esarhaddon about four years after Hezekiah had been succeeded by Manasseh on the throne of Judah. Esarhaddon, a man of blood and iron, succeeded in an enterprise which had baffled both Sargon and Sennacherib when he led an army into Egypt and reduced that country to an Assyrian province. Esarhaddon recorded this campaign on a monumental monolith which graphically depicts Assyrian control over Egypt. Before a great representation of Esarhaddon kneel the puny figures of two Egyptian princes, each with a ring passed through his lip. To these lip-rings one end of a cord is tied, while the other end is gripped in the hand of Esarhaddon. Isaiah refers to this method of humiliating captive rulers: "Therefore I will put my hook in thy nose, and my bridle in thy lips" (*Isaiah* 37:29).

Of his victory over Egypt, Esarhaddon says:

Tarku, king of Egypt and Kush, from Ishupuri to Memphis, his royal city, a march of fifteen days—I smote daily in countless numbers his warriors. Himself I attacked five times with the point of the spear in deadly combat. Memphis, his royal city, I laid waste, I burned it with fire. His children and possessions I carried away to Assyria. The roots of Kush (Ethiopia) I tore out of Egypt. Over the whole of Egypt I placed afresh kings, governors, prefects, overseers, regents.

Esarhaddon greatly extended the dominions of Assyria. Egypt was conquered. Babylonia was rehabilitated. The ancient city of Babylon, which Sennacherib had destroyed, was rebuilt and restored as a royal city. With two royal capitals, Babylon and Nineveh, and many other great cities, Assyria flourished.

Within its own borders Assyria never had the natural wealth and resources to build and maintain the great cities erected by its ambitious monarchs. This wealth had to come from without the national boundaries. But little came from trade. The great bulk of the wealth was tribute wrung from conquered peoples. With treasure torn from wounded lands, the warlike monarchs built gorgeous palaces for themselves and lofty temples for their gods in the various capitals of their empires. The kings of Assyria decorated the walls of their palaces with reliefs depicting the military might of the matchless troops that won for them an empire reaching from the Euphrates to the Nile, and from the Persian Gulf to the hills of northern Syria.

The kings collected more than material treasure. From conquered countries they gathered the ablest inhabitants and transported them to Assyria for service in all walks of life. Many artists and scholars from foreign lands found outlet for their talents in the palaces and temples of the kings of Assyria. The written and pictured records of that distant day are gradually being brought to light to unfold new pages of history. Much of this material evidence illuminates and supplements the work of the editorial annalists who compiled the religious history of the epochs in the Books of *Kings* and the Books of *Chronicles,* and adds fresh lustre to the written work of the immortal Isaiah.

The rise of the Assyrians to empire was marked with a corresponding decline of the Hebraic peoples as a factor in world politics. Israel had vanished as a political entity, and Judah had shrunk to a shadow of its former greatness. However, during this period the Children of Israel were giving to mankind a spiritual heritage priceless beyond the gift of king or potentate. This period produced four outstanding preachers of pure religion who revolutionized religious thought. Amos and Hosea were followed by the mighty-minded Isaiah and the peasant prophet, Micah.

The inspired writings of Isaiah stand unparalleled in the field of religious literature. He gave to the world a new conception of the holiness and the majesty of God. He foretold the coming of the Messiah, outlined the mission of the coming Christ toward the ultimate redemption of mankind, and raised religion from mere ceremonial worship to the realms of spiritual and religious morality.

The part of the written work of Micah which has come down to us in the Old Testament apparently deals with the time when Sennacherib was threatening Jerusalem with destruction. The country-bred young

Micah lacked the finely furnished mind of Isaiah, but lacked nothing in consecration and devotion. He viewed with horror the callousness and wickedness of the inhabitants of the cities of Judah. The vice and violence of the ruling classes in the cities of Judah brought from Micah the burning denunciations found in the first three chapters of his work. Despite his pessimism over the future of Judah he visioned a brighter day, which led him to proclaim: "But thou, Bethlehem Ephratah, though thou be little among the thousands of Judah, yet out of thee shall he come forth unto me that is to be ruler in Israel; whose goings forth have been from of old, from everlasting"—*Micah* 5:2.

With the passing of Hezekiah, and the ascension of Manasseh to the throne, the last vestige of political independence vanished from Judah. During his long reign, Manasseh accepted without struggle the Assyrian overlordship. Probably Manasseh's peaceful policies brought material benefits to Judah. The merchants of Judah could push their trade throughout the far-flung Assyrian Empire. Mingling freely with the Assyrians, the keen-minded Hebrews doubtless absorbed much Chaldean culture. This would be particularly true after B. C. 668, when Esarhaddon was succeeded on the throne by the scholarly Ashurbanipal, the last of the great sovereigns of Assyria.

Prominent among Ashurbanipal's peaceful pursuits was his promotion of culture and education. In his palace at Nineveh he caused to be collected literary works from all parts of his empire. This great library was discovered by Horsmuzd Rassam in 1854. This library included epics, poems, hymns, legends, lessons in languages and in grammar and composition, dictionaries, in fact, every sort of written document which could be found in Ashurbanipal's day. This great collection is now in the British Museum. It is not unlikely that interest in literature was stimulated among the Hebrews at this period, which may have led to the production of the great writings which shortly afterward made their appearance in Judah. Jeremiah, who began his ministry about B. C. 626, did not depend on the spoken word to such an extent as some of his prophetic predecessors. He dictated his sublime messages to his secretary, Baruch, who inscribed them on a roll.

So Manasseh made Judah and the inhabitants of Jerusalem to err,
and to do worse than the heathen.—2 Chronicles 33:9

Manasseh was not content with mere political dependence on Assyria. Religiously he was more Assyrian than Hebrew. Under his guidance the pagan practices of Assyria supplanted the worship of Jehovah throughout Judah (See 2 *Kings* 21:2-9).

14

The defection of Judah from the worship of Jehovah marked a definite break in the prophetic succession. Prophets were not lacking, but religious persecution was driving them to cover. Vice and violence ran rampant in the City of Peace. "Moreover Manasseh shed innocent blood very much, till he had filled Jerusalem from one end to another" (2 *Kings* 21:16).

Evidently Manasseh's administration was not altogether satisfactory to his Assyrian overlords. "The captains of the host of the king of Assyria, which took Manasseh among the thorns, and bound him with fetters, and carried him to Babylon" (2 *Chronicles* 33:11). The Assyrians had touching, though not tender, methods of bringing recalcitrants to time. The refractory ruler of Judah was soon tamed, "and when he was in affliction, he besought the Lord his God." It was a chastened Manasseh who returned to Jerusalem to take up his duties as ruler. After his return from Babylon, Manasseh completely altered his mode of life, and restored the worship of Jehovah.

The brief reign of Amon, who succeeded Manasseh, ended when conspiracy among his palace retinue led to his death. This brought the eight year old Josiah to the throne. His coming brought a period of social and religious reform. During his minority the boy king seems to have been advised by a group of wise and loyal guardians. Reared by God-fearing men in the shadow of the temple, it was but natural that "he began to seek after the God of David his father" (2 *Chronicles* 34:3). Judah now had a king whom the annalists unhesitatingly approved.

When the young king had purged "Judah and Jerusalem from the high places, and the groves, and the carved images, and the molten images" (2 *Chronicles* 34:3) he was now ready to crown his campaign of religious reform by completely restoring the temple. Years of neglect and defilement during the reign of Manasseh had rendered the temple in sore need of repairs. The great building was now over three centuries old. Time had taken its toll from the ancient structure. Heavier than the hand of time had been the hand of the despoiler. Time and again the treasures had been stripped from its holy walls to soothe the sordid palm of the foreign tribute collector. Marred and broken were the polished cedar floors "which the kings of Judah had destroyed" (2 *Chronicles* 34:11). Pagan religious practices had frequently penetrated the sacred precincts, leaving behind them destruction and defilement. Solomon's successors had marred his mighty masterpiece of construction.

The chronicler dwells in detail over the story of the labors of the commission appointed to carry out the restoration of the temple. Here was a subject worthy of his pen. The passing of crowns or kingdoms could be covered with a few phrases, but the Hebrew historians wrote

with rapture of any episode which tended toward the glorification of the
House of the Lord. The restoration of the temple was a labor of love.
Funds were collected not only in Jerusalem and Judah, but from "all
the remnant of Israel." Graft and mismanagement were carefully guarded
against. Priest labored with craftsman. The Chosen People had again
returned to the Lord their God.

*Hilkiah the priest found a book of the law of the Lord given by
Moses.*—2 Chronicles 34:14

Sometime, in the unremembered long ago, some gifted and spiritually-
minded scribe had lovingly copied from ancient tablets "the law of the
Lord given by Moses," and carefully preserved his writings for posterity
by burying them deep in the archives of the temple. Who was this unknown writer? Why was his work so long forgotten that Hilkiah was
amazed when he accidentally discovered it? These questions can be answered only by conjecture. It is clear, however, that these rediscovered
documents were of such potential importance that their finding created
a "nine days wonder" in Judah such as would be occasioned in our world
today were some fortunate archæologist to discover one of the original
documents on which the Pentateuch is based. This fortunate find was an
important factor in the making of the Old Testament as we read it today.

As one reflects on the narrative of the rediscovery of "the Law" it is
possible to picture the patriarchal priest hovering over the busy workmen
to make sure that no injury comes to the sacred objects placed in the temple centuries before by Israel's greatest king, Solomon. As the workmen
disturb the dust in some dim recess, he suddenly sees something which
attracts his aged eye—a roll of manuscript. Carefully removing the dust
of years, he holds it up to a shaft of light streaming down from one of
the "narrow windows" high in the wall of the temple. As he reads the
first few faded words he senses the importance of the document, and
hurriedly sends for Shaphan the scribe. Shaphan is so impressed that he
hurries with the book to the palace and reads it to king Josiah. The
young monarch is so moved by the solemn and sublime contents of the
mysterious manuscript that he unconsciously resorts to the Hebrew method
of expressing deep emotion: he rends his clothes.

Naturally, there arose among the advisors of the king the question, Is
this work genuine? The decision is made to consult Huldah, the prophet-
ess, as to the authenticity of this literary and religious treasure. Evidently
Huldah was a woman of learning, since the chronicler interpolates the
interesting information that "she dwelt in Jerusalem in the college" (2
Chronicles 34:22). The mention of a college as being in existence as
early as B. C. 600 might cause the raising of a questioning eyebrow were

it not known that Schaeffer and Genet discovered at Ras Shamra in Syria the well preserved remains of a college for priests which long antedates the time of Josiah. At the Ras Shamra school twelve languages were taught.*

When Huldah sanctioned the Book of the Law, Josiah called for a general assembly at Jerusalem: "And he read in their ears all the words of the book of the covenant which was found in the house of the Lord" (2 *Kings* 23:2).

The finding of the Book of the Law, and its promulgation in Judah, made a profound impression on the religious thought of the kingdom. The re-establishment of the Mosaic Law as the fundamental law of the land brought about a great revival of religion. We catch an echo of the effect of the rediscovery of the law in the writings of Jeremiah (See *Jeremiah* 11:2-8).

It is the considered judgment of authorities on the component books of the Old Testament that the manuscript discovered by Hilkiah covered the same ground, at least the legal part of it, as the Book of *Deuteronomy* as we read it today. It is fortunate that this priceless literary treasure was discovered before the destruction of the temple, which a not-far-distant day was to bring about.

The wave of religious reform which followed the discovery of "the Law" was accompanied by social and political prosperity. Ashurbanipal, the last of the great Assyrian monarchs, had now grown old, and was peacefully pursuing his hobby of collecting libraries. Probably the old king worried little over Palestine so long as the tribute was promptly paid. Judah was plodding along the paths of peace as faithful vassal of Assyria, undreaming that the end of both Judah and Assyria loomed in the not-far-distant future.

The sovereigns of the Assyrian Period were:

Israel	*Assyria*	*Judah*
Zechariah &	Tiglath-pileser 745-727	Jotham 740-735
Shallum ... 740	Shalmaneser V 727-722	Ahaz ...... 735-715?
Menehem ... 740-736	Sargon II.... 722-705	Hezekiah ... 715-686
Pekahiah...... 736-735	Sennacherib .. 705-682	Manasseh .. 686-641
Pekah 735-732	Esarhaddon .. 681-668	Amon 641-639
Hoshea 732-722	Ashurbanipal.. 668-625	Josiah 639-608

End of the Kingdom.

---

*See *Secrets from the Syrian Hills*, by C. F. A. Schaeffer.

XIV

THE ENDING OF THE KINGDOM OF JUDAH

Thy shepherds slumber, O king of Assyria: thy nobles shall dwell in the dust: thy people is scattered upon the mountains, and no man gathereth them.—Nahum 3:18

O ye children of Benjamin, gather yourselves to flee out of the midst of Jerusalem, and blow the trumpet in Tekoa, and set up a sign of fire in Beth-hacerem: for evil appeareth out of the north, and great destruction.—Jeremiah 6:1

IN the latter days of the kingdom of Judah, there arose a new group of Hebrew prophets who not only foretold the coming downfall of Judah, but with amazing daring prophesied the end of the Assyrian empire which had long dominated western Asia. The outstanding prophet of this period was Jeremiah, but his work was ably seconded by Nahum and Zephaniah. Jeremiah was a son of Hilkiah and of priestly descent, while Zephaniah was a direct descendant of king Hezekiah. Of Nahum little is known. Elkosh, his birthplace, cannot be located today. These three great souls lived and labored at a time when the East was in a turmoil. The scenes on the stage of international politics were rapidly shifting. Evil was approaching "out of the north" in the form of hordes of hardy horsemen who were rolling down through the Caucasus from the wild, wind-blown steppes of Russia. This wave of semi-barbarians was the Scythians, men hard and cruel as the winters of the country which cradled them. Tidelike, they swept down through Syria to the Egyptian border, and threatened to overrun all of western Asia. Rocklike, Assyria stood in the tide of invasion, parting it so that one stream flowed into Asia Minor, while the other moved down through Media. Danger of Assyrian overthrow was, for the time, postponed.

Long before this time, when Assyria was just approaching its greatest glory, Isaiah had proclaimed: "I will punish the fruit of the stout heart of the king of Assyria, and the glory of his high looks" (*Isaiah* 10:12). Zephaniah, who was closer to the coming events, clothed his prophecies with more detail, but it remained for Nahum to present the most vivid pictures of the doom of Assyria and the destruction of Nineveh.

Nineveh at this time must have been one of the most beautiful cities in the world. Three sovereigns in succession—Sennacherib, Esarhaddon, and Ashurbanipal—had brought the treasures of empire to their capital city on the Tigris, and used this wealth to build gorgeous palaces and to beautify the city of Nineveh. Their palaces were built of brick. Against the walls of the rooms were ranged rich statuary and beautifully executed reliefs illustrating the warlike deeds of the mighty kings, while the rest of the walls were lined with rare woods. Towering walls, measuring a distance of twelve miles, guarded the treasures of the royal city.

While Nineveh was in its greatest glory, seemingly secure behind its protecting walls, the varicolored tiles of its turreted towers glittering under the Assyrian sun, Nahum was writing with the realism of an eyewitness his poetic predictions of the coming doom of the city beautiful. Nahum foresaw, twenty-six centuries ago, the shapeless mound of Nineveh into which the archæologist Botta was to plunge the excavator's spade in the nineteenth century A. D. "Nineveh is empty," "Nineveh is laid waste," wrote Nahum.

The disruption and dismemberment of the Assyrian empire did not come suddenly as a result of foreign invasion. Assyria lay like an octopus over western Asia, its grasping tentacles even reaching over into Egypt. Years were required to break the tenacious hold of Assyria on neighboring nations, and bring the day when the combined armies of the Babylonians, the Medes, and the Sythians were to wound Assyria to the heart by capturing Nineveh.

Necho king of Egypt came up to fight against Charchemish by Euphrates: and Josiah went out against him.—2 Chronicles 35:20

Egypt, under the ambitious Necho II, was among the first of the dependencies to throw off the Assyrian yoke. Not content with mere independence, Necho visioned the recovery of the Palestinian provinces which had once belonged to Egypt. Accordingly he marched an army toward the Euphrates in B. C. 609. Gaza and Ashkelon were quickly captured. Other cities fell. The way seemed clear until Josiah, a faithful vassal of Assyria, intercepted the march of Necho at Megiddo. It is difficult to understand this impetuous action of Josiah. Judah could be no military match for Egypt. In the battle which followed, Josiah lost his life. Thus ended a reign which seemed full of promise for better things.

Assyria, seriously threatened from within and without, was in no position to rescue Judah. Judah became a vassal of Egypt. In the chaotic political conditions which followed, some sort of popular election was held in Judah: "Then the people of the land took Jehoahaz the son of Josiah, and made him king in his father's stead in Jerusalem" (2 *Chronicles* 36:1). The choice of a king was not satisfactory to the Egyptian overlord. Necho summoned Jehoahaz to his military camp at Riblath, in Syria. Jeremiah prophesied that the king would never return (See *Jeremiah* 22:11, 12). The Pharaoh deposed Jehoahaz and placed Judah under a heavy fine. "And Pharaoh-nechoh made Eliakim the son of Josiah king in the room of Josiah his father, and turned his name to Jehoiakim, and took Jehoahaz away: and he came to Egypt, and died there" (2 *Kings* 23:34).

Hebrew nationalism was now more shadow than substance. Judah was but a pawn in the great game of international politics played by powerful peoples. Against this dark background the brilliant but bitter writings of Jeremiah were projected. It was Jeremiah's misfortune that the major portion of his ministry fell in a period when world-shaking political events were rendering the national life of Judah hopeless. Under such conditions his writings could not be otherwise than gloomy. Jeremiah, however, was no mere carping critic. Patriot and prophet, he was also a practical politician. A keen, far-seeing student of world affairs, he could see little hope for Judah. His stinging tongue and trenchant pen made him personally unpopular with the rulers of dying Judah. Such skin-lifting sermons as *Jeremiah* 12 and 13 irked the aristocracy of Jerusalem. The keeping of the covenant, not the divine rights of kings, was uppermost in the mind of Jeremiah. He saw the plight of the Chosen People as a result of sin and disobedience.—"But if they will not obey, I will utterly pluck up and destroy that nation, saith the Lord" (*Jeremiah* 12:17). Such preaching did not make for popularity.

Judah remained under Egyptian control for four years. Meanwhile the life stream of Assyria had been ebbing fast. The seeds of dissolution had been sown in Assyria during the latter years of the reign of Ashurbanipal. While the aged king was dreaming over his literary collections and libraries, powerful personalities were plotting against him. The Assyrian empire was not a product of properly handled economic natural resources. It was an empire raised by the point of the sword. What the sword makes, the sword must maintain. Artificial empires won by warfare must be maintained by the sword. Dictatorships are never static. Once the active element of warfare was withdrawn from Assyrian political purpose, Assyria's days of empire were numbered.

Within a year after the death of Ashurbanipal, in B. C. 625, Nabopolasser, who had been Ashurbanipal's viceroy at Babylon, led a successful revolt against Ashur-etil-ili, the successor of Ashurbanipal, and wrested all of Babylonia from Assyrian control. Joining his forces with those of the Medes and the Scythians against whom he had formerly fought, Nabopolasser joined in a series of campaigns against the city of Nineveh, which finally fell before a combined assault in B. C. 612.

There has long been much uncertainty among historians as to the date of the fall of Nineveh. Many authorities place the date as B. C. 606. At that date the armies of Nabopolasser were campaigning in Palestine, and it has been difficult to see how they could have been present at the fall of Nineveh if the city fell during that year. The difficulty as to dates has been cleared up by a Babylonian cylinder now in the British Museum. This cylinder gives a day by day account of historical events of eight years of Nabopolasser's reign. This chronology is well established. It gives the date of the final fall of Nineveh as the fourteenth year of Nabopolasser. This, according to our system of reckoning, would be B. C. 612. The Medes and the semi-barbaric Scythians probably knew little of the art of writing. Although they probably bore the brunt of the warfare before Nineveh, they lacked scribes to immortalize their military glory. Cultured Babylonians kept the records, and characteristically claimed most of the glory for their country.

The fall of Nineveh did not bring about the immediate end of Assyria. When Nineveh fell, the Assyrian army successfully broke through the ring of armies which surrounded the city. Establishing a new capital at Harran, the Assyrians fought on for a few years, but, as a world power, Assyria's day was done.

The rise of the Neo-Babylonian (New Babylonian) empire over the ruins of the great Assyrian empire set the stage for a renewal of the age-old conflict for control of western Asia between the civilization centering on the Nile and that centering on the Euphrates and Tigris. Palestine was again the center of conflict. Judah lay on the perilous path of Mars.

While Nabopolasser was busy reaping the harvest of his victories, and consolidating his gains in Assyria, Egypt under Necho II had successfully entered the arena and occupied considerable territory. On the throne of Judah he had placed his puppet, Jehoiakim. The great question of supremacy on the coast had yet to be settled, however. Necho marched a great army to Carchemish on the Euphrates. Nabopolasser met this challenge by sending his armies under his eldest son, Nebuchadnezzar to meet the invaders. In the battle which followed, Nebuchadnezzar dealt a crushing blow to Egyptian ambition. The battle of Carchemish, B. C. 604, has been extensively dealt with by historians, but none have ever matched the description of defeat penned by Jeremiah (See *Jeremiah* 46). Egypt was overwhelmed. Judah, under Jehoiakim, became a vassal of Babylonia.

While Nebuchadnezzar was pursuing the Egyptians in their panic-stricken retreat from the fatal field of Carchemish, word was brought to him of the death of his father, and the young man returned to Babylon to be crowned king. Thus Nebuchadnezzar became an important factor in the political life of Judah during its declining days.

Jehoiakim was at first apparently loyal to Nebuchadnezzar. At least the tribute was paid. However there developed in Judah a party of political patriots who urged Jehoiakim to throw off the Chaldean yoke. Habakkuk, in his writings, seems to reflect a state of mind which was current in Jerusalem (See *Habakkuk* 1:6-17). Jeremiah, sensing the power of Nebuchadnezzar, raised a strong voice against revolt, but to no avail. In 601 Judah refused to pay the tribute.

Jeremiah's political attitude earned him the distrust of many in high places in Jerusalem. Jehoiakim hated him. He was denied admission to the temple (See *Jeremiah* 36:5). Practically a prisoner, Jeremiah dictated his messages to his faithful secretary, Baruch, and ordered him to read them before the house of the Lord. Political leaders regarded the writings of Jeremiah as seditious and advised Jeremiah to flee. The king ordered the writings of Jeremiah destroyed. Jeremiah disagreed with the prophets who believed that Jerusalem was inviolate and would never fall to foreign foe.

At first Nebuchadnezzar failed to take Judah's puny revolt seriously. He apparently did not deem it worthy of the attention of the Assyrian army. To bring Jehoiakim to his senses he "sent against him bands of the Chaldees, and bands of the Syrians, and bands of the Moabites" (2 *Kings* 24:2). When this guerilla warfare failed to bring the desired results, Nebuchadnezzar came with an overpowering army and invested Jerusalem. About this time Jehoiakim had died, leaving the throne to his young son, Jehoiachin. With the Chaldean army before the gates, there was nothing the young king could do to save the city from destruction but surrender. The king, his mother, and his court, together with seven thousand fighting men and a thousand craftsmen and smiths, were carried captive to Babylon (See 2 *Kings* 24:10-16; also *Jeremiah* 24:1-5).

This removal of the flower of Jerusalem's manhood, the "very good figs," as Jeremiah calls them, might seem to be a brutal military measure, but compared with Assyrian practices on conquered peoples, Nebuchadnezzar's punitive policies must be judged as humane. Assyrian records of military campaigns tell of large numbers of captives flayed alive and of others impaled on stakes, to die in agony as a warning to their fellow countrymen. War is a grim business.

To meet the heavy indemnity which Nebuchadnezzar levied on the city it was necessary to strip the sacred area of its treasures: "And he carried out thence all the treasures of the house of the Lord, and the treasures of the king's house, and cut in pieces all the vessels of gold which Solomon king of Israel had made in the temple of the Lord" (2 *Kings*

24:13). The sacred objects used in the rituals of worship were left untouched, but Jeremiah grimly warned: "They shall be carried to Babylon, and there shall they be until the day that I visit them, saith the Lord; then will I bring them up, and restore them to this place" (*Jeremiah* 27:22).

With Jerusalem thoroughly subdued, Nebuchadnezzar placed another of the ill-fated sons of Josiah on the throne of Judah. This was Mattaniah, to whom Nebuchadnezzar gave the regnal name of Zedekiah. The inhabitants of Judah now had the saddening experience of watching the loot-laden army of the Chaldeans march away from the humiliated city, carrying with them the best and bravest of Judah to dwell in exile on the banks of the Chebar in Babylonia.

The young and inexperienced Zedekiah was left to handle an administrative situation which would have appalled an older man. Such leaders of thought as were left in the city were sharply divided into two political parties, one anti-Chaldean, and one pro-Chaldean. The leader of the anti-Chaldean faction was Hananiah, who was regarded by his followers as a prophet. This party urged a national policy of revolt against Nebuchadnezzar, basing their arguments on the belief that Jerusalem was sacred and could not fall. On the other hand, Jeremiah urged that Jerusalem was being punished for its sins, and that the only safe policy was to submit to the unbreakable power of Nebuchadnezzar, meanwhile repenting and invoking the powers of the Lord God of Israel. Politically, the population was split into a religious and a non-religious party. Jeremiah warned that continued revolt would bring a climaxing disaster; that Jerusalem would fall, "and this whole land shall be a desolation, and an astonishment; and these nations shall serve the king of Babylon seventy years" (*Jeremiah* 25:11). Jeremiah's warning fell on deaf ears.

The bitterness of the conflict between the two schools of political thought in Jerusalem is portrayed in *Jeremiah* 27. Jeremiah even extended his campaign to the exiles in Babylonia by means of correspondence, urging them to make the best of a difficult situation (See *Jeremiah* 29:3-7). Despite the fact that the pro-Chaldean faction was encouraged by the messages of Ezekiel, a young priest of the temple who was now in exile in Babylonia, Jeremiah was fighting a losing political battle. Encouraged by the promise of help from Hophra, king of Egypt, "Zedekiah rebelled against the king of Babylon" (2 *Kings* 24:20).

And it came to pass in the ninth year of his reign, in the tenth month, in the tenth day of the month, that Nebuchadnezzar king of Babylon came, he, and all his host, against Jerusalem, and pitched against it; and they built forts against it round about.— 2 Kings 25:1

Nebuchadnezzar was now determined to settle Judah once and for all. Being an experienced soldier, he made no attempt to take Jerusalem by storm. Slowly, but surely, starvation would bring surrender. His forces were sufficient to invest closely all the other cities of Judah (See *Jeremiah* 34:7). Judah was a country besieged. The situation looked hopeless to the Hebrews. Caught in an ever-tightening iron ring of arms, Zedekiah sent to Jeremiah, saying "Pray now unto the Lord our God for us" (*Jeremiah* 37:3). A repentant king was ready for reform. Internal reforms were promptly proclaimed (See *Jeremiah* 34:8, 9). The beleaguered city, however, soon had a brief period of hope. The siege was temporarily lifted.

Then Pharaoh's army was come forth out of Egypt: and when the Chaldeans that besieged Jerusalem heard tidings of them, they departed from Jerusalem.—Jeremiah 37:5

The invasion of Palestine by Hophra's Egyptian army, and the lifting of the siege of Jerusalem by Nebuchadnezzar, caused great rejoicing in Judah. Jerusalem had not fallen. Jeremiah was duly discredited. Vainly the prophet warned: "Behold, Pharaoh's army, which is come forth to help you, shall return to Egypt into their own land. And the Chaldeans shall come again, and fight against this city, and take it, and burn it with fire" (*Jeremiah* 37:7, 8). The anti-Chaldeans were in the saddle. Jeremiah was truly "a prophet without honor." Jeremiah, about to leave the city on some private business, was accused of treasonable traffic with the Chaldeans, and cast into prison. There he might have been left to rot had not the Chaldeans returned to the investment of Jerusalem. The ancients had a facile forgetfulness for unwanted persons once they were placed in prison.

With Nebuchadnezzar's forces again surrounding the city, starvation once more threatened. The harassed Zedekiah, probably with mingled fear and respect, had Jeremiah taken from the dungeon and confined in the court of the prison. The extremity to which the inhabitants of Jerusalem were reduced through lack of food is reflected in the statement in regard to Jeremiah, "that they should give him daily a piece of bread out of the baker's street, until all the bread in the city were spent" (*Jeremiah* 37:21).

The leaders of the party opposed to Jeremiah were thoroughly provoked by Zedekiah's apparently lenient treatment of the prophet. Coming to the king with a plea that Jeremiah's predictions were destroying the morale of the city's defenders, they demanded that Jeremiah be put to death. "Then Zedekiah the king said, Behold he is in your hand: for the king is not he that can do anything against you" (*Jeremiah* 38:5).

Once in the hands of his enemies, no mercy would be asked or given. The prophet was lowered into a dungeon to await a lingering death: "And in the dungeon there was no water, but mire: so Jeremiah sunk in the mire" (*Jeremiah* 38:6). Jeremiah was in a sorry plight. In the thick mire he could not move about freely. If he attempted to lie down he would suffocate. Without water, without food, he could only pray for death to end his agony. Jeremiah, however, was not destined to die just yet. Through the merciful intervention of a temple negro slave, the king ordered Jeremiah rescued from the pit, and again confined in the court of the prison.

The inhabitants of Jerusalem were gazing into the grim and grisly face of starvation. Only a little time remained. Moved by desperation, Zedekiah finally sought a secret conference with Jeremiah "in the third entry that is in the house of the Lord." In a last counsel of despair the distraught king begged of Jeremiah to "hide nothing from me." After exacting a promise that if he gave counsel he would not be put to death, Jeremiah urged surrender: "Obey, I beseech thee, the voice of the Lord, which I speak unto thee: . . . and thy soul shall live" (*Jeremiah* 38:20). Jeremiah pointed out the terrible alternative which would result from continued resistance. Surrender would prevent the Holy City from being put to the torch. The kingdom might fall but Jerusalem would still stand. The king was convinced and summoned the leaders of Judah for a final conference with Jeremiah. This conference was futile. The obdurate opposition failed to comprehend the gravity of the prophet's warnings: "So they left off speaking with him; for the matter was not perceived" (*Jeremiah* 38:27).

The hesitating Zedekiah delayed too long. Jerusalem fell. In a last wild surge for freedom the imprisoned army broke from the city "by night by way of the gate within the two walls" (2 *Kings* 25:4) and fled toward Jericho. Here on the plain the fugitives were overtaken and slaughtered by the triumphant Babylonians. The last thing Zedekiah saw before his eyes were plucked out, was his own children being put to a dishonorable death. Then the broken king was led away in fetters to fret out his soul in a Babylonian dungeon, until, long later, a kindlier king of Babylon remembered that this blinded wreck of a man had once been a king (See 2 *Kings* 25:27).

> *And they burnt the house of God, and brake down the wall of Jerusalem, and burnt all the palaces thereof with fire, and destroyed all the goodly vessels thereof.*—2 Chronicles 36:19

No city ever built by man has been more frequently destroyed by warfare than Jerusalem. Many a wave of invasion has broken before its walls; many a wave of invasion, unhalted, has swept over its sacred site. Primitive men fought for its limestone caves. The Amorite and the Hittite fought fiercely over the strategic site. As the little city of Jebus, it long defied the Hebrews, until David won it for Israel. Egypt, Assyria, Babylonia, Persia, Greece, and Rome in turn possessed it, before the Moslem hordes came to claim it for their own. The best blood of Europe was gallantly shed to redeem the city in the Christian Crusades; the bravest blood of Islam was as gallantly shed to defend it. Seldom, however, has the sacred city suffered such complete destruction as that inflicted by Nebuchadnezzar.

During the days of the Hebrew kingdoms the city had often been saved from destruction by pouring out the temple treasures as tribute. Gold and silver had saved it. Now it was beyond ransom. Not only the gold and silver must go, but also the brasswork and the bronzework of the Holy House. (See 2 *Kings* 25:13-17). The hand of the despoiler could not be stayed.

The crowning humiliation of the Children of Israel was the destruction of the temple. After four hundred years of glory the great sanctuary lay in shattered ruins. High on the hill its broken, blackened walls stood stark to sentinel a nation's shameful end. Jerusalem was ruined. The departing Hebrews, marching from Jerusalem toward captivity, gazed back on a scene of desolation through their tears. The kingdom of David was done.

For seven centuries the Hebrews had shaped the history of Palestine. They carved out a kingdom in a land where no people has ever kept permanent footing. Land of limited natural resources, lacking in forests and minerals, its scant agricultural and pastoral areas broken by mountain and hemmed by desert, Palestine has broken the imperial ambitions of many proud peoples. Palestine has contributed little to the wealth of the world; her ships have never sailed the seven seas; her exports never gladdened the ports of the nations; but, above all places of the earth, Palestine has fostered God's greatest gift to mankind—the revelation of His Own Oneness and Holiness. Meagre, indeed, was the Hebrew kingdom's contribution to secular history; priceless was its contribution to religious thought.

And them that had escaped from the sword carried he away to Babylon.—2 Chronicles 36:20

In accordance with custom, Nebuchadnezzar carried away many of the inhabitants of Judah to captivity. So far, no Babylonian records of Nebuchadnezzar's capture and destruction of Jerusalem have come to light. During the latter years of Nebuchadnezzar's reign his principal peaceful pursuit was the restoration and rebuilding of temples and cities. Many interesting records of his great building campaigns have been unearthed by various archæological expeditions. Behind him he left more inscriptions bearing his name than any other monarch mentioned in the Old Testament. Perhaps the great king regarded his Palestinian campaign as a minor episode in his military career. In connection with the transportation of a part of the population of Judah to Babylonia, 2 *Kings* 25:12 states that he "left of the poor of the land to be vinedressers and husbandmen." Jeremiah refers to those whom Nebuchadnezzar deemed unworthy of deportation as "evil figs." Nebuchadnezzar refers to this policy in a general way in an inscription which reads, in part: "I captured the enemies, established justice in the lands; the people I exalted; the bad and evil I separated from the people."*

And all the people, both small and great, and the captains of the armies, arose, and came to Egypt: for they were afraid of the Chaldees.—2 Kings 25:26

Only the lower classes and the under-privileged portion of the population of Judah remained in the homeland. Judah was now an impoverished province over which Nebuchadnezzar placed Gedaliah as governor. Many prominent Hebrews who had left Judah during the days of active warfare now returned: "Even all the Jews returned out of all places whither they were driven, and came to the land of Judah, to Gedaliah, unto Mizpah, and gathered wine and summer fruits very much" (*Jeremiah* 40:12). Gedaliah, himself a Hebrew, planned a benevolent administration for his stricken country. Realizing the folly of continued resistance, he urged loyalty to the Babylonian regime: "Fear not to be the servants of the Chaldees: dwell in the land, and serve the king of Babylon; and it shall be well with you" (2 *Kings* 25:24). Since Jerusalem was destroyed, Gedaliah set up a provincial capital at Mizpah, seven miles north of Jerusalem. Here came Jeremiah to second the efforts of Gedaliah in the reconstruction of the remnants of Judah.

War had sown the dragon's teeth of hatred and intrigue. Word was brought to Gedaliah that a renegade Hebrew, Ishmael, was plotting his assassination. Ishmael was in the pay of the Ammonites, Israel's old-time enemy. Gedaliah's informant, Johanan, offered to slay Ishmael in an effort to avoid trouble. Sternly Gedaliah forbade him: "Thou shalt not do this thing: for thou speakest falsely of Ishmael" (*Jeremiah* 40:16). Unfortunately for the trusting Gedaliah, Johanan had spoken only too truly. Ishmael paid a ceremonial visit to Gedaliah, accompanied by ten trusted men. As they sat at table, hospitably breaking bread, Ishmael

*See *Cuneiform Inscriptions of Western Asia*, Rawlinson.

and his men suddenly arose and slew Gedaliah and his household. A delegation of eighty devout Hebrews, who had come to Mizpah on a religious mission, were lured into the house of Gedaliah by Ishmael and seventy of them summarily put to death and cast "into the midst of the pit." Ten men escaped death by pleading that they had valuable stores which they would turn over to Ishmael. Mizpah was at this time really a fortress, or a very small town surrounded by exceedingly heavy walls. Recent excavators have discovered that some of the walls were twenty-seven feet thick. Ishmael raided the place and carried off the inhabitants, including Gedaliah's daughters, and started back to the land of the Ammonites. Hotly pursued by loyal forces under Johanan, Ishmael was forced to abandon his captives, and, with a bodyguard of eight men, flee to safety among the Ammonites.

Beneath the ruins of Mizpah (Tell-en-Nasbeth) an expedition from the Pacific School of Religion, under the leadership of Professor F. W. Bade, discovered a number of large rock-cut pits or cisterns which had been closed up and covered over for many centuries. The stratification above them indicated that they had been undisturbed for twenty-six hundred years. In one of these was a large number of human skeletons. Were these the victims of Ishmael's treachery? This may be open to question. However, the find indicates that such practices were known in Jeremiah's day.

The murder of Gedaliah brought new troubles to Judah. The Babylonians would not be likely to overlook the killing of an appointed governor. Some of the leaders among the Hebrews advocated a mass flight to Egypt. Jeremiah was consulted, and advised that they remain in Judah. Jeremiah was promptly accused of false prophecy. The leaders went to Egypt and forcibly took Jeremiah with them.

In connection with Jeremiah's life in Egypt, a curious prophecy is to be found in *Jeremiah* 43:9, 10: "Take great stones in thine hand, and hide them in the clay in the brickkiln, which is at the entry of Pharaoh's house in Tahpanhes, in the sight of the men of Judah; and say unto them, Thus saith the Lord of Hosts, the God of Israel; Behold, I will send and take Nebuchadnezzar the king of Babylon, my servant, and will set his throne upon these stones that I have hid; and he shall spread his royal pavilion over them." Many commentators have doubted that Nebuchadnezzar ever invaded Egypt. However, a single Egyptian inscription states that he did invade the country in B. C. 577. Tell Defeunch, the site of Tahpanhes, was excavated by Sir Flinders Petrie. Before the ruins of a great royal palace of the Pharaoh he discovered something hitherto unknown in Egyptian excavation. This was a great pavement of brickwork, raised to platform height, measuring one hundred by sixty feet, directly in front of the main entrance. It is a strange fact that such a platform should be found just where Jeremiah said it would be.

Of Jeremiah's later life nothing is known. Probably the tradition that he died in Egypt is well founded. From his writings, one gathers that Jeremiah was a solitary, sensitive soul, misunderstood and mocked by immoral and mercenary political partisans. The political policies he promoted, the prophecies he proclaimed brought him only persecution and imprisonment. Strange product of a turbulent time, his own generation thought him a failure; only posterity could perceive his greatness. He saw the land he loved swept with the sword, his beloved Jerusalem reduced to ashes, part of his people carried into captivity, part of them in voluntary exile, only the unfit residue remaining.

Jeremiah wrote with realism the story of the ending of the kingdom of Judah. His meditations over his people's sins; his eloquent appeals for national repentance; his pen pictures of war-stricken Jerusalem, and the poignant poetry of his lamentations over the fallen city, mark him as one of the great writers of all time.

Dying, Judah produced a flood of ever-living literature. Besides the book which bears his name, the five songs of sorrow in *Lamentations* are dedicated to Jeremiah. The brief Book of *Obadiah* belongs to this period. Habakkuk wrote with wondering worry as he contemplated how Jehovah could allow "the Chaldeans, that bitter and hasty nation," to continue crushing Judah. Finally he found the answer. God was just. Judah was being punished for her sins. The erudite Ezekiel in exile on the banks of the Chebar was beginning to write his brilliant letters. Great prophecies were being combined with "the Law." The Old Testament was gradually taking shape.

Hebrew nationalism was ending, but the great religious movement which originated among the Hebrews was but beginning. For fifteen hundred years the great spiritual idealism had been fettered by Hebrew formalism. Now it found freedom beyond all bounds of nationalism. Religion was denationalized, but was spiritualized and individualized. "The just shall live by his faith" (*Habakkuk* 2:4).

UNCOVERING A BABYLONIAN CITY

Nippur, Babylonia, was the scene of operations of the first "All American" archæological expedition to the Near East.

By permission of The Museum of the University of Pennsylvania

XV

BY THE RIVERS OF BABYLON

By the rivers of Babylon, there we sat down, yea, we wept, when we remembered Zion.—Psalm 137:1

THE knell had rung for Hebrew nationalism. Judah lay devastated in the tyrant tracks of war. Jerusalem was but the burned and blackened ghost of a slaughtered city. Where once had stood the shining temple, shapeless heaps of shattered stones and burnt beams monumented the crowning degradation of Israel. In doleful dirge, a grief-stricken prophet poured his sorrows into the pathetic poems of *Lamentations.*

The fall of Jerusalem marked another turning point in the history of Israel and in the history of religion. With the denationalization of Judah its population was widely dispersed. The bulk of the agricultural population was allowed to remain in the homeland. With them were left the physically unfit and the lower stratas of Hebrew society. Some strong groups had already fled to Egypt to join colonies of former expatriates. Individuals found freedom in other foreign lands. Palestine was beginning to give to the world her two most notable products, enlightened religion and the everlasting Jew.

The long-delayed day of reckoning had arrived. Israel must pay the prophesied penalty for neglecting to keep the covenant: "The Lord shall cause thee to be smitten before thine enemies: thou shalt go out one way against them, and flee seven ways before them: and shalt be removed into all the kingdoms of the earth" (*Deuteronomy* 28:25). The ablest and most directive portion of the population, the best blood of Judah, faced deportation. Hordes of hapless Hebrews were herded together for a forced three months' trek over mountain and desert. With backs bent under the burdens of loot they carried for their conquerors, they turned tear-wet eyes for a last, long, lingering look at ruined Jerusalem, 'ere they took the trail to a strange and distant land. The reed that would not bend was broken.

Only the physically fit would be chosen for such a journey. The Babylonians were seasoned campaigners who would not burden themselves with infants or the aged and infirm. Many a family must have been broken up before the beginning of that pitiful pilgrimage. Even then, only the strongest would survive. Many a grave must have been shaped in the hot sands or flinty slopes along the trail before the green country of the Euphrates was sighted. It must have been a weary, travel-stained remnant of the original contingent, with eyes red-rimmed from the refracted rays of sun on sand, that staggered into Babylonia.

The new arrivals were settled with the former contingent of captives on the banks of the Chebar, one of the great river-like canals which ancient Chaldeans had constructed to divert the waters of the Euphrates to the rich alluvial soils bordering the river. Although they were forbidden to revisit Judah, apparently little restriction was placed upon them. They were free to develop their own community life and enter freely into the commercial life of the country. Coming into Babylonia at a time when Nebuchadnezzar was starting a great building campaign, with its subsequent commercial expansion, many of the Hebrews must have found an outlet for their inherent commercial capabilities in the trade and commerce of Babylonia.

The Hebrew captives were fortunate in that they were enabled to mingle freely with the scholarly and literary-minded Babylonians. Babylon was at that time the great center of culture and education of the then-known world. The Israelites were now in the midst of a culture which had been developing since long before their famous ancestor, Abraham, was born. Abraham, himself, had profited by that country's educational advantages. Ur of the Chaldees, his home town, had been an early center of Chaldean culture. During the centuries since Abraham's day, Chaldean culture had advanced far. Definite advances had been made in art, in literature, and in some of the sciences. Centuries later, the writers of the Golden Age of Greece were to borrow extensively from early Babylonian epics and legends. We of today owe much to the Babylonians for pioneering work in the fields of literature, architecture, mathematics, science, and astronomy. The Hebrews have always been gifted with a keen interest in literature. In this intellectual atmosphere they must have found much to inspire them. Under this stimulus they made remarkable contributions to the religious thought of their day. To this period we owe many of the sublime prophecies and exalted inspirations to righteous living which we read in the Old Testament.

It is difficult to estimate to what extent the Hebrews entered into the social and political life of Babylonia. The Book of *Daniel* indicates that able and representative men found their way into court life. From the writings of Ezekiel we gather than he was familiar with governmental life and political trends in Babylonia.

Despite the fact that the temple had been destroyed and the exiles far removed from the holy City of David, the religious life of the Hebrews did not languish. Free from the fetters of formalism it took on new life and vigor, new trends and forms. Without a temple in which religious life could be centralized, current soul-needs called for its closer human application. Revealed religion took a long step forward. Jehovah was no longer the exclusive Lord God of the Hebrews administering through His Holy Temple in Jerusalem. He, the Holy One, was the Divine Ruler of all mankind, Jew and Gentile alike, and the universe the Kingdom of God.

So thou, O son of man, I have set thee a watchman unto the house of Israel; therefore thou shalt hear the word at my mouth, and warn them from me.—Ezekiel 33:7

A great factor in the altered religious life of the Jews was the work of the prophet Ezekiel. In early life Ezekiel had been a priest in the temple at Jerusalem. Torn from Jerusalem with the first group of exiles deported by Nebuchadnezzar with Jehoiachin in B. C. 597, Ezekiel had kept in touch through correspondence with affairs in his old home city. He had been active in supporting Jeremiah during the turbulent period which preceded the fall of Jerusalem. Much of the earlier part of the book which bears his name consists of warnings to the inhabitants of Judah and predictions that an unrepentant people would bring about the fall of Jerusalem. While he believed that Judah was being justly punished for its sins, he was not lacking in sympathy for the captives who came to join the colony of exiles on the banks of the Chebar. Touched to the heart by the plight of his countrymen, the polished, priestly scholar became the simple pastor of a forlorn people. He gathered groups of the people in their homes for religious and social instruction. The "synagogue" was an outgrowth of this custom.

The king spake, and said, Is not this great Babylon, that I have built for the house of the kingdom by the might of my power, and for the honor of my majesty?—Daniel 4:30

Someone has said that any great business house was but the shadow of the family at the head of it. In the same sense, it might be said that the Neo-Babylonian kingdom, which lasted from B. C. 625 to 538, was the shadow of a single illustrious Babylonian family. No family mentioned in the Old Testament made a more meteor-like flash across the horizons of history than the family that flamed into political prominence with the brilliant Nabopolasser and Nebuchadnezzar, and faded to obscurity with the degenerate Belshazzar. Strangely enough, this family of four known generations left behind it more material evidence of its day on earth than any other family mentioned in the Bible. The archæologists of today owe a wealth of gratitude to the royal family that governed Babylonia while the Children of Israel served in bondage there.

Nebuchadnezzar was the greatest builder of the Old Testament Period. The earlier years of his reign were given up to warfare, but during the latter years his principal peaceful pursuit was to carry on one of the greatest building campaigns the ancient world had ever known. Babylon, the capital city of the empire, was entirely rebuilt and became the largest, richest, and most populous city on earth. Nebuchadnezzar rebuilt and strengthened its defensive walls, and surrounded them with a great moat. Since the region had no stone these walls were built entirely of brick. No city ever built by man had walls of such towering height or amazing thickness. The city was entered through a hundred gates. The most famous of the gates was the magnificent Ishtar gate, the entrance to the inner, or royal, city. This gateway was the beginning of the sacred way over which the processions of Marduk, the principal deity of Babylon, might pass to the temple. On the protecting walls, as well as on the gateway itself, were figures of lions, bulls, and dragons in low relief, executed in brilliantly enamelled titles. These tiles were so excellently made that many of them are just as bright and perfect today as when they glittered on the walls of Babylon twenty-five centuries ago.

Limited to clay products as native building materials, Nebuchadnezzar reared great and imposing structures whose massive ruins amaze the excavators of today. All timber had to be imported. Perhaps some of the timber for roofing and decorative purposes was brought all the way from the distant Lebanons. On a monument at Wadi Brisa in the Lebanons was found an inscription of Nebuchadnezzar which reads, in part: "I cut a road for the cedars and before Marduk, my king, I brought massive, tall, strong cedars, of wonderful beauty, whose dark appearance was impressive, the mighty product of the Lebanon.* With bricks of clay, many of which bear his name and boastful references to his reign, Nebuchadnezzar built gorgeous palaces for himself and great temples for the gods of Babylon. Here was the great temple of Marduk, the famous Hanging Gardens (one of the Seven Wonders of the World), and the Throne Hall on the wall of which Belshazzar saw the handwriting before the fall of the city to the Medes and Persians in B. C. 539.

Although Babylon was Nebuchadnezzar's masterpiece of construction, other cities were not neglected. Throughout the empire palaces, temples, and cities were rebuilt and restored. Interesting records of his building activities have been found at Kish, Ur of the Chaldees, and many other sites. The wide range of territory over which Nebuchadnezzar's identification markers have been found, attest not only the great extent of his

*See *Cuneiform Parallels to the Old Testament*, by R. W. Rogers.

empire, but also the great king's passion for monumental works in brick
and stone. Buildings, roadways, and pavements bear the boastful records
of a building king. An inscription in bronze, found on a temple step, is
typical:

> *Nebuchadnezzar, the king of Babylon (the gate of god) the restorer
> of the temple of Sigila and the temple Zida, the eldest son of
> Nabopolasser, the king of Babylon, am I. For the god Nabu, the
> supreme lord, the lengthener of the days of my kingdom, E-Zida
> his temple in Borsippa afresh I made.*

While Babylon was in its greatest glory, prophets of Israel were
predicting the city's ultimate doom. Long before Babylon grew into
magnificence under the transforming hand of Nebuchadnezzar, Isaiah
proclaimed: "Babylon, the glory of kingdoms, the beauty of the Chaldees'
excellency, shall be as when God overthrew Sodom and Gomorrah" (*Isaiah*
13:19). It remained for Jeremiah, however, to paint the dismal picture
of Babylon as it would appear twenty-five centuries later: "Babylon shall
become heaps, a dwelling place for dragons, an astonishment, and an
hissing, without an inhabitant" (*Jeremiah* 51:37).

Jeremiah's words are a vivid picture of the mound of Babylon as it
appeared when the German Orient Society's expedition, under the direction of Dr. Robert Koldeway, began operations at the site in 1899. After
the city had been left uninhabited, the weather had disintegrated the
upper portions of the brick ruins into a thick bed of clay which covered
the remains of the walls beneath. Wind and weather gradually transformed
the earth over the ruins of Nebuchadnezzar's structures into shapeless
mounds. Only the owl and the jackal haunted the heaps which marked
the site of the greatest city of the ancient East.

The German Orient Society carried on its operations up to the beginning of the World War. To Koldeway and his associates we are indebted
for most of our information as to the appearance of Babylon in the days
of Nebuchadnezzar. Not only did Koldeway uncover the amazing ruins,
but from field measurements he made accurate scale models which enable
us to visualize the great city as it appeared to the disheartened Hebrew
captives wending their way to their future home on the banks of the
Chebar.

Unlike some of the Assyrian cities, Babylon was not a city built by,
or supported by, the sword. The great city was a natural outgrowth of
the natural wealth of the country surrounding it. The soil surrounding
the city was the deep, rich silt of the river flats. Great irrigation systems
supplied plentiful water to the soil. The combination of rich soil, water,
and almost perpetual summer sunshine produced two crops of wheat per

year. Herodotus, the Greek historian and traveler (b. B. C. 484), found it a country of such astonishing richness that he feared his readers would regard his descriptions as gross exaggerations. This country had been the seat of some of the earliest settlements of mankind. Here were some of the earliest cradles of culture. Centuries of economic growth lay behind the city of Babylon. Although frequently ravished, and at times destroyed, by savage warfare, the economic resources of the country promptly restored it. Daring, indeed, were the Hebrew religionists who prophesied its ultimate end. Who could foresee that the grain-laden, palm-decked plain would some day be a desert? Only an inspired prophet could visualize the golden city of Babylon as "heaps" "without an inhabitant."

Babylon did not drop to oblivion overnight. No sudden shock of siege or wave of invasion overwhelmed it. The eyes of the prophets were surveying centuries unborn. Babylon survived the coming of the Medes and Persians. Xerxes sacked it of almost countless treasure. Alexander the Great died within its walls of a fever induced by alcoholism. The Romans overran it. Centuries passed before the desert tribes could ransack its ruins for the last of the city's fabled treasures. Through centuries the city rose to glory; through succeeding centuries it sank to nothingness. Before we pass on the prophet's predictions as merely foretelling the common fate of ancient cities, let us reflect that many contemporary cities still live and flourish. Damascus, one of the oldest cities in the world, is still a city of commercial importance. Sidon, never a large city, still survives. Even Jerusalem, which Nebuchadnezzar reduced to ruins, still lives.

In Nebuchadnezzar's reconstructions of temples throughout the empire, he made one important architectural alteration. Before Nebuchadnezzar's day the interiors of the temples had been a labyrinth of outer and inner sanctuaries to which only priests of varying degree had been admitted. The populace remained outside in the courts. Nebuchadnezzar altered all this by tearing out the inner sanctuaries and converting the structures into auditoriums. He opened up the interiors so that the laity could observe the rituals of worship. Dr. C. Leonard Wooley, Director of The Joint Expedition of the University of Pennsylvania Museum and the British Museum, which, at Ur of the Chaldees, unearthed much material evidence of Nebuchadnezzar's reconstructions, believes that Nebuchadnezzar introduced congregational worship.* This naturally calls to mind the dramatic events recorded in the third chapter of *Daniel* in connection with the king's attempts to make the entire population worship the gods of Babylon.

Nebuchadnezzar showed due regard for the original builders of temples and other buildings he restored. It was his custom, when original identification markers were discovered, to enclose the data of the original

---

*See *Ur of the Chaldees,* by C. L. Wooley.

builders, together with some historical tablets of his own, in the renewed walls; thus preserving much priceless historical data.

Nebuchadnezzar's reign forms the background for the earlier portions of the Book of *Daniel*. The latter part of the book carries over into the Persian Period. The work of Ezekiel also falls into the days of Nebuchadnezzar, since his active ministry began when he was "among the captives by the river of Chebar" (*Ezekiel* 1:1). Although Jeremiah was not in Babylonia, some of his most illuminating prophecies belong to this period.

Our childhood conceptions of Nebuchadnezzar as the cruel king who oppressed the Children of Israel must be modified in the light of modern research. Had the political policies advocated by Jeremiah and his fellow patriots been adopted by the rulers of Jerusalem, the city and the temple might have stood for many a day and the seventy years of captivity been avoided. Jeremiah was a statesman as well as a prophet. Nebuchadnezzar was a truly great king and an able administrator.

When Nebuchadnezzar's long reign of forty-three years came to an end in B. C. 561 he left behind him no worthy successor. His immediate descendants started a wild scramble for the throne. First in succession came his son, Amil-Marduk (the Evil-merodach of 2 *Kings* 25), who reigned less than two years before he was murdered by his brother-in-law, Nergal-shar-user (the Nergal-sharezer of *Jeremiah* 39:13), who had been a commanding officer at the capture of Jerusalem.

Evil-merodach king of Babylon in the year that he began to reign did lift up the head of Jehoiachin king of Judah out of prison.—
2 Kings 25:27

Of the brief reign of Amil-Marduk but little is known from the Old Testament. There is only a brief notation in *Kings*, and similar information in the writings of Jeremiah. These record the historical fact that he released Jehoiachin of Judah, after half a lifetime of imprisonment, and recognized his royal standing. This would seem to indicate that time was healing the wounds of bitterness of war. The Israelites had found their place in the Babylonian economic system. The only material evidence regarding Amil-Marduk that has so far been discovered is an inscription on an alabaster vase, discovered by De Morgan at Susa, where some Edomite conqueror had probably carried it. This inscription reads: "Palace of Amil-Marduk, king of Babylon, son of Nebuchadnezzar, king of Babylon."

Nergal-shar-user reigned for four years and was succeeded by his young son, Labasha-Marduk, who reigned for only a few months. This rapid succession of nondescript kings was disastrous for Babylonia. Powerful peoples in leanly-favored lands were looking longingly toward opulent

Babylonia. Within the empire the seeds of disintegration were being sown. The kingdom which Nebuchadnezzar had inherited and the empire his arms had won were being wrecked by machinations of political parties seeking personal profit through the internal unrest in Babylonia. Absorbed in struggles for political control of the world's richest city, the leaders in the administration of Babylonia failed to observe or underestimated the warclouds gathering in the east where the Medes and Persians were soon to make a bid for world empire. The aging eyes of Jeremiah could clearly foresee the ultimate doom of Babylon: "So Jeremiah wrote in a book all the evil that should come upon Babylon" (*Jeremiah* 51:60), but the Babylonians were not likely to read the works of Jeremiah. Had they read them, they would doubtless have dismissed them as the vaporings of an austere religious fanatic. The handwriting on the wall was not yet discernible in Babylonia.

The contest for the kingship of Babylonia was finally settled in B. C. 556, when a conspiracy of nobles and priests placed another of Nebuchadnezzar's descendants on the throne. This was Nabonidus, the father of the ill-fated Belshazzar who figures so prominently in the stirring story told in the fifth chapter of *Daniel.* It is questionable whether or not this was a wise choice. A stronger king might have postponed Babylonia's evil day. Although Nabonidus was a great improvement over his immediate predecessors, he was not the man of the hour for Babylonia. Nabonidus, a deeply religious man, was more interested in scholarship and archæology than in the administration of his empire. He longed to honor his gods by building and restoring temples, after the manner of his distinguished forbear, Nebuchadnezzar. Pursuing his hobbies, he left the administration of affairs of state largely to his son, Belshazzar, who acted as co-regent.

Nebuchadnezzar had one worthy descendant. This was the Princess Bel-shalta-nana, the brilliant sister of the degenerate Belshazzar. Back in the days when the aged Nebuchadnezzar was still on the throne, the old king had sent this young woman as ambassadress to Ur of the Chaldees to pacify the inhabitants, who apparently were not taking kindly to Nebuchadnezzar's religious innovations in connection with the reconstruction of the temple. At Ur, Bel-shalta-nana made a wonderful record. She became a High Priestess of the Temple of the Moon God. She was a patroness, and probably principal teacher, in the famous "Boys' School" of the city. Her most noteworthy accomplishment was the founding of the first museum of which there is any known record. Rare products and archæological specimens from her own land and from those that found their way into the country through the channels of commerce were carefully collected, mounted and catalogued. Recently, at one of our leading universities, a group of distinguished scholars and leaders in the business world gathered to celebrate the 2480th anniversary of the first museum known to history. Had Belshazzar been gifted with as much character and mental capacity as his sister the currents of history might have run differently.

Probably no short work of literature that ever came from the pen of man has occasioned more comment than the Book of *Daniel*. Many commentators maintain that the book was not written during the days of Daniel. They assert that it was not written until B. C. 168, and was then merely a campaign document to encourage the Jews in their famous rebellion against Antiochus, who was attempting to force the Jews to accept the religion of Greece. The reality of Belshazzar has long been doubted by many. It is true that the name of Belshazzar is not included in the Babylonian records as a king of Babylon. However, evidence is no longer lacking as to the reality of Belshazzar. It is clear that Nabonidus had a son bearing this name, and that this son, Belshazzar, exercised kingly prerogatives in Babylon at the time indicated in the Book of *Daniel*.

The scholarly Nabonidus left behind him many records of his reign. Naturally, most of these have no bearing whatsoever on anything written in the Old Testament. His relationship with Belshazzar is made clear in such statements as:

> *As for me, Nabonidus, king of Babylon, save me from sinning against thy great divinity. A life of many days grant as thy gift. As for Belshazzar, the firstborn son, proceeding from my loins, place in his heart fear of thy great divinity; let him not turn to sinning; let him be satisfied with the fulness of life.**

Nabonidus makes a similar prayer to Marduk for his firstborn son on four clay cylinders found at Ur of the Chaldees, where Nabonidus carried out extensive reconstruction work on the ziggurat. Two tablets in the Yale Babylonian Collection, dated in the twelfth year of the reign of Nabonidus, contain oaths in which the names of Nabonidus and Belshazzar are coupled in approximate equality. Tablets in the collection of Goucher College associate the names of Nabonidus and Belshazzar in connection with the payment of royal tribute. There can no longer be any doubt as to the reality of Belshazzar or as to his functioning as co-regent with his father during the closing years of the Neo-Babylonian Empire. This evidence has important bearing on the historicity of the fifth chapter of *Daniel*.

By the time of Nabonidus, Babylonia was no longer the undisputed overlord of the East. Two new powers had appeared and were making history: Lydia under Croesus, and Media under Astyages. Babylonia,

---

*See *Cuneiform Inscriptions of Western Asia*, Rawlinson.

Media, and Lydia, as three separate units, were in control of all the western half of Asia. The age-old lust for world empire must soon bring armed conflict.

Back in the days when the Babylonians were fighting for freedom from Assyria, the Medes had been their able allies. At the capture of Nineveh in B. C. 612 the armies of king Nebuchadnezzar had fought side by side with the Medes under king Cyaxares. Nebuchadnezzar married the daughter of Cyaxares. It is unlikely that the Medes would have troubled the Babylonians had not a new and powerful personality suddenly appeared on the international scene. This was Cyrus, prince of Anshan.

While Nabonidus was peacefully puttering over his archæological treasures, leaving the administration of Babylonia to the Crown Prince, Belshazzar, Cyrus was plotting a rebellion which finally led to the overthrow of his overlord, Astyages. Welding the Medes and the Persians into a powerful fighting force, Cyrus was ready to start his march toward world empire. Only the Babylonians under the Nabonidus-Belshazzar regime and the Lydians under Croesus stood in his way. The prospect looked inviting. Lydia was rich in minerals, particularly gold; Babylonia was the richest country on earth.

The name of Croesus is always associated with wealth in the world proverb, "Rich as Croesus." Historically, this king of Lydia is credited with the first coinage of gold. Croesus did not wait for Cyrus' attack. Alarmed at the growing prestige of Cyrus, Croesus declared war. The Lydians were famous for their cavalry. Their horsemen had turned the tide of many a battle. Arranging his order of battle, Croesus placed the cavalry in the forefront. To counter this, Cyrus resorted to a strange strategem. In front of his army he placed a battalion of men mounted on camels. Behind these were his infantry and in the rear his cavalry. A camel is unlovely to look at and smells worse than he looks. When the advancing horses of Croesus' army sighted and scented the camels, they refused to go farther, turned, bolted, and threw the Lydian army into confusion. Cyrus won an easy victory. A few days later Croesus was captured at Sardis. Cyrus decided to offer Croesus as a living sacrifice by fire. Fortunately Croesus was saved from this cruel fate. Later he swore fealty to Cyrus and acted as his counsellor.

The mighty men of Babylon have forborn to fight, they have remained in their holds: their might hath failed.—Jeremiah 51:30

There were now but two military powers in western Asia: Babylonia and the Medo-Persian empire. Cyrus had no need to hurry. Under such weak rulership, the end of the Babylonian empire was inevitable. Geographically Babylonia lay in the arms of Medo-Persia. Some day those armored arms would hold Babylonia in a strangling grip. A Nabopolassar or a Nebuchadnezzar would have shattered the power of Persia promptly and effectively. A scholarly old king dreamed, and his profligate son played at being a king, while an empire was slipping from beneath their feet. In B. C. 539 Cyrus began to close in on Babylonia.

The march of the armies of Cyrus to Babylon was little more than a military parade. In a series of battles that were but little more than skirmishes for the powerful invading army, the feeble resistance of the Babylonians was swept aside. Soon a mighty army surrounded the mighty city.

Belshazzar the king made a great feast to a thousand of his lords, and drank wine before the thousand.—Daniel 5:1

The opening paragraphs of the dramatic story told in the fifth chapter of *Daniel* picture a scene of wild revelry in the throne room of the king's palace in Babylon. The decadent aristocracy are staging a defiant gesture in the face of fate. An empire that for nearly a century had dominated all the rising civilizations of the East was rocking to its fall. For months a mighty army had been marching across Mesopotamia toward the great city which was the heart of Babylonia. Nabonidus had depended on his son, Belshazzar, to stem the iron tide which was rolling in from the east. Belshazzar had failed dismally. One by one the lesser towns and cities had fallen before the advancing enemy, some without a blow being struck. On the battlefield of Opis the armies had met in open combat, and the defeated Babylonians had retired behind the towering walls of the capital city. The mighty walls which Nebuchadnezzar had built to guard "the glory of the Chaldeans' pride" were almost impregnable against any offensive military equipment of that day. The highest and heaviest walls that had ever surrounded any city reflected the glare of the campfires of the enemy encamped without. The walls of Babylon could bid defiance to any army for many a weary day. No force of arms could breach them in a night, a month, or even a year. Babylon apparently lay secure. Dark days were ahead, but the lords and ladies of Babylon were not thinking of the morrow as they gathered in the high halls of the palace for a night of Oriental orgies. Joy was king in Babylon on that fateful night.

On a night when a prudent commander might well have called a council of war to plan the defense of the city against a long siege, Belshazzar, the commander-in-chief of the armies, chose to gather the elite of Babylon for a night of unbridled, drunken carousal. Undreaming that the crafty commander of the encircling enemy was already conspiring with disloyal political elements within the city to admit the besiegers that very night, Belshazzar and his guests were reaching new heights of riotous revelry. As a crowning act of impious defiance, Belshazzar ordered that the sacred vessels, which once had graced the "House of God" at Jerusalem, be brought in: "The king, and his princes, his wives, and his concubines, drank in them"—*Daniel* 5:3.

The Hebrew slaves, assisting at the service of the banquet, must have been shocked almost into insensibility by this drunken defilement of the vessels which for centuries had been sacred to the rites of worship of the Lord God of Israel. A greater shock awaited Belshazzar. As the festivities reach their riotous climax the drinking suddenly ceases, the feet of the dancers are stilled, the laughter and the singing die out in a note of terror as the finger of fate writes high on the palace wall the coming doom of Babylon. Belshazzar, shocked sober by terror, in white-lipped agony calls wildly for help from the soothsayers and prophets of "the gods of gold, and of silver, of brass, of iron, of wood, and of stone." Even the prophet of Israel, when finally summoned, can afford no comfort to the stricken Belshazzar, he can only interpret the mysterious message of doom. Babylon's imperial day was done. "In that night was Belshazzar the king of the Chaldeans slain."

Critical scholars find much room for argument as to the exact sequence of events in connection with the fall of Babylon. There is also wide room for discussion as to the personalities who played important parts in the dramatic series of events through which the mightiest city in the world fell into the hands of the Medes and Persians almost without bloodshed. The slimy fingers of treachery, clutching ill-gotten gold, may have played an inglorious part. Regardless of all other factors, however, there must have been excellent generalship and precise military movements to bring to successful culmination a strategic military coup of such magnitude. A city, with surrounding defensive walls stretching for upwards of fifty miles, does not fall in a night without some master mind exercising a stroke of military genius. Some able soldier served Cyrus well that night. Who was this military genius? Was "Darius the Median" of *Daniel* 5:31 the "Gobryus" of the Nabonidus Chronicle? Be the answers what they may, there can be no doubt that the writer of the fifth chapter of *Daniel* lifted the curtain of history to reveal a dramatic highlight on that fateful night when the sceptre of empire passed from the hands of the Semitic races into the hands of the Aryans, and all the currents of history were profoundly altered.

The story told in *Daniel* indicates that the climactic campaign which made Cyrus of Persia the undisputed monarch of the East ended suddenly when the besieging army was enabled to move through the defenses of Babylon without using force. This evidence is abundantly substantiated by

Babylonian records contemporaneous with the recorded events. The Nabonidus Chronicles covering the seventeenth year of the king's reign contain this statement:

> *In the month Tammuz (June-July) Cyrus, when he made battle in Opis, on the banks of the river Zalzallat, with the soldiers of Akkad, conquered the inhabitants of Akkad. When they assembled the people were killed. On the fourteenth Sippar was taken without a battle. Nabonidus fled. On the sixteenth Gobryas, Governor of Gutium, and the soldiers of Cyrus entered Babylon without a battle. Later, Nabonidus was captured because he remained in Babylon. To the end of the month the shield bearers of the land of Gotium assembled at the gates of Esagila. No weapon was taken into Esagila or the temples, nor was the standard raised. On the third day of Marcheswan (Oct.-Nov.) Cyrus entered Babylon.**

The part of the Cylinder of Cyrus which deals with the fall of Babylon, states:

> *Marduk, the great lord, looked joyfully upon the return of his people, his kindly deeds and upright heart. To his city, Babylon, he commanded him (Cyrus) to go; he caused him to take the road to Babylon, going as a friend and companion at his side. His numerous army, the number of which was, like the waters of a river, unknown, marched at his side girded with their weapons. He caused him to enter Babylon without war or battle. He preserved his city, Babylon, from tribulation; he filled his hand with Nabonidus, the king who did not fear him.†*

Critical commentators make much of the seeming conflict of statements between the Nabonidus inscription which states that Babylon fell to Gobryus and the Biblical passage which says: "And Darius the Median took the kingdom" (*Daniel* 5:31). From the Nabonidus inscription it is clear that some days elapsed between the occupation of the city and the formal entry of Cyrus into Babylon. This is not strange. Allenby is credited commonly, and justly, with the capture of Jerusalem in 1918, yet it is well known that he was not the first British officer to enter the city or to be offered its formal surrender. Similarly, Gobryus was one of the commanding officers under command of Cyrus. Naturally, the records give Cyrus due credit, although stating that Gobryus was the officer in command at the fall of the city. Those who associate Gobryus with Darius the Mede may not be taking too great a liberty with history.

The writer of the fifth chapter of *Daniel* framed his narrative into the correct historical setting. There can be no doubt as to the positions of the

---

*See *Transactions of the Society of Biblical Archæology*, Vol. VII.
†See *Cuneiform Inscriptions of Western Asia*, Vol. V. Rawlinson.

conflicting armies at the time. There can be no doubt that Belshazzar was exercising regnal powers as co-regent with Nabonidus. The writer was guilty of no slip of the pen when he refers to Belshazzar as being the son of Nebuchadnezzar, although Belshazzar was two generations removed from that great king. It is customary in the Orient, even to this day, for a man to refer to the most illustrious of his predecessors as his father. The word "father" is not used in the East with Occidental exactitude. The present writer, while working in Asia, has often been addressed as father by his employees.

The *Daniel* story of the gathering of a thousand lords gains color from the description of the room where it probably took place.* The throne room of the palace was of such dimensions that it could easily accommodate the number of guests indicated in the narrative. Of this room Dr. Koldeway, who unearthed it, writes: "To the south lies the largest chamber of the citadel, the throne room of the Babylonian kings. It is so clearly marked out for this purpose that no reasonable doubt can be felt as to its having been used as their principal audience chamber. If anyone should desire to localize the scene of Belshazzar's eventful banquet, he can surely place it with complete accuracy in this immense room. It is seventeen meters (about fifty-six feet) broad and fifty-two meters (about one hundred sixty-eight feet) long." With all due deference to all shades of learned opinion, it must be stated that the fifth chapter of *Daniel* seems to have a sound background of history.

Two generations of Israelites grew up beside the rivers of Babylon. Most of the Jews now living in Babylonia had never seen Jerusalem. Only the aged could remember the sacred city. Gray and bent old people might recount the glories of Jerusalem, but Jerusalem and Judah had lost their spell for the great majority of the Jews. The Jew no longer had a homeland. A remnant of the Chosen People might return to Judah; Jerusalem might be rebuilt; another temple might arise on the holy heights; but Hebrew nationalism, at least for many centuries, could never be more than an unsubstantial dream. Hereafter, the wide, wide world would be the home of the Jew. Already the Jews were widely scattered. Still stood the ancient prophecy: "And the Lord shall scatter thee among all people, from the one end of the earth even unto the other" (*Deuteronomy* 28:64). The wandering Jew was already on his way, picking his appointed path among all nations, but wanted by none. "And thou shalt become an astonishment, a proverb, and a byword, among all nations whither the Lord shall lead thee"—*Deuteronomy* 28:37. The nations that knew the Jews in their brief day of national glory have largely been erased by the running sands of time. No identifiable descendant of the Assyrians

*See *Excavations at Babylon*, by Robert Koldeway.

or the Babylonians remains on earth. Through centuries of hatred and persecution, of slavery and slaughter, the "seed of Abraham" has survived. No other blood stream remains so unsullied. Since the patriarchs of Israel first raised their altars in Palestine many peoples have appeared, risen to political prominence, and perished, but the Jew endures in persistent perpetuity.

The decline and fall of Hebrew nationalism did not destroy the vitality of Israel's inspired spiritual idealism. Beyond the narrow boundaries of nationalism and sectionalism it breathed the freer air of realism, and found the wider field of world activity. Beside the calm waters of Babylon the lofty religious idealism of the Jew was immeasurably broadened. In an atmosphere of enlightenment, leaders of religious thought were preparing the way for the coming of Christianity. In the cold light of secular history the Hebrew kingdoms left little behind them; but, viewed in the warmer light of eternal truth, they left behind them a priceless legacy of spiritual thought.

GOLD BOWL OF MES-KALEM-DUG
The inscription states that this vessel was the property of "The Lord of the Good Land."

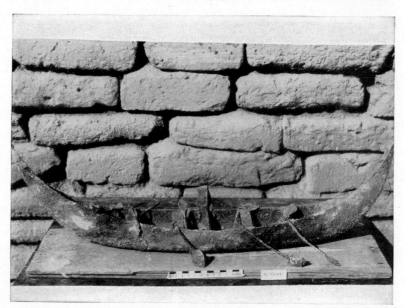

ANCIENT SUMERIAN MODEL OF BOAT
Four thousand years ago the boats that plied the waters of the Tigris and Euphrates were similar in design to many in use on the same rivers today.

By permission of The Museum of the University of Pennsylvania

XVI

THE RETURN OF ISRAEL FROM EXILE

Thus saith Cyrus king of Persia, All the kingdoms of the earth hath the Lord God of heaven given me; and he hath charged me to build him an house in Jerusalem, which is in Judah. Who is there among you of all his people? The Lord his God be with him, and let him go up.—2 Chronicles 36:23

THE fall of Jerusalem marked the beginning of the long exile. In turn, the fall of Babylon ended the exile and paved the way for the return of the Jews to Judah. The fall of Jerusalem and the fall of Babylon are in no sense historical parallels. One marked the end of a little kingdom, the other the end of a great empire. Compared with the downfall of the Neo-Babylonian empire, the destruction of the puny kingdom of Judah was a comparatively unimportant historical event. In the history of religion, however, the fall of Jerusalem looms larger than the fall of Babylon. With the fall of Jerusalem the Hebrews lost their place in the world of nations but found a broader place in the world of religion. Deprived of an earthly kingdom, Israel began to vision a Heavenly Kingdom. On the minds of the Chosen People dawned the deeper meanings of the spiritual idealism which Moses had expounded on Mt. Sinai. During the years of exile, the narrow, tradition-bound religion of Israel was broadened by a newer and nobler conception of the character of God. Great leaders of religious thought, exploring the realms of the spirit and the mind with heaven-born inspiration, visioned a God who would redeem all mankind through the coming Messiah.

The time had passed when little kingdoms, like that of the Hebrews, could live successfully in western Asia. The little kingdoms which had figured so prominently in Hebrew history during the days of the Judges had either entirely disappeared or were sunk in vassalage to more powerful peoples. The Amorite, the Hittite, and the Ammonite would never again appear prominently in political history. Even the powerful Edomites had disappeared by the fifth century B. C. Minor people had been submerged or absorbed by major peoples marching to empire. Nationally, the Hebrews were no longer historically important. In the field of religious thought they were still world leaders.

At the noise of the taking of Babylon the earth is moved, and the cry is heard among the nations.—Jeremiah 50:46

16

The taking of Babylon was a world-shaking event, such as might be occasioned today if London or New York fell into the hands of an invading army. The eyes of all the western half of Asia and of all the rising civilizations of southern Europe must have turned toward Babylon when the fall of the great city set the seal of Cyrus on a new world empire.

The fall of Babylon did not bring about extensive destruction of the city. The great metropolis was spared the havoc of the sword and the torch. The proud old city was to live in glory for many a day. The predictions of the prophets as to the ultimate fate of Babylon were not to be fulfilled until after the beginning of the Christian Era. Many a time were the streets of Babylon to echo the tyrannical tread of the conqueror. Time and again, the despoilers were to "come against her from the utmost border," and "open her storehouses" (See *Jeremiah* 50:26). Persian monarchs exacted exceedingly heavy tribute. When Alexander the Great swept over the East, he paid off his mighty army with loot from the treasuries of Babylon, and added a bonus in gold to every man in the service. Later, the Romans ravished the city of almost countless treasure. Even when the "great nations from the north country" (See *Jeremiah* 50:9) had reduced the great city to nothingness, the wild tribes of the desert reaped a rich harvest of treasure from its ruins. Great was Babylon. Many centuries were to pass between the coming of Cyrus and the days when Babylon would "become heaps" awaiting the spade of the archæologist.

The coming of the Persian conqueror brought dismay to the Babylonians, who had long dominated western Asia and held the rest of the then-known world in check. On the other hand, the coming of Cyrus brought joy to the hearts of many exiles who had been unwillingly transported from their homelands at the heels of conquering Babylonian armies. The proclamation of Cyrus, as given in *Ezra* 1:1-4, was but one of many generous gestures on the part of the Persian monarch. In allowing nationals to return to their own lands, Cyrus was reversing a national policy which was centuries old. The custom of wholesale deportation of conquered peoples may have originated with the Assyrians. With them it was established national policy. Tiglath-pileser carried away part of the population when he raided northern Israel (See 2 *Kings* 15:29). When Samaria fell to the Assyrians most of the inhabitants were carried away (See 2 *Kings* 17:6). Many Assyrian inscriptions boast of this practice. Although Cyrus held nations in vassalage, a new day of individual freedom dawned over the East. Cyrus granted permission to those who were in captivity in Babylonia to return to their own countries and to resume their time-honored customs of worship. Part of the inscription on the Cylinder of Cyrus reads as follows:

The cities beyond the Tigris, whose sites had been founded of old—the gods in them I returned to their places, and caused them to settle in their eternal shrines. All the people I assembled and returned them to their dwellings.*

The liberal policies of Cyrus mark a distinct step forward in the rise of civilization. Individual and religious freedom for subject peoples was a new note in national administrative policies.

The story of Israel's return from exile and the rebuilding of the temple and the walls of Jerusalem is told in the Book of *Ezra* and the Book of *Nehemiah*, supplemented by the writings of Haggai and Zechariah. Ezra will always be remembered in connection with the erection of the second temple; Nehemiah won undying fame as the rebuilder of Jerusalem; but, beyond these material things, they deserve a greater recognition as leaders in the great movement toward the recreation of the racial life of Israel after the exile.

Among Biblical scholars there is wide divergence of opinion as to dates and sequence of events in connection with the rebuilding of Jerusalem. While data may be scattered and scarce and some of the writings rather obscure, allowing wide latitude in interpretation by students, there would seem to be little foundation for much of the destructive criticism put forward by some nineteenth century commentators.

The proclamation of Cyrus covering the repatriation of exiles carried no compulsion. The outlanders were free to go or stay as they wished. Cyrus realized that many descendants of exiles had been born in Babylonia, had grown up with the country, and found their way into civil and commercial life. To uproot these people might inflict unnecessary hardship. Even among the Jews there were doubtless many who preferred life in the fat lands of Chaldea to a weary pilgrimage to a country which had not as yet recovered from the depredations of Nebuchadnezzar's marauding armies.

The passing of the years had depleted the numbers of those who originally marched out of Judah into exile. Only the aged could retain memories of the homeland. To the younger generations Judah with its wonder-city of Jerusalem was known only through tales their elders told. Those of patriarchal years might be drawn by irresistible longing for the hills of home to undertake the return pilgrimage. From Babylonia to Jerusalem was a long journey in those days. The project of a general departure from Babylonia was regarded with apathy by a majority of the Jews.

There were, evidently, two sections of Jewish society eager to avail themselves of the generous permission to return to Jerusalem. One of

*See Rawlinson's *Inscriptions of Western Asia*, Vol. V.

these was the royalist group, which wished to reëstablish the Davidic succession through Prince Zerubbabel, a descendant of the ancient royal line. The other was composed of the religiously inclined, who wished to rebuild the temple and again centralize the worship of Jehovah in Jerusalem. With one group politics was predominant, with the other, religion.

The muster roll of Jewish citizens listed in the second chapter of *Ezra* indicates that only a vanguard of the Jews returned to Judah with the first expedition in B. C. 537. Years were to pass before the great folk-movement attained impressive proportions. Many Jews never returned to the homeland. While their traditional religion had not lost its hold upon them, they were indifferent to the ties of Jerusalem and Judah. The fall of Jerusalem marked the beginning of the dispersion of the descendants of Abraham. Previously they had functioned as a racial unit. Those days were done. The Jews were now living in an expanding world. This was an age of movement. Countries of which their forefathers had never even heard now lay open to the commercially-minded Jew. Jerusalem would always be the sacred city of the Jew, but richer lands were calling. The wandering Jew was on his way. Peacefully penetrating every place that offered opportunity for business, he carried with him the religious ideals which were the heritage of his race. While the home-seeking Jews were rebuilding Jerusalem, the wandering Jews were infiltrating world thought with the higher ideals of Israel. The strength of the Jewish world now lay outside of Jerusalem.

The proclamation of Cyrus, giving individual freedom to the Jews, was no empty gesture. Royal words were backed with kingly deeds. The Jews who remained in Babylonia were asked to contribute funds to finance the return journey of their countrymen. A contribution of funds toward the rebuilding of the temple also was suggested. To the latter project the king generously made a state contribution: "Also Cyrus the king brought forth the vessels of the house of the Lord, which Nebuchadnezzar had brought forth out of Jerusalem" (*Ezra* 1:7). An Eastern potentate returning golden treasure was something extraordinary. A new policy in imperial administration had appeared.

The people of the land weakened the hands of the people of Judah, and troubled them in building.—Ezra 4:4

The country to which the Jews were returning was no longer "a land flowing with milk and honey." During long years of misrule the land of Judah had deteriorated seriously. A country broken and ruined by invasion had been bled white by taxation. The ruins of the temple and the famed walls of Jerusalem lay in the battered disorder into which

Nebuchadnezzar's legions had reduced them. The holy heights of Mt. Moriah looked down on a scene of desolation and decay.

No welcoming committee met the returning Jews with sound of trumpet and roll of drum. The mixed native population regarded the newcomers from Babylon as aliens, and viewed them with sullen suspicion which later flamed into open animosity.

Returning Israel signalized its arrival by rearing an "altar of the God of Israel." Soon the cornerstone and foundation walls of the temple were laid with appropriate ceremonies. The work of rebuilding and resettlement was begun under Sheshbazzar (See *Ezra* 1:8-11), who was soon succeeded by Zerubbabel. With the able assistance of Joshua, the priest, Zerubbabel began the construction of the temple. Into this task the Jews entered with religious zeal. Stone could be readily reclaimed from the ruins of Solomon's massive masonry but timber had to be imported. Again, as in the days of Solomon, timber was brought from Lebanon and handled by workers in wood from Tyre and Sidon. A grand start was made, but the work was soon slowed to a standstill through the interference of "the people of the land."

These "people of the land" were largely of Hebrew blood. Most of them were descendants of the lower classes of Hebrews whom Nebuchadnezzar had deemed unworthy of transportation to Babylonia. They were the offspring of the people whom 2 *Kings* 24:14 classifies as "the poorest sort of the people of the land." Jeremiah refers to these left-at-homes as "evil figs" (See *Jeremiah* 24). This inferior racial stock had deteriorated even further through the admixture of foreign blood from the peoples whom the Assyrians had settled in Palestine through their policy of intertransportation of captive peoples. The race-proud, pure-blooded Hebrews from Babylonia looked down their noses at these mixed-caste Hebrews. Friction between the natives and the newcomers delayed the completion of the temple for years.

New Israel's troubles with the local population were augmented by serious difficulties with the people of Samaria. These difficulties persisted throughout the entire period in which Jerusalem was being rebuilt. Back in the days when Omri ruled the old northern kingdom, he built the city of Samaria as the new capital of Israel (See 1 *Kings* 16:24). The strategic location of the city and its naturally strong defensive position enabled the city on the hill to dominate the entire surrounding district. Even in the days of Our Saviour on earth Samaria constituted a separate district. When the northern kingdom came to an end at the time of Hoshea through the capture of Samaria by the Assyrians, the character of the population was definitely changed. "The king of Assyria took Samaria, and carried Israel away into Assyria" (2 *Kings* 17:6), "and the

king of Assyria brought men from Babylon, and from Cuthah, and from
Ava, and from Hamath, and from Sepharvaim, and placed them in the
cities of Samaria instead of the children of Israel" (2 *Kings* 17:24). By
the time of Ezra and Nehemiah the descendants of this amalgamation of
peoples formed an important factor in the population of Palestine. They
had inherited a form of worship closely resembling that of the orthodox
Jew. Their ancestors had "feared the Lord, and served their own gods"
(2 *Kings* 17:33). When these people came forward with an offer to assist
in the erection of the temple, only to have their offer curtly refused
(See *Ezra* 4:3), they became the bitter and implacable enemies of the Jews.

Denied participation in the rebuilding of Jerusalem and denied recognition as good Jews, the people of Samaria built their own temple of
Jehovah on Mt. Gerizim. This temple stood on Gerizim until B. C. 109
when it was destroyed by John Hyrcanus. The enmity between Jew and
Samaritan persists in Palestine to this day. This mutual animosity is
referred to in New Testament writings. Perhaps the most striking illustration occurs in the recorded interview of Jesus with the woman at the Well
of Jacob: "Then saith the woman of Samaria unto him, How is it that
thou, being a Jew, askest drink of me, which am a woman of Samaria?
for the Jews have no dealings with the Samaritans" (*John* 4:9).

*And hired counsellors against them, to frustrate their purpose,
all the days of Cyrus king of Persia, even until the reign of Darius
king of Persia.*—Ezra 4:5

The writers of the Old Testament, interested primarily in recording
the rise and development and presenting the ultimate aims of a great
religious movement, sometimes span long periods of secular history with
a phrase or a paragraph. With the words, "all the days of Cyrus king of
Persia, even until the days of Darius king of Persia," Ezra covers a time-
space which saw two changes of rulers and one change of dynasty in Persia.
The period spanned by the text also saw great changes in the picture of
international politics. The peoples of the countries on the northern
shores of the Mediterranean were making history. The Greeks were
making their initial movements toward world empire. During the
coming century they would challenge the Persians for the sceptre of world
dominion. Ezra, however, was interested only in the rebuilding of the
temple and the sacred city, and troubled only by the efforts of non-
religionists to delay the work.

When Cyrus died in B. C. 529 he left his great empire to his son
Cambyses. Like many another son of an illustrious sire, Cambyses lacked
the sterling qualities which had distinguished his famous father. He
inherited his father's ambition for empire, but failed to inherit the great

ability of Cyrus for administration and for the pacification of conquered peoples. His greatest weakness was lack of self-control. This mental and emotional instability led to his untimely death. In B. C. 525 Cambyses led his armies into Egypt, overran the country, and marched up the Nile as far as the First Cataract. His conquests availed him little. As he returned toward his own realm, he was driven frantic by learning that during his absence in Egypt a pretender, Smerdis, had laid claim to his throne. Smerdis claimed to be a younger brother of Cambyses. Cambyses, himself, had murdered this younger brother years before, and doubtless could have easily disposed of this usurper who was posing as the dead brother, but in his rage he took his own life at Damascus in B. C. 522.

The death of Cambyses caused a period of great political unrest throughout the entire Persian empire. The claim of Smerdis to the throne failed to impress the princes and nobles of Persia. With Oriental deftness, they wafted him into another world and installed one of their own number, Darius, on the throne. The coming of Darius threw Persia into political turmoil. Rebellion broke out in every province of the realm. Darius spent nearly three years in restoring political stability within the empire.

It is probable that these years of political unrest added to the difficulties which beset the Jews in rebuilding the temple. At any rate, the temple lay unfinished while the colonists interested themselves in material gain. This lackadaisical attitude on the part of the Jews toward a great enterprise aroused the ire of Haggai. The prophet issued a ringing appeal to his countrymen to complete the work on the temple. Haggai was ably aided by his fellow prophet, Zechariah, whose scholarly exhortations have come down to us in the book which bears his name. Aroused by the call of duty, the Jews returned to the building of the temple, and exerted every effort toward completion of the sacred task (See Ezra 5:2).

The second temple lacked the ornate richness and architectural magnificence of the great edifice erected by king Solomon. No palaces and courts or royal residences surrounded it. No luxurious landscaping linked it to its site. Stark and alone, it rose above Jerusalem, a renewed symbol of the Lord God of Israel's eternal covenant with his Chosen People.

News of the great building campaign in Jerusalem soon reached the ears of "Tatnai, governor on this side of the river." Since Tatnai was the governor of the provinces on this side of the river (the Euphrates), it was his duty to investigate this unusual activity. Here was a pretty problem for the petty politicians who were attempting to frustrate the work and hiring counsellors to hinder its completion. Tatnai made a complete report to king Darius, certifying the names of those engaged in the enterprise. When the official report reached Darius, a search for the original charter issued by Cyrus was instituted. Fortunately a copy of the charter was found "at Achmetha, in the palace that is in the province of the Medes" (*Ezra* 6:2). The representations of the Jews at Jerusalem being found correct, Darius issued a supplementary decree covering the completion of the work.

The detailed description of the documents issued in connection with this decree of Darius suggests that the writer of the fifth and sixth chapters of *Ezra* may have had access to the original documents. It might be remarked in passing that thousands of documents of the Persian Period have been recovered by archæologists. These are usually dated with the day of the month, month of the year, and year of the king's reign. All documents had to be signed by the principal parties and the scribe and duly attested by the witnesses. Among the collections of the University Museum, Philadelphia, may be seen many business documents from the records of Murashu and Sons, bond brokers of Nippur, Babylonia, in the period of Darius II. Many of these business documents appeal to our imaginations as "modern." Here recorded on clay tablets in cuneiform script are salary vouchers, balance sheets neatly ruled in columns, guarantees of the worth and durability of goods sold, leases and sales records of property, adoption of children documents, marriage dowries, divorce contracts, wills, notes on the purchases of slaves, records of criminal and civil suits, income tax and property records.

Freed from official interference, the Jews rushed to completion the erection of the temple. Finished in the sixth year of Darius, B. C. 516, it was dedicated with due solemnity. The temple was now complete. Jerusalem still lay in ruins.

Then said I unto them, Ye see the distress that we are in, how Jerusalem lieth waste, and the gates thereof are burned with fire: come, let us build up the wall of Jerusalem.—Nehemiah 2:17

The outstanding historical figure in connection with the rehabilitation of Jerusalem was Nehemiah. The book that bears his name is largely biographical and deals principally with his reconstruction work at the Holy City. Much of the story is told in the first person. The opening scene is laid in the ancient rose-red city of Susa in Elam. Here Nehemiah is visited by his brother Hanani and a delegation of Jews from Judah. In answer to his queries regarding the welfare of their co-religionists throughout the empire, his visitors tell only a tale of unmitigated woe: "The remnant that are left of the captivity there in the province are in great affliction and reproach: the wall of Jerusalem also is broken down, and the gates thereof are burned with fire" (*Nehemiah* 1:3). Nehemiah is shocked at the recital of Israel's woes. Graphically he pictures his grief over the deplorable conditions at Jerusalem. He tells of his prayers for the relief of the sacred city. He adds the laconic statement: "For I was the king's cup-bearer."

Behind the reticence of Nehemiah as to his position in the king's court one may read much. Only a young man of commanding presence and great personal charm could occupy the position of cup-bearer at the sumptuous court of Artaxerxes, king of kings. Here was a devout young Jew, a youth of great personal piety, occupying a position of trust in the palace of the ruler of a country where morals were loose and ideals shockingly low. Early in life Nehemiah must have shown promise of the great abilities which brought him outstanding success in later life.

Nehemiah longs to be of personal service in the restoration of the city of his fathers. Great difficulties stand in his way. He has never labored. His life has fallen in pleasant places. Jerusalem means unwonted hardship. Although he may be willing to exchange the ease of court life for the hardships of construction work, he can attain this end only through the consent of the august Artaxerxes. The cup-bearer must petition the king. Before he enters the royal presence to serve the wine he breathes a prayer to the God of Israel: "Prosper, I pray thee, thy servant this day, and grant him mercy in the sight of this man." Despite his appeal to Jehovah he is nervous and downcast as he takes up the wine and gives it to the king. In his story, Nehemiah omits telling that he tasted the wine in the king's presence before serving it. No Eastern monarch would take any risk of drinking poisoned wine. The king quickly notices something unusual in the cup-bearer's demeanor. When the king questions him as to why he is sad, Nehemiah is "very sore afraid." Behind the king's questioning may lurk a shadow of suspicion. Despite his fears, Nehemiah prays "to the God of heaven" and replies to the king. His prayers to God and his answers to the king must have been simultaneous. A moment's hesitation might have brought a knife blade to his throat. Oriental monarchs can never afford to take chances. Probably the king sighed with relief when he learned that all that was troubling his servant was that Jerusalem lay in ruins. The plight of Jerusalem might be of nightmare proportions to his Jewish servant, but to the Emperor of the World this was a trifling matter easily remedied.

Artaxerxes graciously permitted Nehemiah to visit Jerusalem. He also furnished him with the necessary official letters to provincial governors and equipped him with a military escort. The journey to Jerusalem must have taken two months or more. Nehemiah tells nothing of the long trip over the desert, nor does he mention the journey through the pleasant countryside of Damascus. He does relate that as he neared his journey's

end, and had reached Samaria, he suffered some discourtesy at the hands
of Sanballat and his servant. Nehemiah had good reason to remember
Sanballat. He had met a man who was to be his lifelong enemy.

On his arrival at Jerusalem, Nehemiah found conditions worse than
his brother had pictured. The great prophets of Israel had only visioned
Jerusalem in ruins. Nehemiah saw it in actuality. The goal toward which
Israel had marched through a thousand years of glorious history; the
city where David had established the capital of Hebrew nationality, where
Solomon had reigned in splendor; the city in whose rocky foundations
were sepulchred the bones of Israel's mighty kings, lay in shattered ruins
scattered over the lonely hills. As he gazed on the burnt and broken
ruins of a once-great city, Nehemiah must have realized that the rebuilding
of the ramparts of Jerusalem was a task for an experienced engineer, rather
than for a youth fresh from the courts of a Persian king. The magnitude
of the task would have appalled a less resourceful man.

After he had been in the city three days, Nehemiah decided to make
a personal survey of the work to be done. Slipping out in the dark of
night with only a few trusted attendants, he made a circuit of the ruined
walls. The extent to which the walls were broken down, and the surface
of the ground cluttered with debris, is clearly indicated by the statement:
"Then I went on to the gate of the fountain, and to the king's pool:
but there was no place for the beast that was under me to pass"
(*Nehemiah* 2:14). The "gate of the fountain" is the Water Gate opening on the path leading down to the Gihon spring, "the Virgin's
Fountain." The fact that the ground around the city's principal source
of water supply was still so obstructed by debris that a horse could not
pass is eloquent testimony of the thoroughness of Nebuchadnezzar's
demolition of the walls of Jerusalem.

Before Nehemiah's lonely night ride was finished he had arrived at
some definite decisions. The restoration of the walls of Jerusalem was a
question of man-power. The ruins of Solomon's and Hezekiah's masonry
would furnish the necessary materials. Labor to put the materials in
place was the great need. There was no money to pay for labor. The
entire population must volunteer its time and talent. If Nehemiah could
but rouse Israel to a sense of duty, the walls of Jerusalem would be rebuilt.

> *Then I told them of the hand of my God which was good upon
> me; as also the king's words that he had spoken unto me. And
> they said, Let us rise up and build. So they strengthened their
> hands for this good work.*—Nehemiah 2:18

Nehemiah's appeal for constructive action brought ready response.
City and countryside rallied to the call of religious duty. Everyone was

ready to lend a hand. Strange types, indeed, were many of the laborers. Jerusalem was not without skilled mechanics, but on a work of this magnitude their labors must be supplemented by many who knew nothing of building work. Builders came from every walk of life. Eliashib, the high priest, was not above working on the sheep gate. "From above the horse gate repaired the priests, everyone over against his house" (*Nehemiah* 3:28). The goldsmiths and the apothecaries, the aristocrats and the merchants, even the Nethinims, who were inferior servants of the temple, contributed their labor. The Nethinims' portion of the wall abutted on "the great tower that lieth out." Evidently, "the tower that lieth out" had not been destroyed by Nebuchadnezzar. A substantial part of it still stands today. It was uncovered by J. G. Duncan in 1926, and is now preserved as a national monument.

> But it came to pass, that when Sanballat, and Tobiah, and the Arabians, and the Ammonites, and the Ashdodites, heard that the walls of Jerusalem were made up, and that the breaches began to be stopped, then they were very wroth. And conspired all of them together to come and to fight against Jerusalem, and to hinder it.—Nehemiah 4:7, 8.

Sanballat had hated Nehemiah from the day the latter first entered the country. The more Sanballat saw of Nehemiah the less he liked him. Sanballat, being a Samaritan, had hated the young Jew on sight. He had encountered Nehemiah when the latter passed through Samaria en route to Jerusalem. He would have liked to have turned him back, but, since the young man carried warrants signed by Artaxerxes, it was impossible to do so. He could keep a watchful eye on him, however. When Sanballat learned that the young Jewish upstart was contemplating the restoration of the walls of Jerusalem, he had laughed the young man to scorn, and contemptuously inquired if Nehemiah was planning rebellion. Fortifying a city within the Persian realm was a serious matter. Few young men can face ridicule. Nehemiah was young, but the warrant of his king and his faith in Israel's God, gave him poise. To his tormentor he administered the withering rebuke: "The God of heaven, he will prosper us; therefore we his servants will arise and build: but ye have no portion, nor right, nor memorial, in Jerusalem" (*Nehemiah* 2:20). Sanballat might be governor of Samaria, but Nehemiah was running things in Jerusalem.

When the walls of Jerusalem began to rise above the ruins, Sanballat decided that something must be done about it. Despite the fact that his satellite, Tobiah, laughingly declared: "Even that which they build, if a fox go up, he shall even break down their stone wall" (*Nehemiah*

4:3), Sanballat saw that the time had come for action. Swords were weightier than words. When one-half the wall was completed, Sanballat started his first overt action. He and his allies came "to fight against Jerusalem, and to hinder it."

The hostility of the non-Jewish peoples, led by the crafty Sanballat, brought Nehemiah a train of troubles. With the work but half finished, many of the Jews grew weary of well-doing. Nehemiah had labor troubles. Labor difficulties are not a product of the machine age. They are as old as labor itself. Whispering tongues told the weary workmen of danger from conspirators without the walls. To the harassed Nehemiah the workmen complained: "The strength of the bearers of burdens is decayed and there is much rubbish; so that we are not able to build the wall" (*Nehemiah* 4:10). This trouble with labor was not altogether new. At the beginning of the work, Nehemiah had noted that the "nobles put not their necks to the work of the Lord." This latest trouble was at the middle of the work, when the toilers, and perhaps Nehemiah himself, were soul-weary. The fine enthusiasm with which they had begun the work had dwindled to depression. Firm foes without, faint friends within, threatened to halt Nehemiah's work, leaving the half-finished walls to monument a young man's foiled ambition.

Nehemiah's testing hour had arrived. To repel prowling trouble from without, Nehemiah posted a guard over every working family. To dispel the troubles within was the real test of Nehemiah's executive ability. Could he handle men? Could he encourage a dispirited Israel to keep on keeping on? Would his great project fail through his inability to handle the unstable human equation? In the first chapter of his book Nehemiah stresses how he prayed when he had merely learned by hearsay of Jerusalem's troubles. Now, in the midst of still greater troubles, he does not tell of his prayers, but stresses the answer to them: "And God had brought their counsel to naught, that we returned all of us to the wall, everyone unto his work" (*Nehemiah* 4:15).

Failure to halt Nehemiah's rebuilding work with ridicule and threats, the artful Sanballat resorted to guile. Under various pretexts he attempted to entice Nehemiah outside the walls of Jerusalem. Nehemiah was too wary to be entrapped. Beneath the smooth words of Sanballat's invitation to "meet together in some one of the villages in the plain of Ono" Nehemiah saw the gleam of the assassin's dagger. Nehemiah was a match for Sanballat in the dark diplomacy of the Orient.

Checkmated in his endeavors to draw Nehemiah out of Jerusalem, Sanballat decided to strike from within. In the city there were many who regarded Nehemiah with jealousy and suspicion. Some of the malcontents held high places in Jerusalem. Sanballat conspired with some of these who lived within the very shadow of the temple to lure Nehemiah to his doom. It was Shemaiah, who had access to the temple, who treacherously whispered in Nehemiah's ear that that night someone from without was coming to slay him, and urged him to seek safety behind the locked doors of the temple. This time, Nehemiah's personal courage saved him from the knife of treachery. Scorning to skulk like a hunted thing within the sacred walls, Nehemiah gave the priestly conspirator an answer that sounds the keynote of his character: "Should such a man as I flee? and who is there, that, being as I am, would go into the temple to save his life? I will not go in" (*Nehemiah* 6:11). Again Sanballat had failed.

Rising above all difficulties, Nehemiah carried the great work to completion. "So the wall was finished in the twenty and fifth day of the month Elul, in fifty and two days" (*Nehemiah* 6:15). Israel assembled for triumphant procession and the solemn ceremonies of dedication. Nehemiah's first mission to Jerusalem was complete.

Many scholars have doubted the historicity of the Books of *Ezra* and *Nehemiah*. Some extremely liberal scholars have suggested that Ezra was not a personality. They suggest that he was a scribe-created personification of the great movement toward the reorganization of the religious life of the Jews that took place in the fifth century B. C. It has been maintained by some liberal scholars that the Artaxerxes who was the friend and patron of Nehemiah was not Artaxerxes I (B. C. 466-425) but Artaxerxes II (B. C. 404-358). Others, basing their arguments on the writings of Josephus, place the time of Nehemiah as during the reign of Darius III (B. C. 337-331). Josephus places Sanballat, the governor of Samaria, in the reign of Darius III, the last of the Persian kings, and states that Sanballat deserted to Alexander the Great and died during the siege of Gaza by Alexander.*

These pages have already mentioned the ascension of Darius I to the throne of Persia in B. C. 521. Darius had a long and successful reign, although in his latter years he had considerable trouble with his subjects in the Ionian Peninsula. The troubles among the Ionians were fomented by the Greeks of Europe. Darius decided to end this trouble by subjugating the Greeks. His efforts in this direction brought only disaster, culminating in a decisive defeat at Marathon in B. C. 490. In the midst of this campaign Darius died. He was succeeded by his son Xerxes I (B. C. 486-466). Xerxes carried on the war against the Greeks, only to lose a large fleet at Salamis and suffer a crushing defeat on land at Plataea. This ended all attempts at conquest in Europe by the Persians. Persia had

*See Josephus, *Antiquities of the Jews,* Book XI, Chapter VIII.

passed the period of her greatest imperial glory. Over a century was to pass, however, before the Greeks became dominant in western Asia.

The next ruler of Persia was Artaxerxes I (B. C. 466-425). This would seem to be the king who commissioned Nehemiah to rebuild Jerusalem and under whom Sanballat was governor of Samaria, Josephus to the contrary notwithstanding.

A great deal of light has been thrown on this period and on the perplexing problems of Biblical scholars, by the discovery of what is known as the "Elephantine Papyri." The first group of these remarkable documents was discovered in 1895 on the southern end of the Island of Elephantine, which lies in the Nile just below the First Cataract near the borderline between Egypt and Nubia. A second lot of the papyri was found at the same site in 1907. Many of these papyri date from the period of Ezra and Nehemiah. In the days when Nehemiah was rebuilding the walls of Jerusalem, temple scribes at Elephantine were writing a strange chapter in the history of the Jews.

The Elephantine papyri opened to the astonished eyes of scholars a new and startling chapter in the history of Israel. The documents were written in the fifth century B. C. and date from 494 to 400. They reveal that there was a strong Jewish colony on the Island of Elephantine at the time the temple in Jerusalem was rebuilt and the walls of Jerusalem restored. Strangest of all their revelations is that this colony of Jews had long before erected a temple of Jehovah on the island. This was no mere synagogue or place for worship only, it was a real temple. Burnt offerings, meal offerings, and frankincense, were placed on the altar with the same ceremonials as were employed at the temple in Jerusalem. It has always been assumed that according to "the Law" no other temple than that at Jerusalem could be erected. Until the discovery of these papyri, there is no known mention in sacred or secular history of any Jewish temple other than that at Jerusalem at this early date, unless Isaiah is referring to this temple when he says: "In that day shall there be an altar to the Lord in the midst of the land of Egypt" (*Isaiah* 19:19).

Whence came these Jews? What led a colony of Jews so numerous that they could build a great temple so far up the Nile? These questions can be answered only by conjecture. Evidently many in the colony were soldiers, since the temple was built "in Yeb, the fortress." The temple had been built long before the dates of the documents. According to one document Cambyses of Persia when he overran Egypt in 525 spared this temple when "the temples of the gods of Egypt were overthrown." This document, a letter to Darius II, is dated the 20th of Marcheswan,

(Oct.-Nov.) year 17 of Darius the king. This would be B. C. 407. Therefore the temple must have been built more than a century earlier.

This long and interesting letter was written to Bagohi (Bagoas), the Persian governor of Judah. The writers complain that during the absence of Arsames, the Persian governor of Egypt, some priests of the Egyptian god Khnub had bribed the acting governor, Waidrang, to destroy and burn the temple of Jehovah at Elephantine. The work of destruction was carried out by Egyptian forces under the leadership of Waidrang's son, Nephayan. The temple with its "pillars of stone" and "five gates of stone" was broken down and the furnishings and "the roof which was of cedar wood" were burned.

The petitioners go on to explain that they have been mourning their temple three years and are anxious to rebuild, and crave the permission of Bagohi to do so. They also state that they had formerly written to Jerusalem about this matter, but had received no reply. The text reads:

> *Also formerly, at the time this shameful deed was done to us we sent a letter unto our lord, and unto Jehohanan, the high priest, and his associates, the priests who are in Jerusalem, and unto Ostan, the brother of Anani and the elders of Judah, but a letter they have not sent unto us.**

Failing to receive assistance or even a reply from Jerusalem, the petitioners make an appeal direct to the Persian governor. They add the astonishing statement:

> *Also the whole is told in a letter we sent in our name to Dalajah and Shelemjah, sons of Sanballat, governor of Samaria.*

The writers must have been moved almost to desperation before they would appeal to the Samaritans, Dalajah and Shelemjah. Between the Jews and the Samaritans was undying hatred. Only as a last resort would a Jew appeal to a Samaritan for aid in securing permission to build a Jewish temple. The interesting point, however, is that two sons of Sanballat were in positions of authority in Samaria in B. C. 407. If Sanballat served as governor of Samaria during the reign of Darius III (B. C. 337-331), as many liberal scholars maintain, how could his sons be serving in similar positions seventy years earlier? It would take a curious twist of the family tree to allow Sanballat's sons to serve the state seventy years before their father. It would seem clear, therefore, that Nehemiah and Sanballat both served under Darius II, as the Old Testament indicates.

---

*See *Aramaic Papyri Discovered at Assuan*, Sayce and Cowley.

Among the Elephantine papyri there is a letter from one Hananiah to
the Jews at Elephantine in regard to the observance of the Passover in the
fifth year of Darius. In *Nehemiah* 7:2 we read "that I gave my brother
Hanani, and Hananiah the ruler of the palace, charge over Jerusalem."
Were the Hananiah of the text and the Hananiah of the Elephantine
letter one and the same man? Perhaps there is no connection, but it would
seem a strange coincidence if two men of the same name were in positions
of authority in Jerusalem at approximately the same time.

In a letter of introduction, sent from the Jewish colony at Elephantine
to a group of Jewish leaders in Jerusalem these words are to be found:

> *And whatever thing Seha and Hor may desire of you, stand ye*
> *before them so that no cause of blame may be found in you.*
> *With you is the chastisement which without cause has rested on*
> *us, from the time Hananiah was in Egypt until now. And whatever*
> *you do for Hor you do for yourselves. Hor is known to Anani.*
> *Do you sell cheaply from our houses any goods that are at hand;*
> *whether we lose or do not lose, is one to you. This is why I am*
> *sending to you: He said to me: "Send a letter before us." Even*
> *if we should lose, credit will be established because of him in the*
> *house of Anani. What you do for him will not be hidden from*
> *Anani. To my lords, Jedoniah, Uriah, and the priests and the Jews.*

This letter would indicate that Anani was someone of great importance
in Jerusalem. The writers were extremely anxious to secure his goodwill.
Some conservative scholars, apparently with good reason, connect Anani
with Hanani, the brother of Nehemiah.

Regardless of divergence of opinion between liberal and conservative
scholars, it would seem clear that the honor of reëstablishing the racial
and religious life of the Jews in Jerusalem and of rebuilding the city
and the temple belongs to Ezra and Nehemiah, with supplementary
honors for Haggai and Zechariah.

When the time came that Nehemiah must temporarily leave Jerusalem
to return to Susa, he could look back over a great work well done.
Behind him he was leaving a city he had raised from ruins. The
religious and racial life of his people was again centered in Jerusalem.
After the prophetic seventy years of exile, Israel had come home.

STELA OF UR NAMMU

Fortunately for the scholars of today the ancient Sumerians made monumental reliefs and inscriptions bearing on their building operations. In lower right hand corner Ur Nammu is shown receiving the tools of the builder from the priest.

MILKING SCENE FROM TELL-EL-OBEID

This dates from at least B. C. 3000. Note strainer and storage jar, also position of the milkers. Lower panel is a "bull panel" from a temple.

By permission of The Museum of the University of Pennsylvania

XVII

THE COMING OF THE EUROPEAN CONQUERORS

FTER the exile, there was little to lure the Israelites back to
Palestine. The lands where the kingdom of David and Solomon
had flourished were but the "Beyond River" provinces of the
Persian empire. Assyrian and Babylonian conquerors had plundered the
wealth of the country and carried the intellectual and physical cream of
the population into captivity. All, "save the poorest sort of the people of
the land" (2 *Kings* 24:14), had been deported. These low-grade Hebrews
who had escaped exile had mingled through marriage with foreigners
implanted in the country by successive conquerors. The half-caste offspring
of this amalgamation formed a considerable portion of the population.
This inferior people could gather little from the soil above the toll of
the tax-gatherer. A once rich land was now miserably poor. Civil
governors, appointed by the Persian king, kept a semblance of law and
order, but were principally interested in collecting the revenues. Strange
desert peoples were drifting across the land, including the restless
Arabians, the rude forerunners of the hordes who would some day claim
Palestine for their own.

The drab and dismal outlook for the future of Palestine would not
appeal to materially-minded Jews, the majority of whom had emigrated
to richer and more promising lands. Jerusalem held the heartstrings of the
Hebrew, but the pull of the pursestrings was more powerful. The learned
literary colony, snugly settled in centers of Chaldean culture, was loath
to leave that intellectual atmosphere for the rude surroundings of rebuilt
Jerusalem. Seventy years had shifted the centers of Jewish influence.
The strength of Israel lay beyond the boundaries of Palestine. The
rebuilding of Jerusalem and the rehabilitation of Judah were tasks for
religious heroes.

Doubtless many ardent nationalists cherished the iridescent dream
which has since become a part of the Hebrew heritage—an independent
Jewish people in a strictly Jewish country. Hope for independent
nationalism rested on a faulty foundation. Political power is usually a
product of the working out of economic law. However the Israelites
builded better than they knew. Temporal power was denied the Hebrews
but a politically impotent people found new power in the spiritual world.
The dream of earthly empire vanished before a vision of a realm of
righteousness which would endure through God's eternal years. The

17.

remnant of Israel which resurrected Jerusalem from ruins formed the nucleus of an hitherto largely unexplored conception of the Kingdom of God—the Messianic Kingdom. Firmly the foundations were being laid for religious developments which would find full fruition with the coming of the Great Redeemer.

Although nationalism was impracticable, even impossible, the restoration of Jerusalem sent a wave of patriotic fervor through the Jewish world. Even the Jews who failed to return to Judah felt its influence. The taproots of religion reach deep into the soul-soil of the Israelite. Jerusalem became more than ever the symbolic center of Israel's religious life. The Holy City was the sacred capital of an invisible religious empire. Regardless of where his wandering feet had led him, the Jew was rededicating himself to the service of the Lord God of Israel.

The experiences of exile had a cleansing effect on the religion of Israel. The forms of worship were forever purged of pagan practices which formerly frequently polluted the pure stream of Mosaic teaching. In this revitalized religion lay the potential powers of New Israel. During the days of exile the synagogue had come into being as the center of social and religious instruction. Under such circumstances the solemn ceremonials of Hebrew religion had not been strictly observed. Israel now had a temple. Leaders of religious thought deemed it advisable to return to the ancient forms of temple worship. Ethical thought and righteous living would be reinforced by rigid ritualism. Ezra, who was a noted scribe, "even a scribe of the words of the commandments of the Lord" (Ezra 7:11), was a leader in this movement. The prophets Haggai and Zechariah ably aided his efforts.

Ezra was a stickler for the racial purity of the Jews. The priestly scribe was shocked to find that mixed marriages were common among the people and the practice countenanced by the priesthood. Ezra gave vent to his grief through the Hebrew custom of rending his garments and plucking hairs from his beard.

On Nehemiah's return to Jerusalem, after some time spent in Susa, he, too, was horrified to learn that the custom of mixed marriages had become common, penetrating even the sacred precincts of the temple. In fact, Eliashib, the high priest, was one of the chief offenders. He was entertaining in the courts of the temple his grandson, who had married a daughter of Sanballat, Nehemiah's ancient enemy. With all his old-time vigor, Nehemiah instituted drastic marriage reforms. Nehemiah was too practical a man to pull out his own beard. He pulled the other fellow's. He added punch to precept when he "smote certain of them, and plucked off their hair, and made them swear by God, saying, Ye shall not give your daughters unto their sons, nor take their daughters unto your sons, or for yourselves." Evidently Nehemiah's policy of prayer, precept, and punch was highly effective, since he reports: "Thus cleansed I them from all strangers" (*Nehemiah* 13:30). Nehemiah had handled these Jerusalem Jews before.

Only the deeply religious had returned to Jerusalem. They were responsible for the rebuilding of Jerusalem and the temple. Resolutely they set to work to restore ancient religious forms and usages and resume the ancient covenant with Jehovah. The ceremonial usages of the Mosaic order, broadened to meet current needs, were restored to the temple. The blood stream of Israel was protected from contamination through the forbidding of mixed marriages. The rigid observance of the Sabbath and the sabbatical years were restored. The Hebrews, as a race, were placed in position to survive the successive waves of European invasion which engulfed the great empires of western Asia during the succeeding centuries.

After the rebuilding of Jerusalem, the real rulers of Judah seem to have been the high priests. Judah, as a Persian dependency, had a civil governor appointed by the Persian king. Most of these civil governors appear to have been Jews. The real power, however, rested in the hands of a succession of high priests, of whom Eliashib, Joida, Johanan, and Jaddua seem to have been most outstanding.

From the versions of the Scriptures which most of us read we can learn little of the history of the Jews during the centuries which elapsed between the rebuilding of Jerusalem and the coming of Jesus of Nazareth. From the standpoint of history, with the exception of prophetical history, our Old Testament ends with the rebuilding of Jerusalem. Much, of course, may be sifted out from the "Apocryphal" books, which have been excluded from most versions of the Old Testament since the time of the Reformation. The term "Apocrypha" is Greek, and properly means "hidden," or "secret." In the last two centuries before the beginning of the Christian Era many books were written which were not considered authentic by orthodox Jews. Some of these books claimed secret or mystical qualities and thus came to be looked upon as spurious. Soon, all spurious books, whether secret or not, came to be called "apocryphal," and the word took on its present disparaging meaning. These Apocryphal books, as they appeared in ancient versions, were: Esdras 1, 2, 3, 4; Tobit; Judith; The Rest of the Chapters of the Book of Esther; Wisdom of Solomon; Ecclesiasticus; Baruch; The Song of the Three Holy Children; The Story of Susanna; Bel and the Dragon; Prayer of Manasses; Maccabees 1, 2, 3, 4. Some of these books are of no historical value. Others will be referred to later in the text.

Some small portion of the credit for the rebuilding of Jerusalem should accrue to the liberal sovereigns of Persia, who rendered supremely important service to the Hebrew race. Such helpful sovereigns as Cyrus, Darius I, and Artaxerxes I, deserve especial mention. Unfortunately for Israel, at the very time Artaxerxes was rendering such signal service to his friend Nehemiah, his own empire was slipping toward its fall, and Greece was soon to supplant Persia as the dominant power in western Asia.

As far back as the days of Darius I (B. C. 521-486), the Ionian subjects of Persia were causing serious trouble by rebellion. Darius decided to end this trouble by subjugating the entire Hellenic Peninsula. His first expedition, in 492, met with disaster. Returning again in 490, the Persians made a direct attack on Athens by sea and landed an army a short distance east of Marathon. The appearance of such a formidable force at Marathon so alarmed the Athenians that a runner, Pheidippides, was dispatched to Sparta for aid. The air-line distance is more than a hundred miles, much farther by road, but by reaching Sparta within forty-eight hours the messenger set a record which has become historical. Fame is a fickle jade. The names of only a few military leaders have bridged the centuries since the Battle of Marathon, but the "modified Marathon" races of today keep green the memory of an athlete. The reinforcements from Sparta arrived too late to do more than view the bodies of slaughtered Persians at Marathon. The battle was already over. Persian invasion had failed.

Xerxes I, the son and successor of Darius, renewed the warfare against the Greeks. After overrunning Egypt, Xerxes marched a mighty army from Sardis, bridged the Hellespont (now known as the Dardanelles) and marched against Athens. A strong supporting fleet followed the coastline. The Greeks offered battle at the Vale of Tempe, but were soon forced to retreat. A stand was made at Thermopylae. Here, in the famous pass, the Greeks held back the Persians for three days, until a column of Persians, having found another pass, appeared in the rear of the Greeks. Retreat was now a necessity. Disaster to the Greek army was averted when Leonidas volunteered to hold the pass with three hundred Spartans long enough to enable the Greeks to retreat to new positions. The Spartans were joined by 700 Thespians and 400 Thebans, who preferred death to retreat. For one whole day the gallant little band held back the Persian hosts. All, save one who was ill, died on the field of battle.

Once through the pass at Thermopylae, the armies of Xerxes rapidly overran the peninsula. City after city fell to the Persians, until even Athens was occupied and burned. The fleet of Xerxes did not fare so well. Storms and unfamiliar coasts were taking a terrible toll. Still, there came a day when Xerxes, seated in state above the narrows at Salamis, to watch his huge fleet annihilate the inferior Greek fleet which his sea forces had cornered, saw, to his horror, the smaller fleet of the enemy completely outmaneuver and outfight the vaunted sea power of Persia. With his sea power gone, there was only one course open to Xerxes, retreat. Leaving the main portion of his forces in Thessaly, under Mardonis, Xerxes returned to Susa. In the following year, B. C. 479, Mardonis was completely defeated and the Persian army forced to flee. Never again did a Persian army invade Europe. The Greeks had discovered their power. Over a century was to pass, however, before the Greeks could successfully invade Asia.

Defeat in Europe hastened the downfall of the Persian empire. This was not the primary cause, however. Persia was treading the inevitable path of uncontrolled autocracies. The blood-stained wealth of empire was leading to moral decadence and national decay. In the cities, vice and violence were rampant. Uncontrolled lust, encouraged by the obscene rites of the religion of the shadows, was sinking a once sturdy people into a moral morass.

Meanwhile the Greeks, freed from the threat of Persian invasion, entered the great age of Grecian culture—the age that produced Pericles and Plato, Socrates and Aristotle, the tutor of Alexander the Great. This "Golden Age of Greece" witnessed amazing advancement in the production of literature; sculpture and the plastic arts flourished; a start was made in the organized study of political and natural science; a school of philosophical thought was organized which has inspired scholars even unto our day. Just as the Hebrews centuries before began to revolutionize religious thinking and later made Jerusalem the religious capital of the world; so the Greeks of this period through their life, their literature, and their culture, led the world in the substitution of civilization for barbarism, and made Athens the great world-center of culture and education. No dream of world conquest disturbed the cultured Greeks until the coming of Philip of Macedon and his amazing son, Alexander the Great.

Historians, in appraising the astounding career of Alexander, frequently fail to accord due credit to his distinguished father. A favorite phrase of historians and eugenists is, that "great sons are the product of great mothers." If so, Alexander would seem to be an exception to the rule. His father, Philip, was one of the great men of his day, a man of broad vision and of a high order of intelligence, a really great monarch. On the other hand, his mother, Olympias, was a strong-willed, evil-minded woman, deep-steeped in semi-Oriental cult worship with its orgiastic practices and obscene rites. Philip and Olympias, although reigning monarchs, led the proverbial "cat-and-dog life" so often the accompaniment of ill-mated marriage. Alexander was the strange product of this strange wedlock.

Philip was born in the little semi-Greek state of Macedonia which today forms a part of Albania. Then, as now, it was rough and wild. Coming to the throne of this barbaric little state in B. C. 359, Philip soon brought most of Greece into a strong confederacy with himself at the head of it. Philip had great dreams of empire, which he strove to impart to his son. As a boy in school under the erudite Aristotle, as a youth at court and in the field of battle, Alexander was constantly trained under his father's watchful eye for imperial administration. Philip visioned his son at the head of a great Graeco-Persian empire, which he himself would win for him. In B. C. 336 he sent his first troops into Asia, intending to follow them shortly. This was not to be. An assassin's dagger ended the life of the king.

Alexander, although only a youth of twenty when he came to the throne, was fully fitted to attain his father's great ambition—a universal empire controlling the world of his day. Realizing that before he dare take his armies deep into Asia he must destroy the sea power of Persia, he marched along the coast of Asia Minor destroying port after port. On the banks of the Granicus the Persians offered battle, only to be defeated and destroyed. Two years later Alexander encountered a great army of Persians under Darius III on the plain of Issus, and so completely routed his Asiatic enemy that Darius abandoned even his harem as he fled from the field.

Alexander now marched down the Phoenician coast. Sidon surrendered. The new city of Tyre, built on an island, held him up for seven months before it fell. Gaza surrendered after a sixty-day siege. As cities fell into the grasp of Alexander they were very thoroughly plundered and the inhabitants sold into slavery. The victorious Alexander now swung into Egypt. The Egyptians offered no resistance. Two centuries of Persian rule had rendered them passive. Egypt could not "exalt itself any more above the nations" (See *Ezekiel* 29:15). Persian or Macedonian master mattered little.

Since Alexander had destroyed many of the Mediterranean seaports, it became necessary to build new maritime trading centers. One of these seacoast cities was Alexandretta, north of Tyre; another was Alexandria in Egypt, at one of the mouths of the Nile. Both of these cities flourish to this day. Alexandria was for a long time one of the great cities of the world. It became noted as an educational and literary center. As we shall see later, the city figured prominently in the translation and production of the Old Testament as we read it today. At one time so many learned

Jews flocked to Alexandria that it became the greatest Jewish city in the world and contained more Jews than Jerusalem.

By B. C. 331 Alexander was ready for his great adventure—the invasion of Persia. Deep down in Assyria, at Arbela, near the ancient mound of Nineveh, he found Darius waiting for him with an immense army. Before the Macedonian cavalry the Persian phalanxes fell like ripened grain before the reaper, and were swept like chaff from the field before the merciless Macedonians. Darius, in panic-stricken retreat, abandoned his chariot for a mule cart. Next morning Alexander stood beside a deserted mule cart and gazed on what had once been a king. Darius was dead; slain by his own officers. A beardless boy held in his hands the direction of world destiny.

It is not the purpose of this narrative to follow Alexander on the military journey of seven years which took him through the wilds of Turkestan, down through the Khyber Pass into India, along the coast to the Persian Gulf, and finally back to Susa. Our purpose is to note the effect of the introduction of Hellenism into Palestine on the life and culture of the Jews. By "Hellenism" is meant the characteristic culture expressed in Grecian institutions, art, literature, and life. The coming of Alexander brought disaster to many an Asiatic people, but to the Jews the introduction of Hellenism opened wide the gates of educational opportunity. Contact with Greek culture broadened the relationship of the educated Jew with the literary world of his day.

If Alexander had any plans for the consolidation and development of his vast empire, he did not live long enough to see them carried out. He left behind him only a record of conquest. Regent of Greece at 16, king of Greece at 20, he died, master of the world, at the early age of 33 at Babylon, and the empire his sword had won fell into fragments. The empire was divided among the generals of Alexander's army. Most of the old Persian empire in Asia fell to Seleucus, who founded a dynasty. This is generally referred to as the "Seleucid of Syria." Egypt came into the possession of Ptolemy, who founded the dynasty generally referred to as the "Ptolemies of Egypt." Fortunately for the Jews, Ptolemy secured Palestine, although the Jews engaged in some sporadic fighting to dispute his overlordship.

Under the Ptolemies, Egypt prospered and this prosperity spread over into Palestine. The location of Egypt made it safe from the plundering Gauls, who later raided and ravished most of Asia Minor. These Gauls are generally supposed to be the forerunners of the Galatians of St. Paul's day. The favorable location of Alexandria made it a leading seaport and trade center. The city vied with Athens as a center of cultural activity. Attic (Athenian) Greek became the literary language not only of Egypt but also of all of Palestine, and remained so until long after the beginning of the Christian Era.

Fortunately for Jewish life and thought, fortunately in fact for the world of letters, Ptolemy I was a scholar. Ptolemy was interested in every branch of culture and education. At Alexandria he established a Medical College. He also established the great school known as the Museion (Museum), where all branches of learning were taught at the expense of the state. To aid the instructors he began the collection of books which grew into the famous Alexandrian Library, one of the wonders of the ancient world. This library was an encyclopedic conception. All the literary treasures of the earth were collected, and carefully copied on papyrus for permanent preservation. Despite the laborious and tedious nature of the hand copying, the number of volumes in the library finally totaled above a half million. The loss of this great library was a tragedy to the world of learning. Part of it was destroyed by fire during the siege of Alexandria by Julius Caesar. Part of it was destroyed by fanatic Christians in 391 A. D. The balance of the manuscripts furnished fuel for six months for the Arab conquerors, under the Caliph Omar in 641 A. D.

Hellenism widened the intellectual horizons of the Jews and led to a broader, fuller life than was possible under the Assyrians, the Babylonians, or even the more tolerant Persians. Centers of Hellenic culture sprang up all over western Asia. The Palestinian Jews were welcome in these centers where they became familiar with Greek art, architecture, literature and customs. For those who were interested in higher education, the great cultural centers of Athens, Antioch, and Alexandria were available. On every hand the Jew heard Greek spoken; he learned the language; even read the great literature of his own race as translated into that tongue.

Under the easy-going Ptolemies Judah was making definite progress. Regardless of civil governors, the real power at Jerusalem lay in the hands of the high priests. Jaddua was high priest at the coming of Alexander the Great. After that time the succession of the high priesthood is often impossible to follow. Naturally, there were many points of conflict between the intellectual self-centeredness of Hellenism and the traditional religious exclusiveness of Judaism. The orthodox Jew clung tenaciously to ancient customs and habits of thought: the liberal Jew adopted the newer mode of life and thought.

During the reign of Ptolemy Philadelphus (B. C. 285-247) the scholars at Alexandria became greatly interested in the richest literary treasure trove that the minds of mankind have ever produced—"the Law" of the Hebrews—the work we know today as the Old Testament. Realizing the monumental nature of the task, Demetrius Phalerius, the director of the Alexandrian Library, appealed to Philadelphus for aid. According to apparently well-founded tradition, and to Josephus,* Philadelphus released all the Jewish slaves in Egypt, so that scholars among them could assist in the translation. Under the urging of one Aristeus, Philadelphus sent to Eleazer, the high priest at Jerusalem, for trained Jewish temple scholars to supervise the actual translation. Eleazer responded by sending seventy scholars to Alexandria. On their arrival at Alexandria, the seventy scholars were taken to the island of Pharos where they could work in seclusion. Working in pairs, they are reputed to have prepared seventy identical translations in seventy days. Since the work was accomplished by seventy men, this translation is commonly called the "Septuagint." While none of the original manuscripts have survived, several copies from originals are still in existence in various museums. The Septuagint version is still in use in the Eastern Church.

The orthodox Jews in Palestine refused to accept this Greek translation, basing their objections on alleged inaccuracies in the text. There is no authentic record of other translations into Greek before the opening of the Christian Era. In the second century A. D., non-Palestinian Jews produced three separate versions of the Old Testament in Greek. One of these was by Aquila, a converted Jew, who lived in Asia Minor; another was by Theodotion; and the third was by Symmachus. The work of Theodotion was so excellent that his translation of the Book of *Daniel* was substituted for the earlier translation in the Septuagint. In the following century, the Alexandrian Christian scholar, Origen, and his assistants, produced the monumental work that is known as "the Hexapla." In the Hexapla, six separate translations are given in parallel columns. No original manuscripts of Origen's work are in known existence. Some fragments of a copy are in the library at Cambridge University, England, and a portion of the *Psalms* is in possession of the Ambrosian Library at Milan, Italy.

Under the stimulating influence of Hellenism education was becoming more widely disseminated. Politically, the Ptolemies paid little attention to Palestine as long as the tribute was paid. In Jerusalem the local administration of government was a peculiar combination of practical politics and religious practices. Some of the priests were more interested in politics than in the duties of their sacred calling and used their high office as a means of extortion and oppression. This use of political power widened the gap, already discernible, between what we of today might call "right wing" and "left wing" Jews. On the right were the strictly orthodox Jews, who clung to the literal interpretation of "the Law." On the left were the Hellenized Jews, composed of groups more ready to mingle socially and politically with the cosmopolitan peoples who were all about them. One

*See *Antiquities of the Jews*, Book XII, Chapter II.

of the leading groups which turned toward the left was the Sadducees. The conservative Jews were highly exclusive. The liberal Jews, while loyal to their faith, were not above a little judicious proselyting. This may account for the wide divergence in types of Jews that may be seen today in any great Asiatic commercial center, where one may note, among peoples who have been Jews for many centuries, distinct strains of blood which could never have come down direct from Abraham.

By the second century B. C. the great strength of Israel was no longer in Palestine. With the fall of Jerusalem the Jews began to migrate in every direction. The introduction of Hellenism into Palestine accentuated this migratory movement. Every country, every great commercial center, from the Tiber to the Persian Gulf, and from far up the Nile to the Balkan Mountains, had Jewish commercial and cultural colonies. Jerusalem was still the religious capital of the Jewish world, but that world had no political boundaries. The Holy City was a truly religious capital. No animal deemed unclean by orthodox Jews could be brought into the city. No foreign emblem, no graven image, could pass through the city gates. The Sabbath was so strictly observed that, at a slightly subsequent date, the city fell to invaders who attacked on the Sabbath, when the Jews were forbidden to fight. In the strictly material sense, however, Jerusalem was the vulnerable spot through which the Hebraic race could most easily be attacked. Jerusalem, capital of a far-flung religious empire, lay on what was still the military crossroads of the world.

The Seleucids of Syria had long coveted the Palestinian provinces. At the division of the old Persian empire they had made a determined effort to secure them, but the prize had gone, with Egypt, to the Ptolemies. The eyes of the Seleucids had never left them, however. With the weakening of the Ptolemies the Seleucids prepared for attack. In B. C. 198 the Seleucids under the able leadership of Antiochus of Syria wrested Palestine from the Ptolemies. Antiochus had ambitious plans to conquer Egypt. The rising Romans, who were now preparing to make their own bid for world empire, sensing the danger of allowing their rich resources of Egypt to fall into the hands of Antiochus, barred his way with the strength of the Roman legions.

Antiochus now attempted to form a pan-Hellenic league which would be able to overwhelm, or at least successfully resist, the threatening power of Rome. After two crushing defeats, at Thermopylae in 191 and at Magnesia in 190, he was forced to yield all of Asia north of the Taurus range to Rome and pay an indemnity of 15,000 talents. While plundering a temple in Susiana to make this payment, he lost his life. Rome now entered the political picture in western Asia.

Antiochus Epiphanes (B. C. 176-164), the grandson of Antiochus the Great, attempted to carry out his grandfather's great ambition. When the Romans turned back his attempted invasion of Egypt, he appeased his wrath by attempting to completely Hellenize Palestine by force. Aided by many Jews who were politically allied with the Greeks, he captured Jerusalem and turned it into a truly Hellenic city. The reading of the Scriptures was forbidden, the high priesthood dispersed, and the keeping of the Sabbath abolished. As a crowning act of desecration an altar to Olympian Zeus was erected in the sacred courts of the temple, and the flesh of swine presented as a burnt offering. This sacrilegious performance filled the pious Jews with horror, and brought on that turbulent period in Jewish history when, with a heroism unsurpassed in history, the Maccabeans fought for the liberation of Judaism. History contains few historical episodes more thrilling than those reflected in *Maccabees* 1 and 2.

Under the tolerant Ptolemies the influence of Jewish religious thought had been immeasurably broadened. Greek culture opened innumerable avenues through which Israel's great gifts of moral development and religious knowledge reached the non-Jewish world. Able writers were placing in permanent literary form the priceless Hebrew heritage of divine revelation and prophetic teaching which forms the Old Testament.

XVIII

THE DARK BEFORE THE DAWN

NO document which forms a recognized part of the Old Testament tells the story of Israel from the days of the prophet Malachi to the eve of the coming of Our Saviour. The great prophetic age ended with Malachi, but the great movement which was the prime purpose of Israel's mission did not end with the passing of the prophets. Neither did this historical movement end with the coming of Jesus of Nazareth. With His coming the greatest of all religious movements took on new life, new trends, new dynamic energy, in shaping the channels through which the knowledge of God's grace could reach the hearts of men. Nearly twenty centuries earlier, a tiny seed of spiritual truth had sprouted in the soul-soil of Israel. The centuries had seen this puny plant grow like a time-tried tree. Now the time had come for grafting of newer and more fruitful growth. Subsequent centuries have seen the new growth overshadow the parent stem, but it still draws sustenance from ancient roots deep anchored in eternal truth.

Although their names, their deeds, and their devotion to the religion of their race are unrecorded in the sacred pages of the Great Book, the last two centuries before the beginning of the Christian Era produced a galaxy of Hebrew heroes well worthy of distinguished place in history. Although there arose in Israel no prophet to reflect their glory in historical highlight; no psalmist to weave their story into sacred song; although the numbering of their years is unrecorded in any document deemed worthy of inclusion in the Old Testament, time cannot tarnish the fame of the great Israelitish leaders whose names lend lustre to what is known as the Hasmonean or Maccabean period. Faced with apostasy among powerful political groups of their own people, confronted with the relentless ambition of the Seleucids to Hellenize Judea, they fought with such fanatical fury for freedom to worship God that for a brief period they achieved complete political independence for Israel. With a heroism unsurpassed in the history of any people, tens of thousands of unsung, unheralded Hebrews fell, fighting for their ancient faith.

Dark was the gloom which descended over Israel just before the dawning of the Christian Era. Israel was seemingly sinking in the shadows when suddenly the Light Eternal appeared to illuminate the pathway of the great historical movement. Removed from its setting of spiritual idealism and stripped from its background of religion, the history of the

Hebrew is but a tragic tale. Only for a trifling stretch of time has the Jew ever enjoyed political power and prominence. The trail he has trod through secular history has largely led through valleys of sorrow. Only for a little day did his pathway through history lead him to the mountain tops which rise above the clouds to political place in the sun. Even his little day of political glory—the day of the Hebrew kingdoms—presents a meager measure of accomplishment. Only in relation to the great religious movement which originated with his race does the Hebrew rise to historical glory. The earthly kingdoms of Israel were but trifling toys of time; the ideals of Israel are eternal, more potent today than when the white walls of Solomon's temple shone above the walls of Jerusalem.

Plentiful as is the material evidence left behind by the Hebrews in Palestine, it is as nothing to the archæological evidence left behind by imperial peoples who were contemporary with the Hebrews during Old Testament days. The Assyrian empire, the Babylonian empire, even the Roman empire, greatest of them all, are monumented by shattered ruins, decayed by time, despoiled by barbarians. Today the uncouth Arab shatters the walls of Hellenic temples and palaces, of Roman theatres and hippodromes, for materials to build his squalid huts and ramshackle villages. "Nineveh is laid waste" (*Nahum* 3:7). "Babylon is fallen" (*Revelation* 14:8). Egypt has become "the basest of the kingdoms" (*Ezekiel* 29:15). The cruel conquerors who reared these mighty cities and swept their way to empire with the sword are largely remembered only through well-earned infamy. The universal empires are all gone; Hebraic nationalism lives only in the pages of history; but the great historical movement which originated in distant Chaldea still flourishes, enduring, endless, eternal.

By the beginning of the second century B. C., Israel had long since ceased to be an isolated people packed in Palestine. Israel had penetrated the farthest reaches of civilization. Not only were there great colonies of Jews in Babylonia, Asia Minor, Egypt, and Greece, but in all parts of the rising Roman empire. Wherever the sons of men gathered for commerce or culture, there would the Jew be found. With him he brought his inherited Jewish culture plus the culture his race had borrowed from all the rising civilizations of the East. Although Jerusalem was still the center of Israelitish religious life, and the temple still the symbol of Jehovah's covenant with His Chosen People, the numerical strength of the race lay outside the confines of Palestine. Strong ties of blood and the still stronger ties of traditional religion turned the reverential thought of the Jew toward Jerusalem, but no national boundary restricted the mental and spiritual growth of Israel. The iron heel of the conqueror might obliterate Jewish nationalism, Jerusalem might fall and rise and fall again; but the divine mandate vouchsafed to Abraham defied both time and tyrant. The sword of the Seleucids might sweep over Judea; the rapidly rising Romans might slaughter Jews by thousands and sell survivors into slavery by tens of thousands; still a resilient Israel would pursue its historic task of preparing the way for "the day of fulfillment."

The opening of the so-called "Maccabean Period" found Judea prostrate at the feet of the Seleucids under Antiochus Epiphanes, B. C. 175-164. The Seleucid general, Apolonius, had torn down the walls of Jerusalem, deposed the Jewish high priest, turned the temple of Jehovah into a pagan temple of Zeus. Israel was apparently cowed into complete submission. When, however, the insolent invaders defiled the altar with a burnt offering of swine flesh, the supreme abomination of the Jew, the wrath of the horror-stricken Hebrews knew no bounds. Death was preferable to such dishonor. Once more the Hebrews nerved themselves to show the world that the race still possessed the materials from which martyrs are made. They must dislodge the Seleucids or die in the attempt. A long period of bitter guerrilla warfare ensued.

Israel was not long in finding a leader worthy of the Hebraic tradition of heroism in warfare. This leader was the patriarchal Mattathias, the leading citizen of the little town of Modein, which lay between Jerusalem and Joppa. When a detachment of soldiers visited the district to enforce the worship of the Greek gods by the inhabitants, Mattathias not only refused to worship but when a renegade Jew approached the altar to offer sacrifice he slew his craven countryman and overturned the altar. In the ensuing melee, Mattathias and his sons killed the commandant of the troops, Apelles, and several of his soldiers. Mattathias and his family fled to the mountains, where they were joined by many orthodox Jews who rallied to the standard of revolt.

Israel was now engaged in a Holy War, battling for religious freedom. The aged Mattathias soon died. He was succeeded by his son, Judas, whose exploits in battle won him the name of "the Maccabee." Maccabee means "the Hammer." Judas met in battle and defeated Apolonius, the general who had sacrificed the swine in the temple. Apolonius was killed, and thereafter Judas wore the sword of the arch-enemy of Israel. At Bethhoron, Judas overthrew the army of Seron, the successor of Apolonius.

Irked by these repeated reverses in desultory warfare, Antiochus Epiphanes decided to dispatch to Judea an expeditionary force of sufficient strength to wipe out these troublesome Jews. He decreed that Jerusalem must be destroyed and its inhabitants reduced to the deepest degradation of slavery. Accordingly a great army was organized by Lysias, acting vice-regent of Syria, and marched into Judea, under the leadership of three generals, Ptolemy, Nicanor, and Gorgias. This army established military headquarters at Emmaus. Before this mighty host lay the meager, ill-armed troops of Israel. Gorgias had a brilliant idea. With picked troops, guided through the darkness by renegade Jews, he would fall on the contemptible little army of Judas and destroy it in sudden night attack. When his troops rushed the Jewish camp, which still had its watchfires burning brightly, they found it deserted. Judas had turned the tables on him. When Gorgias returned to his own base, he found that Judas had captured and burned it. Such of its defenders as had escaped the sword were scattered far and wide. The invaders retreated, leaving the spoils of war to the triumphant Israelites. Hope now burned high in loyal Hebrew hearts. They had proved their mettle.

Lysias now determined personally to undertake the task at which his generals had failed. Judas met and defeated him in a great battle at Beth-zur in B. C. 165. A triumphant Israel now rallied at Jerusalem. Israel had recovered the great essential—freedom to worship God. The temple was thoroughly cleansed and restored. A new altar was dedicated with the ceremonious lighting of the Menorah or seven-branched temple candelabrum. The anniversary of this ceremony is still observed by devout Jews as the Day of Dedication or Feast of Lights.

The temporary loosening of the iron grip of the Seleucids did not bring peace to Judea. The Palestinian provinces were in the midst of a political maelstrom. Provincial neighbors eyed with envy the rising power of Judea. To resist territorial encroachment, Judas found it necessary to engage in a running series of minor wars. Ably assisted by his brothers John and Simon, he waged military campaigns which ranged all over the country included in the proverbial "from Dan unto Beersheba" and beyond, as well as reaching over into the trans-Jordan country. Military mercy was unknown in those days. As cities fell before the arms of Israel all the male inhabitants were slain and the cities given to the torch. Judas conquered a territory larger than the kingdom of David, and used the rich spoils of war to enrich Jerusalem.

During all this time the Seleucids of Syria claimed a provisional protectorate over all of Palestine, including Judea. A Syrian garrison still held the citadel in Jerusalem. Meanwhile Antiochus Epiphanes had died. His son Antiochus V, a minor, succeeded him, with Lysias as co-regent. Judas now determined to oust the Syrians from the citadel in Jerusalem, from which they had been troubling the Jews. His siege of the citadel brought a great army hurrying down from Syria under Lysias, and Judas was in turn besieged in the temple. Serious internal troubles in Syria, where a usurper was claiming the throne, forced the Syrians to make peace with Judas.

COURTYARD OF SUMERIAN HOUSE

This house dates from the "Larsa Period" (when Abraham lived at Ur). The houses, two stories high and frequently containing ten or twelve rooms, were so built as to admit of a considerable degree of comfort.

WOOL ACCOUNT TABLET

The Sumerians had no coined money. Taxes were paid in grain, dates, wool and other products. Carefully balanced accounts were kept of receipt and disposal of the goods. The above tablet shows amounts of wool issued to female weavers, the amounts of cloth returned, with charges against the women for household supplies issued.

By permission of The Museum of the University of Pennsylvania

The famous regnal line of the Seleucids was now nearing its end. The young king was murdered by Demetrius, a usurper, after a reign of only two years. In B. C. 160, Demetrius sent an overwhelming army into Judea. At Bethzetho, Judas, with a remnant of his fighting force, was surrounded. Scorning to surrender Judas died as he had lived, with his face toward his enemies. The remains of Judas were reverently conveyed to Modein, the little town his fighting family had made famous, and laid to rest while Israel mourned her famous son.

Jonathan, the brother of Judas, now became the chosen leader of the Jews. For a long time he could accomplish little. Lacking men and military resources, he was obliged to remain away from Jerusalem. For a time he lived like an outlaw in the upper Jordan country around Lake Huleh. Here he played military hide-and-seek with the forces of Bacchides, the Syrian general who was seeking to destroy him. Bacchides was finally lured into an attack on the village of Bethagla, which Jonathan had garrisoned with troops under his brother Simon. While Bacchides was attacking he was suddenly beset by Jews under Jonathan, who had advanced on his rear. Bacchides was compelled to sign a truce and retire to Syria.

While Jonathan was an able warrior, it was as a diplomat that he scored his greatest successes. A ruthless adventurer, Alexander Balas of Smyrna, was laying claim to the throne of Demetrius of Syria, and eagerly sought the aid of Jonathan and his fighting Jews, offering rich rewards for assistance. Demetrius, in turn, offered what practically amounted to independence for Judea for a little timely help. Not knowing which would win, Jonathan played them one against the other, claiming constantly increasing concessions until he was recognized as the civil and military governor of Judea and the high priest of Israel.

When Demetrius was killed in battle, Jonathan swung his favor to Alexander. When Alexander was displaced by Demetrius II, Jonathan espoused the cause of the new king, and was rewarded by the removal of many taxes and a considerable addition to the territory of Judea. Once firmly on the throne, Demetrius was about to recall his generous decree on taxes, when suddenly the pendulum of political power in Syria again swung wide. A successful conspiracy was launched against Demetrius by Tryphon, who placed Antiochus, the young son of Alexander, on the throne. Jonathan, now recognized as a man of power at the court of Syria, raised a great army to definitely defeat Demetrius, and firmly establish the boy king on the throne. In gratitude, Antiochus granted wide political powers to Jonathan and raised his brother Simon to high military command in Syria. Judea was now such a political power in the

18

East that the country sent ambassadors to other powers, even to the august court of Rome.

The crafty Tryphon, so far successful in his machinations, now coveted the crown of Syria for himself. The great barrier to his nefarious ambition was the powerful Jonathan. The assassination of the stripling king would be a trifling matter, but the disposal of Jonathan would be a difficult and dangerous undertaking. Tryphon marched an army to the valley of Jezreel, where he met Jonathan at the head of 40,000 picked men. Tryphon immediately sent word to Jonathan that he had not come for war, but on a goodwill mission to turn the city of Ptolemais and the surrounding district over to Jonathan. Feigning friendship, Tryphon suggested that, with a few troops each, they journey to Ptolemais for a conference. Jonathan consented. Once within the closed gates of Ptolemais, the treacherous trap was sprung. Jonathan's bodyguard was slain, and Jonathan made prisoner. The jackal had trapped the lion.

The mantle of the Maccabees now descended to the last remaining brother, Simon, probably the ablest member of this historical family. Simon was immediately placed in a troublesome dilemma. Tryphon marched into Judea, bringing with him his famous prisoner, Jonathan. The infamous Tryphon now offered Simon an embarrassing bargain. He offered to exchange Jonathan for one hundred talents of silver and two young sons of Jonathan, who were to be kept as hostages as an assurance that Jonathan would not take up arms against Syria. Simon realized that this proposition was merely an effort to ensnare him. Tryphon would take the money and the boys, but would not return Jonathan. If, however, he refused to negotiate with Tryphon for the release of his brother, the calumnious tongues of his enemies in Israel would immediately clamor that he had sacrificed his brother to his own advantage. After deliberation with his leaders, Simon delivered the money and the hostages. The other side of the bargain was never kept. Instead of releasing Jonathan, Tryphon killed him. Later, Simon recovered his brother's bones from Basca, where he had been buried, and interred them in the family burying place in his home village of Modein. Over the graves of his mother, his father, and his five fighting brothers who had died for Israel, he erected seven great pyramidal monuments which centuries later still marked the resting place of the heroic Maccabean family.

Tryphon treacherously disposed of young king Antiochus, and announced that the youth had died under the knife during a surgical operation. Once on the throne, however, Tryphon soon revealed his true colors. His despotism brought on revolt in the army, and the kingdom was offered to Cleopatra, widow of Demetrius. Cleopatra married Antiochus, the brother of Demetrius. With the aid of Simon, Antiochus repeatedly defeated Tryphon, who finally fell while his army was besieged in Apama.

The establishment of the Maccabean kingdom, which lasted from B. C. 143 to 63, marks the beginning of one of the most important and progressive periods in Jewish history. During these eighty years of practical independence Israel made important advancement in the fields of education, culture, literature, and particularly in collating and coördinating the written expressions of religious thought. The ancient Hebrew theocracy—the government of the state by Jehovah administering through the priesthood—was revived and strengthened. Devout Jews were studying and teaching, in Hebrew and in Greek, a version of the "Law" that was fundamentally and practically the same as we read in the Old Testament today.

Simon, although reigning as a sovereign, wisely refrained from adopting the title of king. A grateful people, enthusiastic over the recovery of long-lost independence, were eager to shower honors on their great leader. When Simon refused kingship, the populace made his office of high priest hereditary in the Hasmonean family. Then began the "Cycle of Simon," and Judea took its place in the family of nations. No foreign tribute was paid. Judea issued its own coinage and collected its own taxes.

During this period the two great factions which had arisen in Judea's religious and political life were drifting farther apart. The Pharisees were the "Puritans" of their day. To them the observance of the letter of "the Law" was the great essential. Theirs was an exclusive doctrine. The Jews must be a holy people prepared for a Holy God. The opposing party, the Sadducees, took their name from Zadok, the priest of David (See 2 *Samuel* 8:17). This party was headed by worldly-minded priests who were deeply interested in politics. The Sadducees, while strict in the matter of worship and religious observances, were more open to the influences of Hellenic life and culture. The bitter antagonism which grew up between these factions had a profound effect on later Jewish history.

The comparatively peaceful and prosperous reign of Simon came to an end through the treachery of his son-in-law, Ptolemy, who killed the unarmed Simon at a family feast, seized his mother-in-law and her two young sons, and attempted by force to usurp the high priesthood of Judea. When Ptolemy rushed to Jerusalem to claim the high office, he was driven from the city by the enraged inhabitants, who had already installed John Hyrcanus, son of Simon, as the ruling high priest.

John Hyrcanus (B. C. 135-105) was a great success as a warrior, but rather a failure as a high priest. He waged a successful war against Samaria, destroyed the city, and burned the temple built on Mt. Gerizim by Sanballat in the days of Nehemiah. Samaria, as well as Perea and Idumea, was annexed to Judea through conquest, and the territory of Judea widely extended.

John Hyrcanus was extremely worldly-minded for a high priest. When in need of money for his military operations he did not hesitate to open the tomb of David and remove 3,000 talents of treasure. He obtained possession of Beth-shan through open bribery. His irreligious conduct so displeased the Pharisees that they asked him to resign his holy office as high priest. This turned his sympathies to the Sadducees, and thus emphasized the religious and political differences of the day.

With the passing of John Hyrcanus in B. C. 105 the power of Judea began to wane. The government was left in the hands of his wife, and his son Aristobulus was made high priest. Aristobulus promptly had his mother seized and imprisoned, and proclaimed himself king of Judea. His reign was brief. He died the year following his coronation. He was succeeded by his brother, Alexander Jannaeus (B. C. 104-78), a cruel and vengeful despot. Alexander Jannaeus was an unworthy scion of the Hasmonean House. Fortunately, while he was engaged in his many wars, the affairs of state fell into the hands of his queen, Alexandra, an extremely able woman. Alexandra was a devout Pharisee. Although she had a strong mind of her own, she turned to the Pharisees for political advice. The Pharisaic faction became the real power behind the throne. On the whole, this worked out well. Elementary schools were established in connection with the synagogues, and the education of youth placed in the hands of the scribes. The Great Assembly was reorganized under the name of the Sanhedrin, and the scribes admitted to membership. The yearly temple tax for Jews all over the world was instituted. This was an important legislative measure since it tied world Jewry into a powerful religious empire with its capital at Jerusalem.

After the death of Alexander Jannaeus, Alexandra ruled alone for nine years. After her death in B. C. 69, Judea was plunged into civil war through a dispute over the line of succession. The right of Hyrcanus to the high priesthood was disputed by his brother, Aristobulus. Aristobulus was defeated. Hyrcanus secured control.

Long before this time, the center of world political power had shifted to the banks of the Tiber. Rome was in the ascendant, rising rapidly toward the zenith of her power. By B. C. 63 Syria had become a Roman province. Pompey was at Damascus reorganizing Rome's Asiatic possessions. The Pharisees at Jerusalem, disturbed by the civil war which was raging between the followers of Hyrcanus II and the supporters of Aristobulus, sent ambassadors to Pompey to inform him that their party would support a Roman invasion if Pompey would guarantee that their religious liberties would not be interfered with. Pompey promptly responded by sending an army. Jerusalem fell. Judea was annexed to Rome. Jewish nationalism was ended.

During the eighty years of Judean independence the influence of Jewish thought had widened greatly. The unpolluted blood stream of the Jews, developed for two thousand years, had given them a peculiar racial identity. Generations of thinkers, gifted with deep spiritual insight, had bequeathed them distinctive gifts of moral development and religious knowledge. The migrating Jews were carrying to the outermost rim of civilization their inspired ideals of man's spiritual relationship with his God. Wherever the Jew might travel he found colonies of co-religionists. The Jews were a people apart, but the hand of the Jew was ever open to the Jew. He could obtain sustenance, shelter, money, and business aid. Thus developed a world-wide religious brotherhood bound together by racial tradition and intense realization of the unchallengeable power of the Lord God of Israel. Kept in touch with symbolic Jerusalem by "the Law" and the synagogue system of instruction, as well as the annual temple tax, the Jews maintained a solidarity unknown to any other people. The majority of the world population of Jews had never seen Jerusalem, or set foot on the soil of Palestine, but in the secret shrines of the soul they cherished Israel's religious idealism. Rome acquired more than a puny Palestinian province. It secured control of the political destinies of a vast religious empire that knew no geographical boundaries.

At about the time the Old Testament was being translated and given definite literary form, a flood of religious and semi-religious writings began to appear. Many of the literati of the day produced writings in which they attempted to reconcile the philosophy and logic of the Greeks with the teachings of "the Law" of the Hebrews. This movement produced several of the "Apocryphal" books and much of what is known as "Pseudepigrapha" or falsely assigned literature, of the day. Much apocalyptic (prophetical) literature also appeared. Despite the difficulties imposed by the slow process of hand copying, these writings obtained a comparatively wide circulation. This movement continued for fully a century and a half after the coming of Our Lord. The writings of Philo, a contemporary of Jesus, were widely studied and taught. Paul apparently encountered the effects of this type of teaching: "Beware lest any man spoil you through philosophy and vain deceit, after the tradition of men, after the rudiments of the world, and not after Christ" (*Colossians* 2:8).

The arrival of the Roman eagles at Jerusalem marks the end of the Old Testament Era. Pompey appointed an "Ethnarch" in place of the king, and made the deposed Hyrcanus II high priest. The Hasmonean House was replaced by the Idumean family headed by Antipater, as state administrators of Judea. The Decapolis, or League of Ten Cities (See *Matthew* 4:25; *Mark* 5:20; 7:31), was formed from the ten cities with predominating Greek populations. These were free cities. Judea, however, was far from pacified. The turbulent followers of Hyrcanus and Aristobulus, despite the loss of national independence, were always ready for free-for-all fighting, to which the various religious sects were only too willing to lend a hand.

The shadow of another of the great figures of the world now reached Judea. This was that of the impulsive and dissolute super-soldier, who later fancied himself as superman and demi-god—Julius Caesar. The civil war which followed the Triumvirate in Rome was settled when, in B. C. 48, the armies of Caesar and Pompey met at Pharsalos in Thessaly. Pompey, defeated, fled to Egypt and assassination. Caesar, victorious, moved on to the greatest glory any Roman ever knew.

Caesar, now lord of the East, made Hyrcanus ethnarch and Antipater procurator. Antipater's son, Phasael, became governor of Jerusalem. Herod was made governor of Galilee. Western Asia was held in an iron hand. Dictators are mortal. Four years later in the Senate Chamber at Rome, the mighty Caesar dropped to the floor with a knife-blade in his throat and lay dying at the foot of the statue of Pompey, his former great rival.

The temporary division of power after the death of Caesar brought Cassius, one of the murderers of Caesar, to the East. Herod soon so ingratiated himself with Cassius that he was made governor of Syria and was promised the throne of Judea. Antipater soon slipped from the scene. The friends of Hyrcanus II had given him a little poison.

After the Battle of Philippi in B. C. 42, in which Cassius was killed, Antony became Roman administrator in the East. Antony is best remembered for his amorous adventures with the glamorous Cleopatra of Egypt, but he, too, played his part in the Palestinian drama. Historians have a penchant for placing halos on undeserving heads, and hiding the habiliments of the harlot under the robes of romance. Cleopatra met Julius Caesar when he was a bald, girthy Roman who had seen fifty-four summers, with little resemblance to his statue in the temple, which named him the "Unconquerable God." Even before the sword of the assassin settled the fate of Caesar, the coy Cleopatra was casting her eye on the impressionable Antony. When Antony and Octavian engaged in a death struggle for control of the Roman Empire, Cleopatra kept careful watch of all parts of the political picture. She clung to Antony until his success seemed doubtful. At the naval battle of Actium she suddenly withdrew her supporting fleet of sixty ships and sailed for Egypt. Antony left his fleet to its fate to follow Cleopatra to Alexandria. Here the romantic pair were hemmed in by Octavian. Antony committed suicide. When Cleopatra found that Octavian was cold to her charms, she invited death by the fangs of an asp, not for love, but through fear of being paraded on the streets of Rome as a prisoner.

During his day of administration in the East, Antony had made the ambitious Herod and his brother Phasael governors of all Judea. Hyrcanus II was reduced to the rank of high priest. Herod was apparently on his way.

Herod's progress to power now suffered a rude interruption. This was an invasion by the Parthians. The Parthians were one of those semi-barbaric Indo-European peoples who from time to time swept down from the north in waves of invasion. They were at home on horseback and exceedingly skillful with the bow and arrow. Fine fighters, they frequently served as mercenaries in the many wars which racked the East. Antigonus, son of Aristobulus, was keeping up a show of armed resistance against Hyrcanus II and his administration as high priest. Antigonus induced Orodes, the Parthian king, to take up arms in his behalf against Herod and Hyrcanus. In B. C. 41 Orodes invaded Syria, induced the whole of Galilee to rebel, and chased Herod and his betrothed, Mariamne, out of Asia. Antigonus was duly installed at Jerusalem.

Herod made his way to Rome by way of Egypt. The Senate passed a decree making him king of Judea. Returning to Judea in B. C. 39 Herod was soon in armed conflict with Antigonus. Assisted by Roman soldiers, Herod captured Jerusalem. Antigonus was sent in irons to Rome. There he met the fate of unsuccessful would-be kings. Herod married Mariamne, and was triumphantly crowned king of the Jews in B. C. 37.

Herod was a product of the blood-stained days in which he lived. By birth an Edomite, he professed to be a Jew. Perhaps this claim was well founded. Back in the days of John Hyrcanus, that doughty warrior had conquered Edom, and used a persuasive procedure in proselyting the surviving population. He gave them a choice of being dead Edomites or live Jews. Probably Herod's forefathers conceded a point of religion at the point of the sword. Herod was undoubtedly a man of great ability and an excellent administrator. With all his daring as a soldier, his bravery as a man, his passion for building monumental works in brick and stone, his unswerving loyalty to his Roman masters, he was a ruthless, relentless tyrant, guilty of cruelties worthy of a demon from the pit, ready to stain his soul with the blood of his own wife and children to satisfy his inordinate ambitions. Herod wrote history in blood.

Once he held the reins of power in his hands, he removed all opposition with his own simple formula of slaughter. He destroyed the Sanhedrin by murdering forty-five nobles. He appointed his own high priest, one Ananel, a Babylonian. This appointment raised a domestic storm in his own household. Mariamne, his wife, claimed that her brother, Aristobulus III, was the logical candidate. Mariamne, being a woman, had her own way. Ananel was deposed. Aristobulus was made high priest, but Herod took pains to see that the new high priest was ducked so deep in the Jordan that he was dead when he came up. Herod had plenty of family trouble. Incited to insane jealousy by his mother and his serpent-tongued sister, Salome, Herod had the faithful Mariamne done to death.

Herod's power was greatly increased by Augustus Caesar (B. C. 27-14 A. D.). These were the parties in power when Our Saviour was born in Bethlehem. Augustus made Herod ruler over Syria, Palestine, Arabia, and Egypt. Herod now had full scope for his great ambitions. He decided to Romanize the Near-East. He began to build great palaces, temples, theatres, and hippodromes in the Roman style of architecture. He constructed great cities on Roman models. Roman civilization, culture and customs were introduced. With taxes wrung from the people, Herod started the most ambitious building campaign the East had seen since the days of Nebuchadnezzar. The walls of Jerusalem were rebuilt and three great new towers added to its defenses. He rebuilt Samaria and renamed it Sabaste, the Greek for Augustus, in honor of his emperor. Around the city he built a colonnaded street, many of the pillars of which still stand upright today. In many cities he erected great temples which were dedicated to Bacchus. Many remains of these temples have been unearthed recently, and lamps, bronzes, marbles, pottery, and other exhibits from their ruins may be seen today in the great museums of the world.

About B. C. 18 Herod began one of his most notable reconstructions. This was the rebuilding of the Jewish temple at Jerusalem. The ancient structure which had been built in the days of Ezra and Nehemiah from the ruins of king Solomon's mighty sanctuary probably looked dingy and dilapidated in comparison with the splendid structures that Herod had erected at Jerusalem. Herod had difficulty convincing the Jews that the temple should be disturbed. However, when he promised them that alien hands would not be permitted to defile the sacred structure, a start was made. Many priests served as masons and stone cutters. The

Jews would permit no changes in the ground dimensions from those originally planned by David and Solomon, but the new temple was higher than the old. This was the temple Our Saviour knew. Here, at the time of the Passover, when He was twelve years old, Mary and Joseph found Him "sitting in the midst of the doctors, both hearing them, and asking them questions" (*Luke* 2:46). This was the temple from which He drove the money changers. Although the walls of this temple had been erected in eighteen months, the building was never entirely completed during the earthly lifetime of Our Lord. During His day on earth the work dragged drearily on. It was still far from completion when the Jews questioned Jesus: "Forty and six years was this temple in building, and wilt thou rear it up in three days?" This temple was not completed until 64 A. D., and six years later it was destroyed by Titus.

The ruthless rule of Herod aroused great resentment among all classes of society. From hovel to palace the country was permeated with conspiracy. Plots and counter-plots were weaving a web of death around the hated House of Herod. Scarcely had Herod settled the order in which his three sons should succeed him, Antipater, Alexander, and Aristobulus, than Herod's scheming sister, Salome, poisoned his mind with a story that the young princes were plotting his assassination. Herod, on the advice of Augustus, called the council which sentenced his own sons to death.

The political atmosphere of Palestine was now fraught with suspicion and terror. Two of Herod's sons, Alexander and Aristobulus, were put to death in B. C. 7, but this did not clear the atmosphere. The ever troublesome Jews were proclaiming that the appearance of the Messiah was imminent. Many theories were being advanced by the Jews as to the character and scope of the Messianic Kingdom. The more materially minded looked for a militant Messiah who would sweep the Gentiles from the land and restore Israel to the glories of the Solomonic empire. The more thoughtful and spiritually minded among the Jews looked for the ushering in of a new religious era, and visioned the coming Messiah as the Redeemer of all mankind. Crude conceptions of the great coming event gave rise to many wild rumors. This mysterious undercurrent of expectancy was extremely disturbing to Herod. Naturally he feared that in a spirit of religious exaltation the Jews might be led into active rebellion. He must be ever on his guard. When rumor reached him that the Messiah was to be raised up to his own brother, Pheroras, Herod took prompt action. Pheroras was put to death.

During the latter years of Herod's life he was an embittered old man. Throughout his mature life he had been dominated by two ambitions, his own political advancement and the establishment of the power of Rome in the Near-East. Herod had but one answer to political opposition, slaughter. To satisfy his own inflamed egoism and serve his Roman masters he had sacrificed all that a saner man would have held dear. Not only his natural enemies, but formerly trusted followers, his own wife and two of his sons, as well as his brother, were put to the sword. Now, in his declining years, he was called upon to cope with a situation which was difficult to completely comprehend. The current belief among the Jews that the Messiah would be born in Bethlehem offered opportunity for action and the slaughter of the babes of Bethlehem resulted.

After Herod's death his dominions were divided between his sons. Herod Antipas governed Galilee. Archelaus ruled Judea. His rule was weak and he was soon banished to Gaul by Augustus. In 6 A. D. came the first of the Roman procurators or governors. The fifth procurator was Pontius Pilate, who officiated at the trial of Our Saviour (See *Matthew* 27). About 40 A. D., the powerful and ruthless Agrippa I became supreme ruler of all Palestine. Agrippa came to power at a time when both the Romans and certain political sections of the Jews were attempting to stem the rising tide of Christianity with pitiless persecution. It was before Agrippa that St. Paul made his remarkable plea in the court scene pictured in *Acts* 26, a plea so convincing that "Agrippa said unto Paul, Almost thou persuadest me to be a Christian."

During the administration of the last of the procurators, Gessius Florus, the passive resistance of the Jews to Roman oppression flamed into active rebellion. They refused to offer the required daily sacrifice in the temple to the gods of Rome. The Roman emperor, Nero, promptly sent his legions to Palestine under the leadership of Vespasian. In 68 A. D., Vespasian succeeded Nero on the throne at Rome and the crushing of the Jewish rebellion was turned over to his son Titus. In April of 70 A. D. Titus appeared before Jerusalem. The Jews stubbornly held the city until the 8th of September, when Jerusalem capitulated. Titus completely destroyed the Herodian temple Our Saviour knew. Jewish nationalism was apparently a thing forever done.

Driven from Jerusalem, the center of religious thought drifted to Jamnia. Here flocked Jewish scholars and leaders of religious thought. In this intellectual and religious atmosphere the time was ripe for critical consideration of the canonicity of the various books included in the Scriptures. At Jamnia, about 90 A. D., the Old Testament was shaped practically into the form in which we know it today, and many late writings which lacked canonical authenticity were excluded.

The present writer has refrained from comment, at this time, on the many references that Jesus of Nazareth made in His teachings to the Old

Testament. That will form a part of a companion volume to the present work. However it may be said in passing that Jesus made extensive use of the Old Testament in His teaching. In over one hundred instances He made direct quotations from, or allusions to, passages in the Scriptures. The broadly educated St. Paul was an authority on the works included in the Old Testament. Great religious leaders who devoted their lives to the spread of Christianity, some of them to the extent of suffering martyrdom for their faith, believed implicitly in the Old Book. It formed a part of the foundations of their faith.

In the dark days just before the dawning of the Christian Era the faith of many advanced thinkers differed but little from the faith of the early Christians. Many Jewish scholars no longer believed in an exclusive predestined preëminence of the Hebrew in the Creator's relationship with His creatures. Old ideas of an exclusive "Lord God of the Hebrews" were breaking down before an inspired vision of a God who was the loving father of all mankind. The earliest Christians were recruited from the Jews. The fundamental difference revolved around the personality of Our Lord. His followers saw themselves as the true Israel. They did not abandon the Old Testament. To them it was the great guide to righteous living. They merely added to it a newer and a greater Gospel. Like Simeon they had seen "a light to lighten the Gentiles, and the glory of thy people Israel" (*Luke* 2:32).

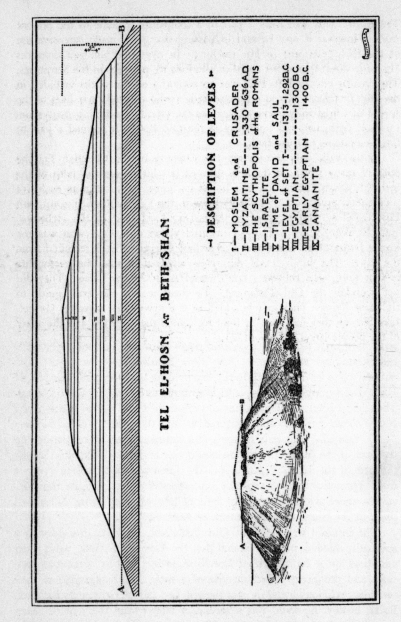

TEL EL·HOSN AT BETH-SHAN

DESCRIPTION OF LEVELS

I—MOSLEM and CRUSADER
II—BYZANTINE——330–636A.D.
III—THE SCYTHOPOLIS of the ROMANS
IV—ISRAELITE
V—TIME of DAVID and SAUL
VI—LEVEL of SETI I——1313–1292B.C.
VII—EGYPTIAN——1300B.C.
VIII—EARLY EGYPTIAN 1400 B.C.
IX—CANAANITE

XIX

TRACING THE STEPS OF HISTORY

THE Bible is our best known book. Year after year it leads the lists of "best sellers." Printing presses pour an ever-increasing flood of literature into our homes, but the Great Book still holds premier place. Oldest of books, its age but adds to its charm.

Most of us evaluate the Bible according to our own peculiar needs. Some seek solace for the soul in its sacred pages. Many value the book for its preëminence as the literary legacy of the ages. To the historian and the archæologist it is the indispensable handbook. Few of us however realize that the Old Testament is an important consulting medium for those interested in several branches of science, particularly those branches which seek to probe the inchoate infancy of civilization. Those interested in ethnology, anthropology, sociology, and other branches of science where a knowledge of the early progress of mankind is essential, find much to interest them in the Old Testament.

The earliest books of the Old Testament go back to the beginnings of civilization. Part of the original records on which these documents rest must have been written by men who never knew pen, ink, or paper. The earliest original records must have been inscribed on clay tablets with pointed bone or sharpened reed. From many archæological sources we know that writing was in vogue in several places before the days of Moses. The ancient ideals of Hebrew justice were shaped into law by Moses, "and Moses wrote this law, and delivered it unto the priests" (*Deuteronomy* 31:9), but what materials he used is a question open to conjecture. In the days of the Judges the professional scribe appeared: "they that handle the pen of the writer" (*Judges* 5:14). Jeremiah wrote with a "pen of iron" (*Jeremiah* 17:1), probably on prepared skins. Despite the difficulties under which these early authors labored, their work holds first place in the hearts of men: *Literature immortal!*

The inspired writers of the Old Testament, in telling the story of a spiritually-minded people's search for the One True God, wove their narratives on a framework of Israelitish history. Their marvelous messages and prophecies reflect the rise of a race. The background of their matchless religious literature was the rise and fall of Hebrew nationalism. Racial history, however, was a secondary matter with the writers. They were primarily interested in recording the rise, development, and inter-

[269]

pretation of "the Law." All their other writings were incidental to this prime purpose.

The writers of the Old Testament claim no distinction for their race for pioneering work in the rise of civilization. Rather they picture their race as emerging from an advancing civilization, from Chaldea (See *Genesis* 11:31). Civilization—as distinct from culture—began when men first lived in settled communities.

In a strictly material sense, the parts the early Hebrews played in the rise of civilization are distinctly minor. Save for a few brief centuries of glory they have always been a secondary people. As a race they never invaded unknown, virgin lands to found new centers of civilization. They were inheritors, rather than originators, of such civilization as they knew. The cities they made famous were largely built by others: "And I have given you a land for which ye did not labour, and cities which ye built not, and ye dwell in them" (*Joshua* 24:13). No mighty pyramids, no sculptured monoliths in enduring stone, mark the resting places of their great kings; instead they slumber in obscurity in the rocky recesses of the ridge they made famous as the hill of history. However, no people, past or present, no nation this old world has ever known, have left behind a memorial to themselves greater than the deathless documents the Old Testament Hebrews gave to mankind. More powerfully than any other race of the sons of men the Old Testament Hebrews have affected the faiths and the religious thought of the world. In the language of the Revelator, "They . . . rest from their labours; and their works do follow them." With them "the pen was mightier than the sword."

Since the days when the latest of the Old Testament writers penned their religious literature the centerline of civilization has shifted ever westward. Newer peoples in newer lands have risen to political power and prominence. Economic resources have become more potent than the sword in shaping the course of empire. The awakening of the West has left the East to slumber in the shadows of its romantic history. Time-distance has shadowed the story of the ancient Hebrews with the mists of unreality. Modern man is preoccupied with material concerns. The achievements of science have swept us into a new and troubled world, still, fundamentally, men live by ancient faiths. The Ten Commandments and the Sermon on the Mount are more potent today than when they were first formulated. It is small wonder that we look with interest on the ever-increasing volume of material evidence which the spade of the archæologist and the notebook of the scientist are revealing to supplement the story told in the Book of Books.

Save for some slight historical supplementation, the records of the Old Testament stood unsupported by external evidence for over two thousand years after the latest of the narratives was written. Material evidence as to the historicity of the writings was entirely lacking. The tortuous trail over which Israel trod to national glory had largely been obliterated by time and the hand of the despoiler. Some of the cities which Israel made famous still stood, but the majority of them had been reduced to shapeless heaps to which the natives gave the name of "Tells," so called because of the ruins which lay beneath their sand-swept surfaces. The cities which still remained, even sacred Jerusalem, were ruled by the Moslem, who held scant welcome for Christian traveler or explorer.

Unlike the Egyptians and the Chinese, the Hebrews built up no long-continuing civilization. Although their racial history is unbroken for two score centuries it has largely found its setting in the midst of alien civilizations. Nevertheless the Hebrews have left a stratum of material evidence behind them, buried deep in the dust and debris of civilizations mightier than their own. It is not a continuous stratification. Save for their meagre day of nationalism in Palestine the history of the Hebrews is a story of unhappy movements. Slavery, captivity, and exile do not contribute mounds of material evidence. Here and there, however, archæologists are finding rich pockets of evidence which indicate that the Old Testament writers were trustworthy reporters.

It is to the traveler, the trader, the explorer, and the soldier that we owe the beginnings of modern Biblical archæology. About the beginning of the nineteenth century travelers began to bring back to Europe tales of strange discoveries in Bible lands. Interesting were the stories of massive mounds which covered the ruins of long-lost cities, but more interesting still was the material evidence dug from their depths. In the first year of the nineteenth century, the British East India Company had a shipment of tablets sent from Babylonia to its offices in London. A little later, C. J. Rich, of the same company, made some superficial examinations of such well known sites as Babylon and Nineveh and forwarded a report on them. These discoveries aroused great interest, but scientific exploration was still in the far future.

Many of the great archæological "finds" of the nineteenth century were purely accidental discoveries, or resulted from fortunate circumstance. The famous Rosetta Stone, which furnished the linguistic key which unlocked for scholars the hieroglyphic inscriptions on the monuments of ancient Egypt, was found by a young French officer serving in Napoleon's army of invasion. An old peasant woman, digging in her little garden, discovered the first-found tablet of the Tell el-Amarna letters. A young British officer, Henry Rawlinson, found on a precipitous cliff in the Zangers Mountains in Persia the great inscription of Darius I which enabled him to give to the world the key to the cuneiform inscriptions of ancient Assyria and Babylonia. A missionary, traveling in the land of Moab, accidentally discovered the memorial stone of Mesha, king of Moab, which had been erected to commemorate Moab's deliverance from Israel's domination.

Many other great discoveries were made by amateur, and sometimes by professional, archæologists, working in more or less "hit or miss" fashion. Since the beginning of the present century, however, and particularly since the close of the World War, governments in control of regions in which are located important archæological sites have closely limited permits for excavation to well established educational institutions which are in a position to preserve important historical treasures and properly display them for study by the public.

The scientific investigation of the ruins of an ancient city is an important undertaking involving large expenditure of funds. Naturally such a work calls for highly trained specialists, not only for work in the field, but also in the museum, where the findings of the excavators have to be cleaned, repaired, treated to prevent deterioration, properly classified and catalogued, mounted, and displayed in such a manner that they may be systematically studied by students and the public at large.

The proper assembly of broken tablets requires much patience as well as extensive training and experience. Part of a tablet may be in one shipping crate and another part in any one of perhaps a hundred or more other cases. After the contents of the cases are spread out on tables and cleaned the work of matching begins. This at first is by color and type of clay, as well as by shape. Then comes the matching for continuity of text. This is a task for specialists.

Many a romantic story might be told of the matching of parts of archæological finds. In 1927 the University Museum, Philadelphia, acquired a rare head of a statue of Gudea made in Lagash over four thousand years ago. Meanwhile the headless body of a statue of Gudea was being exhibited in the Bagdad Museum. In 1935 it was suggested that the head in Philadelphia might match with the body in Iraq. This surmise proved to be correct. Casts were made and exchanged, the parts fitted perfectly. Now both museums can exhibit their respective parts in the proper setting.

Sometimes extensive preliminary work is necessary in the field before beginning a "dig." Living quarters for the staff must be erected, and arrangements made for a supply of potable water. Sometimes unusual conditions must be met. Desert conditions may prevail or, on the other hand, the district may be malarial, and drainage work to eliminate stagnant water and infected mosquitoes must be carried out.

VIEW IN EGYPTIAN ROOM OF MUSEUM

The sphinx was found in the Temple of Ptah at Memphis. The limestone columns, pylons and other large sculptures in the Palace of Merenptah at Memphis.

By permission of The Museum of the University of Pennsylvania

As the work of excavation is carried out, each step must be properly surveyed and accurately mapped. Elevations must be definitely determined. As objects are uncovered, each must be photographed *in situ,* given identification numbers and marking, and entered in catalogue files at field headquarters. Absolute accuracy is at all times essential. Owing to the delicate nature of some of the operations, the actual excavation is essentially hand work. The spoon and the camel-hair brush must be frequently and painstakingly used by well trained workmen under vigilant supervision.

The excavation of an individual Biblical city may mean much or little to the Biblical scholar. Some cities, while extremely interesting to the archæologist and the historian, may lack definite contact with personalities or historical episodes mentioned in the Bible. Some cities grew to importance after the Hebrew conquest of Palestine, others were important places even before the patriarchs penetrated the country. A detailed survey of all the sites of Biblical cities is beyond the limitations of this volume, but a level-by-level study of a single site may prove of interest to the reader. Probably the most significant site where active excavation is still being carried on is Beisan, the Scythopolis of the Decapolis or League of Ten Cities mentioned in the Gospels, and the Beth-shan of the Old Testament. The story of Beth-shan is the story of Palestine.

About fifty miles north of Jerusalem and approximately thirty-five miles east of the shore of the Mediterranean Sea, the little Arab village of Beisan occupies an outlying portion of the site of Beth-shan. A little river, the Jalud, coming down from the Plain of Esdraelon, hurries past the village to join the Jordan four miles to the eastward. Between the village and the Jalud looms a mighty mound, nine hundred feet long and over two hundred feet high, called by the natives "Tell al Hosn," which means in Arabic "the Mound of the Fortress."

Located just where the valley of Jezreel drops down to meet the valley of the Jordan, from time immemorial down to the days of the Crusaders the citadel at Bethshan guarded the gateway to the lands beyond the Jordan. Its strategic location enabled it to dominate the military and commercial highway leading from the Mediterranean and the junction of that highway with the north and south highway which ran along the banks of the Jordan. Military control of Beth-shan was the indispensable key to military and commercial control of northern Palestine.

The strategic location of Beth-shan made it the magnet which drew to the ancient city all the great peoples and many of the great personalities mentioned in the Old Testament. The citadel on the "Tell" was in turn an Amorite, Hittite, Egyptian, Philistine, Hebrew, Assyrian, Babylonian, Persian, Greek, Roman, Arab, and Crusader stronghold. Each of these peoples and many others left buried deep in the dust and debris of the

19

Tell material evidence which tells with unchallengeable accuracy the story of the rise of civilization during the period when the Children of Israel were working out the dramatic racial history which is reflected in the immortal narratives related in the Old Testament.

Beth-shan was a flourishing town when the adventuring Abraham came from his native Chaldea. The patriarchs of Israel must have known the place well. During the days when the Hebrews were submerged in semi-slavery in Egypt, the Pharaohs who oppressed them were building great palaces and lofty temples within the walls of Beth-shan. Israel, returning to the Promised Land after the sojourn in Egypt, found in Beth-shan one of the barrier cities which delayed the completion of the conquest of Canaan for centuries. In the vicinity of Beth-shan the Hebrews fought long with the Canaanites and later with the Philistines for the control of the fertile valleys which surrounded the town. The grim walls of Beth-shan frowned down on the futile efforts of the Judges to complete the conquest of the country. Within sight of the city Israel's first king, Saul, went to his death when the armies of Israel were overthrown by the hosts of the Philistines. Inside the city there remain to this day the foundation walls of the temple where Saul's armor was placed, as well as the ruins of the temple where his head was fastened before his mutilated body was hung on the wall. Around Beth-shan David fought the climactic campaign of the conquest of Canaan. The city was the center of one of the administrative districts of Solomon's kingdom. During the days when the Hebrews were divided into the twin kingdoms of Israel and Judah, Beth-shan was the scene of many dramatic historical episodes. Under the Greeks and the Romans Beth-shan was a place of outstanding military and commercial importance.

Beth-shan was much more than an Old Testament city. It was an important military outpost of the Roman empire during the boyhood days of Our Lord in nearby Nazareth. In His day Beth-shan rivalled Jerusalem in commercial importance. As Scythopolis it was the only city of the Decapolis west of the Jordan. Tradition associates Jesus with Beth-shan.

Encouraged by a knowledge of the town's eventful past, an expedition maintained by the University Museum, Philadelphia, has been at work at the Tell since 1921. Already ten historical levels have been in part uncovered, while beneath them an equal number of strata have been sounded and lie ready for investigation.

Although years must elapse before the story of Beth-shan, as read in material evidence, is complete, it is possible to find much of interest to the student of the Old Testament as we follow the spade of the archæologist down through the dust of historical epochs in the story of mankind.

The archæologist reads history backward. He numbers his levels from the top as he works downward, but, to avoid the obvious difficulties of reading history backward, we will study the evidence by periods rather than by archæological levels.

STEP ONE: PERIOD, PREHISTORIC TO AMORITE-HITTITE

Far back beyond the dim dawning of history the site of Beth-shan was chosen by man for a habitation. Here he built the most primitive village yet discovered in Palestine. Probably primitive man chose the site because the red soil of the surrounding valleys yielded easily to his crude methods of agriculture and the countryside was well adapted to his pastoral pursuits. Undreaming of the dramatic events succeeding centuries would bring, he chose, perhaps unwittingly, a strategic location for his little village.

When a stronger and more advanced people crowded the original settler from his poor fields and squalid village, a new day dawned for Beth-shan. With the beginnings of trade the cattlepaths grew to caravan trails, and trails developed into highways, and Beth-shan became a quiet little market town in an agricultural district which was inhabited by Amorites, who had displaced the original settlers.

Some time previous to B. C. 2000 the warlike Hittites swept down from Cappadocia, and Beth-shan's peaceful days were over. The Hittites, after a period of warfare, amalgamated with the Amorites to form the people known in the Old Testament under the generic name of Canaanites. Beth-shan, in common with several other cities in northern Palestine, was strongly fortified by the Canaanites. Guarding the eastern gateway, Beth-shan became of great strategic importance in military and commercial operations in northern Palestine.

The Amorite-Hittite, or Canaanite, civilization cannot be regarded as that of a purely tribal people. The Amorite-Hittites built up an empire that covered Palestine, Syria, and the major portion of Asia Minor. From their capital in Kadesh they established a definite national administration that governed all the country. Probably, as in all the history of Palestine, many tribal peoples were drifting about the country when Abraham first appeared in the land of Canaan.

STEP TWO: PERIOD, EARLY CANAANITE

Abraham is the central figure in many of the *Genesis* narratives. The scenes of most of the narratives are laid in Canaan. Although the history of the Hebrews as a race properly begins with Abraham, it would seem unsound to form conceptions of the rise of the Jewish race without taking into account the effect of Chaldean culture on the forefathers of Israel. Abraham was a product of Chaldea. The *Genesis* portraiture of the personality of Abraham presents him as a product of civilization. From the early chapters of *Genesis* we learn of settled communities and cities long before the days of Abraham. Scientific investigation proves this information to be correct. Cities and civilizations rise simultaneously. The earliest cities must have arisen close to the cradle of mankind. Where has the scientist found the earliest evidences of settled community life? Where has he found the oldest floorings from which civilization began its first feeble rise? Just where *Genesis* indicates they would most probably be found, in Mesopotamia. Of the two oldest city sites now known to science —Tepe Gawra and Uruk—one is mentioned in *Genesis* 10:10. The Sumerian "Uruk" is the "Erech" of *Genesis*.

It seems reasonably clear that the patriarchal clan-families of the Israelites held aloof from the Amorite-Hittites, or Canaanites. They may have mingled freely with them in the grazing grounds and trading centers, but looked with disdain, if not with horror, at intermarriage with the natives (See *Genesis* 24:3; 28:1, 2).

Apparently the four generations of patriarchs of Israel who moved about Palestine before the sojourn in Egypt were little more than outlanders wandering about in a strange land and doing fairly well in a material way for themselves. Outwardly, this was an ordinary migratory movement in an age of migration; inwardly, however, this apparently aimless movement had deep significance. The seed of Abraham were already a people apart. They were a people motivated by a unique religious idealism. They were already convinced that through the mandate of the Unseen God their descendants would at some time inherit Canaan as a national home: Canaan was already the Promised Land. This was a monumental exhibition of faith. A few clan-families firmly believed that their race "in the fullness of time" would control a land already well populated with warlike peoples and guarded by strongly fortified cities. St. Paul in his survey of Hebrew history (*Hebrews* 11) attributes the national rise of the race to their remarkable faith. The faith of Israel gave new meaning to the life of mankind. A faith that would not die separated Israel from a world of paganism.

Outwardly the patriarchs could have differed but little from their Canaanite neighbors. The Amorites, the Hittites, and the Israelites were each of Semitic origin. Their manners and customs were much alike. Although the patriarchs worshipped Jehovah they used the same methods of marking their sacred places as did the Canaanites. The *massebah* or standing stone had long been a symbol of pagan worship among the Canaanites. These pillars have been found at many city sites in Palestine at the Canaanite levels. Amid the ruins of Beth-shan may be traced all the steps in the transition of pagan sanctuaries from the "high place" with its sacred stone to the temple with altars. Jacob, after his vision at Bethel, "took the stone that he had put for his pillows, and set it up for a pillar, and poured oil upon the top of it" (*Genesis* 28:18). It will be noted, however, that when Jacob later returned to build an altar (*mazbeah*) he ordered his household to "put away the strange gods that are among you, and be clean" (*Genesis* 35:2). Jacob is making a clear distinction between the "sacred stone" of the Canaanites and the "altar" of the Lord.

The patriarchs were not strict monogamists. This is in keeping with the customs of the time and place. However, the narratives in *Genesis* dealing with the subject indicate clearly that the mothers of Israel were of selected Chaldean descent. No half-caste could aspire to place in the councils of Israel. The blood stream of the Chosen People must be kept unsullied.

During the patriarchal period Canaan was dominated by the Hittites. They had subdued, and, to a certain extent, amalgamated with the Amorites who had been in the country before them. The Philistines were gradually moving in to occupy the grain-growing districts on the coastal plains. The seed of Abraham were still in the clan-family stage, differing little from their neighbors save in religion and their inheritance of Chaldean culture. Ancestral ties were strong among the forefathers of Israel. After a hundred years among the Canaanites Abraham still referred to Chaldea as "my country" (*Genesis* 24:4).

Although the first Biblical mention of Beth-shan occurs in *Joshua* 17:16, it is highly probable that the Patriarchs of Israel knew well the country about Beth-shan. Tradition associates them with the ancient city. The old Jewish Book of Jubilees, written in Hebrew by a Pharisee between the years B. C. 135-105, states that:

> *Jacob crossed the Jordan and dwelt beyond the Jordan, and he pastured his sheep from the sea of the heap (Galilee) and unto Dothan, and he sent to his father Isaac of all his substance, clothing and food, and meat, and drink, and milk, and butter, and cheese, and some dates of the valley.*

STEP THREE: PERIOD, CANAANITE, HYKSOS, EARLY EGYPTIAN

During the period in which the Chosen People were sojourning in Egypt profound political changes took place in Palestine. Egypt became a prime mover in Palestinian affairs. About the time the patriarchs were living in Canaan, Egypt began to expand commercially and territorially. The natural avenue of expansion was toward the Asiatic mainland. This expansive movement was sharply halted by the Hyksos. The Hyksos not only drove the Egyptians back to their own country but forced them far up the Nile. Unfortunately, the Hyksos left little material evidence behind them outside of their remarkable pottery and the disparaging historical comments of their unwilling Egyptian hosts.

Israel evidently entered Egypt during the period when all of lower Egypt was in control of the Hyksos. The Hyksos, like the Israelites, were a Semitic people. The Hyksos, Asiatics themselves, would have little reason to resent the intrusion of another Asiatic people. This renders the Joseph narratives more intelligible. A Hyksos Pharaoh, or "Shepherd King," of Egypt, might well welcome an intelligent, educated youth from a cultured Hebrew family at his court, and amicably receive the family of the young man when they appeared in the country later on. The Biblical accounts of Joseph's adventures have the correct historical setting.

The expulsion of the Hyksos from Egypt changed the political picture not only in Egypt but in Palestine as well. In B. C. 1479 the Egyptians invaded northern Palestine and occupied the country as far east as the Jordan. Save for one short period the Egyptians dominated Palestine for nearly three hundred years. This invasion had an important bearing on subsequent Hebrew history. Long-continued warfare with the Egyptians broke the power of the Amorite-Hittites. Egypt was paving the way for a later successful invasion of Canaan by the Israelites. The Hebrew kingdom was erected on the ruins of Canaanite civilizations.

The extension of Egyptian domination over widely extended territories had an immediate effect on the fortunes of Israel. Man power became scarce in Egypt. Egyptian Pharaohs, engaged in extensive building campaigns as well as warfare, found it necessary to resort to labor levies. This was an age-old custom often exemplified on Egyptian monuments. The Israelites, a part of the despised Asiatics, offered a ready reservoir of forced labor. Many Egyptian records attest the historical accuracy of the picture presented in *Exodus* 1:9-14; 5:4, 5.

Forced labor was the inevitable lot of Israel. While this savors of slavery, it was not slavery in the commonly accepted sense of the term. Labor levies were called up in rotation to serve the state. Forced labor called for strong military guards. Before the date of the Exodus, Egypt, threatened by foreign invasion, found it necessary to employ foreign troops to garrison the Palestinian strongholds and guard the mines in the Sinai Peninsula. The introduction of mercenary troops from the countries bordering the northern shores of the Mediterranean had a strong influence on the future of Palestine. These troops introduced the manners and customs of their countries. Many evidences of their stay are found in the ruins of the cities of northern Palestine. The evidence from the citadel and the great cemetery at Beth-shan shows that the city was held by mercenary soldiers for a long period. In Palestine the races of southern Europe mingled with the Amorite-Hittite population and the representatives of their Egyptian overlords. Palestine had a polyglot population.

The story of this step is told in the evidence from "City Level IX" as marked on the records of the Palestinian Expedition of the University Museum, Philadelphia, now working at Beth-shan. This level dates to the Late Canaanite Period when Beth-shan was under the rule of Egypt. When Thotmes III defeated the tribes at Megiddo in B. C. 1479, Beth-shan passed into the control of Egypt. Scarabs bearing the name of the king have been found at various levels on the Tell. A scarab of Queen Hatshepsut, with whom he was co-regent for many years, was also discovered.

On this level are two buildings which were Canaanite temples. These are known as the "northern temple," and the "southern temple" of Thotmes III. Both are made of brick with stone foundations and have low brick pedestals on their walls, evidently for the purpose of holding the posts supporting the boards with which the buildings seem to have been screened. The southern temple, the larger of the two, was made for the local god "Mekal, the lord of Beth-shan," while the northern building was evidently built for his female counterpart. In a room adjoining the northern temple were found cult objects used in the ritual of worship. These figurines and bowls decorated with serpents indicate that ophiolatry, or serpent worship, was practiced at Beth-shan at that date.

The great southern temple of Thotmes III is really a complex of rooms and corridors built around an inner sanctuary. The inner sanctuary, which was reserved for the priests, contains two altars, one of brick and one of stone. Upon the brick altar, which has a stone libation bowl beside it, were originally placed the various cult objects, jewelry, beads, pottery, figurines, lamps, and many other articles which were found on the ground round about. The inner sanctuary also contained a portable altar stand of basalt with a cross in high relief on top.

The southern temple is an interesting combination of a Canaanite "High Place" and a temple with altars. Here may be seen the transition from one form of idolatrous worship to another. Here the Canaanites had worshipped the "mazzebah," the sacred stone that was emblematic of the local god, Mekal. When later the Egyptians came to use the temple, they could not worship a simple stone. Their gods were all in the forms of animals or men. Their representation of "Mekal, the lord of Beth-shan" had the attributes of a man.

High Places of the Canaanites were common in Palestine before the coming of Israel. Originally some high-placed natural rock served the purpose. The most famous of these "rock altars" is the one now covered by the Mosque of Omar at Jerusalem. At some high places the Canaanites set up monolithic stones in a curved line. Gradually these developed into crudely walled sanctuaries, generally open to the sky. Under Egyptian influence, these developed into temples with altars.

In connection with the sanctification of the infant Samuel (See 1 *Samuel* 1:24, 25) we learn that the Israelites sacrificed young bullocks. The Canaanites also practiced similar rites of sacrifice. In addition to bones of bullocks, the excavators at Beth-shan found the sockets for the poles on which the carcasses of the animals were hung for dressing, the sacrificial dagger, and the ornaments with which the live bull was dressed for sacrifice.

In the room of a temple dedicated to Ashtoreth, the Queen of Heaven, were found evidences of a type of worshipful offering which later roused the anger of the prophets of Israel when the Hebrews adopted the practice in some of their many defections from the worship of Jehovah. These were in the form of baked offerings. "Seest thou not," thundered Jeremiah, "what they do in the cities of Judah and in the streets of Jerusalem? The children gather wood, and the fathers kindle the fire, and the women knead their dough, to make cakes to the queen of heaven" (See *Jeremiah* 7:17, 18). Here were temple ovens with charcoal still in the fireplaces and evidences of flour and sesame seed "to make cakes to the queen of heaven." Later, cakes of clay were substituted. These were stamped "daily offering."

Although driven from their cities, the Canaanites still retained control of the outlying territories for many years. An inscription of Thotmes III of Egypt, dated about B. C. 1470, mentions them as holding northern Syria. *Judges* 1:27 indicates that they were still powerful and troublesome after the death of Joshua. Even the mighty Tiglath-pileser I of Assyria (about B. C. 1120) calls the Canaanites ringleaders in rebellion. They are prominently mentioned in the Tell el-Amarna letters. The Old Testament abounds with narratives of their gallant attempts to bar the onward way of the advancing Hebrews.

During the latter part of the period in which the Israelites were sojourning in Egypt, successive Egyptian Pharaohs built great temples and fortresses in the cities of northern Palestine. Throughout these eras Beth-shan was an extremely cosmopolitan city. The city is called Biti-sani in the Egyptian records. Travelers from many lands traversed the trade routes which centered in Beth-shan and bargained in the bazaars that lay under the shadow of the citadel on the Tell.

During the reigns of Amenophis III and Amenophis IV there was a strong return of Hittite influence in the cities of northern Palestine.

The official records of the excavators at Beth-shan list almost innumerable Hittite articles found belonging to this period. In this connection we must remember that according to the Tell el-Amarna correspondence between Amenophis III and Amenophis IV of Egypt and their governors and other officials in Western Asia, the Hittites were intriguing against Egypt in northern Syria. We also learn from the same correspondence that bands of nomadic Semites, including the Khabari and Suti, were advancing in Syria and Palestine. Some scholars identify the former with the Hebrews. Egypt's power was waning.

STEP FOUR: PERIOD, LATE EGYPTIAN, PHILISTINE, EARLY HEBREW

Israel returned to Canaan at an opportune time. The empire of the Hittites which held sway in Palestine for nearly a thousand years had been ruined by almost continuous conflict with Egypt. Egypt, still clinging to a shadow of power in the East, still held a few cities in northern Palestine. The Philistines were taking advantage of the lack of political authority to increase their holdings of agricultural lands. There was no national administration. When Joshua and his conquering horde of Hebrews appeared in the south Jordan country such military power as the country still possessed lay largely in the north. Joshua's military opposition came largely from minor city-kingdoms, each forced by circumstance to fend for itself. The advantage of position favored the defenders. They held the fortified cities and a distinct superiority in arms. Joshua held the advantage in the great number of his hard-bitten, desert-bred warriors. Only when the Hebrews threatened to completely overrun the entire country did the rulers of the city-kingdoms combine to offer united opposition.

In open field warfare Joshua was more than a match for the various coalitions of Canaanite kings. However, some of the cities presented a totally different problem. Joshua was able to hem the Philistines into a district dominated by five cities in southern Judea (See *Joshua* 13:3). The chain of fortified cities which guarded the plain of Esdraelon from Dor, on the coast, to Beth-shan, four miles west of the Jordan, defied the Hebrews till long after the days of Joshua (See *Joshua* 17:11). Jebus defied the Hebrews until the days of David. Gezer was handed to the Hebrews by the Pharaoh of Egypt in the days of Solomon (See 1 *Kings* 9:16). The historicity of this political picture is verified by archæological exploration.

Excavations at the sites of the Philistine cities mentioned in *Joshua* 13 show clearly that the cities were in possession of the Philistines at the time of Joshua. The northern cities mentioned in *Joshua* 17:11 were in the hands of the Egyptians until after the death of Rameses III in B. C. 1167. During the reign of Amenophis IV Egypt had lost control of these cities. They were recovered by Seti I in B. C. 1313, and remained in Egyptian possession until long after the death of Joshua.

After the death of Joshua the campaign for the control of Palestine came to a standstill. Historically, Israel was merely marking time. There was much sporadic fighting but most of it was mere guerilla warfare between predatory bands of Canaanites and tribal detachments of Israelites.

In the days of the later judges a new menace to Israel's nationalistic ambitions appeared. When the Egyptians withdrew from the cities of northern Palestine the cities were left in the hands of imported mercenary troops. These mercenaries apparently welcomed into the strongholds the Philistines against whom they had formerly fought. The Philistines, rather than the Israelites, threatened to become masters of the Promised Land. Israel was now faced with a formidable foe ready to fight to the death. This was probably one of the principal reasons for the Israelitish clamor for a king (See 1 *Samuel* 8:5) which eventually brought Saul to the throne of Israel.

The climactic campaign for the control of Palestine was fought in the neighborhood of Beth-shan. Near the town on the slopes of Mt. Gilboa Israel met with a stunning defeat at the hands of the Philistines. Saul and his three sons were slain.

In the beautifully written chapter which closes the first Book of *Samuel* it is related that after the battle the armor of Saul was put in the "house of Ashtoroth: and they fastened his body to the wall of Beth-shan." The version given in 1 *Chronicles* 10, which was written later, states that "they put his armour in the house of their gods, and fastened his head in the temple of Dagon." In addition to earlier Canaanite temples discovered at Beth-shan the excavators found the two temples mentioned in the Scriptures in connection with the defilement of the body of Saul by the Philistines.

Beth-shan was rebuilt by Rameses II of Egypt (whom many regard as the Pharaoh of the Israelitish oppression) in the ninth year of his reign. This would be B. C. 1283. At this time he built a strong citadel with two temples enclosed within it. These temples had a long and dramatic history. They stood watch while the power of Egypt passed from the Palestinian scene. They saw the Philistines replace the Egyptians at Beth-shan. They witnessed the life-and-death struggle of the Philistines with the invading Hebrews for the control of northern Palestine. Under Philistine control the northern temple became the "house of Ashtoroth" where the Philistines placed the armor of Saul, and the southern temple was "the temple of

Dagon" where the head of Israel's fallen king was placed before "they fastened his body to the wall of Beth-shan."

The two temples stood side by side with only a narrow corridor between them. The lintel of the door of the temple of Dagon bears an inscription giving the name and the titles of the builder. It also bears a relief showing the builder with his hands raised in adoration of his sovereign.

The discovery and positive identification of these two temples are a remarkable example of the supplementary material evidence which modern scientific investigations so frequently reveal. In the northern temple was found a stela showing the figure of the Canaanite warrior-goddess dressed as Ashtoreth. Before the crown of the goddess are two lines of text which read: "Antit, the Queen of Heaven, the mistress of all the gods" (Comp. *Jeremiah* 44:17-19).

It will be remembered that news of the overthrow and death of Saul was brought to David as he was encamped at Ziklag. David rallied Israel to wreak vengeance on the Philistines. In David's great campaign, Beth-shan was captured and burned. The famous temples were partly destroyed by fire, but fortunately enough remained to make their identification certain. The power of the Philistines was definitely broken. Beth-shan passed into the control of the Hebrews.

STEP FIVE: PERIOD, HEBREW

This step covers the most important period in Hebrew history. The story is very fully told in *Kings* and *Chronicles*. Over four centuries of history are covered in these books. Although the recorded events are not arranged in exact chronological order, there is no reason to doubt their historicity. The annalists, in addition to their own observations, had excellent sources to which they could refer to check their material. Some of these they mention: "Now the acts of David the king, first and last, behold, they are written in the book of Samuel the seer, and in the book of Nathan the prophet, and in the book of Gad the seer" (1 *Chronicles* 29:29). "And the rest of the acts of Solomon . . . are they not written in the book of the acts of Solomon?" (1 *Kings* 11:41). The Book of the Chronicles of the Kings of Israel and the Book of the Chronicles of the Kings of Judah are referred to as well as the writings of the prophets. The great writing prophets sometimes acted as national historians and recorders.

Israel reached its greatest glory during the reigns of David and Solomon. Over the ruins of the Amorite-Hittite civilizations the Hebrews built an empire. Israel, at last, had a national home, and Jerusalem became a truly national capital. The annals of the Kings picture the completion of the conquest under David, Israel's rise to national glory under Solomon, then the long period of division, deterioration, decay, and destruction, of the most phenomenal adventure in nationalism known to history.

During the days of Solomon, Beth-shan was incorporated in the district administered by Baana (See 1 *Kings* 4:12). It was the duty of Baana to provide victuals for the royal table for one month each year.

During the reigns of David and Solomon, Israel consolidated its conquests and built up a powerful kingdom. Occupying a strategic location between mighty empires, it naturally drew the covetous attention of the Egyptians and Assyrians. Both of these empires were preparing for armed conflict over control of the Near-East. While Solomon lived, no foreign power dared attack. The division of the kingdom after the death of Solomon opened the way for invasion.

Quick to take advantage of a divided Israel, king Sheshonk I of Egypt staged a raid into Palestine, and plundered Beth-shan. This was about B. C. 932. This raid is recorded in 1 *Kings* 14:25 and 2 *Chronicles* 12:7-9, and verified by the Egyptian king's inscription on the Amen Temple at Karnak. This was the first of many historic invasions of Palestine during the last thousand years of Old Testament history.

In B. C. 737, the Assyrians under Tiglath-pileser invaded Syria and Palestine and collected tribute. When they next returned there was not sufficient portable treasure to meet the indemnity, so part of the northern kingdom was annexed to Assyria, Beth-shan passed into the control of Assyria, although the city remained essentially Hebrew.

Beth-shan next passed into the control of the Scythians. The Scythians were Indo-Europeans from the far north who, between B. C. 630 and 625, entered western Asia, overran Syria and Palestine, and halted only at the border of Egypt. This invasion destroyed the power of Assyria in Palestine.

Following the break-up of the Assyrian Empire, Pharaoh Necho of Egypt swept through Palestine in B. C. 608 (See 2 *Kings* 23:29, 30; 2 *Chronicles* 35:20-24) en route to the Euphrates. After capturing Gaza and Askelon, he defeated Josiah, king of Judah, on the plain of Esdraelon. For a little while Beth-shan was again in the hands of the Egyptians. Pharaoh Necho, in turn, was defeated by Nebuchadnezzar, whose father Nabopolasser had founded the Neo-Babylonian empire on the ruins of the Assyrian empire. Beth-shan now suffered the fate common to Palestinian cities under Babylonian control.

STEP SIX: PERIOD, GREEK, ROMAN

The New Babylonian empire did not last very long. In B. C. 538 Cyrus the Persian captured Babylon. The coming of the Macedonian conqueror, Alexander the Great, put an end to the Persian empire in B. C. 332. Three years after the death of Alexander, in B. C. 323, Ptolemy, the son of Lagos of Egypt invaded the country but retired. He returned, however, in B. C. 302 and subdued the entire country, and occupied Beth-shan.

Under the Ptolemies Palestine had a period of comparative peace which lasted almost a century. Beth-shan prospered. The introduction of Hellenic culture broadened the intellectual horizons of the Jew. Israelitish idealism under the impetus of contact with Greek art, literature, and life began to spread throughout the civilized world. The tolerant Ptolemies worried little over Palestinian cities as long as the tribute was paid. Greek influence was shown in the architecture of Beth-shan, which reflected the general prosperity of the country.

In B. C. 198 the Seleucids of Syria wrested control of Palestine from the Ptolemies. Under the able Antiochus III, the Syrians had twice previously invaded the country, once in B. C. 218, when he captured Beth-shan, and again in B. C. 202.

The attempt of Antiochus Epiphanes (B. C. 176-164) to force the Jews to accept the religion of Greece brought about the rebellion of the Jews under Mattathias. This revolt, after long and bloody fighting, brought the Jews a brief period of complete independence. John Hyrcanus, grandson of Mattathias, in B. C. 108, bribed Epictates, the Syrian general, to betray Beth-shan into his hands. Once again Beth-shan passed into Jewish control. The Jews held Beth-shan until the arrival of the Romans, under Pompey, in B. C. 64.

The arrival of the Romans brought revival to Beth-shan. The city was rebuilt by Gabinius, a Roman proconsul who came to Palestine in 57 B. C. Under the name of Scythopolis, it now became a self-governing city and became greater than Jerusalem in population and commerce. It became chief city of the Decapolis or League of Ten Cities (See *Matthew* 4:25, *Mark* 5:20). The great extent of the ruins, stretching out over the valley, testify to the importance of the city during the Roman Period.

Now came the great turning point of all history. The life, the culture, and the faith of a large proportion of mankind, in fact, all the currents of human history, were profoundly altered by the coming of Jesus of Nazareth. Beth-shan was one of the most important cities in the homeland of Jesus. Part of His boyhood was spent in the adjacent town of Nazareth. Presumably, He was more or less familiar with Beth-shan. Traveling down to Jerusalem, when the family of the carpenter Joseph went to pay the annual taxes, the Holy Child must have seen the great Temple of Bacchus with which the Romans crowned the summit of the Tell.

With the coming of Our Lord the Old Testament portion of the history of the Hebrews was done. Over a period of twenty centuries the Hebrews shaped the foundations for the faiths of the three great living religions which worship only one God. Then came One from a carpenter's shop in Nazareth to give to a waiting world messages direct from God. He built no earthly empire. He knew no empire save that of the Romans which oppressed His people. He met none of the great ones of earth save those who tried Him for His life. Behind Him He left no great books of prophecy, or even a single known written line. He knew and revered "the Law" as we have it in the Old Testament. His simply spoken sermons were all delivered within three years of His death. Stable-born, manger-cradled, living the life of the lowly, dying a dishonored death, leaving no estate save a few poor garments for His executioners to gamble over, He became the greatest of civilizing forces by revealing the simple avenues through which man could reach his God.

HIS TRUTH ENDURETH!

INDEX OF ILLUSTRATIONS

INDEX OF MAPS

INDEX OF SCRIPTURE REFERENCES

GENERAL INDEX